Hegel, Nietzsche and
the criticism of metaphysics

Hegel,
Nietzsche
and the criticism
of metaphysics

Stephen Houlgate

RESEARCH FELLOW IN PHILOSOPHY

UNIVERSITY OF EDINBURGH

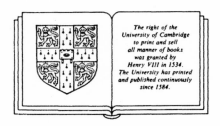

The right of the
University of Cambridge
to print and sell
all manner of books
was granted by
Henry VIII in 1534.
The University has printed
and published continuously
since 1584.

CAMBRIDGE UNIVERSITY PRESS

CAMBRIDGE

LONDON   NEW YORK   NEW ROCHELLE

MELBOURNE   SYDNEY

PUBLISHED BY THE PRESS SYNDICATE OF THE UNIVERSITY OF CAMBRIDGE
The Pitt Building, Trumpington Street, Cambridge, United Kingdom

CAMBRIDGE UNIVERSITY PRESS
The Edinburgh Building, Cambridge CB2 2RU, UK
40 West 20th Street, New York NY 10011–4211, USA
477 Williamstown Road, Port Melbourne, VIC 3207, Australia
Ruiz de Alarcón 13, 28014 Madrid, Spain
Dock House, The Waterfront, Cape Town 8001, South Africa

http://www.cambridge.org

First published 1986
First paperback edition 2004

A catalogue record for this book is available from the British Library

Library of Congress cataloguing in publication data
Houlgate, Stephen.
Hegel, Nietzsche, and the criticism of metaphysics.
Bibliography.
Includes index.
1. Hegel, Georg Wilhelm Friedrich, 1770–1831.
2. Nietzsche, Friedrich Wilhelm, 1844–1900.
3. Metaphysics – History – 19th century. I. Title.
B2948.H66 1986   193   86-6831

ISBN 0 521 32255 3 hardback
ISBN 0 521 89279 1 paperback

For my mother and father

Contents

vii

Preface

This book is an attempt to compare and contrast the philosophies of Friedrich Nietzsche (1844–1900) and G. W. F. Hegel (1770–1831), and in particular the criticisms made by these two philosophers of the mode of thinking they both call 'metaphysics'. I have undertaken this project in order to challenge the claim which is sometimes made that Nietzsche's writings represent a revolution in philosophical thinking, which makes any thought of a return to more traditional conceptions of philosophy, in particular to the great conceptual systems of German Idealism, impossible. This book tries to show that, *pace* Nietzsche, a return to Hegel is defensible, and indeed that the inadequacies of Nietzsche's own philosophy became fully manifest when his 'Dionysiac' vision of life is contrasted with the dialectical thought of Hegel. The point of the book is not, however, simply to maintain that Hegel is more consistent than Nietzsche, or that he deals with areas of experience – such as political and economic life – which Nietzsche largely ignores, though these are claims I would wish to uphold. The point is rather to show that Hegel is more far-reaching and more profound than Nietzsche in precisely the area in which Nietzsche's philosophy has been held to be so revolutionary: the critique of the conceptual distinctions and oppositions (*Gegensätze*) of metaphysical thought, and in particular the distinction between the subject and the predicate. It is this common ground which, I believe, makes the comparison of Hegel and Nietzsche intelligible, and perhaps even essential, and which gives to a Hegelian interpretation and critique of Nietzsche a special interest.

Before comparing and contrasting the criticisms of metaphysical distinctions and oppositions made by Hegel and Nietzsche, I offer in chapter 1 a general survey of the wide variety of positions that have been taken up in the Hegel–Nietzsche debate, and I indicate what contribution my own work is trying to make to that debate. Chapter 2

examines Nietzsche's own view of Hegel's philosophy and the sources
for that view, and counters the opinion, held, for example, by G.
Deleuze, that Nietzsche was a reliable and incisive critic of Hegel. The
path is cleared by this chapter for an understanding of the relation
between Hegel and Nietzsche which differs greatly from Nietzsche's
own understanding of that relation.

In chapter 3 I examine Nietzsche's conception of metaphysical,
oppositional thinking, and his own philosophical alternative to such
thinking. In chapters 4 and 5 I then examine the conception of
metaphysical thinking and the philosophical alternative to such
thinking offered by Hegel. The main difference which emerges between these two figures is that Nietzsche criticises metaphysical
thought by confronting it with his vision of shifting, chaotic 'life',
whereas Hegel criticises metaphysical thought by articulating the
speculative, dialectical form immanent in such thought itself. Chapters 6 and 7 develop this Hegelian idea that the dialectical character of
rationality is immanent in the forms of human thought and consciousness by considering Hegel's treatment of the dialectical character
of the judgement and of the modes of consciousness discussed in the
Phenomenology. These two chapters also continue the theme of the
second part of chapter 5, namely that Hegel's dialectical understanding of thought brings with it the redefinition of what has traditionally
been thought of as the subject. In chapter 8 I briefly compare the
dialectical conception of the subject put forward by Hegel with the
heroic, 'Dionysiac' conception of the subject promoted by Nietzsche,
and then in the main body of the chapter I seek to bring the fundamental difference between Hegel and Nietzsche into sharper focus
by looking at the way the two philosophers deal with the theme of
tragedy.

This book has inevitably oversimplified many issues and neglected
many others. Nevertheless, I hope that it has perhaps opened up a way
of contrasting Hegel and Nietzsche which others will find it valuable
and profitable to pursue.

In the course of preparing this book (which formed my Ph.D thesis)
many friends, students, teachers and colleagues have given me
encouragement, criticism and advice for which I am extremely grate-
ful. In particular I would like to mention J. P. Stern and my Ph.D
examiners, Raymond Plant and Barry Nisbet, all of whom made very
helpful suggestions for improvements to the text. Above all,

however, I should like to express my deepest gratitude to my thesis supervisor, Nicholas Boyle, who, over seven years, was the most conscientious and thoughtful reader of my work, and who has also been the most generous and helpful of mentors.

The original inspiration for my thesis and for this book came from lectures on Hegel given by Duncan Forbes which I attended when I was an undergraduate at Cambridge. These lectures – which I still regard as probably the best introduction to Hegel's philosophy available in English – laid the foundation for my understanding of Hegel, and I should like to acknowledge my debt to Duncan Forbes here.

I should like also to thank my two Cambridge colleges – Trinity Hall and Girton – for the friendship and support that they offered me during my years at Cambridge, as well as my colleagues in the Department of Philosophy at the University of Edinburgh for the encouragement they have given me since my arrival from Cambridge in 1984. I am particularly indebted to the late Mistress, Brenda Ryman, and the Fellows of Girton, and to the Faculty of Arts at the University of Edinburgh for granting me the financial support of research fellowships. Further financial support was awarded to me by the DAAD for two years' study in Germany: one year as an undergraduate in Freiburg-im-Breisgau, during which I made my first prolonged study of Nietzsche, and one year as a graduate in Tübingen, when I was able to spend several months in detailed study of Hegel's *Science of Logic*, and also to attend lectures on the *Logic* given by Klaus Hartmann. For this opportunity to study German philosophy in Germany itself, I am especially thankful.

Finally, I should like to thank my parents and my wife, Mary, for all their encouragement, practical assistance and enduring patience over many years of what must have seemed remote and obscure research. Without the loving support of my two families this work would not have been completed. Since, however, my parents have had to endure my obscure research for substantially longer than my wife, I dedicate this book to them.

Abbreviations and translations

The following abbreviations are used in the notes for texts by Hegel, Nietzsche and Schopenhauer, and the translations indicated are the ones on which I have drawn for the quotations in English which are given in the book. Unless otherwise indicated the dates given refer to the date of publication of each text.

TWA   Hegel, *Theorie Werkausgabe*, edited by E. Moldenhauer and K. Michel, 20 Vols. and Index (Frankfurt, 1969–)

FS   *Frühe Schriften* (*Early Writings*), written 1793–1802 (*TWA*, I)
Translations from G. W. F. Hegel, *On Christianity: Early Theological Writings*, translated by T. M. Knox, with Introduction, and Fragments translated by Richard Kroner (Chicago, 1948; New York, 1961)

Phän   *Phänomenologie des Geistes* (*Phenomenology of Spirit*), 1807 (*TWA*, III)

Translations from *Hegel's Phenomenology of Spirit*, translated by A. V. Miller, with Analysis of the Text and Foreword by J. N. Findlay (Oxford, 1977)

NHS   *Nürnberger und Heidelberger Schriften* (*Nuremberg and Heidelberg Writings*), written 1808–17 (*TWA*, IV)

WL   *Wissenschaft der Logik* (*Science of Logic*), 1812–16, second edition, 1832 (*TWA*, V, VI)

Translations from *Hegel's Science of Logic*, translated by A. V. Miller, with Foreword by J. N. Findlay (London, 1969)

PRecht   *Grundlinien der Philosophie des Rechts* (*Philosophy of Right*), 1820 (*TWA*, VII)

Translations from *Hegel's Philosophy of Right*, translated with Notes by T. M. Knox (Oxford, 1952)

E I   *Enzyklopädie der philosophischen Wissenschaften (Encyclopaedia of the Philosophical Sciences)*, 1830, Vol. I, *Wissenschaft der Logik* (*TWA*, VIII)

Translations from *The Logic of Hegel*, translated from the *Encyclopaedia* with Prolegomena by W. Wallace (Oxford, 1874)

E II   *Enzyklopädie (Encyclopaedia)*, Vol. II, *Naturphilosophie* (*TWA*, IX)

Translations from *Hegel's Philosophy of Nature*, edited and translated with Introduction and Explanatory Notes by M. J. Petry, 3 Vols. (London, 1970)

E III   *Enzyklopädie (Encyclopaedia)*, Vol. III, *Philosophie des Geistes* (*TWA*, X)

Translations from *Hegel's Philosophy of Mind*, being Part Three of the *Encyclopaedia* (1830), translated by W. Wallace, together with the *Zusätze* in Boumann's text (1845), translated by A. V. Miller, with Foreword by J. N. Findlay (Oxford, 1971)

BS   *Berliner Schriften (Berlin Writings)*, written 1818–31 (*TWA*, XI)

PGesch   *Vorlesungen über die Philosophie der Geschichte (Lectures on the Philosophy of History)*, delivered in Berlin, 1822–31 (*TWA*, XII)

Translations from G. W. F. Hegel, *The Philosophy of History*, with Prefaces by Charles Hegel and the translator, J. Sibree, and new Introduction by C. J. Friedrich (New York, 1956)

Ä   *Vorlesungen über die Ästhetik (Lectures on Aesthetics)*, delivered in Berlin, 1820–9 (*TWA*, XIII, XIV, XV)

Translations from G. W. F. Hegel, *Aesthetics: Lectures on Fine Art*, translated by T. M. Knox, 2 Vols. (Oxford, 1975)

PRel   *Vorlesungen über die Philosophie der Religion* (*Lectures on the Philosophy of Religion*), delivered in Berlin, 1821–31 (*TWA*, XVI, XVII)

Translations from G. W. F. Hegel, *Lectures on the Philosophy of Religion. Together with a Work on the Proofs of the Existence of God*, translated from the second German edition by the Rev. E. B. Speirs and J. Burdon Sanderson, edited by the Rev. E. B. Speirs, 3 Vols. (London, 1895)

GPhil   *Vorlesungen über die Geschichte der Philosophie* (*Lectures on the History of Philosophy*), delivered in Heidelberg and Berlin, 1816–31 (*TWA*, XVIII, XIX, XX)

Translations from G. W. F. Hegel, *Lectures on the History of Philosophy*, translated from the German by E. S. Haldane, 3 Vols. (London, 1892–6). (Much of the text of this translation is arranged in a different order from the text of the *TWA* edition since it follows an earlier German edition.)

Werke   Nietzsche, *Werke*, edited by K. Schlechta, 3 Vols. and Index (Munich, 1954–)

HKG   Nietzsche, *Werke und Briefe: Historisch-kritische Gesamtausgabe*, edited by H. J. Mette, W. Hoppe and others, 9 Vols. (Munich, 1933–)

KG   Nietzsche, *Werke: Kritische Gesamtausgabe*, edited by C. Colli and M. Montinari (Berlin, 1967–)

GT   *Die Geburt der Tragödie* (*The Birth of Tragedy*), 1872

Translations from F. Nietzsche, *The Birth of Tragedy* and *The Case of Wagner*, translated with Commentary by W. Kaufmann (New York, 1967)

PTZG   *Die Philosophie im tragischen Zeitalter der Griechen* (*Philosophy in the Tragic Age of the Greeks*), written 1873–6

Translations from F. Nietzsche, *Philosophy in the Tragic Age of the Greeks*, translated with Introduction by Marianne Cowan (Chicago, 1962)

ÜWL   *Über Wahrheit und Lüge im außermoralischen Sinn* (*On Truth and Lie in an Extra-moral Sense*) written 1873

ÜPW   *Über das Pathos der Wahrheit* (*On the Pathos of Truth*), written
       1872

       Translations of both *ÜWL* and *ÜPW* from *Philosophy and Truth: Selections from Nietzsche's Notebooks of the early 1870s*, translated and edited
       with Introduction and Notes by Daniel Breazeale, with Foreword
       by W. Kaufmann (New Jersey and Sussex, 1979)

UB   *Unzeitgemäße Betrachtungen* (*Untimely Meditations*), 1873–6

       Translations from F. Nietzsche, *Untimely Meditations*, translated by
       R. J. Hollingdale, with Introduction by J. P. Stern (Cambridge,
       1983)

ÜZBA   *Über die Zukunft unserer Bildungsanstalten* (*On the Future of our
       Educational Institutions*), delivered in Basle, 1872

       Translations from F. Nietzsche, *On the Future of our Educational
       Institutions; Homer and Classical Philology*, translated with Introduction by J. M. Kennedy (Edinburgh and London, 1909), in *The Complete Works of Friedrich Nietzsche*, edited by Oscar Levy, Vol. VI

MA   *Menschliches, Allzumenschliches* (*Human, All-too Human*), 1878

       Translations from F. Nietzsche, *Human, All-too Human: A Book for
       Free Spirits*, Part 1, translated by Helen Zimmern, with Introduction
       by J. M. Kennedy (Edinburgh and London, 1909), in *The Complete
       Works of Friedrich Nietzsche*, edited by Oscar Levy, Vol. VII, Part
       1

VMS   *Vermischte Meinungen und Sprüche* (*Miscellaneous Maxims and
       Opinions*), 1879
WS   *Der Wanderer und sein Schatten* (*The Wanderer and his Shadow*),
       1880

       Translations of both *VMS* and *WS* from F. Nietzsche, *Human, All-too
       Human: A Book for Free Spirits*, Part 2, translated by Paul V. Cohn
       (Edinburgh and London, 1911), in *The Complete Works of Friedrich
       Nietzsche*, edited by Oscar Levy, Vol. VII, Part 2

M   *Morgenröte* (*Daybreak*), 1881

Translations from F. Nietzsche, *Daybreak: Thoughts on the Prejudices of Morality*, translated by R. J. Hollingdale, with Introduction by Michael Tanner (Cambridge, 1982)

FW   *Die fröhliche Wissenschaft* (*The Gay Science*), 1882

Translations from F. Nietzsche, *The Gay Science. With a Prelude in Rhymes and an Appendix of Songs*, translated with Commentary by W. Kaufmann (New York, 1974)

ASZ   *Also sprach Zarathustra* (*Thus Spoke Zarathustra*), 1883–5

Translations from F. Nietzsche, *Thus Spoke Zarathustra: A Book for Everyone and No-one*, translated with Introduction by R. J. Hollingdale (Harmondsworth, 1961; reprinted with new Introduction, 1969)

JGB   *Jenseits von Gut und Böse* (*Beyond Good and Evil*), 1886

Translations from F. Nietzsche, *Beyond Good and Evil: Prelude to a Philosophy of the Future*, translated with Introduction and Commentary by R. J. Hollingdale (Harmondsworth, 1973)

GM   *Zur Genealogie der Moral* (*The Genealogy of Morals*), 1887

Translations from F. Nietzsche, *On the Genealogy of Morals*, translated by W. Kaufmann and R. J. Hollingdale, and *Ecce Homo*, translated by W. Kaufmann, edited with Commentary by W. Kaufmann (New York, 1969)

FWag   *Der Fall Wagner* (*The Case of Wagner*), 1888

Translations from F. Nietzsche, *The Birth of Tragedy*, and *The Case of Wagner*, translated with Commentary by W. Kaufmann (New York, 1967)

GD   *Götzendämmerung* (*Twilight of the Idols*), written 1888, published 1889
A   *Der Antichrist* (*The Antichrist*), written 1888, published 1895

Translations from both *GD* and *A* from F. Nietzsche, *Twilight of the Idols* and *The Anti-Christ*, translated with Introduction and Commentary by R. J. Hollingdale (Harmondsworth, 1968)

EH   *Ecce Homo*, written 1888, published 1908

Translations from F. Nietzsche, *On the Genealogy of Morals*, translated by W. Kaufmann and R. J. Hollingdale, and *Ecce Homo*, translated by W. Kaufmann, edited with Commentary by W. Kaufmann (New York, 1969)

WM   Notes from Nietzsche's *Nachlaß* (posthumously published writings) of the 1880s, collected under the title *Der Wille zur Macht* (*The Will to Power*), by Elizabeth Förster-Nietzsche

Translations from F. Nietzsche, *The Will to Power*, a new translation by W. Kaufmann and R. J. Hollingdale, edited with Commentary by W. Kaufmann (London, 1968)

VWSG   *Über die vierfache Wurzel des Satzes vom zureichenden Grunde* (*On the Fourfold Root of the Principle of Sufficient Reason*), 1813

Translations from A. Schopenhauer, *On the Fourfold Root of the Principle of Sufficient Reason*, translated by E. F. J. Payne, with Introduction by Richard Taylor (La Salle, Illinois, 1974)

WWV   *Die Welt als Wille und Vorstellung* (*The World as Will and Representation*), 1818, second edition, 1844

Translations from A. Schopenhauer, *The World as Will and Representation*, translated by E. F. J. Payne, 2 Vols. (New York, 1958; revised edition, 1966)

GPE   *Die beiden Grundprobleme der Ethik* (*The Two Fundamental Problems of Ethics*), 1841

Translations from A. Schopenhauer, *On the Basis of Morality*, translated by E. F. J. Payne, with Introduction by Richard Taylor (Indianapolis, 1965)

PP   *Parerga und Paralipomena* (*Parerga and Paralipomena*), 1851
Translations from A. Schopenhauer, *Parerga and Paralipomena: Short Philosophical Essays*, translated by E. F. J. Payne, 2 Vols. (Oxford, 1974)

Translations from the works of other writers such as F. A. Lange, J. Burckhardt, M. Heidegger, G. Deleuze, G. Frege, K. Löwith and

R. Wagner are taken from the English versions listed in the bibliography. Translations from texts for which no English versions are listed here or in the bibliography are in all cases my own.

I have used published translations wherever possible since they are likely to be the texts most commonly consulted by students. However, I have frequently amended translations or substituted my own, so the wording of quotations in this book will not always match the wording in the English versions to which I refer. When citing or referring to passages from French and German texts in the notes, I have first given the reference to the edition which I myself used, and then, wherever possible, the date of a letter, a paragraph number or a page number in brackets in order to enable the reader to find the relevant passage in the corresponding English translation. Where I have referred in the notes to a French or German text for which no suitable English translation is available, and I have just cited a few words which are not intended as a quotation but merely as a signpost to help the reader locate the precise passage in question in the original text, then I thought it sensible to cite those few words in the original language.

1
The
Hegel–Nietzsche
debate

Anyone attempting a comparison of the philosophies of Hegel and Nietzsche is immediately confronted with what seems to be an intractable difficulty, for the two men represent 'fundamentally divergent types of philosophical style and temperament'.[1] Hegel is a systematic philosopher who places his faith in the rigorous and methodical unfolding of dialectical reason, whereas Nietzsche is an unsystematic, highly literary writer, the champion of brilliant isolated perceptions and colourful, arresting metaphors. Linguistically the philosophers are worlds apart. Hegel's speculative discourse, whatever its intrinsic merits and purpose, strikes many, including Nietzsche, as cumbersome and obscure,[2] whilst Nietzsche's lively and lucid style seems, as B. F. Beerling puts it, to defeat with its light-footedness the innate ponderousness of the German tongue.[3] These differences raise awkward questions for the commentator: Why should we undertake a comparison of Hegel and Nietzsche? And how are we to undertake that comparison? Are not the philosophers simply too far apart from each other to warrant or even to allow comparative evaluation? In this chapter we will survey some of the answers that have been given to these questions.[4]

The effort of comparing Hegel's speculative philosophy with Nietzsche's Dionysiac philosophy of life has been justified on many different grounds. The most direct justification has come from Gilles Deleuze. In his somewhat unorthodox view, we should compare Hegel and Nietzsche because Nietzsche himself saw Hegel as the

1

primary target of his philosophical assault on nihilism.[5] For Deleuze, therefore, the reason why there exists a debate between Hegel and Nietzsche is that Nietzsche's own polemic against Hegel initiated it.

Walter Kaufmann, on the other hand, has justified comparing Nietzsche with Hegel (rather than, say, with Schopenhauer) for exactly the opposite reason. In his view, Nietzsche's philosophy is not opposed to that of Hegel at all, for if we compare Hegel's concept of sublation (*aufheben*) with Nietzsche's concept of sublimation (*sublimieren*) we can detect a 'truly amazing parallel'.[6] Whether or not Kaufmann is correct in the details of his analysis, he suggests enough of a superficial similarity between Hegel and Nietzsche to warrant comparing them. Elsewhere, however, Kaufmann has put forward an argument which suggests an even more obvious reason for studying Hegel and Nietzsche together: that is, simply, that Hegel and Nietzsche are the two nineteenth-century philosophers who have exercised the greatest influence on the thinking and life of the twentieth century.[7] Even if one might wish to qualify Kaufmann's assertion and say that Nietzsche and Hegel are two of the nineteenth-century philosophers who have most influenced our century, it nevertheless remains true that both have enough authority and stature in our eyes to call each other to account.

The most persuasive argument has, however, been put forward by Daniel Breazeale. In his view we should compare Hegel and Nietzsche because the two philosophers share (and are perceived by us to share) a common aim, that is of bringing to an end the tradition of Western metaphysics and of initiating a radically new way of thinking:

Surely Hegel, just as appropriately as Nietzsche, could have thought himself 'a destiny' (*EH*, IV), even while he had the better taste not actually to *say* so. Not just in their own opinion, but in that of many reflective persons today, the work of one (or both) of these thinkers represents a decisive culminating and turning point in the history of Western thought and culture.[8]

If both philosophers want to offer their philosophies as liberating alternatives to metaphysics, it seems not only warranted, but incumbent upon us, to compare and evaluate what they have to offer. Nor is the debate between Hegel and Nietzsche a purely regional problem of interest only to Hegelians and Nietzscheans. Much of our thinking from Marxism to linguistic analysis, from Heidegger and Wittgenstein to Derrida, has been concerned precisely with the problem of criticising and surpassing what is understood to be 'metaphysical' philosophy:

In the context of such considerations, the Hegel–Nietzsche problem is part of the larger problem of comprehending the crisis of modern thought, and an expression of our desire to establish our own intellectual identity, with respect both to the 'tradition' and its breakdown.[9]

In view of its importance, therefore, it is all the more surprising that no full-scale study of the Hegel–Nietzsche problem has been attempted. The discussion has been fragmented and scattered amongst articles and chapters of books, and it is to this fragmented and varied discussion that we now turn.[10]

Summarising the work of previous commentators who have compared Hegel and Nietzsche is made difficult by the fact that no single theme or approach has guided their research. The reason for this is, however, clear. Both Hegel and Nietzsche are extremely wide-ranging thinkers who have turned their philosophical attention, amongst other things, to religion, art, history, ethics, metaphysics and language. Furthermore, the notorious complexity of their thought, sometimes exaggerated and sometimes disguised by the philosophical and political prejudice of their commentators, has given rise to many varied and often contradictory interpretations, by no means all of which can be supported by the texts. As a consequence, therefore, discussion of the relationship between Hegel and Nietzsche has taken on radically different forms.

The most barren approach has without doubt been the attempt to bring Hegel and Nietzsche together by associating them both with the aims of National Socialism. The two short articles in *National-sozialistische Monatshefte* (December 1931), printed under the heading 'Hegel und Nietzsche', do not present any formal philosophical comparison of the two thinkers, but assert their inestimable common value for the Nazi cause. The value of Nietzsche, as is to be expected, is seen in his espousal of the 'manly' virtues which the author maintains lie at the heart of National Socialism: 'discipline, courage, hardness, sobriety, freedom, service, activity'.[11] Hegel, on the other hand, whose dialectical method grows out of 'the formative expressive power of the German character [*des Deutschtums*] in general, that is, the German language',[12] has bequeathed to National Socialism the quintessentially German concept of *Aufhebung*, the unification or sublation of different moments into a higher totality. This concept, we are told, is important for National Socialism, because it encapsulates the central aim of the movement, which is to *aufheben* the two sides of Germany – the liberal bourgeoisie and the German international proletariat – into a true, free *Volkstum* or nationhood.[13]

Such overt abuse of Hegel and Nietzsche for political motives has of course only confirmed popular prejudice against the philosophers. H.C. Graef's article, 'From Hegel to Hitler', published, it should be said, during the Second World War, exemplifies the unthinking acceptance by many commentators of the allegedly sinister implications of Hegel's and Nietzsche's philosophies. Hegel is identified as a direct ancestor of the Nazis because of his alleged doctrine of the unlimited power of the state – 'the individual as such is insignificant and unable to develop into a moral personality . . . Thus when Hitler proclaimed the Totalitarian State he only carried to the extreme what was already given in Hegel's philosophy.'[14] Nietzsche's philosophy, on the other hand, is held by Graef to be that of 'unbridled egotism' and the 'unfettered individualism of the superman',[15] and thus to be directly opposed to Hegel's 'deification' of the state. Yet Graef concludes that these utterly different thinkers meet in apparently undisturbed harmony in the Nazi *Weltanschauung*:

> Hegel furnished it with the theory of the absolute superiority of the State to which the individual must sacrifice everything, and which, itself, is not subject to any international laws. Nietzsche, on the other hand, was called in to provide *Lebensraum* for those whose will to power was too strong to submit to the World-Spirit as embodied in the State. He proclaimed the Superman which became incarnate in the Fuehrer, whom all the little sub-Fuehrers are striving to imitate.[16]

Fortunately such views do not represent a major trend in the Hegel–Nietzsche debate. They rest on wilful misreading of the original texts or on unscholarly prejudice, and have been criticised many times over. They are mentioned here only for the sake of historical interest and comprehensiveness.[17]

The main corpus of literature pertaining to the Hegel–Nietzsche debate can be divided into three categories: (a) those commentators who clearly take Nietzsche's side against Hegel, (b) those who are primarily interested in pointing out certain similarities between the two philosophers, but who may also lean more towards one than the other, and (c) those who use Hegelian arguments to criticise Nietzsche.

[Handwritten marginal note:] no better than saying all Jews are sinister – a facile critique based on popular thought devoid of one a reading

R. J. Hollingdale, for example, falls into the first category. Hollingdale acknowledges that Nietzsche owes a great debt to his mentor, Arthur Schopenhauer, since Schopenhauer was the philosopher who directed Nietzsche (as he directed other philosophers) towards the irrational and the subconscious as the source of human motivation. Yet although it is true to say that Nietzsche 'came after' Schopenhauer, Hollingdale believes it would be better to say that he came after *Hegel* 'inasmuch as Hegel summarised and brought to completion a tradition which ... constituted his [Nietzsche's] real "predecessor" '.[18] In Hollingdale's view, Hegel is the last major representative of that tradition of Western philosophy which finds its most incisive critic in Nietzsche. Hegel is committed to the belief that the structure of reason and the structure of reality are identical, the belief that absolute spirit constitutes the 'real' world behind the inferior, 'apparent' world of our experience, and the belief that the world has a moral structure in which justice is rewarded and injustice punished – and all of these are philosophical beliefs which, according to Hollingdale, Nietzsche consistently denies.[19]

In my view Hollingdale is right to see Nietzsche as a vehement critic of Western philosophy, but wrong to consider Hegel to be a traditional philosopher in all of the senses just outlined. Hegel does not, for example, understand absolute spirit as the essential reality *behind* empirical phenomena, but as the rational self-consciousness of man.[20] That being said, however, it is true that Hegel believes the world to have a rational structure, and it is Nietzsche's opposition to *this* belief which distinguishes Hegel's this-worldly ontology from Nietzsche's own.

The most celebrated advocate of Nietzsche's critique of Hegel is Gilles Deleuze. In Deleuze's view, as I have indicated already, there can be no question of a compromise between Nietzsche and Hegel. Nietzsche's philosophy is 'an absolute anti-dialectics'.[21] Deleuze's argument rests upon his acceptance of Nietzsche's qualitative typology of life.[22] Living things, in fact all natural things, are distinguished for Deleuze according to the kind of force they represent – active or reactive – and according to the kind of will to power or mood they exhibit – affirmative or negative.[23] (Action is usually informed by affirmation and reaction by negation, but Deleuze insists that the qualities of force and the qualities of will to power that may inhere in force are not to be confused with one another. A negative will to power can, for example, 'infect' active forces and render them reactive.)[24]

The characteristic of affirmative, active force is a strong, vigorous sense of oneself and of one's own power – 'some fundamental certainty which a noble soul possesses in regard to itself'.[25] The values and interpretations generated by such active force are thus rooted in the affirmation by that force of its own strength and vitality. To demonstrate what is meant by this, Deleuze gives an example of an evaluative proposition typical of the active force: 'I am good, therefore you are bad [*méchant*].'[26] The premise of this proposition is the positive affirmation of the self, and the negative evaluation of the other is a secondary consequence of that initial affirmation. That negative evaluation is thus not the product of a fundamentally negative will to power, for the active force does not begin by denying or suppressing the other; it begins rather by affirming its own unique value and worth and by appreciating its own specific, qualitative *difference* from the other. An affirmative, active mode of being is thus one that rejoices in the hierarchy of qualitatively different and highly individual forces.[27]

By contrast, the characteristic of the negative, reactive force is its lack of a powerful sense of its own individuality and worth. The evaluative proposition typical of it is: 'You are bad, therefore I am good.'[28] The initial premise of this proposition is a negative evaluation of the other, and the 'affirmation' of the self is *derived* from that premise. This reactive force has no vigorous sense of itself and of what specifically differentiates it from other forces; in effect, therefore, its negative 'evaluation' of the other is simply an indiscriminate negation of the other. The reactive force thus begins by positing the other as a mere 'non-ego' (*non-moi*) and only acquires an 'affirmative' grasp of itself by understanding itself as the negation of that 'non-ego'. The utterer of the reactive proposition constructs his self dialectically by negating his negation.[29]

For Deleuze, this dialectically constituted, Hegelian self, and the negation of the other on which it is based, is the product of a wholly negative mode of will to power – one which conceals the specific differences between forces beneath abstract, and therefore fictional, concepts such as 'non-ego'.[30] Such a procedure, in Deleuze's view, is uncritical because the other is reduced to an abstraction which, though conceptually *opposed* to the self, is nevertheless legitimated by being treated as a necessary moment in the dialectical construction of the self. The other is not differentiated or evaluated qualitatively by an affirmative, active force, but is absorbed or dissolved into dialectical rationality. Dialectical thinking such as Hegel's thus submits all life to the dialectical 'labour of the negative'[31] and fosters an attitude of uncritical acquiescence in the fictional necessity of what 'is' and what is objectively 'rational'. For this reason, Deleuze sees in Hegelian dialectic the product of a tired, nihilistic will which is 'weary of willing' (*las de vouloir*),[32] and he contrasts it with the Dionysiac affirmation of the self that is celebrated in Nietzsche's philosophy.

Deleuze's interpretation of Nietzsche is persuasive, if rather too schematised; his view of Hegel, on the other hand, is a distortion.[33] Hegel's dialectic is not in fact based upon an initial *external* negation of the specific differences between things, and does not therefore constitute a flight into an abstract world of fictional concepts as Deleuze asserts. Dialectical negation for Hegel is not something brought to bear on a positive premise from the outside, but is inherent in that premise from the start. According to Hegel's *Science of Logic*, a thing must be *in itself* the negation of something else (which is also negatively determined) if it is to have any determinate characteristics – and indeed be differentiated from anything else – at all. The notion of something real or specific which is not negatively determined, or mediated, is precisely what dialectical philosophy shows up to be an impossibility.[34]

However, Deleuze fails to see Hegel's point. For Deleuze, negation is always either a denial of already qualitatively specified forces, or the secondary consequence of the self-affirmation of already qualitatively specified forces. It is never conceived as that which specifies and differentiates such 'forces' in the first place. The affirmation of the specific 'differences' between forces does not therefore involve seeing those forces as necessarily the 'negation' of one another, as necessarily mediated by one another. Affirmation and negation for Deleuze are quite distinct. If we are predominantly negative beings, we begin with the external negation of existing forces and derive an abstract notion of selfhood by a conceptual dialectical process; if on the other hand we are predominantly affirmative beings, then we begin with the affirmation of ourselves and of what differentiates us from other forces, and conclude with a negative evaluation of certain of those other forces. In both cases, however, existing forces are conceived by Deleuze as the 'irreducible', 'original' (and thus, for Hegel, insufficiently mediated or determined) foundation.[35] Deleuze thus rules out the possibility that true, concrete selfhood is to be understood in terms of the negation of, or mediation by, the other.

The only true sense of selfhood for Deleuze is that of the affirmative, active mode of being which affirms its own specific qualities 'immediately', and does not conceive of itself as inherently mediated by negation, as *intrinsically* the negation of the other. In active forces 'affirmation comes first, negation is never more than a consequence, like a crowning joy [*comme un surcroît de jouissance*]'.[36]

Yet despite his theoretical opposition to Hegel, Deleuze in practice confirms Hegel's dialectical view, for he also determines affirmation as essentially *opposed* to negation (in the sense of the negative will to power). Deleuze thus defines affirmation as logically incorporating the moment of negation (in the sense of opposition) within itself: 'Negation and affirmation are opposed as two qualities of the will to power . . . each is an opposite [*un contraire*], but also a whole which excludes its opposite.'[37] However, Deleuze will not acknowledge that negation is inherent in affirmation as Hegel does. Instead he insists that negation is either a quality of will to power distinct from affirmation or merely a subordinate consequence of affirmative premises.[38]

What are the consequences of Deleuze's failure to appreciate Hegel's somewhat rarified point of logic? Does it actually matter that he does not recognise negation and mediation to be immanent in affirmative being? In my view, it matters a great deal, because it means that for Deleuze there is no qualitative identity between affirmative and negative modes of being; the master and the slave do not share a common human identity because the master does not share the slave's mediated existence and dependence. Deleuze's hostility to various forms of codification and to attempts to objectify and institutionalise human equality are rooted in this belief in the inalienable typological difference between men.

A further consequence of Deleuze's undialectical view of human life is that selfhood for him is conceived in an asocial, virtually anarchic way. The strong man's affirmative sense of himself and of his specific difference from the other is rooted in his *own* feeling of power and vitality. In contrast to Hegel, Deleuze does not believe that genuine self-consciousness requires consciousness of the other's recognition of oneself: 'the one who says "I am good", does not wait to be called good . . . He names himself and describes himself thus to the extent that he acts, affirms and enjoys.'[39] The dependence upon, and mediation by, such recognition is for Deleuze a sign of weakness, and Hegel's dialectical treatment of the master–slave relation, which relies so heavily on the notion of recognition, is consequently dismissed as the slave's view of the matter.[40]

The second category of commentators to be considered comprises those who wish to highlight the similarities which they recognise between Hegel and Nietzsche. As the range of similarities which are suggested is extremely wide, however, this category does not have any real thematic unity.

Walter Schulz, for example, has suggested a general affinity between the philosophers. In his view, Hegel and Nietzsche are both metaphysicians who conceive of being in terms of circular movement. Moreover, they are both specifically modern metaphysicians because they are concerned with the problem, unknown to the Greeks, of how the philosopher who announces the circular character of being can understand himself in terms of that circle. Both answer the problem, Schulz argues, by seeing the philosopher as the locus of the self-knowledge and self-reflection of being.[41]

However, Schulz is of course aware of the great differences that obtain between Hegel and Nietzsche. In Hegel's case the process of cosmic self-reflection takes place only once, whereas in Nietzsche's case it is a continually recurring event. Furthermore, Schulz believes that at times Nietzsche begins to 'surpass' metaphysics by presenting his doctrine of the eternal recurrence, not as the definitive truth of being, but merely as the highest perspective that life or will to power has produced until the present. Unlike Hegel, therefore, Nietzsche oscillates between commitment to what he believes to be true, and commitment to what he sees as an interpretation of being. In Schulz's view, however, Nietzsche's dilemma is not to be dismissed as a simple contradiction; rather it is the result of a genuine reflection on the possibility of metaphysics. That is to say, Nietzsche is alleged to be caught between the metaphysical desire to understand the world as an objective, systematic totality, and the critical insight into the will to power which underlies that metaphysical desire. According to Schulz, Nietzsche has thus begun to challenge metaphysics, but has not yet freed himself from it. This problem is only resolved, Schulz argues, in the radically non-metaphysical philosophy of the later Heidegger, who ceases to conceive of being as the determinate condition or foundation of things, but who conceives of being – usually written in Heidegger translations as Being – as 'in itself not understandable' (*an ihm selbst unverstehbar*), as what Schulz calls the 'pure' condition of our life.[42]

In contrast to Walter Schulz, the work of Karl Brose owes more to Marx and Adorno than to Heidegger. Brose is particularly concerned with the philosophy of history and he studies the views of Hegel and

Nietzsche on history looking for elements of what he calls 'critical history'.[43] The theories of history put forward by Hegel and Nietzsche are 'critical' in Brose's eyes to the extent that they undermine 'moral' (in particular, Christian) interpretations of historical events, interpretations that served to suppress the real character of historical change in the name of the restricted codes of value of nineteenth-century German society.[44]

The main critical thrust of their views of history lies for Brose in the emphasis that both Hegel and Nietzsche are said to place on the role of great individuals. Both philosophers show that the historical 'greatness' of individuals resides in qualities which from a moral point of view can only be considered to be 'immoral'.[45] Great figures like Socrates came into conflict with, and eventually destroyed, a whole culture's beliefs and values; others like Napoleon or Caesar were motivated by personal ambition and thirst for action to carry out acts of conquest. History in the view of Hegel and Nietzsche is not therefore the arena where moral intention and action hold sway, but it is carried forward by personal ambition and passion. The narrow 'moral gloss' (*moralische Beschönigung*), which, according to Brose, was put on historical events and on nineteenth-century society by such uncritical historians as Treitschke, is thus revealed by the perspectives of Hegel and Nietzsche to be a falsification of historical reality.[46]

Brose's admiration for Hegel and Nietzsche is, however, qualified. Whilst recognising that Nietzsche's critique of historicism is more a critique of the consequences of Hegel than of Hegel himself,[47] Brose still adopts the Nietzschean (and Marxian) view that Hegel's is to a large extent itself an idealistic distortion of actual historical reality. Hegel may well put figures like Socrates and Caesar beyond moral censure, but his 'immoral' historical individuals in fact serve a higher ethical goal; they are the vehicles of a rational 'world-spirit'. Consequently, Hegel fails to achieve an adequate understanding of the material and economic dimension of historical change and interprets history in terms of the single unifying principle of 'reason'.[48] By contrast, Brose finds Nietzsche's view of history more sensitive to human practice, to 'life'. Nietzsche dispenses with Hegel's 'cunning of reason' and interprets action solely in terms of '*individual* power'. As a result, we no longer find in Nietzsche, as we do in Hegel, 'a rounded, total view of history', but rather an individualised, multi-faceted, perspectival view of events.[49]

The limitation of Nietzsche's view, however, is that it is too individualistic; it does not display sufficient awareness of the social context of individual action which Hegel (albeit in an idealistic way) recognises.[50] Furthermore, Nietzsche lacks any explicit awareness of the 'dialectical' character of power which Hegel uncovers, awareness, that is, of the inherent dependence of the powerful upon the impoverished. For Nietzsche, the powerful and the weak are always antagonistically opposed to one another (*feindlich konfrontiert*). In this respect, therefore, Brose finds Nietzsche uncritical, because once he has revealed will to power as the basic motive behind historical action up to and including the present, he does not then follow Hegel and highlight the essential dependence and consequent vulnerability of all power; in fact Nietzsche's 'immoralism' is a function of his celebration of power in its most 'heroic' form.[51]

On the other hand, Brose does detect traces of an unconscious 'dialectic' in Nietzsche's notion of strength, for Nietzsche takes the phenomenon of weakness so seriously that he cannot conceive of strength 'without reference to the weak'.[52] The strict dichotomy which Nietzsche sets up between the strong and the weak is thus, for Brose, 'erected . . . artificially' (*künstlich . . . aufgerichtet*)[53] – a fiction, perhaps, to preserve the powerful, heroic individual from any sense that his strength might need and depend on weakness in order to flourish.

Brose's final qualification of Nietzsche is to suggest that despite their common 'critical' dimension, Nietzsche and Hegel share a profoundly uncritical admiration for the universal as against the particular. For all his commitment to individualism, therefore, Nietzsche's great individuals are representatives of the universal will to power just as Hegel's individuals are vehicles of *Geist*; 'the question arises', Brose comments, 'whether this Hegelian universal, the "cunning of reason", is not at work in Nietzsche's "will to power" '. In their uncritical subordination of the individual to the universal, Hegel and Nietzsche thus prefigure, though are not responsible for, the 'cult of the total' and the 'subsuming . . . of millions of people' which later descended on Germany.[54]

In contrast to Brose (and also to Deleuze) two commentators – Robert L. Zimmermann and Walter Kaufmann – have pressed the claim that there is a conscious and highly important dialectical strand to Nietzsche's philosophy. According to this interpretation Hegel and Nietzsche are agreed that the underlying reality – whether it is called 'spirit' or 'will to power' – must be conceived as 'essentially active, as self-diremptive and eternally self-overcoming'.[55] They are both, in Kaufmann's phrase, 'dialectical monists'.[56]

Zimmermann begins his article, 'On Nietzsche', by distinguishing two important traditions within philosophy. One he calls the Pythagorean tradition. This tells us that 'in the beginning, man existed in an ideal, profoundly happy, virtually divine state', but that in the course of history man' "fell" from his state of perfection and became the imperfect, profoundly unhappy creature that he is ... a soul imprisoned within a body, a repressed, broken animal'.[57] For this tradition, which Zimmermann finds exemplified by thinkers like St Augustine and Rousseau, as well as Pythagoras, man's true state was the initial state of harmony that has been lost.

The second tradition Zimmermann calls the Hegelian one. For Hegel, beginnings or origins are merely immediate states of being: 'at its beginning a thing is neither fully developed nor fully real and complete'. In order to become truly what it is to be, a thing must move away from its origins and pass through 'mediation, change, alienation, and development'. The question Zimmermann poses is this: 'is Nietzsche to be classified as a Pythagorean or an Hegelian? More specifically, does Nietzsche interpret the Christianizing of the master as a fall from a metaphysically privileged state or a step in the evolution of man?'[58]

At first sight, we are told, Nietzsche appears very much to be a Pythagorean. Nietzsche describes an initial state of natural, instinctual innocence and shows how Judaeo-Christian religion has disrupted that natural state by introducing the concept of guilt and repression into man's life. The once noble animal has been tamed and weakened by the ascetic ideal. But, Zimmermann argues, the impression that Nietzsche sees Judaeo-Christianity as wholly destructive is mistaken. In fact Nietzsche has 'an Hegelian, which is to say dialectical, notion of negation'. In Zimmermann's view, Nietzsche sees the negation of the initial noble state as leading to the creation of a new state of being which is 'more definite and more complexly propertied'. The master was destroyed, 'but a new *more evolved, higher* type being was created'.[59]

Before Christianisation man was a purely natural being, whose behaviour was guided by his instincts. Christianity, however, repressed that natural life and gave man the power to negate himself, to defy the natural order and make an unnatural thing of himself. This power, of course, can be and has been misused by man to weaken and 'castrate' himself, but it can also be used to spiritualise and sublimate the natural instincts into higher (for example, aesthetic) drives. When this is achieved man acquires the capacity to determine his own life and to direct his natural energy freely and consciously. Such a man – the superman (*der Übermensch*) – is, as far as Zimmermann is con cerned, the true goal of history for Nietzsche. Zimmermann concludes: 'it thus seems clear that Nietzsche is an Hegelian. He conceptualises the state of the master as a foundational state from which, as a basic original stuff, man, i.e. fully realised and developed, self-made man, is to come.'[60]

Zimmermann has highlighted an important feature of Nietzsche's thought. He is undoubtedly correct that Nietzsche does not wish to bring about the resurrection of the 'blond beast', but the sublimation of him. To that extent Nietzsche's philosophy does indeed exhibit the familiar Hegelian structure of immediacy–reflection–mediated immediacy, or self–negation of self–new self, a structure that is clearly related to the Christian notion that man must die to himself in order to be born into new life.[61] Zimmermann's interpretation is in this respect an improvement upon that of Deleuze, for although Deleuze maintains that the affirmative master comes to harness the weak, negative mode of will to power to his own purposes, he does not suggest that the master is thereby 'honed', transformed or sublimated.[62]

But is Zimmermann's Nietzsche truly Hegelian? I believe not, for the 'dialectical' negation and re-creation of the master is, from a Hegelian point of view, incomplete. The master is transformed into a new master, but, just as in Deleuze's interpretation, and indeed as Karl Brose's account implies, the typological distinction between the master and the slave is not broken down. The dialectic that Zimmermann describes merely modifies the master's mode of being in an external way; 'one adds more reality to it, so to speak, by crystallising out of it new and enriching dimensions'.[63] But the basic character of the master as vigorously individual and self-assertive is not affected, as the model of the *Übermensch* demonstrates. The master is not transformed into a mode of being which finds its strength in its common identity and humanity with all men.

The same criticism could be levelled against the attempt to draw a parallel between Hegel and Nietzsche made by Walter Kaufmann, who greatly influenced Zimmermann's article.[64] In Kaufmann's view, as I suggested earlier, there is a remarkable similarity between

Nietzsche's notion of sublimation and Hegel's concept of *aufheben*, in that both involve 'a simultaneous preserving, cancelling and lifting up' of what is being changed. For both Hegel and Nietzsche, therefore, the sublimation of the instincts, rather than the repression or indulgence of them, is the goal of human life.[65]

Kaufmann makes out a case for the similarity between Hegel and Nietzsche that is *prima facie* quite convincing. However, if we look more closely at how Kaufmann defines Nietzsche's concept of sublimation, it becomes clear that it bears only superficial resemblance to Hegel's *aufheben*. To understand the sublimation of an instinct, Kaufmann suggests, we must distinguish the essential force within that instinct – will to power – from its accidental or changing attributes, for example its manifestation as sexual appetite or hunger. In sublimation the will to power is what is preserved and the accidental manifestation is what is cancelled.[66] The fundamental feeling of potency remains, but it comes to be manifested in a new form, for example in aesthetic creativity or in reason.

Now, whatever the value of Kaufmann's theory as an explanation of Nietzsche's notion of sublimation, it certainly does not explain what Hegel means by *aufheben*. Kaufmann's metaphysical distinction of essence and accident means that the sublimation of, say, the sexual drive, whilst preserving the energy of the drive, effectively cancels its specifically sexual orientation.[67] For Hegel on the other hand, as he explains in the *Science of Logic*, the *Aufhebung* of something only involves the negation of the immediacy of the thing's specific character; it does not involve cancelling that specific character altogether in favour of a more refined manifestation of an underlying essential quality. When something is *aufgehoben*, it is reconciled with whatever it is opposed to in its immediacy, but 'it still has, therefore, *in itself* the *determinateness from which it originates*'.[68] The *Aufhebung* of sexuality, from a Hegelian perspective, would thus involve both preserving its initial sexual orientation and reorienting it towards 'higher', more ethical goals by transforming it, for example, into a moment of spiritual love.

Kaufmann also defines sublimation in a slightly different way, however, which might accord more with Hegel's notion. In this second sense, sublimation involves the employment of impulses *by* reason, rather than the transformation of impulses *into* reason.[69] Sublimation in this sense might be said to involve the subordination of impulses, in their original specification, to rational goals. Even in this sense, however, Nietzsche's sublimation and Hegel's *aufheben* are not identical processes. For Nietzsche, in Kaufmann's eyes, sublimation can be defined as self-overcoming, the domination and control of the instinctual self by the rational self. Sublimation is thus a function of the individual's will to power; it is a process in which the individual's will to power is fulfilled by being turned against itself, by being converted from power over others to power over self. But for that very reason the fundamental orientation of the individual's will towards dominance is not altered – will to power remains will to power.[70]

This leads Kaufmann to posit a dualism within the unity of the individual's will to power, for 'in overcoming or sublimating itself, . . . it is both that which overcomes (e.g. reason) and that which is overcome (e.g. impulse)'.[71] Kaufmann claims that this dualism finds a parallel in Hegel's view that *Geist* is both substance and subject, both activated and activating force. However, unlike Kaufmann's 'reason', subjectivity for Hegel is not a *force* that overcomes and dominates its 'other', i.e. substance; subjectivity, in this sense, is rather the inner rationality or self-contradictory character of substance – the mediation of substance's independence by what is insubstantial. Hegel's dialectical *Aufhebung* of the impulses does not, therefore, merely take the form of the control of one instinctual mode of will to power by another rational mode, a process which leaves the individualistic, self-assertive essence of the will to power untouched and which indeed actually fulfils that essence in the very exercise of control. The *Aufhebung* of the impulses is the dialectical working-out of the self-contradiction at the heart of the will to power itself, that is the working-out of the self-contradiction involved in the inherent dependence of the will's masterful freedom on what it seeks to dominate. The result of Hegel's *Aufhebung* of the will is therefore not merely individual self-control, but the explicit socialisation of man's interest. It is the explicit recognition by the will that the satisfaction of individual needs lies in *social* interdependence and interaction.[72] For Hegel, this dialectic actually transforms a will geared primarily to individual self-assertion into one that finds individual self-fulfilment and power in community. For Nietzsche, however, in Deleuze's or Kaufmann's interpretation, no such profound change in the orientation of the will can take place. The individualistic will to power remains the fundamental character of man; genuine common interest is, therefore, illusory and is merely a fiction produced by a weak, 'democratic', form of will to power.

Finally in this category we come to a number of commentators who
have discerned what to my mind is the most important similarity between Hegel and Nietzsche: the parallel, stressed by Daniel Breazeale,
between the two philosophers as 'critics of is/ought, this world/other
world dualism'.[73] M. Theunissen, for example, has described Hegel as
a critic of 'the theory of two worlds which Nietzsche attributed to
Plato';[74] B. F. Beerling has argued that 'the thought of Hegel is hardly
any less opposed to the beyond than that of Nietzsche';[75] and several
commentators, including M. Greene, I. Soll and Beerling have drawn
attention to the similarity in the critical analyses that Hegel and
Nietzsche have undertaken of alienated, other-worldly consciousness: 'that which Hegel exposed as the unhappy consciousness . . .
recurs in Nietzsche's work in a more acute form as the *ressentiment* of
those beings "who are denied the true reaction, that of deeds", and
who compensate themselves with an "imaginary revenge" '.[76]

This parallel, it seems to me, is the main topic with which the comparative study of Hegel and Nietzsche should be concerned. 'The
starting-point for any serious consideration of their relationship is a
recognition that they are *allies* in the struggle against metaphysical,
moral and epistemological dualism. It is the common ground which
makes a study of their differences so interesting.'[77] Other topics, such
as 'history', 'the importance of science' or 'freedom and will', could
also yield interesting results; but for us to reach a proper understanding of the ways in which Hegel and Nietzsche treat such topics, they
would have to be studied in the light of the philosophers' criticisms of
dualism. Since, however, this common concern of Nietzsche and
Hegel is discussed in later chapters of this book I will not go into
details here.

The third category of commentators to be considered in this review
comprises those who use Hegelian arguments to criticise Nietzsche.
The general character of such a critique is suggested by Beerling's
article, 'Hegel und Nietzsche'. Beerling's main intention is to show
how Hegel's 'pathos of the concept' and Nietzsche's 'pathos of the
will' both sound the death-knell of 'the ideology of the beyond which
is founded on the "ought" '.[78] However, Beerling is fully aware of the
substantial differences which separate Nietzsche from Hegel.
Nietzsche's criticism of dualism, he says, is carried out in the name of
aristocratic radicalism, whilst Hegel's is based on an appeal to 'the
rational'.[79] Furthermore, although both are critics of romantic sen-

sibility, Nietzsche, in Beerling's eyes, always remains much more of a romantic than Hegel. Hegel was able to overcome the division and disharmony within the romantic soul by finding infinity present *within* finite reality and not beyond it, by reconciling man and the world. In this, Beerling says, Hegel was close to Goethe. Nietzsche, on the other hand, never achieved such harmony or 'divine calm' in his vision of man. Nietzsche's opposition to romantic dualism led him to reject any yearning for the beyond and to affirm the infinity of the finite world itself; but, Beerling points out in an astute comment, the excessive pathos and vehemence of Nietzsche's strained apotheosis of the finite world reflects the very romantic disharmony he sought to transcend.[80]

A similar charge is made by Stanley Rosen. Rosen identifies both Hegel and Nietzsche as critics of nihilistic 'self-lacerated spirit'. Like Beerling, however, Rosen argues that Nietzsche is unable fully to free himself from self-laceration. For Hegel 'the transition from pure nihilistic distraction to the eventual overcoming of nihilism lies in the self-consciousness of the distracted . . . spirit'. Spirit is distracted because it is conscious of its internal diremption, but precisely because it knows itself as that which bears and sublates that inner diremption, it is unified within its diverse moments. Hegel thus directs our attention to 'the *consciousness of consciousness*, or to the unity of the spirit that speaks within its mutually inconsistent thoughts'.[81]

Nietzsche, on the other hand, denies the primacy of self-consciousness. The essence of man, in his view, is what is unconscious – the will to power. Self-consciousness is thus not the discovery of true unity in diremption, but merely a mistaken interpretation of our unconscious nature. Nietzsche, ostensibly opposed to all forms of the 'beyond', in fact alienates man as self-consciousness from nature as unconscious becoming.[82] As a result of rejecting the unity of self-consciousness as a fiction, Nietzsche cannot find freedom from nihilistic self-division as such, but rather attributes the overcoming of decadent nihilism to the non-self-conscious creativity of noble nihilism.[83] But this, Rosen says, is to make nihilistic self-division the permanent 'sense' of human experience. Nietzsche's solution thus deprives man of his consciousness of consciousness, of his unified, universal sense of 'I', and confines him to a truth which is particular and personal. Against this, Rosen argues, Hegel reminds us of what, thanks to Nietzsche, we have lost: 'We can learn from Hegel that, if philosophical truth is *mine*, then there is no truth, but only opinion (*meinen*).' We can learn, therefore, that if truth is to be found, it is in the unity, direction and purpose of man's universal self-consciousness.[84]

The absence of an adequate grasp of self-consciousness in Nietzsche's thinking is also highlighted by Murray Greene in his difficult and at times obscure article, 'Hegel's "Unhappy Consciousness" and Nietzsche's "Slave Morality" '.[85] In contrast to Rosen, however, Greene's case is not just that Nietzsche lacks a sense of the unity of consciousness; it is rather that Nietzsche fails to understand the moment of mutual recognition and social mediation which in Hegel's view all true selfhood requires.

Greene contrasts the accounts given by Hegel and Nietzsche of 'self-negating' consciousness. Hegel's account, we are told, is a phenomenological analysis of consciousness in terms immanent to the mental realm as such. This analysis is rooted in the fact that consciousness is only certain of itself as consciousness insofar as it is conscious of other objects. This, in Greene's phrase, is 'consciousness's "being for self" in its "otherness" '. Greene shows that desire, which is the first mode of self-consciousness Hegel discusses, seeks to 'verify its certainty of self in its other by destruction and consumption of the object, an independent natural life'. In this way desire transforms what is merely other into an object *for consciousness*, an object which reflects consciousness back into its own sense of self. But precisely because it consumes the object, desire destroys the element which is to reflect its power as conscious desire. The truth of desire thus 'turns out to be rather that self-consciousness can attain its being-for-self only in another self-consciousness'. For Hegel, true self-consciousness is only possible when consciousness knows itself to be *recognised* as self-consciousness by another self-consciousness, which in turn is recognised by it. In order that it may achieve recognition as self-consciousness, therefore, consciousness ceases being mere natural desire and becomes social.[86]

In Hegel's analysis, self-consciousness is mediated by the recognition accorded to it by another self-consciousness. But the relationship between the self-consciousnesses goes even deeper than that because the other self-consciousness is actually the standing reflection of self-consciousness's *own* identity. In the other self-consciousness, self-consciousness confronts itself. The further development of consciousness in Hegel's phenomenological analysis thus involves consciousness *explicitly* uniting itself with its other self. In the unhappy consciousness this process is partly fulfilled. The self still confronts another self, but the other self to which the self relates is now the essential unity of *both* self-consciousnesses in the relationship. In the other, therefore, consciousness confronts not merely itself, but the unity of itself and the other. The 'unchangeable essence' or alienated God which the unhappy consciousness faces is therefore the alienated truth of its social, mediated identity.

The important elements in Hegel's analysis for Greene are (a) that self-consciousness is inherently mediated by, and united with, its other, and (b) that the negation of natural desire is an essential stage on the road to the full realisation of self-consciousness's mediated character. In Nietzsche's analysis, Greene argues, these two elements are missing. The moment of self-negation involved, for example, in morality is not understood by Nietzsche in terms of a logic of self-consciousness, but in terms of physiological force. The negation of desire is thus not motivated by the need of self-consciousness to enter into a relationship of mutual recognition and social identity with another. Rather it is motivated by the will within the weak mode of force to preserve itself *against* the other. The weak slave is impotent before the master and is therefore resentful of the master's instinctual vitality. Consequently, he turns vengefully against that vitality. But in thereby espousing the values of self-abnegation and 'meekness', the slave negates his own instinctual life as well and so develops a bad conscience about it.[87]

Although not rooted in the inherent self-reflectedness of consciousness, this turning of self against self does take on the form of a *social* relationship. The relationship is that of creditor to debtor, which Nietzsche considers to be the most primitive human relationship. What happens, in Nietzsche's account, is that the slave self with its bad conscience comes to understand itself as a guilty consciousness *in debt to* another, untainted self. The God of the Judaeo-Christian religion, Nietzsche maintains, is to be conceived as the maximisation of the creditor figure who, through his perfect manifestation of the slave's ideal, reinforces the slave's sense of guilt.[88]

In Greene's view, however, Nietzsche's account of the creditor–debtor relationship is unsatisfactory. By explaining the relationship in terms of self-negating force, Nietzsche does not take it seriously as a relationship between self-consciousnesses. As a consequence, he fails to account for the moment of reciprocity which the relationship involves. A relationship of debt in which something of value is owed by one person to another would seem to require at least the prior acceptance on the part of each that the other can determine value and that each has the 'right' to his evaluation. 'Without an adequate account of self-reflectedness as *sine qua non* of the original relationship of exchange', Greene concludes, 'Nietzsche's whole construction seems to be hanging in the air.'[89]

Furthermore, since Nietzsche does not see his 'forces' as essentially reflected into themselves in the other, he does not construe their character as mediated by, and united with, the other. So the alienated God in Nietzsche's account cannot represent, as it does in Hegel's account, the alienated *truth* of consciousness's inherent identity with its other. Such a God, for Nietzsche, is merely the projected, fictional antithesis of man's 'own ineluctable . . . instincts'.[90] The negation of man by a deity 'over there' remains for Nietzsche wholly negative; it does not contain immanent within itself the promise of the ultimate reconciliation of man and his true, divine nature. The future, therefore, does not rest with the slave, as it does in Hegel's famous discussion of the master–slave dialectic; positive value does not emerge from the slave's self-negation, but has its source outside the slave in the master: 'In contrast to the determinate emergence of the positive from the negative in Hegel, the positive for Nietzsche comes "like fate", appears "as lightning". Like the work of the "conqueror and master race" which founds the state, the positive is an "instinctive creation and imposition of forms".' Thus the emergence of the positive in no sense takes place through a 'mediation' as in Hegel.[91]

Greene's arguments are complex, but to my mind they represent an incisive critique of Nietzsche, and echoes of that critique will be recognised in my criticisms of Deleuze, Zimmermann and Kaufmann above. Hegel's emphasis on the identity of self and other in mutual recognition does not *reduce* the other to a mere moment of the abstract rationality of the self, as Deleuze would have us believe. Rather, the self is transformed and expanded by its need for self-consciousness into the unity of itself and the other, into a non-Cartesian, socially constituted self. In the light of Hegel's understanding of selfhood as enriched by mutual recognition, it is in fact Nietzsche's understanding of selfhood as 'life', 'force' or 'will to power', essentially at odds with the other, which appears as a reduction and improverishment of the self.

Nietzsche is opposed to the idea that there is 'identity' in life, because he understands the identity of elements as an abstraction from, or reduction of, their specific individuality. But an examination of Hegel's concept of the concrete identity of self and other reveals that identity need not be conceived in that reductive way. In Hegel's terms, we must learn to distinguish identity as conceived abstractly by the understanding or *Verstand* from identity as conceived concretely by reason or *Vernunft*. This point has been made forcefully by W. Seeberger. Seeberger points out that Hegel well recognises the importance of analytical understanding, but that he sees the understanding only as a moment or subordinate form of consciousness as a whole: 'It is therefore a grave error for the understanding to be simply equated with the human mind.'[92] Nietzsche's failure, Seeberger maintains, is precisely that he equates consciousness and the understanding. Nietzsche correctly sees that the role of understanding is to destroy the immediacy of life and to characterise it in reflective terms, but he concludes from that that consciousness *as such* is opposed to life. For Nietzsche, therefore, consciousness is unable to articulate life and life ultimately eludes the unity and coherence of thought. In Seeberger's view, Hegel would be prepared to agree with Nietzsche that life and formal understanding are 'opposed' to one another,[93] but unlike Nietzsche Hegel believes that consciousness can become *vernünftig* and thus can think life.

Seeberger's criticism of Nietzsche has strongly influenced the argument of the present book. In my view, Nietzsche is bewitched by the opposition of life and thought. Since he does not distinguish abstract, reductive identity from the concrete identity of differentiated or opposed moments, Nietzsche pictures life without any conceptually articulable identity at all as discontinuous and shifting. Since that is the way life is and since thought is irredeemably abstract, there is no purpose to be served by undertaking an immanent critique of the categories of the understanding as Hegel does. But since Nietzsche does not undertake such a critique, he cannot grasp the inherently dialectical, 'living' character of those categories which that immanent critique reveals. Thus he has no reason for doubting the distinction between life and consciousness. The mismatch between life and consciousness forms the axiomatic foundation of Nietzsche's thinking. But that, of course, means that it provides Nietzsche with a dogmatic reason for not following Hegel's procedure of immanent criticism and for not being open to the challenge Hegel presents to the Nietzschean view of life.[94]

That concludes our survey of the major positions in the Hegel–Nietzsche debate. My intention in this book is to lend support to those commentators, such as Beerling and Breazeale, who see Hegel and Nietzsche as critics of dualism. However, I wish to extend the parallel between the two philosophers beyond what these commentators are suggesting. Not only are Hegel and Nietzsche both critics of 'reality-behind-appearance' dualism or 'other-worldly' consciousness; they are both critics (at least in intent) of *all* conceptual oppositions or *Gegensätze*.[95] This belief in conceptual oppositions, which – almost invariably for Nietzsche, and frequently for Hegel – manifests itself in the belief in a world 'beyond' our ordinary experience, but which is not necessarily reducible to that belief, is identified by both these philosophers as 'metaphysical'. My own study will thus concentrate on the different ways in which Hegel and Nietzsche seek to surpass such metaphysical thinking in the hope that it may prepare the ground for a proper treatment of the other issues linking the philosophers. The overall aim of the book is not, however, simply to catalogue the similarities which exist between Hegel and Nietzsche. It is also to present, from the perspective of Hegel's philosophy, a critique of the way in which Nietzsche deals with the metaphysics they both identify. My study thus in fact falls into the third category of commentators considered in this review: those who use Hegelian arguments to criticise Nietzsche.[96]

In chapter 2 I will examine Nietzsche's own reception of Hegel's philosophy and the sources on which he draws. By this means I hope to show that Nietzsche himself was not, as Deleuze would have us believe, a reliable interpreter or critic of Hegel. In chapters 3 and 4 I will then try to demonstrate that Hegel and Nietzsche are both critics of a mode of thought which they characterise as metaphysical. I will argue that Hegel's conception of metaphysics differs from Nietzsche's in certain ways, but that his criticisms nevertheless apply to the metaphysics which Nietzsche describes. My conclusion will be that Nietzsche's critique of metaphysics is based upon the opposition of life and metaphysical understanding or *Verstand*, but that within Nietzsche's own terms this opposition is itself a metaphysical one. Nietzsche's critique is therefore vitiated by his failure to challenge the antithesis of these terms. Hegel's critique, on the other hand, is an immanent critique of *Verstand* and resolves all categorial *Gegensätze*, including that between thought and life. Hegel's method is therefore truly 'non-metaphysical' and avoids the self-contradiction which besets Nietzsche's philosophy.

Chapters 5 to 7 then attempt to show that Hegel's alternative to metaphysical thinking – his speculative, dialectical conception of rationality[97] – is, in his understanding, immanent in human thought, language and consciousness. In these chapters certain differences between Hegel's and Nietzsche's views of, and use of, language are also discussed. In the final chapter I will try to show how Hegel's speculative philosophy can be turned against Nietzsche's 'heroic' philosophy of life in the very area in which Nietzsche considers his understanding to be most original and most profound: the discussion of tragedy. I will try to show that Nietzsche's failure properly to appreciate the dialectic of tragic hubris causes him to overlook the process whereby individuality is transformed into a moment of truly *sittlich*,[98] communal identity. My conclusion will be that Nietzsche's devaluation of the sense of selfhood which resides in association, institutionalised social life and religious community is rooted in this oversight.

2
Nietzsche's
view of
Hegel

In the opinion of Gilles Deleuze, as we saw in the last chapter, Nietzsche is to be seen as a powerful critic of Hegelian dialectic. Deleuze not only claims that Nietzsche knew Hegel's texts well, he also maintains that Nietzsche exposes once and for all the life-denying 'slave' mentality underlying Hegel's philosophy.[1] This is an opinion which I find hard to share. Nietzsche, as far as I can tell, did not study Hegel's texts in any depth and relied mainly on secondary sources for his interpretation and his evaluation of Hegel's thought. Furthermore, his understanding of Hegel's philosophy was in my view superficial and largely misconceived. The purpose of the present chapter, therefore, is to explain how Nietzsche understood Hegel and what the sources of that understanding might have been.

In general, Nietzsche seems to have relished criticising great philosophers rather than actually reading them. He studied at first hand almost none of the major philosophers in whose tradition he followed and whose thought he sought to surpass – with the exception, that is, of the ancient Greek philosophers and of Schopenhauer.[2] The only explicit reference Nietzsche makes to having read any texts by Hegel comes in a letter to Hermann Mushacke of 20 September 1865.[3] However, the flippant tone of Nietzsche's comment does not suggest that he was applying himself very seriously to the study of Hegel's philosophy: 'with coffee I eat a little Hegelian philosophy which spoils my appetite, so I take some Straußian pills such as *The Wholes and the Halves*'.[4] Various comments Nietzsche made about

Hegel's style also imply that he read sections of Hegel's original texts, but of course Nietzsche's opinions in this matter were probably gleaned from other writers such as Schopenhauer as well.[5] Even what seem like direct quotations from Hegel do not necessarily testify to any detailed knowledge on Nietzsche's part of the passages in which they appear in Hegel's work. In the preface to *Daybreak*, for example, Nietzsche cites Hegel's 'celebrated dialectical principle . . . "contradiction moves the world, all things contradict themselves" ', and whereas he may well have taken this quotation directly from Hegel's work, the very word 'celebrated' suggests that he could have learnt of Hegel's principle from any popular source.[6]

Although of course it is difficult to prove that Nietzsche did not study Hegel in depth, nothing in his work suggests that he accorded more than cursory attention to Hegel's texts. Nor, *pace* Deleuze, can we assume that Nietzsche was well acquainted with the works of Hegel's immediate successors either, except perhaps Feuerbach and D. F. Strauß.[7] Nowhere does he mention having read either Marx or Engels; his comments on Bruno Bauer suggest that he was concerned more with Bauer's reading of his own work than with his reading of Bauer's, though he did apparently read Bauer's *A Guide to the Bismarck Era (Zur Orientierung über die Bismarck'sche Aera)* in March 1881;[8] he only decided to read Kierkegaard towards the end of his active life and never, as far as is known, actually read him;[9] there is uncertainty about whether he had any first-hand knowledge of the work of Max Stirner,[10] and his only connection with Arnold Ruge seems to have been that Ruge's second wife was a Nietzsche.[11] It seems, therefore, that Nietzsche's understanding of Hegel was not founded on a close study of either Hegel's own works or of the works of those who might most obviously be expected to have known Hegel's philosophy well, but that it was derived rather from other secondary sources.

What, then, were Nietzsche's sources for his view of Hegel? The major source, at least for Nietzsche's early ideas about Hegel, is likely to have been Schopenhauer. Nietzsche discovered Schopenhauer at the end of October 1865 in Leipzig soon after he first mentions reading Hegel for himself,[12] and his philosophical interest was absorbed by his new discovery before he can have progressed very far with Hegel's original texts. It is true that Nietzsche does not explicitly identify Schopenhauer as the source of his view of Hegel, but he admits as much implicitly by writing in 1866 that it is Schopenhauer who has removed 'the blindfold of optimism from our eyes'.[13] In fact

Nietzsche was so overwhelmed by Schopenhauer's thought when he first encountered it that his view of Hegel, as of all philosophy, cannot fail to have been deeply influenced by it, as this proclamation to his friend Carl von Gersdorff indicates: 'would that all who do philosophy were followers of Schopenhauer!'.[14]

Nietzsche's opinion of Hegel was not, however, formed solely by Schopenhauer, but also by other writers more highly esteemed for their scholarship than was Schopenhauer himself. In 1870, for example, Nietzsche attended lectures given by Jakob Burckhardt, his friend and distinguished colleague at Basle. These lectures, which dealt with the study of history and which discussed Hegel's philosophy of history in particular, clearly found favour with Nietzsche and were considered by him to be a worthy contribution to the Hegel centenary celebrations.[15] In a note written some years later, between the spring and summer of 1875, it becomes clear that Nietzsche values not only Burckhardt's exposition of Hegel, but also his critique of Hegel. Burckhardt is portrayed in this note as the only man living who is defending the study of history against the spirit of rationalistic optimism. Since later in the same passage Nietzsche identifies Hegel as one of the culprits responsible for the spread of historical optimism in Germany, it is obvious that he saw Burckhardt's thought as a valiant defence against Hegel, too.[16]

Friedrich Albert Lange's *The History of Materialism* (*Geschichte des Materialismus*) was also read enthusiastically by Nietzsche, and it is probable that he took note of Lange's extensive comments on Hegel. In a letter to Mushacke of November 1866, for example, Nietzsche refers to Lange's book as 'the most significant philosophical work that has appeared in the last decades', and he adds emphatically: 'Kant, Schopenhauer and this book by Lange – I don't need anything more.'[17] It should be said, however, that despite his general enthusiasm for Lange there is no direct evidence that Nietzsche considered Lange to have written anything important about Hegel in particular.

Other possible sources for Nietzsche's understanding of Hegel are Überweg's *History of Philosophy* (*Geschichte der Philosophie*), which Nietzsche requested in 1868, Eugen Dühring's *Course of Philosophy* (*Cursus der Philosophie*), which he read in 1875, 1885 (and perhaps also in 1881), and E. von Hartmann's *Philosophy of the Unconscious* (*Philosophie des Unbewußten*), which he first mentions reading in 1869.[18] None of these writers is ever mentioned by Nietzsche in direct connection with Hegel, however, and all are seen to be in some way deficient as philosophical thinkers, so it is unlikely that Nietzsche would have relied much on them as interpreters of Hegel.[19] Nietzsche also read, or at least ordered, several other minor philosophical works by such people as Teichmüller, Roberty and Martensen, some of which include occasional comments on Hegel; but he gives no indication that any of these works were important for his understanding of Hegel.[20] Since none of these works, with the exception of Martensen's *Outline of the System of Moral Philosophy* (*Grundriß des Systems der Moralphilosophie*), offers a view of Hegel which deviates substantially from that presented by Schopenhauer, Burckhardt and Lange, and since Nietzsche did not consult Martensen's work until 1880, by which time his view of Hegel had already been formed, I will not consider these works any further.[21]

Schopenhauer, Burckhardt and possibly Lange can therefore be considered to be the main influences on Nietzsche's view of Hegel. Amongst these three, Schopenhauer's influence, at least initially, was the greatest. Even Burckhardt and Lange are praised by Nietzsche largely because they are interpreted as furthering the Schopenhauerian cause. Nietzsche claims to see in Lange, for example, 'a highly enlightened Kantian and student of nature [*Naturforscher*]', and he remarks to his friend Gersdorff, after briefly sketching Lange's philosophical position as he understands it: 'you see, even judged against this most severe critical standpoint, Schopenhauer still remains ours, in fact he almost becomes ours all the more'.[22] Lange's critical method is seen by Nietzsche to enhance Schopenhauer's authority and thus indirectly lends support to the latter's critique of Hegel. Similarly, as a letter of Nietzsche's to Erwin Rohde suggests, Burckhardt's attraction for Nietzsche also stemmed to a large extent from his affinities with Schopenhauer.[23]

What view of Hegel did Schopenhauer have then? Three main points recur in Schopenhauer's somewhat repetitive, and not always consistent, diatribes against Hegel. Firstly, that Hegel is philosophically in error; secondly, that he is a charlatan; and thirdly, that his influence on German culture is pernicious. Schopenhauer's vehement hostility to Hegel was fuelled by two bitter personal disappointments: his abortive attempt to draw students away from Hegel's lectures in Berlin in 1820 by arranging his own lectures at exactly the same time as Hegel's, and his failure in 1840 to win a prize from the Royal Danish Society of Sciences for his essay on the foundations of

morality because, in the judges' verdict, he had amongst other things
neglected to take proper account of Hegel's contribution to the study
of ethics.[24] However, Schopenhauer does also have genuine philosophical reasons for disapproving of Hegel, and two in particular are
important. The first charge Schopenhauer makes against Hegel is
that he misconstrues the nature of concepts. Schopenhauer defends
the 'Kantian' principle that concepts can only be employed to understand and classify the objects of empirical or a priori intuition.
Without an intuited content, therefore, concepts for Schopenhauer
are empty forms which tell us nothing.[25] The problem with Hegel's
philosophy in Schopenhauer's view is that it sets out to be a science of
'pure' concepts and tries to generate philosophical knowledge
without reference back to intuition. This means that it either produces what are in Schopenhauer's opinion wholly misconceived
thoughts about the world which pervert the mind of the young, or it
produces no thoughts at all, a mere 'display of words' (*Wortkram*),
which yields no information and simply bores and disgusts the reader
with its abstractness.[26] In fact Schopenhauer believes that Hegel is not
really interested in truth at all, but is only concerned to mystify and
bemuse his audience – and perhaps to dazzle and impress the unsus-
pecting – with his vertiginous word-play. Hegel is therefore a dishonest charlatan, masquerading as a philosopher, but in reality out to
achieve mere 'effect'.[27]

The second philosophical disagreement Schopenhauer has with
Hegel concerns the latter's philosophy of history. Schopenhauer
believes that Hegel's attempt to look for a plan in history betrays both
'a crude and shallow realism' and 'shallow optimism', neither of
which, clearly, Schopenhauer approves of. Hegel is guilty of crude
realism because he ignores Kant's distinction between appearance
and reality 'in itself'. He holds temporal, historical experience –
which Schopenhauer considers to be mere 'appearance' – to be 'the
being-in-itself of the world', and he believes that such experience is
what should concern the philosopher. Consequently, he ignores the
Schopenhauerian truth that only the will within man, not the external
forms of man's historical existence, constitutes the real 'thing in
itself'. Hegel is guilty of optimism on the other hand because he constructs an overall plan of purposeful development for history,
whereas in fact history reveals in an apparent multiplicity of forms the
never-changing selfish will of man and the actions and sufferings of
man which follow from that will. The goal of such 'purposeful' history
in Schopenhauer's view is 'a comfortable, substantial, fat state', and

here again Schopenhauer detects Hegel's dishonesty; for in proposing a philosophy of history, Hegel is not actually serving the interests of philosophical truth, he is serving the ignoble ends of the state.[28]

As we shall see, Nietzsche, especially in his writings prior to 1876, takes over from Schopenhauer many of the latter's arguments against Hegel. He agrees that Hegel is an un-Kantian thinker; he echoes Schopenhauer's view that Hegel's philosophical style dulls and exhausts the mind (though he does not explicitly take up Schopenhauer's point about the proper use of concepts), and he also accuses Hegel of false historical optimism and the deification of the state. Nietzsche's treatment of Hegel is, however, different from Schopenhauer's in two important ways. First of all, it is noticeable that Nietzsche is less concerned with the untruth of Hegel's philosophy and with Hegel's alleged personal dishonesty than with the cultural effects of Hegel's philosophy on subsequent generations. This is of course a reflection of the fact that Nietzsche is writing some thirty to forty years later than Schopenhauer and does not see himself in personal competition with Hegel. But perhaps it is also a reflection of the fact that Nietzsche's overriding concern is always more with cultural reform than with philosophical truth. This interest of Nietzsche is obvious in the *Untimely Meditations*, but even in the later philosophy, where Nietzsche deals with many traditional philosophical issues, his aim, as we shall see, is to promote a particular mode of human existence and not merely to present neutral, philosophical truths.[29] The second difference between Schopenhauer and Nietzsche is that Nietzsche is much more interested in Hegel's view of history than in his use of words, whereas most of Schopenhauer's comments seem to be directed against Hegel's *Wortkram*. This difference reflects the different philosophical interests which we have just mentioned, but it may also have been promoted by Nietzsche's friendship with Jakob Burckhardt.

Burckhardt's view of Hegel does not offer any challenge to Schopenhauer's, though as a historian his emphasis is clearly much more on Hegel's philosophy of history. The introduction to the course on the study of history which Nietzsche attended in the winter of 1870–1 contains Burckhardt's most direct statement of his opposition to Hegel. Burckhardt writes:

Hegel . . . tells us that the only idea which philosophy *brings with it* to the contemplation of history is the simple idea of reason, the idea that the world is rationally ordered, that the history of the world is a rational process, and that the conclusion yielded by world history *must (sic!)* be that it was the rational, inevitable march of the world-spirit – all of which should first have been proved and not just 'brought to' the contemplation of history. He speaks also of the 'purpose of eternal wisdom', and calls his study a theodicy . . . We even find him cautiously putting forward the doctrine of perfectibility, that is, our old familiar friend called progress.[30]

Burckhardt then remarks that the error of all such philosophies of history is to believe that 'our time is the consummation of all time, or very nearly so'.[31] This critique of Hegel is not delivered with the same vehemence as Schopenhauer's, but its implications are the same. For Burckhardt, as for Schopenhauer, Hegel's view of history is optimistic. History is misinterpreted as progressing towards a continuingly improving future and the present is thus justified as the rational goal of historical development, or as a rational stage in that development.

In contrast to Burckhardt, F. A. Lange was not particularly impressed by Schopenhauer; in fact he finds in him 'a decisive step back behind Kant'.[32] However, Lange, like Schopenhauer, considered himself a follower of Kant, so some of Schopenhauer's 'Kantian' arguments against Hegel find an echo in Lange's book. Like Schopenhauer, for example, Lange criticises Hegel for failing to take account of the Kantian distinction between human experience and the nature of things in themselves. For Lange the distinction between 'essence' and 'appearance' in Hegel's philosophy is nothing but a distinction between two forms of *human* understanding. As a result, Lange concludes, Hegel's philosophy fails to appreciate Kant's critical point that human experience is limited: 'The great relapse of Hegel compared with Kant consists in his entirely losing the idea of a more universal mode of knowing things than the human mode of knowing them.'[33] Lange's criticisms of Hegel's conception of thought are also made in a Kantian vein and parallel Schopenhauer's remarks. Like Schopenhauer, for example, Lange criticises 'the prejudice that there must exist a sensationless, quite pure, quite abstract thought', and like Schopenhauer he casts doubt on the rigour of Hegel's logic.[34] Finally, Lange even suggests that Hegel's teaching that the real is the rational has furthered absolutism (though he refrains from suggesting that Hegel actually *aimed* at serving the interests of the Prussian state).[35]

Lange's view of Hegel is close enough to that of Schopenhauer for Nietzsche to see in him someone who confirms rather than challenges Schopenhauer's view of Hegel. And yet, though Nietzsche does not explicitly admit as much, there are aspects of Lange's view of Hegel which foreshadow some of the positive remarks Nietzsche was to make about Hegel in the 1880s. The precise influence of Lange on Nietzsche's later view of Hegel is hard to establish, but it certainly seems as if Lange's work might have played a part in weaning Nietzsche away from Schopenhauer's philosophy and from Schopenhauer's passionate dislike of Hegel. The most obvious difference between Lange's and Schopenhauer's views of Hegel is Lange's scholarly, though critical, moderation. Indeed, Lange explicitly states that in his opinion, although Hegel has little or nothing to contribute to the problem of materialism, it is inappropriate to look down upon him 'with the contempt [*Geringschätzung*] . . . which has now [i.e. around 1866] almost become fashionable'.[36] In a generous, and therefore un-Schopenhauerian vein, Lange also suggests that Hegel did not consider his philosophy to be the definitive conclusion of scientific enquiry, as many of Hegel's detractors claim (though he does think that Hegel undervalued the findings of natural science).[37] The most important comment that Lange makes about Hegel from our point of view, however, is one which directly anticipates the later Nietzsche's own positive comments about Hegel: this is Lange's view that Hegel has made subsequent generations aware of *change* in man's understanding of the world through his doctrine 'that concepts develop by antitheses'.[38] Hegel's 'poetry of concepts' (*Poesie der Begriffe*), in Lange's opinion, has been of enormous value in furthering the study of history and in particular the study of cultural history.[39] Although Lange's impact on Nietzsche was initially to confirm Nietzsche's admiration for Schopenhauer, Lange's positive evaluation of Hegel must have impressed Nietzsche when his admiration for Schopenhauer waned, because it is precisely Hegel's developmental understanding of concepts which Nietzsche singles out as important in *The Gay Science*.[40] Though Nietzsche may not explicitly state that Lange had an influence on his view of Hegel, therefore, it seems likely that he both confirmed the early Nietzsche's negative evaluation of Hegel and also prepared the way for Nietzsche's more positive evaluation of Hegel in the 1880s.[41]

Having considered the possible sources for Nietzsche's interpretation and evaluation of Hegel's philosophy, we should now look in more detail at Nietzsche's own comments on Hegel. When he first began to investigate Hegel's philosophy for himself, Nietzsche

appears to have taken an immediate dislike to it. In the letter of 20
September 1865 to Hermann Mushacke which was quoted above, for
example, Nietzsche declares that he finds Hegel's philosophy dis-
tasteful, though he does not explain precisely what it is that offends
him.[42] This distaste remains characteristic of Nietzsche's attitude to
Hegel throughout his 'early' period from 1865 to about 1876. His
fundamental objection to Hegel's philosophy during that period was
that it was hostile to critical thinking, and he expressed this objection
in a number of different ways. In discussing the 'coarse realism' of D.
F. Strauß, for example, Nietzsche blames Hegel (and Schleiermacher)
for obscuring from Strauß's view Kant's insight into 'the extreme
relativity of all science and reason'.[43] In this case, therefore, Hegel's
'uncritical' spirit is manifest in his failure to appreciate Kant. Another
feature of Hegel's philosophy which is opposed to critical thinking,
we are told, is his style. Where Heine's style assaults the eye with its
'electric' play of colours, Hegel's style, Nietzsche says, dulls the eye
(and by implication the critical spirit) with its 'contemptible grey'
(*nichtswürdiges Grau*).[44] On one occasion in his early writings Nietzsche
suggests that there might be a parallel between the Hegelian dialectical
method and his own attempt to draw out the truths hidden in the
literary tradition by being sceptical of the assumptions of that tradition.
However, even in this case Nietzsche clearly wants to preserve an
ironic distance between himself and the style or terminology of the
Hegelians, as the presence of the little word *etwa*, 'perhaps', in this
sentence shows:

ein Hegelianer also würde etwa sagen, daß wir die Wahrheit durch die Negation der Negation zu ermitteln suchten.

So a Hegelian would perhaps say that we were trying to ascertain the truth
through the negation of the negation.[45]

What disturbs Nietzsche more than anything, however, is the effect
of what he sees as Hegelian 'historical optimism' on subsequent
generations of German intellectuals.[46] Nietzsche is in no doubt that
Hegel's philosophy has exercised a tremendous influence on German
culture in the nineteenth century and he is equally convinced that
that influence has been bad.[47] The problem, in Nietzsche's view, is
that Hegel's philosophy encourages an attitude of uncritical acceptance of historical 'necessity' by arguing that whatever occurs in history is determined by an all-powerful, rational 'Idea'. Hegel's
philosophy, Nietzsche alleges, thus transforms what is into what must

be, and thereby fosters two dangerous trends in modern German society which Nietzsche sees as related: the neutral, 'scientific' veneration of facts, and the naked admiration of political power and success. Instead of furthering the creative, critical anger which Nietzsche thinks is essential to the overcoming of German philistinism, Hegel's perverse philosophy encourages the belief that the modern age as such is the fulfilment of history, and thereby effectively sanctions the rise to power of any modern cultural or political movement, whatever its intrinsic value or worth.[48] Hegel's philosophy for Nietzsche is thus hostile to the independence of the critical and self-critical mind. It seeks to subordinate the individual to the prevailing authority – be that history, the 'spirit of the times' or the authoritarian state – and does nothing to encourage the individual to be sceptical of that authority.[49]

Such views, expressed in the essays, aphorisms and notes compiled before 1876, were strongly influenced by Schopenhauer's diatribes against Hegel. However, as Schopenhauer's status as philosopher and sage began more and more to be questioned by Nietzsche, the latter's attitude to Hegel ceased being quite so hostile.[50] This is not to say that Nietzsche's more positive remarks about Hegel suddenly start appearing in 1877, but such remarks do become noticeable in the writings of the 1880s. Nietzsche's reference to Schopenhauer's 'unintelligent rage against Hegel', for example, bears witness to the fact that there was a connection in his mind between the revaluation of Hegelian philosophy and his increasing criticism of Schopenhauer.[51] Further evidence of this connection is provided by a fragment from the *Nachlaß* in which Nietzsche directly attributes Schopenhauer's 'absurdity and naivety' to his unhistorical mode of philosophising, and in which he contrasts Schopenhauer with Herder and Hegel, who, as Nietzsche puts it, passed through 'that strong schooling in history'.[52] By the mid-1880s, therefore, Nietzsche had come to recognise the value of Hegel's emphasis on history, something he had not done in 1873 when he completed the second of his 'untimely' meditations. Nietzsche's revaluation of Hegel did not by any means go hand in hand with a complete rejection of Schopenhauer, however; indeed in *Beyond Good and Evil* Nietzsche actually praises both Schopenhauer and Hegel – 'those two hostile brother geniuses' – for their opposition to the 'English–mechanistic stultification of the world [*Welt-Vertölpelung*]'.[53] Nevertheless, Hegel's stock did rise as Nietzsche's attitude to Schopenhauer became more and more critical.

Among Nietzsche's later remarks about Hegel there are thus several which are positive in tone. Some of these remarks, however, leave the reader in a certain amount of doubt as to how 'positive' they actually are. When Nietzsche writes: 'Hegel's value. "Passion" ', for example, we are, I presume, intended to take this as a statement praising Hegel's passion and commitment, though in fact the comment is so cryptic as to be well-nigh unintelligible.[54] Similarly, when Nietzsche points out that Hegel (along with Goethe, Heine and Schopenhauer) was a 'spirit who *means something* to Europe', 'a *European* event . . . and *not merely* a parochial, a "national" one', we are, one supposes, to understand this as a laudatory comment.[55] Hegel is being counted amongst that select group of German writers who were respected throughout Europe and he is thus being contrasted favourably with contemporary German figures whom Nietzsche considered provincial. But being hailed as a European figure by Nietzsche does not of itself guarantee Nietzsche's approval, so we cannot be quite sure what the intention of Nietzsche's remark is. After all, when Nietzsche declares: 'Hegel is a *taste* . . . And not merely a German, but a European taste! – A taste Wagner comprehended!', are we to understand that as a compliment?[56]

There is no equivocation, however, when Nietzsche draws attention to what he feels is the main value of Hegel's philosophy, that is Hegel's introduction of the notion of 'development' into science. In the fifth book of *The Gay Science*, for example, which was written in 1886, four years after the rest of the text was published, Nietzsche talks of 'the astonishing stroke of *Hegel*, who struck right through all our logical habits and bad habits when he dared to teach that species concepts [*Artbegriffe*] develop *out of each other*'. By emphasising that everything in the world is 'developing', 'becoming', Hegel encouraged in philosophy the suspicion that the category of 'being' might not after all be applicable to the world. In this way, Nietzsche claims, Hegel's philosophy cast doubt on the definitiveness of human logic and reason, and by so doing gave expression to a mistrust of human logic instinctive to the German spirit.[57] In the preface to *Daybreak*, also written in 1886, Nietzsche highlights a similar affinity between Hegel and 'the Germans of today' by pointing to Hegel's stress on the contradictory nature of things:

We Germans of today, late Germans in every respect, still sense something of truth, of the *possibility* of truth behind the celebrated dialectical principle with which in his day Hegel assisted the German spirit to conquer Europe – 'contradiction moves the world, all things contradict themselves' –: for we are, even in the realm of logic, pessimists.[58]

By revealing a world driven by contradiction and in continual flux, Hegel's philosophy appears to Nietzsche to contain the seeds of a critical pessimism. By the mid-1880s, therefore, Nietzsche was prepared to acknowledge that Hegel's philosophy might implicitly challenge the certainty of man's convictions about logic and the world, a possibility which in his early writings he had denied. Whereas in *On the Uses and Disadvantages of History for Life* Nietzsche had insisted that Hegel exploited his historical method purely in order to deify contemporary values, by the time he wrote the fifth book of *The Gay Science* and the preface to *Daybreak*, Nietzsche could see in Hegel a potential subversive.

Other passages from the 1880s confirm Nietzsche's recognition of the critical element in Hegel's thought. 'At bottom', Nietzsche remarks at one point, '[Hegel] generalised German criticism and German romanticism.'[59] Similarly, in the passage from *Daybreak*, where, as open as he ever becomes in his praise of his predecessor, Nietzsche states that 'of the celebrated Germans, none perhaps possessed more *esprit* than *Hegel*', Nietzsche does not intend a mere pun on Hegelian *Geist*, but is claiming to detect in Hegel French *esprit*, the incisive, critical spirit of the Voltairean *écrasez l'infâme*. The kernel of the Hegelian sentence is thus seen by Nietzsche as 'a witty, often indiscreet inspiration on the most intellectual subjects, a daring and subtle phrase-coinage [*Wortverbindung*], such as is appropriate to the *society of thinkers* as a condiment to science'.[60] (Compare with this Nietzsche's earlier assertion that historical consciousness, and by implication Hegelian consciousness, employed all its powers 'in paralysing, stupefying or disrupting all those quarters where fresh and powerful movements might be expected to appear'.)[61]

Yet despite the challenge to human reason implicit in his philosophy, Hegel nevertheless remains a predominantly conservative thinker in the eyes of the later Nietzsche, one whose thought is ultimately aimed at discouraging criticism of, and revolt against, faith in reason: 'Hegel seeks reason everywhere – before reason one may *submit* and *acquiesce*.'[62] As in the *Untimely Meditations*, Nietzsche thus still sees Hegel's philosophy as indulging the tendency of the modern age to reject personal independence and responsibility:

The nineteenth century looks instinctively for *theories* that seem to justify its *fatalistic submission to matters of fact*. Already *Hegel's* success against 'sentimentality' and romantic idealism was due to his fatalistic way of thinking, to his faith in the greater reason on the side of the victorious, to his justification of the actual 'state'.[63]

But whereas the early writings considered Hegel to be justifying whatever is given (including moral and cultural values, and political and social institutions), the later notes concentrate almost exclusively on the religious and ethical conservatism alleged to be inherent in Hegel's thought. Indeed, at one point Nietzsche suggests that any attempt to use Hegel's religious conservatism to justify the preservation of political power by any particular faction constitutes an abuse of Hegel's philosophy[64] (although the passage just quoted does talk of Hegel's 'justification of the actual "state" ' (*Rechtfertigung des wirklichen 'Staates'*)).

Nietzsche's main argument against Hegel in the 1880s concerns the latter's failure to accept the 'death of God' which historical scholarship and modern science in Nietzsche's view were helping to bring about. Hegel delays the triumph of atheism, we are told, by interpreting history as the revelation of a deity or a rationality which so fashions existence as to make human salvation inevitable: 'Hegel in particular was its [atheism's] delayer par excellence, with his grandiose attempt to persuade us of the divinity of existence, appealing as a last resort to our sixth sense, "the historical sense".'[65] For all his valuable emphasis on the historical nature of man, therefore, Hegel's basic philosophical motivation still has a *'moral* origin'.[66] He saw history not as a challenge to the eternal truths of religion and morality, but as the gradual revelation and confirmation of these truths. God or Moral Reason may now be conceived as a *developing* reality, but history nevertheless serves to prove that such a divine, moral reality does exist.[67] On one occasion, where Nietzsche associates Hegel's philosophy with pantheism, he suggests that Hegel's might in fact be a philosophical attempt to overcome the 'moral God'.[68] But elsewhere Nietzsche sees Hegel's 'pantheism' as actually defending the existence of God by absorbing evil, error and suffering into divinity itself.[69] It is in this respect, therefore, that Hegel can never be for Nietzsche a genuine philosopher who challenges the old values and creates new ones, but will always remain, like Kant, a philosophical 'labourer' whose task it is 'to take some great fact of evaluation – that is to say, former *assessments* of value [*Wert*setzungen], creations of value which have become dominant and are for a while called "truths" – and identify them and reduce them to formulas, whether in the realm of *logic*, or of *politics* (morals) or of *art*.[70]

Although Hegel shared the critical *esprit* of the French, and the Germans' instinctive mistrust of human reason – both qualities which Nietzsche admires – he is chastised by Nietzsche because he was beset by a 'German' fear of the threat that such *esprit* might pose to traditional morality: the fear 'that it [*esprit*] may put out the eyes of morality'.[71] In this sense Hegel remained a 'counterfeiter', a deceiver who betrayed his wit and insight for the sake of his faith in morality and reason; he was a German philosopher in pursuit of mystical 'depth' and 'thoroughness' and thereby lacking the intellectual purity and honesty of self-understanding which Nietzsche prized so highly in himself.[72] Like Richard Wagner, whom Nietzsche called 'the *heir of Hegel*', Hegel remained in Nietzsche's view uncritically convinced of the infinite significance of his work; like Wagner, 'he invented a style for himself charged with "infinite meaning"'; like Wagner, therefore, Hegel was 'his life long the commentator of the "Idea"', a man who believes himself mysteriously in tune with the spirit of the universe.[73]

For all his emphasis on the historicity of human life, Nietzsche's Hegel still believes that human history is under the guiding control of what Nietzsche calls 'a pre-existing "Idea"'.[74] This 'Idea' or 'God' may be interpreted as developing within history and time, but *it* and not human life is what determines the course of events.[75] I shall argue that Nietzsche is right to contend that Hegel 'delayed the triumph of atheism' by preserving faith in the 'Idea', but that he is wrong to understand that Idea as pre-existing, transcending or riding roughshod over the actions of men. In order to show this, however, two things must be demonstrated: firstly, that Hegel is in fact an ally of Nietzsche's in his critique of transcendent rationality; and secondly, that such a critique may lead, not to the Nietzschean understanding of reason as a fiction imposed on life by man, but rather to the Hegelian view that reason is the immanent form of life itself. I shall try to show this by comparing and contrasting Hegel's and Nietzsche's understanding of metaphysics.[76]

3
Nietzsche
and
metaphysics

Nietzsche's critique of metaphysics

In this chapter we will examine what Nietzsche means by metaphysics, what his alternative to metaphysics entails and, finally, why I believe that alternative itself rests on foundations which, in Nietzsche's own terms, may be characterised as metaphysical. I should add that it is not my intention to address the problem of the historical accuracy of Nietzsche's view of metaphysics. What I am concerned with is the phenomenon which, after 1876, Nietzsche himself describes as metaphysics and how he proposes to criticise it. Nor do I consider the chronological development of Nietzsche's views on metaphysics or of his philosophy as a whole during his 'mature' period. I do not deny that Nietzsche's views on many matters, as well as his manner of expression, undergo obvious development and change throughout the 1880s, but I share Karl Schlechta's opinion that, for all the variety of formulation and detailed insight in Nietzsche's writings, there is overall a remarkable monotony in the statement of his philosophical position.[1] Despite the unsystematic twists and turns of his mature philosophy, therefore, Nietzsche's fundamental belief in the divorce between language and life and in the primacy of selfishness in human motivation remains in my view unchallenged.

What, then, does Nietzsche mean by metaphysics?[2] Perhaps the most obvious characteristic of metaphysical thinking for Nietzsche is *its hostility to the transience, contradictoriness and pain of human* experience – 'the *ressentiment* of metaphysicians against actuality', or what Nietzsche calls the philosophers' 'hatred of even the idea of becoming'.³ Metaphysical thinking, according to this description, refuses to accept the view, which Nietzsche holds to be self-evident, that everything in human experience – the values, ideas and characteristics of man – has emerged in time and will one day pass away, but it yearns instead for a true world, an unconditioned world, a world free of contradiction, a world of being.⁴

From the time he began working on *Human, All-too-Human* at the end of 1876, Nietzsche's thinking was dominated by the conviction that everything has its origins in time and history, and that consequently everything in the world is finite and is destined to be destroyed. Previous philosophers in Nietzsche's view, however, have been committed to the contrary belief that many of our values, ideas and characteristics are 'essential' to man and constitute his 'substantial' identity or soul, and consequently are eternal and unchanging. Such philosophers for Nietzsche have thus understood man as 'an *aeterna veritas*, as a thing that remains constant in the midst of all turbulence [*ein Gleichbleibendes in allem Strudel*], as a sure standard of things'.⁵ They think that what is substantial and eternal cannot have its source in time and history and cannot have come into being, and they thus see a complete divorce between being and becoming: 'what is, does not *become*; what becomes, *is* not'.⁶ But if man's substantial character and values do not have their source in history, then, so metaphysicians of all ages have argued, they must have their source elsewhere – in another world of eternal, permanent and immutable being behind the world of time and transience: the things of the highest value 'cannot be derivable from this transitory, seductive, deceptive, mean little world, from this confusion of desire and illusion! In the womb of being [*im Schoße des Seins*], rather, in the intransitory, in the hidden God, in the "thing in itself" – that is where their cause must lie and nowhere else!'⁷ In Heidegger's words, the metaphysical philosopher 'always goes beyond beings and crosses over to Being'.⁸

According to Nietzsche, however, metaphysics does not simply distinguish two separate spheres of being and becoming; it attributes to each of those spheres a different status and value. The other world beyond time is held to be the true world, the essential core of reality, and by contrast, temporality and history are relegated to the inferior position of being merely apparent or *scheinbar*. Nietzsche holds this metaphysical hierarchy of true and apparent worlds to be the utter negation and inversion of the actual state of affairs. In his view, time and becoming are what is truly real in our experience, and the metaphysical world of unchanging being is a mere fiction designed to protect us from the suffering which temporal existence causes us.[9]

Nietzsche's major criticism of metaphysical philosophy is therefore that it believes in 'substance', in 'a world of being' (*eine seiende Welt*), in fixed, continuous, clearly defined identity and form.[10] In Nietzsche's view, belief in this self-identical, *seiend* form underlies a number of concepts that have established themselves in our thinking. Amongst such metamorphoses of being Nietzsche includes 'the body, God, ideas, laws of nature, formulas etc.', all of which for Nietzsche are mere fictions which distort the irregular character of our experience.[11]

The God of the Christian tradition, for example, has been construed (so Nietzsche argues) as just such a timeless, substantial being removed from the temporal flux of nature and history. Nietzsche ignores the immense importance of divine incarnation in Christian belief, and treats the Christian God as the complete antithesis of life, time and human existence, indeed as hostile to man (*menschenfeindlich*).[12] Particularly pernicious from Nietzsche's point of view is the exclusive character of the Christian God. The Christian deity is presented as a being which can tolerate no rival to its authority. Consequently, it imposes an exclusive, unchanging set of values on its subordinate worshippers and condemns alternative sets of values as 'evil': 'one demands that no *other* kind of perspective shall be accorded any value after one has rendered one's own sacrosanct with the names "God", "redemption", "eternity" '.[13] Such a forcible reduction of possible human viewpoints to one exclusive perspective represents for Nietzsche a violation of the essential plurality and diversity of life. Polytheism on the other hand, particularly in its Greek form, was a celebration and deification of precisely that plurality.[14]

Christianity in Nietzsche's conception is also committed to belief in a substantial, unified soul. The notion of the soul is conceived by Nietzsche in the same terms as the concept of God; it is, as it were, an instance of the original divine principle. The soul is a fixed self-identical unit, without change and without diversity: 'something indestructible, eternal, indivisible ... a monad ... an *atomon*'.[15] Nietzsche associates such an idea with the gray, frosty mists and shadows of the metaphysical beyond and contrasts it vividly with the sunlight and gaiety of the multiple, dynamic self. 'In contrast to the metaphysicians', therefore, Nietzsche is 'happy to harbour in himself not an "immortal soul" but *many mortal souls*.'[16]

Not only does Nietzsche criticise the reductive character of the metaphysical conception of the soul, he also objects to the idea that the soul should transcend what for him is earthly, temporal reality. As far as Nietzsche is concerned, the soul has been conceived as an 'immortal' entity which has its real home 'somewhere else' and which is merely contingently related to this or that body. The association of such a soul with a body, Nietzsche asserts, does not therefore affect the essence of that soul, nor does it condition it in any way.[17] For Nietzsche the notion of an immortal soul belongs with other notions such as 'ego', 'spirit', 'free will' in the realm of fictitious 'causes' which he wishes to dispense with.[18] In Nietzsche's view man has no continuous spiritual identity or form. All we are is body, a multiplicity of changing desires, sensations and instincts – some purely physical, some sublimated into 'spiritual' drives. Man is thus not ultimately responsible for what he does, because he has no free will, no independent centre of his being from which he can govern and control his bodily energy and activity. Man does not freely determine his own behaviour; he does not decide what to do and then act upon that decision, but he 'is acted upon' by his raw and his sublimated drives.[19] Our sense that we are determining agents derives from the feeling of power which accompanies our instinctual activity and which we misinterpret as evidence of our conscious control. In reality, however, that feeling of power merely signals the beginning of our instinctual activity, but is not its 'cause'.[20]

Belief in spiritual causality, Nietzsche maintains, is the belief that we can separate an agent from any activity that occurs in the world and identify that agent as the ground of that activity. In this way we posit a substratum or subject as the single source of that activity. In Nietzsche's view we commit a double error here. We simplify the activity by giving it *one* source instead of a complex multiplicity of sources working together; and by dissociating the agent from the activity we raise the question: Need such and such have happened, if X had acted differently? – a question which for Nietzsche is out of place. There is thus no real question of freedom or necessity in action as far as Nietzsche is concerned because there is no doer behind the doing; there is only the doing.[21] Whatever 'freedom' Nietzsche does acknowledge in human life, therefore, is bestowed on man, not by any autonomous, rational consciousness, but by birth, nature and history; for in Nietzsche's view such 'freedom' is only acquired when man's instinctual life is itself strong enough to coordinate and discipline its

own conflicting desires and direct them along a single, clearly distinguished path.[22] (Nietzsche's attack on causality, on the notion of
substantial subjects behind or beyond physical existence, is directed
of course at any concept of activity being initiated by a transcendent
'Idea';[23] and at this point we are reminded of the reason why Nietzsche
is critical of Hegel. Despite its historical dimension, Hegel's 'Idea' in
Nietzsche's eyes is just such a transcendent power.)

In the same way as he rejects the distinction between agent and
action, Nietzsche also dismisses the idea of a distinction between a
thing and its relation to other things. As far as Nietzsche is concerned
the idea of a 'thing in itself' which underlies all relations into which an
object is held to enter is a myth. Without relating to other things a
thing could have no properties; it could not be hard, soft, dangerous,
colourful and so on, and therefore it could not be anything specific.
There are therefore no essential *things* which enter into relations;
there are only assemblages of relative properties which we interpret
as pointing back to a fixed centre.[24]

Nietzsche criticises past philosophers because he maintains they
have believed in 'being', in regular, ordered, fixed identity. For
Nietzsche no such identity exists outside our imagination; life is multiple, changing, chaotic – a dance of ever fluctuating relations between ever fluctuating desires and instincts. There is no transcendent
order or form to the world, no law governing nature;[25] there is no total
system or divine teleological pattern guiding activity;[26] in short, there
is no overreaching, monistic unity to life, but only difference and
diversity.[27] Yet Nietzsche insists that the world nevertheless forms a
totality: '*nothing exists apart from the whole!*'.[28] Is there not a paradox
here? How can the world form a whole and yet lack all unity? The
answer to this question lies in the character of the unity which
Nietzsche rejects. What Nietzsche believes in is a concrete, internally
differentiated totality, a *sum* of radically different but interrelating
forces and activities. What he rejects, however, is the notion of the
'unity' of life which overrides that manifold differentiation and
reduces life to a monotonous, uniform structure: 'any comprehensive
unity [*übergreifende Einheit*] in the plurality of events is lacking'.[29]
Nietzsche's attack on the idea of unity is in fact not an attack on
wholeness, as one might imagine, but on the dualistic division of life
into 'underlying' unity and 'apparent' differentiation and flux,
because monistic belief in the unity of being and dualistic belief in the
distinction between 'underlying' unity and 'apparent' differentiation

are understood by Nietzsche as essentially the same phenomenon.[30] Nietzsche actually makes his criticism of this monism–dualism in the interests of wholeness, in the interests of the integrity of life. This same concern for wholeness informs Nietzsche's critique of that moral evaluation of life which he sees as implied by past philosophers. Philosophers, Nietzsche maintains, have employed the ideal of the 'true' world as a standard by which to devalue the sphere of diversity and becoming. For them, becoming is without order, unstable, difficult to pin down, deceptive and therefore immoral.[31] From Nietzsche's point of view, however, becoming is all there is. The philosopher's negative moral evaluation of becoming is therefore interpreted by Nietzsche as life's condemning itself by reference to a standard of value that is purely fictitious. Life is therefore divided against itself; it considers itself responsible for, and even feels guilty about, a nature it cannot alter. Nietzsche's rejection of the 'true' world of 'being' is therefore his way of eliminating the standard whereby life condemns itself, it is his way of restoring life to wholeness and the innocence of becoming: 'that the world is a unity neither as sensorium, nor as "spirit", *this alone is the great liberation* – thus alone is the *innocence* of becoming restored'.[32]

In a passage from *Human, All-too-Human*, Nietzsche suggests that the origin of the metaphysical belief in '*a second real world*' and in the dichotomy between man's soul and his body lies in man's dreams. In primitive cultures, Nietzsche claims, men were able to 'see' people in their dreams whom they knew to be dead, and thus concluded that the souls of such people lived on in another, transcendent realm.[33] In a later passage from the 1880s *Nachlaß*, however, Nietzsche suggests a different explanation. Men believe in another world because of their wish that there might be a realm of 'being' in which the suffering and pain of this world might be evaded. This desire for escape from suffering inspires blind faith in the simple conceptual distinctions and oppositions (*Gegensätze*) of reason, and leads man to the erroneous conclusion that because one concept – 'becoming' – corresponds to something real, then the opposite concept – 'being' – must also correspond to something real.[34] In Nietzsche's view, it is this belief that there are *Gegensätze* in the world which constitutes the most fundamental characteristic of metaphysical thinking; metaphysics thus not only imposes a uniform identity and regularity onto life, it also, at the same time, imposes all manner of rigid oppositions and distinctions onto things:

Der Grundglaube der Metaphysiker ist *der Glaube an die Gegensätze der Werte.*

The fundamental belief of the metaphysicians is *the belief in antithetical values.*[35]

Selfishness and selflessness, desire and disinterested contemplation, the will to deceive and the will to truth – all of these human qualities are treated by metaphysics as wholly opposed to one another in value and as deriving from different sources.[36]

In Nietzsche's view all belief in such *Gegensätze* is false; what appear to be opposites are in fact simply different modes of the same thing – the phenomenon of altruism is not therefore opposed to egoism, but is rather a sublimated mode of egoism. Similarly, what we refer to by the words 'warm' and 'cold', for example, are not qualitatively contrasting states, but 'differences of degree' or 'transitions'.[37] The distinction between true and apparent worlds, however, is clearly the most frequent target of Nietzsche's critique of *Gegensätze*. In fact at the end of his short, but virtuoso 'history of an error' in *Twilight of the Idols* – 'How the "True World" at last Became a Myth' – Nietzsche explicitly identifies his personal mission with the abolition of the dualism of true and apparent worlds. Nietzsche argues that the idea of a true world beyond time has gradually lost its purpose and persuasiveness and has become irrelevant to our earthly concerns. As a result he declares: 'let us abolish it!' But with the abolition of the true world comes the abolition of the merely apparent world, too, for without a true world it no longer makes any sense to characterise time and history as merely *apparent*. The whole metaphysical dichotomy is thus dissolved. And it is at this point that Nietzsche's own philosophical conception of life enters the historical scene as his bold assertion 'INCIPIT ZARATHUSTRA' confirms.[38] The metaphysician fails to follow Nietzsche in his abolition of such dichotomies, however, because he is seduced – and *wishes* to be seduced – into believing in fixed identity or 'being' by the categories of human logic and language.[39]

Language, truth and 'truth'

Strictly speaking, it is not language that produces the fiction of identity. Nietzsche maintains that it is our senses which create the original impression that things are in some sense identical, in order to meet the need, which all of us feel to a certain extent, for a sense of stability and regularity within life.[40] But language builds upon and confirms what the senses have created. Language thus acts as the constant advocate for man's fictions.[41] In Nietzsche's view language and the judgements we form in language falsify life either by simplifying the complexity of living processes or by distorting and overlooking the unique character of our experiences. Language abstracts from the concrete individuality of experience and describes it in terms of universal qualities and properties. It talks, for example, of leaves as if all leaves shared a common form of 'leafness', but it thereby neglects what makes each leaf unique and special.[42]

The major charge Nietzsche levels against language, however, is that it is unable to articulate or express the flux and instability of life, because with words we always turn things into substances which have an immutable form: 'linguistic means of expression are useless for expressing "becoming"; it accords with our *inevitable need to preserve ourselves* to posit a crude world of stability, of "things", etc.'.[43] Through the discreteness of our words, therefore – particularly the discreteness of the grammatical subject and predicate – we create the impression that there is a stable distinction between a subject and its properties or between subject and the activities which that subject performs, whereas in Nietzsche's view there is in fact merely the chaotic array of complex, unstable activities and relations. The simple phrase 'I think', for example, contains a welter of bold assumptions such as that there is an 'I' that thinks, indeed that any 'thing' thinks; that thinking is an activity performed by an agent which is the cause of that activity; and finally that there is an identifiable process called 'thinking' which can be understood and explained. All of these assumptions are questionable, Nietzsche maintains – by which he means false – and are the consequence of grammatical habits through which we interpret our behaviour as being under the control of something we identify as our subjectivity.[44]

In Nietzsche's view metaphysical thinking is thinking which believes in the reality of the ideal forms that language creates or confirms. Belief in grammar is indeed characterised by Nietzsche as 'the metaphysics of the people' (*Volks-Metaphysik*).[45] Nietzsche's own philosophy, on the other hand, can be seen as a persistent attempt to undermine linguistic categories in such diverse spheres as morality, psychology, aesthetics and history. That is not to say that Nietzsche wants us to do without language – he does not think that is possible – but that he wants us to recognise that the simple distinctions with which we operate are *linguistic*. Nietzsche wants to destroy what he sees as our naive faith in language and to make us aware of how we are the artistic creators of our linguistic world.[46]

Now this of course means that in a post-Nietzschean age we are to dispense with the idea that there *is* actually any God, any human soul, any true world of being at all. Truth in the ontological sense of 'the true world' is abolished; there is for Nietzsche no world which corresponds to our logical and linguistic forms; there is only the one chaotic, dynamic world of temporal life. But Nietzsche believes that all language operates with stable grammatical forms, whatever metaphysical or non-metaphysical reality the words are held to refer to. Language and linguistic consciousness cannot therefore articulate the dynamic life that Nietzsche holds to be real either.[47] So truth in the epistemological sense must be abolished too. This is perhaps Nietzsche's most disturbing assertion: there is no such thing as truth, no such thing as the accurate, faithful representation by linguistic consciousness of what life really is. Nietzsche rejects the ideas of *Geist* or the soul as pure fictions, pure lies,[48] but he does not replace those notions with his own unequivocal truths. What status do Nietzsche's anti-metaphysical statements have then? What does it mean for Nietzsche to say 'everything has come into being' (*Alles . . . ist geworden*) or '*This world is the will to power – and nothing besides!*'?[49] Are these statements meant to be true?

The answer to this question is suggested in Nietzsche's 1873 essay, *On Truth and Lie in an Extra-moral Sense*. In this essay Nietzsche insists that all language falsifies life; all language imposes on living processes a form and structure which renders them thinkable. Life – 'the individual', 'the actual' (*das Wirkliche*) – knows no conceptual unities, no 'species', but is 'only . . . an X which remains inaccessible and indefinable for us'. And in order to stress that he means that *all* language distorts life, Nietzsche goes on to say that even the distinction between 'individual' and 'species' which he has used to demonstrate the falsity of language is only an approximation to the real state of affairs. The word 'individual' is itself therefore a simplification of, and abstraction from, actual shifting individuality: 'even our contrast between individual and species is something anthropomorphic and does not originate in the essence of things'. Thus when Nietzsche asks the question 'What is truth?', he does not simply mean 'What is the status of the metaphysical ideas which have previously been held to be true?' (although he does mean this as well); he is asking the much more problematic question 'What is the status of any idea or proposition that might be held to be true – including my own?' Nietzsche's well-known answer must apply to his own language as well as to that of metaphysics: truth is a hoard of metaphors, anthropomorphisms, relative perceptions of things, 'poetically and rhetorically intensified', that have come over time to be seen as canonical and binding. Truths are illusions which one has forgotten *are* illusions.[50]

In all our language we give expression to our *relative* view of things and project that view onto life.[51] We treat the stone as hard and the tree as green, for example, when in fact these adjectives only describe how we perceive these things;[52] and we simplify the world by dividing it up into subjects and properties, causes and effects, or indeed by talking simply of 'life', 'becoming' and 'individuality' as Nietzsche himself does. In all cases what is real ultimately eludes our language; in our language we operate with fictional forms, with signs, images and metaphors for an inaccessible reality – and Nietzsche himself is no exception to this. What distinguishes Nietzsche from the metaphysicians in his own view is that he is aware that language distorts. He can therefore use words as conscious metaphors for life as he sees it, without pretending that they are accurate representations of that life or of 'being'.

Nietzsche claims to know that life is unstable, chaotic, and that it cannot be articulated 'adequately' in language.[53] This means, therefore, that his own characterisation of life cannot be adequate either. All it is is a metaphorical description of reality whose pictorial content is more appropriate to the chaotic nature of life than the description yielded by metaphysics. But Nietzsche's metaphors, like those of nineteenth-century scientists in his view, remain as relative, as *bildlich*, as simplified and alien to the real complexity of life, as did the abstract notions of metaphysics:

'Explanation' is what we call it, but it is 'description' that distinguishes us from older stages of knowledge and science. Our descriptions are better – we do not explain any more than our predecessors ... We have perfected the image [*das Bild*] of becoming without reaching beyond the image or behind it.[54]

Although not wholly beyond metaphorical 'description' in language, therefore, life is ultimately beyond 'explanation' in language. Compared with metaphysical propositions Nietzsche's own statements about the nature of life are intended to be more 'realistic', but at the same time they are still relative interpretations and simplifications of life, which in theory could be improved upon.[55] Nietzsche's language is thus meant neither to be pure truth nor pure fiction, but to undermine and suspend the simple distinction between the two; for 'what compels us to assume there exists any essential antithesis between "true" and "false"? Is it not enough to suppose grades of apparentness [*Stufen der Scheinbarkeit*] and as it were lighter and darker shades and tones of appearance – different *valeurs*, to speak in the language of painters?'[56] Like Zarathustra, therefore, Nietzsche presents himself both as a poet or *falsifier*, and as a prophet of *the truth*, that is as a thinker who produces interpretative, relative, metaphorical 'truths'.[57]

The point should be made here that Nietzsche's use of the terms 'sign', 'symbol', 'metaphor' and 'image' is extremely loose. He seems to draw no systematic distinction between them in the way Hegel does, for example.[58] Nietzsche simply uses the terms to indicate that words are negations of what is real. For Nietzsche, all words are by definition 'prejudices' and 'masks'.[59] This view commits Nietzsche to a thoroughgoing scepticism about any attempt to articulate the character of life adequately in words. But it also allows him uncritically to blur the distinction, which Hegel, for example, would want to preserve, between the metaphorical and the literal uses of words. For Nietzsche there is no literal use of language. In Nietzsche's texts, therefore, what would be for Hegel metaphorical and literal meanings frequently slide into one another without warning. Nietzsche's declaration that philosophy means 'living voluntarily among ice and high mountains', for example, is a statement whose literal and metaphorical senses are fused into one: the real mountains of Switzerland are imbued with figurative significance and thus become concrete manifestations of Nietzsche's image of the loneliness and superior vision associated with philosophy.[60] In this way, through the frequent use of genuine metaphors and through the fusion of those metaphors with more straightforward uses of words, Nietzsche demonstrates in his style the theoretical argument that *all* his linguistic characterisations of life are in fact metaphors.[61]

Nietzsche denies that there is any literal truth in language and linguistic judgements. He treats the human intellect as a mirror which reflects life, but he maintains that the reflection and life never quite match.[62] Life itself provides no ultimate justification for the dogmatic, simplified judgements which we make about it. Now, in order to cast doubt on the capacity of language to determine the precise character of life in this way (and indeed to 'justify' his own metaphorical descriptions), Nietzsche must clearly have some sense of what reality or life is, against which to measure the adequacy of linguistic forms. What, therefore, counts as real for Nietzsche?

The first thing to point out is what Nietzsche does not intend reality to be. Nietzsche does not wish it to be confused with the notion of the 'thing in itself', which he believes falls under the category of a metaphysical concept. There is for Nietzsche no substantial being or essence beyond our reach: 'the world that we have *not* reduced to our being, our logic and our psychological prejudices, does *not* exist as a world "in itself"; it is essentially a world of relationships . . . its being is essentially different at every point'.[63] This is why Zarathustra comes to realise that life is not 'unfathomable' (*unergründlich*), that is that life does not have a substantial, self-identical, but inaccessible foundation or *Grund*. Zarathustra reports that life has told him: 'I am merely changeable and untamed and in everything a woman, and no virtuous one.'[64] Life thus eludes conceptual and linguistic grasp because it is changeable, fickle, 'feminine', not because it has any hidden depth or substance[65] – though we may mistake changeability for depth and look for life's (or woman's) mysterious heart where there is none.[66]

What is real for Nietzsche is 'becoming' – flux, multiplicity, change. Nietzsche uses many different terms to denote this flux, including 'primal unity' (*das Ur-Eine*), 'life', 'occurring' (*Geschehen*), 'chaos', and 'continuum' (this latter, of course, in the sense of continuous change and movement, not in the sense of stable continuity or identity); frequently he just speaks loosely of 'the world', 'reality' and 'actuality' (*die Wirklichkeit*), or he might even say simply that 'everything is fluid'. But always the meaning is the same: becoming is restless primordial indetermination.[67] In an early text such as *The Birth of Tragedy*, 'primal unity', though dynamic and shifting rather than substantial and self-identical, was conceived as an all-pervasive 'cosmic' will underlying appearance, and to that extent still remained a consciously 'metaphysical' notion. After 1876, however, when his romance with Schopenhauerian metaphysics draws to an end, Nietzsche begins more and more to equate 'becoming' directly with this-worldly nature and biological life, and in particular with the complexity and uniqueness of *human* action and experience.[68] The question that now raises itself, of course, is this: How can Nietzsche be sure that life eludes the grasp of the intellect and language? In other words, what is the justification for Nietzsche's opposition between language and life?

One possible answer to this question is that Nietzsche does not actually claim to have any direct knowledge or sense of life with which to compare linguistic concepts, but rather that he is methodologically committed to being sceptical about language. According to this view, Nietzsche's sceptical attitude towards language and logic might rest on his quasi-Kantian insight into the antinomies of reason, that is his view that contradictory propositions about reality can be derived from the basic assumptions of logic. This insight, so it could be argued, has led Nietzsche to the method of mistrust (*Mißtrauen*), to the belief that the capacity of logical thinking to reveal the nature of reality is called into question by the contradictions to which it gives rise.[69] Nietzsche's starting-point on this interpretation would be the following conviction: we are not sure what reality *is*, but we are committed to the view that it is not as thought articulates it – 'what can be thought must certainly be a fiction'.[70] To support this interpretation of Nietzsche one could point out, for example, that he wants us to *conclude* (*hinschließen*) that there is invisible life in bodily action, whether or not we have direct access to such life.[71]

It seems beyond doubt that Nietzsche is committed to the view that life is not exactly as logical and linguistic categories articulate it. This commitment is evident in Nietzsche's frequent use of negative definitions and of the supremely indeterminate word 'something' (*etwas*) to characterise life.[72] However, is it true to say that Nietzsche's commitment to see reality as the antithesis of language and logic is based *solely* on his quasi-Kantian analysis of the self-contradictory character of logical categories? Or does not Nietzsche after all have recourse to direct 'knowledge' of that 'something' to underpin that commitment? A number of points suggest that this is indeed the case. The first is that at various times Nietzsche makes comments which are critical of the ultimate validity of Kant's project. How is it possible, Nietzsche asks, for an instrument such as reason to criticise itself?[73] Nietzsche's criticism calls into question the view that he was persuaded to adopt a sceptical method of thinking by the 'rationality' of a Kant-style critique alone. Indeed, in *The Birth of Tragedy*, Nietzsche seems rather to value Kantian critical philosophy as a mode of speculation which simply prepared the ground for his own *dogmatic*, 'Dionysiac' wisdom.[74] Moreover, there are several passages in Nietzsche's work which clearly suggest that his criticism of language and consciousness rests on the foundation of intuition, sensation and feeling. In *On Truth and*

Lie in an Extra-moral Sense, for example, Nietzsche states explicitly that the free mind is now 'guided by intuitions rather than by concepts'; in passages from the *Nachlaß* he exposes what he sees as the falseness of our conscious experience of 'things' by comparing that experience directly with 'the formless unformulable world of the chaos of sensations' or with the 'medley of sensations' (*Sensationen-Wirrwarr*); and in *Daybreak* he describes consciousness as 'a more or less fantastic commentary on an unknown, perhaps unknowable, but felt text'.[75] The contrast between 'unknowable' and 'felt' neatly encapsulates the basic dichotomy, in Nietzsche's thinking, between language and intellect on the one hand, and feeling, intuition and sensation on the other. Furthermore, it reminds us that Nietzsche's strictures against truth are primarily meant to call into question the truth of our ideas and judgements, but do not necessarily preclude all authentic feeling or vision. We may not be able to know life in reflective terms, but if, like Nietzsche, we are sensuous, sensual and sensitive enough, we may nevertheless be able to 'experience' life vividly.

When criticising language, therefore, Nietzsche seems to operate with a two-tiered conception of human awareness. There is the level of linguistic, reflective consciousness, but there is also the pre-linguistic level of feeling, sense or vision, at which we can be more 'aware' of what life is. It is on the basis of this pre-linguistic vision of life, this 'world of unworded experiences',[76] that Nietzsche is able to justify his criticism of language, for he claims to be able to compare his nuanced sense of the complexity of life with the simplified reflection of life in language.[77] Nietzsche's scepticism about language is without doubt a feature of his methodological commitment to mistrust, but that commitment itself rests firmly on the foundation of pre-linguistic insight into life.[78]

However, this is not to say that Nietzsche is necessarily claiming unmediated access to a reality outside man. It is true that Nietzsche does maintain in *Twilight of the Idols* that the senses are not 'lying' when they show becoming, transience and change, and that this implies that sensation *reveals* reality in a purer way than reflective consciousness.[79] However, the implication of that passage is clearly contradicted by a passage from the *Nachlaß* where Nietzsche explicitly denies that sensation reveals the real character of the world as such. The 'chaos of sensations' to which he refers in that passage in order to determine that the world of 'things' is 'phenomenal' and 'adapted to our needs' (*zurechtgemacht*), does not give us direct access to the world 'out there', but is itself '*another kind* of phenomenal world'; so Nietzsche is in fact using one level of 'interpretation' of the world to criticise another.[80] This, I believe, is how Nietzsche would want to justify his critique of consciousness; not by comparing human fictions directly with the 'other', with the life outside us, but rather by comparing human fictions with a more complex level of human interpretation itself. This is evident, for example, in the preface to *The Genealogy of Morals*, where Nietzsche clearly describes the method of the 'positive' spirit as that of replacing 'the improbable with the probable', or even 'possibly one error with another'.[81] Nietzsche's practice of criticising one level of human interpretation by reference to another should not be confused with Hegel's phenomenological method in the *Phenomenology*, which is discussed in chapter 7. Nietzsche does not draw out the complexity inherent in a particular level or form of consciousness itself, as Hegel does, but rather shows up the limits of the 'simplified' interpretations made by one level of consciousness by contrasting them with those made by another, allegedly 'deeper', more 'complex' level.

What allows Nietzsche to talk of a contrast between 'reality' and consciousness, or 'life' and language, is the fact that that more complex level of human interpretation, the complex world of our feelings, instincts and sensations, is felt by him to constitute what is fundamentally real *in our experience*, to be the life which is our own and which we cannot evade. Nietzsche is not claiming that what human beings experience as 'life' or as 'reality' would necessarily be experienced as fundamentally real by other conceivable beings, though, as we shall see, he does understand the reality or life outside us on the analogy of human life; nor, indeed, is Nietzsche claiming that we can have a perfect, unmediated awareness of the full complexity of our sensations and instincts – in fact he is denying that we can have any such perfect awareness. However, Nietzsche is claiming that if, like him, we are attentive enough, we can 'sense' that our feelings, sensations and instincts are genuinely much more complex than the stable world of language, and that they constitute the irreducible foundation of human experience, the authentic core of human life. In *Beyond Good and Evil* Nietzsche makes this point clear by suggesting that the only 'reality' to which we can have access within our experience and which we can *know* to be distorted and simplified by language and logic is the chaotic reality of our own ever-changing, instinctual life; 'that nothing is "given" as real except our world of desires and passions, that we can rise or sink to no other "reality" than the reality of our drives'.[82] It is thus not so much the case that Nietzsche compares conscious understanding with the complexity of the external reality which feeling and sensation are alleged to reveal; but rather that he compares conscious understanding with the more complex *interpretations* of the world which our sensations and feelings yield, and with the complex, felt *reality* of those interpreting sensations, instincts and feelings themselves. The phenomenal world of consciousness, therefore, is contrasted with the dynamic reality of our own physiological life, but it must always be remembered that that life is only the most fundamental reality to which *we* can have access in our experience, that that life itself gives us its own interpretations of the world, and, indeed, that that life goes to make up another much richer, more complex phenomenon than consciousness, namely the body.[83] Nietzsche's criticism of language or human reason is thus founded on his insight into the way that human beings falsify the 'reality' of their own drives, the 'phenomenon' of their own body, and their own 'phenomenal' physiological experience of the world around them; and it is on the basis of this insight into human self-deception that he is able to 'justify' his claim that we are essentially falsifying beings and that the character of life itself, of the reality outside us, is falsified by our language. Strictly speaking, of course, if Nietzsche cannot allow himself direct access to the world outside man, he cannot allow himself direct access to the experiences of other people either. Nietzsche's insight into the 'fact' that *all* human beings falsify their 'phenomenal' experience can thus itself only be justified on the basis of generalising from his awareness of the extent to which he falsifies the complex content and character of his own 'phenomenal' feelings and sensations. The ultimate warrant for Nietzsche's critique of language and for his belief in the primacy of interpretation can in fact only be his own self-knowledge, therefore.[84]

We are now in a position to clarify how it is possible that Nietzsche can deny that there is any truth and yet also assert that he speaks the 'truth'.[85] What Nietzsche denies is that we can accurately and definitively articulate the character of life in words, but he does not deny that we can be aware of the complexity of human life in various ways and use words to point to (*bezeichnen*) what we are aware of; nor does he deny that we can register the contradiction he detects between what we feel and what we are able to say.[86] The 'truths' of

Nietzsche's own philosophy are therefore metaphorical characterisations and simplified interpretations of life – 'forbidden metaphors and unheard-of combinations of concepts' – by means of which different aspects of Nietzsche's vision, different Nietzschean 'perspectives', are intimated;[87] or they are factual statements which point to the relation of distorted mirroring which obtains between language and life, to 'the truth that [man] is eternally condemned to untruth'.[88] In neither case does Nietzsche conceive of the 'truth' of his statements in the sense he has prohibited, for in neither case does he claim to be able to articulate or formulate the actual character of life. There is not therefore any contradiction between Nietzsche's rejection of truth and his retention of 'truth', because in each case the term is employed in a different sense. Indeed, Nietzsche's conception of 'truth' as metaphorical reference to an elusive life necessitates his rejection of truth as literal reference:

Nietzsche denies the fundamental correspondence between the signifier and the signified ... If the strict univocal reference between word and object, word and meaning, is thus denied, it follows that the classical concept of propositional truth becomes an impossibility – and this is due precisely to the primacy of metaphor.[89]

It should be noted, however, that Nietzsche does not reject reference altogether. In contrast to metaphysics, Nietzsche acknowledges his philosophical 'truths' to be simplified, perspectival, interpretative, and therefore unjust. But these 'truths' are also more appropriate to his sense of what life is, more *realistic* than metaphysical concepts. They describe chaos, becoming, will, rather than substance, being and identity. Nietzsche thus relies on an albeit attenuated concept of correspondence between his own 'truth' and human life in order to criticise both the concept of metaphysical entities and the notion that there can be an *exact* correspondence between reality and linguistic form. It seems, therefore, that in his commitment to interpretative 'truths' Nietzsche is still to a certain extent pursuing what he sees as the traditional goal of realism.[90]

In his writing, Nietzsche always endeavours to emphasise the prelinguistic life that underlies his language; the *real* Nietzsche is his body, blood, instinct and will, and language and intellect are mere vehicles of that physiological reality.[91] Yet Nietzsche is also obsessed with the idea that his words alone cannot adequately communicate his fundamental physiological sense or experience of life's complexity.[92]

Nietzsche's texts are not therefore designed to introduce the reader to utterly new thoughts and experiences. His words are meant to serve as signs to remind us of thoughts we have already had, but which perhaps we have suppressed. Nietzsche's personal experience of life, it seems, can only be communicated in a very imperfect way, but if we have had similar experiences, we can be reminded of them by Nietzsche and our understanding of those experiences can be deepened. The intensity of the reader's own experience of life is thus what entitles him to understand Nietzsche's 'truth'.[93] The reader is therefore intended himself to supply the experiences which give Nietzsche's metaphors substance. The metaphors themselves only lay down the limits of interpretation. In the first main speech by Zarathustra, for example, the metaphors of the camel, lion and child delimit the experience of self-burdening, of wild, 'leonine' freedom and of innocent wholeness, but the vagueness of the metaphors means that the reader must draw upon his own individual experience to give precise meaning to the text. It is this experiential base which is meant to provide the context for deciding the sense of Nietzsche's utterances. However, it also means that we can never *define* precisely what Nietzsche's own experience of life is. Nietzsche's words do not take us 'into' the complexity of his experience; they leave us uneasily on the surface of his world. Only our own experience of life can take us 'inside' Nietzsche's.

In all of his writings Nietzsche's pre-linguistic sense of life provides the authentic base, the dogmatic conviction, from which he proceeds. Nietzsche's 'truths', his metaphorical statements describing life, are thus nothing other than *truthful* expressions of his own experience of life. Nietzsche's personal experience is indeed his main criterion of philosophical 'truth'.[94] This of course puts Nietzsche's philosophy beyond any rational criticism which is independent of the 'experience' of life. Any terms of the public language which we might use as a frame of reference for such a criticism are repudiated by Nietzsche on the basis of his unassailable experience.[95] The only way of criticising Nietzsche, therefore, is by showing that his subordination of language and reason to experience and life, itself rests on questionable conceptual presuppositions that are drawn from the public language he repudiates.

Nietzsche's physiological perspectivism and
hypothetical ontology

Having set out Nietzsche's critique of metaphysics and his attack on what he regards as the traditional conception of truth, I shall now consider Nietzsche's own anti-metaphysical philosophy.[96] The central tenet of that philosophy, based on his experience of his own 'life', is that we are wholly natural, physiological beings, that we are nothing other than a complex of primitive and sublimated bodily desires.[97] The material of human life is made up of our nervous stimuli (*Nervenreize*), our physical sensations, and our instincts, feelings, needs and emotions. These various instincts and emotions interpret our sensations (and indeed each other) in various ways, and the interpretations produced, Nietzsche insists, are always more or less distorted impressions of what is being interpreted.[98] Although Nietzsche grants, therefore, that we can genuinely 'sense' that our own bodily instincts, sensations and emotions are much more complex than our linguistic 'simplifications', and that they constitute the fundamental core of human life, he insists equally that we can never have any awareness of the complex content and character of those sensations, instincts and emotions which is wholly unmediated, undistorted or 'pure'.

When we think, we believe we are following the logic of our interpretations, we believe we are being led by the inherent rational connections between ideas from one idea to another. In fact, however, we are merely the victims of our battling instincts, each of which is struggling to assert its interpretations over all the others. Our most precious thoughts and convictions, Nietzsche says, are simply the '*judgements of our muscles*'.[99] In reality, therefore, there is no 'essential' self, no independent rational mind or soul which rides free of the influence of bodily desires and forces. We have no faculty or organ devoted exclusively to knowledge or truth. What we are is simply a plurality of moods and instincts held together by a more or less dominant instinct or will.[100]

Although, as we have seen, language falsifies life to varying degrees, Nietzsche believes that it is nevertheless also a product and a part of life. The physiological interpretations which become conscious and linguistic are thus to be counted among the various 'grades of apparentness' which are continually changing and replacing one another within the one world 'which is of any concern to us' (*die Welt, die uns etwas angeht*). As was suggested above, therefore, the 'life' which language falsifies includes not just our physiological drives and forces, but also the shifting play of linguistic and non-linguistic fictions produced by these forces.[101]

The interpretations we produce have two main functions in Nietzsche's view. The first is the straightforward one of satisfying the basic need for self-assertion in all drives. Man's instincts are fundamentally egoistical in Nietzsche's eyes, and the activity of falsifying the other is an expression of that egoism.[102] The second function which interpretations can serve is that they can mask the flux and instability of life. This is an idea that Nietzsche insists on throughout his philosophical career. In *The Birth of Tragedy*, for example, Nietzsche outlines the debilitating effect that unrelieved intuitive awareness of the chaotic, 'Dionysiac' character of life can have on man. When man is confronted by an unstable world, he is overcome by an overwhelming sense of futility: How can he ever achieve anything in such a world? Only by veiling his eyes with fictions can he give himself the illusion that he can achieve something in the world, and only on the basis of that illusion can he actually act.[103] In *The Gay Science* a similar idea is set out, only this time in more pragmatic terms. Beings who are too aware of the flux of experience are likely to be cautious and sceptical in their behaviour; on the other hand, beings who falsify, who impose a false identity onto things, render them thereby more manageable and are able to act with greater sure-footedness in life. Their greater certainty helps them act in more decisive ways than the tentative sceptic, but that certainty is purchased at the price of distorting the way things are. Nietzschean confidence does not, therefore, come from any religious sense of being at home in the world, but from wilfully masking the threateningly precarious character of man's environment.[104]

All life therefore has to falsify and distort itself to a certain extent, but it does so in order that, despite its self-awareness, it may remain creative and active. The great danger Nietzsche sees is that our weaker instincts will try to establish a firm foothold in life once and for all by clinging to certain interpretations as 'the only ones that are possible'. When that happens, when man is seduced into believing that certain interpretations are permanent, unquestionable 'realities', man suppresses or overlooks the need for new interpretations, and his creative instincts atrophy. In such a case the interpretations which are designed to serve life and creative action actually threaten it.

Nietzsche feels that this has been the case with the ideas of the Christian religion and of metaphysical philosophy.

Nietzsche launches his attack on metaphysics in order to undermine the apparent firmness of metaphysical ideas and to challenge the belief that they constitute the only possible interpretation of life. Nietzsche thereby aims to release the creative energy which produces new interpretations and which has previously been inhibited. In doing this, of course, he must challenge the belief that metaphysical concepts represent real forms.

Now, Nietzsche seems here to fall into a paradox. On the one hand he argues that fictions are essential to protect life from debilitating self-awareness; on the other hand he challenges the concepts of metaphysics by reminding us of precisely that chaotic reality which we try to protect from our view. The solution to this paradox lies in the fact that Nietzsche does not seek to strip away all our protective illusions and leave us exposed to life. That would not only debilitate life, it would be to deny the moments of falsification and self-concealment which in Nietzsche's view are essential to all instinctual life. Nietzsche reminds us of life's chaotic character in order to highlight the fact that our protective interpretations are just that – protective *interpretations*. Only by being aware that they are created fictions can we be prevented from mistaking them for definitive truths and from suppressing the creation of new fictions.

In Nietzsche's view, man needs fictions to mask life, but at the same time he must affirm what life is in order to prevent the ossification of his fictions into fixed 'realities'. In the terminology of *The Birth of Tragedy*, we need to enjoy illusion (*Schein*) as self-conscious illusion, and we need to affirm 'Dionysiac' insight in order to emphasise the importance of the continual creation of new illusion.[105] For this reason Nietzsche's own 'truths' incorporate both the moments of realism and of artistic falsification. They serve both to give expression to his Dionysiac insight and also to satisfy a pragmatic need for a simplified, aesthetic vision of life. Nietzsche endeavours to be as open as possible to the creative–destructive character of life, but he also recognises that one must be an artist if one is to bear that openness. The difference between the 'weak' metaphysician and the 'strong' Nietzsche, therefore, is that the metaphysician tries to suppress life through his fictions, whereas Nietzsche tries to affirm it.

Nietzsche believes that man has been seduced and bewitched by his weaker instincts to accept metaphysical fictions as realities and to

suppress the creativity of life. Attempts to reassert the value of creative life (such as the Renaissance) have in Nietzsche's view always
been undermined by the seductive power of the Christian religion and
of metaphysics; our vital instincts have never been able to break the
spell. A breakthrough on the part of creative life could only be
achieved when the weaker instincts themselves began to lose faith in
their own metaphysical notions. This waning of faith has actually
been brought about through the emergence of science and Kantian
critical philosophy (both of which, paradoxically, are products of the
metaphysical commitment to truth which have cast doubt on that
truth). [106] Science and Kantian philosophy have thus provided the historical context of scepticism towards metaphysics within which
Nietzsche has been able to affirm his own vitality as more real than the
metaphysician's 'world of being'. Although Nietzsche's rejection of
metaphysics has been made possible by the historical development of
science and Kantian self-criticism, it does not ultimately rest on these
historical phenomena, however, but on Nietzsche's own physiological
sense and affirmation of the Dionysiac character of life. The course of
historical events in this scheme of things is not therefore seen to lead
to insight into the developing historical character and continuity of
man (as it does for Hegel); rather it is seen to make possible the
recovery and reaffirmation (albeit in a refined form) of man's ahistori-
cal, physiological nature. [107] Despite his commitment to historical
philosophising, Nietzsche believes that true insight is ultimately
rooted in critical self-observation; history and historical consciousness are really only the means to make genuine self-observation
possible. [108]

Nietzsche's frequent references to his 'taste', or his insistence on
the sensitivity of his nose, are the rhetorical devices whereby he
emphasises the fact that his insight is physiological and pre-linguistic,
and that his linguistic formulations are merely 'transfigurations' of
that physiological sense. [109] For Nietzsche, in fact, all human awareness is physiological. All we know is what we (more or less strongly)
sense and feel and what our various instincts make of what we feel. We
are caught in the web of our bodily perspectives on things, the
perspectives of our nerves and our individual instincts, the dominant
perspective of our body as a whole and the perspective of the species
to which we belong. [110] In emphasising the bodily nature of consciousness in this way, Nietzsche is of course drawing on his great mentor,
Schopenhauer. [111] Schopenhauer, however, believed it was possible to

free consciousness from its enslavement to bodily desires and to achieve a form of direct, unmediated awareness. This was possible, Schopenhauer thought, in asceticism and also in aesthetic experience in which the mind focuses on the Ideas or pseudo-Platonic forms which underlie spatio-temporal objects. Nietzsche emphatically rejects Schopenhauer's escape route from the body; indeed, his resolute insistence on the irreducibly perspectival character of human awareness of the world is intended as a direct assault on Schopenhauer.[112]

All human awareness of others is therefore partial, relative, 'phenomenal', never pure or direct. We cannot, says Nietzsche, know the other itself, but only the changes which the other produces in our lives and in our moods. We can only register how *we* respond to the other, how *we* relate to the other. All perception of other people and things is therefore unjust. All friendship, generosity and love incorporates and depends upon this moment of unfairness towards the other, this moment of mutual misunderstanding and superficiality, because we always relate to another whom we have fashioned into our own.[113]

The problem which this raises is this. How can Nietzsche develop a positive philosophy of his own which is more than a collection of relative observations about the world? How can Nietzsche develop an ontology, an account of life 'out there', for example? In any literal sense, of course, he cannot develop an ontology; but what he can do is suggest an ontological interpretation of the world which is based on *an analogy with human life and experience and on metaphors drawn from natural science*. Accordingly, Nietzsche sketches a hypothetical ontology using the scientific notion of force (*Kraft*) and the analogy of human will: 'There is nothing for it: one is obliged to understand all motion, all "appearances", all "laws", only as *symptoms* of an *inner* occurrence [*eines* innerlichen *Geschehens*], and to employ man as an analogy to this end.'[114]

By means of these metaphors Nietzsche conceives of reality as dynamic, active and forceful, and he rejects the metaphysical idea that there may be real 'things', entities or substances in the world.[115] Furthermore, this non-metaphysical reality for Nietzsche is plural – a totality of radically different forces or concentrated points of will (*Willens-Punktuationen*).[116] Metaphysical monism is consequently dismissed by Nietzsche as a sign of inertia.[117] The individual forces which populate Nietzsche's world do not have any stable identity or being, but are always changing and shifting, always coming to be and passing away. Moreover, these forces for Nietzsche only exist and have definite character in various different *relations* to other forces. If we eliminate the conceptual forms which we impose on life, we are left with 'dynamic quanta, in a relation of tension to all other dynamic quanta, and whose essence lies in their relation to all other quanta, in their "effect" upon the same'. Reality as a whole, therefore, is simply 'the totality [*Gesamtspiel*] of these actions'.[118]

Now, in Nietzsche's view, to relate to another means to assert oneself against another, to impose one's own force onto the other and therefore to distort the other in a particular way. (Alternatively, of course, it means to be distorted or interpreted in a particular way.) Reality is thus to be seen as the constant process of 'creating, logicising, adapting, falsifying'.[119] Nietzsche also calls this most fundamental ontological activity the activity of 'interpreting' (*Interpretieren*), and his choice of this word exemplifies perfectly how he employs terms from human experience as metaphors to describe non-human reality.[120] Nietzsche draws on the activity of reading and interpreting texts – an activity with which he as a classical philologist was of course very familiar – and himself *interprets* reality in terms of that activity. He, for example, interprets physiological processes in nature, such as the formation of organs in bodies, as acts of *interpretation*.[121] In this way he can both suggest that human and non-human processes are basically the same, and yet also adhere consistently to his conviction that non-human processes can only be described metaphorically by analogy with man.[122]

According to Nietzsche, therefore, reality is the process whereby forces interpret and distort one another in specific ways. This creative activity is not, it should be noted, creation *ex nihilo*; it is the creative remoulding and transformation of real forces in nature. In Nietzsche's conception, therefore, reality unites two qualitatively different levels of being. The primary level is that of the shifting forces which interpret and are interpreted:

es muß ein wachsenwollendes Etwas da sein, das jedes andre wachsenwollende Etwas auf seinen Wert hin interpretiert.

there must be present something that wants to grow and that interprets the value of whatever else wants to grow.[123]

The secondary level of being is that of the interpretations themselves. The forms into which forces are moulded themselves exist and constitute *created* existence. Nietzsche's example of the production of physiological forms through 'interpretation' demonstrates just how material such created forms can be. Similarly, language exists in the world as a potent reality even if its forms are fictional. Created existence is thus incorporated by Nietzsche into his ontology: '"appearance" itself belongs to reality'.[124]

Reality is thus posited by Nietzsche as the constant shifting and interrelating of forces and the shimmering play of the forms or fictions that are the product of those interrelations. Such a reality is without permanent, stable form, but is the eternal process of creating and destroying new modes of itself. Nietzsche's hypothetical ontology is therefore his aesthetic alternative to what he sees as the metaphysical ontology of the Platonic–Christian tradition, an alternative wherein nature and man replace God as the creators of the world. This is Nietzsche's aesthetic justification of life: to see reality as creative, and at the same time to create a simplified vision of that creativity which we can bear. The culmination of this project will be Zarathustra's ecstatic affirmation of the myth of the eternal recurrence, in which creativity is given its most 'perfect', most 'beautiful' form.[125]

Here is the point at which to highlight, though not for the last time, an inconsistency in Nietzsche's thinking which may have puzzled the reader. It has been stressed that Nietzsche's ontology is intended to be non-metaphysical. It is metaphorical and hypothetical rather than literal, thus challenging the metaphysician's faith in language; it presents a dynamic rather than a static conception of reality, thus challenging the metaphysician's faith in the concept of being; and it is pluralistic rather than monistic, thus challenging the metaphysician's faith in unity and continuity.[126] The forces which make up Nietzsche's world are not discrete substances or atoms, but exist only in shifting relations to one another. However, the only kind of relation which Nietzsche acknowledges is that of the interpretation of one individual by another, or of one group of individuals by another. When one force interprets another, it moulds and distorts it; it conceals the primary level of being of that force behind its secondary, interpreted, fictional mode. Behind their apparent, fictional forms, forces remain chaotic, specific forces. Although all forces exist in relation to other forces, therefore, they do have a level of existence which is not actually constituted by their relations with others, namely their specific potential to act and react in certain ways.[127] In conceiving of forces in this way, Nietzsche seems to be employing a distinction between being-for-another and being-in-itself which in his own terms can only be called metaphysical. Nietzsche may well abolish what he sees as the metaphysical division of reality into two worlds, and he may well do away with the idea of substantial, stable being 'in itself' behind appearance; but within his one dynamic world of forces he retains a distinction between primary and secondary levels of existence, between real force, activity and becoming on the one hand, and fictional stability and identity on the other. This contradiction, I will argue at the end of this chapter, invalidates any claim that Nietzsche might make to have produced a truly non-metaphysical philosophy.

To return to our exposition of Nietzsche's ontology: one of the most important metaphysical conceptions that that ontology is designed to replace is that of causality. Nietzsche understands the idea of causality to be equivalent to that of one-way linear determination: X causes Y, Y causes Z and so on. As far as Nietzsche is concerned, however, all that we are dealing with here is a necessary temporal sequence, and the fact that there is necessary temporal succession in the world does not imply that what comes first in any way determines or 'causes' what succeeds it.[128] For Nietzsche there is in fact no simple linear determination but only a chaotic struggle of various centres of power, each attempting to gain ascendancy over the other forces and to determine their character according to its own will. Nietzsche thus replaces causality by complex interaction and struggle.[129] This means that Nietzsche is not a mechanical determinist. It is true that in §106 of *Human, All-too-Human* Nietzsche adopts a determinist position, but one should not overlook the polemical function of that passage; Nietzsche is there taking up a position which is in direct antithesis to the metaphysical belief in free will.[130] This habit of taking up a position in direct antithesis to one that he considers false is a feature of many of Nietzsche's texts and does not necessarily indicate that the position he adopts is one that he whole-heartedly supports. If, however, we are to take that passage at face value, then it is incompatible with the main thrust of his later writings, in which he repudiates determinism. In *The Gay Science*, for example, Nietzsche insists that there is necessity in the world; but he is emphatic that necessity should not be conceived as a determining order imposed upon the forces in reality – a view confirmed in a note from the 1880s *Nachlaß*: ' "Necessity" not in the shape of an overreaching, dominating total force, or that of a prime mover.'[131]

Yet if Nietzsche does not conceive of necessity as an overreaching, determining power or fate, what does he mean by the word? The answer is that the necessity in which Nietzsche places his faith is nothing other than the actual nature of forces in reality:

> The absolute necessity of similar occurrences in the course of one world, as in all others, is in eternity *not* a determinism governing occurrences, but merely the expression of the fact that the impossible is not possible; that a certain force cannot be anything other than this certain force; that it can react to a quantum of resisting force only according to the measure of its strength; occurring and necessarily occurring is a *tautology*.[132]

This means that *amor fati*, Nietzsche's affirmation of 'what is necessary in things', is not to be construed as acquiescence in an alien necessity, but is simply an affirmation of what is real and of all the change, diversity, negation and unpredictability that reality involves.[133]

Nietzsche's visionary theory of eternal recurrence may seem to contradict what has been said here, because it seems to present the past as a force which dominates and dictates what is to occur in the present. However, according to Eugen Fink, that is a misinterpretation of Nietzsche's intention. What the theory asserts, in Fink's view, is that what does occur in the present will always recur and is therefore never ultimately lost. Moments that recur eternally are not subordinated to the past, but are raised to the level of eternal presence and ultimate indestructibility. The sheer contingency and unregulated specificity of the present is not thereby abolished. What happens in 'future' cycles is thus not the result of what has happened in 'past' cycles, but is what *does* happen in every cycle, what is eternally present. The notion of 'future' and 'past' cycles is indeed rendered meaningless by the notion of the constant recurrent presence of the one cycle of events.[134]

Nietzsche's concept of necessity does not appear to be very illuminating; it simply defines what is necessary as what is. Indeed, the indeterminacy of Nietzsche's notion is compounded by such assertions as that what there is is '*being specific*, definitely acting and reacting thus and thus, as may be the case'.[135] However, this notion of specificity is not completely meaningless and empty, for it serves an important function in Nietzsche's thought. The characterisation of reality as indeterminately diversified specificity is central to Nietzsche's assault on the metaphysical concept of being. The concept of fixed identity or being is for Nietzsche a mere fiction, the relative form that one force imposes upon another. If one understands 'being' in this metaphysical sense, therefore, then 'it is' in fact means nothing more than 'it is deemed to be' (*es gilt*).[136] By contrast, Nietzsche uses his own concept of specific being to posit reality as unfixed, as constantly acting and reacting in ways that are not adequately determinable by us. Nietzsche's seemingly empty description of the real as the specific thus highlights the fact that the real forces in nature elude accurate, definitive formulation in words – both in metaphysical concepts (including of course 'essence', 'identity' or 'being') and in Nietzsche's own terminology. Nietzsche is constantly reminding us that what is real differs from what can be said, and it is for this reason that he will often resort to the indeterminate word 'something' in order to indicate what there is or what we are at our most basic, instinctual level.[137] The words 'specificity' and 'something' remind us that the marginally more determinate words that Nietzsche employs in his ontology (such as 'force') are intended only to be simplified characterisations of what there is. Nietzsche thus uses words like 'force' and 'will' to challenge the notions of metaphysics, but he uses words like 'something' to relativise his own non-metaphysical terms.

To say that being real is *being specific* is to imply two things: firstly, it is to say that real things relate to one another in individual and particular ways – a view which is totally consistent with Nietzsche's pluralism; secondly, it is to say that *all* forces can be characterised as specific in this sense. All forces thus manifest the universal form of shifting specificity and particularity. In order to give this universal specificity a less abstract, more comprehensible form, Nietzsche draws on his experience of the 'something' which is human life and ventures the hypothesis that all forces in reality are basically will to power, that 'the only reality is *the will to grow stronger of every centre of force*'.[138]

But with Nietzsche's hypothetical theory of will to power there emerges a major problem. Does not Nietzsche fall back into the very monism he has so consistently criticised? Has not Nietzsche resurrected the notion of a stable metaphysical identity or essence underlying temporal particulars, and does he not thereby manifest the metaphysician's aversion to mere transience as Heidegger suggests?[139]

There is one passage in the *Nachlaß* which certainly suggests that this is the case. There Nietzsche describes will to power in uncomfortably metaphysical terms; it has not come into being, we are told, but is the *cause* of all becoming and development.[140] We should note, however, that Nietzsche frequently uses metaphysical terms as metaphors for his non-metaphysical vision, so we do not know in this case that the term 'cause' (*Ursache*) is meant to be understood in a straightforward way. Moreover, there is overwhelming evidence that Nietzsche rejected the idea that will to power constitutes a unified monistic principle. One of his major objections to Schopenhauer and 'the philosophers' is that they reduce what is in fact a complex, shifting nexus of desires and instincts to a simple unity, 'will'. Will, in Nietzsche's view, is a diverse plurality, not a monistic metaphysical unity: 'there is no will; there are only concentrated points of will'.[141]

But it is nevertheless true that Nietzsche does talk of there being *one* basic will in reality, will to power.[142] How are we to resolve this apparent contradiction? The solution, it seems to me, is this: we know Nietzsche rejects the dualistic conception of a stable, true world underlying temporal experience; therefore we may presume that will to power is not to be construed as such a metaphysical essence.[143] On the other hand, precisely because Nietzsche turns his back on dualism, he wants to recover the idea that reality is one homogeneous whole, that nature and life are of one kind.[144] Nietzsche's hypothesis is therefore that all the various centres of force that make up the world and all the diverse instincts within each force are *intrinsically* of the same character: all of them desire power and dominance for their own specific mode of being. The term 'will to power' does not refer to a transcendent unity or essence, but rather to the inherent, immanent homogeneity of all things: 'All "purposes", "aims", "meanings" [*Sinne*] are only modes of expression and metamorphoses of the *one* will that inheres in all occurring [*der allem Geschehen inhäriert*]: the will to power.'[145]

Will to power cannot be abstracted from the manifold individual forces which act and react in the world; it is not therefore the underlying *cause* of activity in the world. Will to power is, rather, an anthropomorphic metaphor for what Nietzsche calls the 'pathos' within existing forces;[146] it characterises their inner dynamism and orientation and 'explains' why they are inherently relational and shifting, why they constantly seek to grow at the expense of others and why they consequently strive to impose new, changing interpretations on their fellows.[147] It is therefore as the informing character of complex individual forces, *not* as an underlying substratum, that will to power can be said to be 'the most elemental fact from which a becoming and effecting first emerge'.[148] In my view it is only the name or formula 'will to power' that might give rise to the belief amongst readers of Nietzsche that will exists as a unified essence or principle. The reality to which that name, that metaphor is intended by Nietzsche to refer is, rather, a homogeneous plurality, 'a chaotic and contradictory diversity of elementary impulses'.[149]

To the extent that Nietzsche wants to see the diversity of life as homogeneous, he is of course seeking a form of that 'unity in multiplicity' which is the goal of Hegel's philosophy. However, in contrast to Hegel, Nietzsche does not acknowledge that there can develop any true 'identity' within the diversity of life, but always rejects as a metaphysical fiction the explicit unity and continuity of personal self-consciousness and the explicit unity and equality of human beings which Hegel sees as made possible by human self-awareness and language. Nietzsche's homogeneous plurality thus always remains fundamentally diversified and in conflict with itself, and is not only opposed to the metaphysical idea of a self-identical, timeless substance underlying existence, but also to the Hegelian idea that the explicit unity of consciousness can emerge *within* the diversity of temporal existence – because for Nietzsche the metaphysical and the Hegelian ideas are not significantly different.

Strength and the re-orientation of philosophy

In Nietzsche's view, all life, and most importantly all human life, is motivated by will to power. All living forces are thus essentially egoistical and are concerned with their own preservation, growth and advancement. Not all forces, however, display precisely the same kind of egoism.[150] Once we have got rid of the metaphysical fiction of the subject which 'has' being, Nietzsche says, we are left with various different degrees of being itself, various different degrees of egoistical will to power.[151] The metaphysical picture of a world peopled by identical subjects, all of which are equally 'free' and 'responsible' agents, thus gives way to a Nietzschean hierarchy of many different modes or kinds of activity. Nietzsche's hierarchy of modes of being is not quite as multiple and varied as he would like to think, however, and it can in fact be reduced to a hierarchy of two basic modes: a superior and an inferior one. Nietzsche therefore divides humanity into two basic types: those who are informed by what he calls a strong will to power and those in whom the will to power is weak. The former are imbued with a sense of their own sovereign strength, vigour and independence, whereas the latter feel themselves downtrodden, underprivileged and subjugated by the strong. These two types of people are distinguished by Nietzsche as the masters and the slaves.[152]

Now, Nietzsche maintains that all life, all interpreting activity involves evaluation of some kind or another: all life imposes its moral values onto things and judges them to be good, bad or evil from its own perspective.[153] For this reason all evaluations in Nietzsche's view are relative, dictated by the physiological needs and interests of living things. Moral evaluations, such as 'pity is good' or 'violence is bad', cannot be taken as objective statements of moral truth, but are symptoms of the mode of being that produces them.[154]

The masters and the slaves thus each evolve a system of moral values in accordance with their own physiological strength or weakness. The masters, characterised by a superabundant sense of energy, glorify that energy in their morality. For them the term 'good' is to be applied to the characteristics they themselves have; 'good' thus means powerful, rapacious, rich, exuberant and self-fulfilled. The term 'bad', on the other hand, is to be applied to the characteristics of the slaves – unsure, tentative, impoverished, dependent upon others and so on.

The weak slaves evolve an alternative moral code in accordance with their characteristics. For the slaves the term 'good' is applicable to the characteristics which make them incapable of asserting themselves against the strong. What is good, therefore, is mildness, help for others, dependence on others, pity and so on. Nietzsche maintained that the Christian ideal of selfless love for others, together with the Schopenhauerian ideal of pity with which he confused Christian love, are products of an essentially slave morality.[155]

The value which the slaves oppose to 'good' is 'evil', and with that term they vilify all the sovereign energy of the strong. The reason why the slaves operate with the terms 'good' and 'evil', instead of 'good' and 'bad' lies in their notion of human responsibility. In the value system of the masters things are simply evaluated according to what they are felt to be; they are either praised or condemned as the masters see fit. The masters assert their superiority and independence through their value-judgements and are indifferent to the problem of whether or not the weak can help being weak. As far as the masters are concerned, pity is dismissed as weak or bad whatever its cause. The slaves, on the other hand, do not enjoy such manifest physiological supremacy; they are the downtrodden underdogs. By rejecting the characteristics of the strong, they remain in a position of inferiority, still fearful of what for them is bad.

The way the slaves establish a degree of superiority over the masters is by appealing to a standard of dominance which the masters do not understand. The slaves invent the idea of free will and responsibility.[156] They argue that the masters are responsible for their aggressive nature and that because they are responsible for it, it is 'evil'. The masters' natural energy is therefore transmuted into 'evil' intention, whereas the slaves' natural weakness becomes the product of a superior, more altruistic moral choice. The slaves thus turn the tables on the masters and make a virtue out of necessity.

Nietzsche believes that in this way the slaves have taken spiritual revenge on the masters by appealing to a completely illusory sense of responsibility and by infecting the masters with bad conscience.[157] The masters, who are at home in the domain of instinctual creativity, are unable to fight back on equal terms with the slaves, fall victim to this fiction of the free will and are thus alienated from their true strength. In this way Nietzsche relates the triumph of Christianity, and indeed the whole creation of a realm of metaphysical spirituality, back to the desire for dominance of a frustrated weak will to power. The weak, who are motivated by a sense of impotence and resentment towards the strong, repress and deny the vitality of the strong by seducing them into believing in the fiction of the responsible self and in the unnatural moral ideal of freely chosen self-denial for the sake of others. Belief in the linguistic fiction of the subject and in the supreme moral value of asceticism and charity is thus interpreted by Nietzsche as a symptom of decadence, a symptom of a mode of life which is seeking to negate vitality and which tries shamefully to belie its own natural instincts.[158]

As a result of this conviction that ideas and values are *symptoms* of a certain mode of being, Nietzsche develops his famous genealogical or genetic method: by showing, for example, that the source of metaphysical ideas is a weak, life-denying mode of being, Nietzsche demonstrates what he considers to be the value – i.e. the harmfulness (and limited usefulness) – of these ideas for life, and the question of their objective validity is rendered largely redundant.[159]

Nietzsche's critique of metaphysics is not therefore a straightforwardly cognitive one. Although Nietzsche does think that metaphysical ideas are false, his intention is not simply to present an alternative set of *true* ideas and persuade the weak of their error. Physiology determines what people think and experience, so the weak cannot be converted to new ideas.[160] Only those few who experience life with the same degree of creative intensity as Nietzsche will respond fully to his critique of metaphysics. Nietzsche's intention is therefore to vilify the weak mode of being and its fictional 'realities', and to promote the creativity and the interpretative 'truths' of a new, self-consciously sceptical and perspectival mode of strength. His hope thereby is that, by following his example, the strong can once more master the weak (and the weakness within themselves), and recover their creative confidence. By casting off the fictions of metaphysics, the strong will be able to release their authentic strength and again become the guiding cultural force. With Nietzsche's celebration of strength, therefore, history reaches the final stage of its 'development'. Stage one saw creative strength in its original, naive form, initially confident of the superiority of its own energetic views and values, but nevertheless vulnerable to the fictions of the weak because – perhaps – it was not yet fully aware that all moral evaluations and linguistic judgements are perspectival *falsifications* of life and therefore to be treated with a healthy mistrust. Stage two saw creative strength succumb to, and be weakened by, the metaphysical spirituality of the Judaeo-Christian religion and its ideals of Goodness and Truth. Stage three saw the sceptical self-negation of Judaeo-Christian values, and the descent of man into the dark night of modern nihilistic disillusionment and disorientation. Stage four, finally, brings the decisive overthrow of the metaphysical 'idols' of Goodness and Truth in the name of life, and the reaffirmation by Nietzsche of strength in an enriched, self-consciously sceptical form, a form which is to dominate the new dawn.[161]

Nietzsche's criticism of metaphysics, which marks the end of the old era, does not therefore rest on the firm foundation of objective truth and rational persuasion; it sets out to be deliberately interpretative and perspectival, to present 'truths' which can be espoused by, and serve the interests of, the strong will to power.[162] And this radical repudiation of truth is perhaps the most striking feature of Nietzsche's new philosophy of strength. Metaphysical philosophy, according to Nietzsche, is dominated by the belief that truth is the highest value and the supreme goal of man. The foremost aim of the metaphysician is thus to present an account of the world in language that is true and accurate and which can be recognised as such by others. This aim also underlies science and even modern atheism, Nietzsche tells us.[163] In Nietzsche's own philosophy this aim is no longer dominant. Philosophy is no longer concerned with presenting true propositions about the world, but with promoting a stronger, higher mode or style of being.

Nietzsche effects this reorientation of philosophy not only because he dismisses the suggestion that the weak can ever be converted by propositions and ideas, but also because he believes truth in the sense of the literal or definitive description of a state of affairs or events is actually impossible. What are considered to be truths in philosophy or science are all more or less perspectival interpretations of a life which eludes definition; the idea of literal truth itself is therefore an illusion. Those who seek literal truth as their highest aim – the weak – are pursuing a goal they can never attain.

However, not only are such people pursuing an illusory ideal, they are motivated by different impulses from those they themselves acknowledge. They *think* they value truth for the insight into reality that it gives them, but in fact, Nietzsche maintains, what they really value is the sense of security that the fixed forms of language afford them.[164] That sense of security and firmness gives the weak a feeling of power over the subliminal chaos at the heart of their life. Their will to truth is thus in fact a physiological will to conceal life behind the fictions of language. The weak actually value the firmness of truth as a *fiction* although they do not acknowledge this to be the case. In their eyes they are only concerned with objectivity, fairness and justice.

In Nietzsche's view, interest in truth is essentially a form of will to power over life.[165] The criterion by which people decide what they believe to be true is thus not simply an objective standard of empirical evidence or of logical coherence, but the personal feeling of power and security that these ideas give them.[166] This is the basis of Nietzsche's revaluation of truth. He calls into question our deepest motives and asks: Is it really insight that man is interested in in his pursuit of truth? Or is it not rather the case that man's concern for truth is in fact merely a manifestation of his profound wish to be deceived by fictions, and that whatever psychological, scientific or sceptical insight truth-seekers may have achieved has been achieved despite their deepest intentions?

What distinguishes Nietzsche's strong, life-affirming, but sceptical individuals from the life-denying weak is that they do not pretend to value the ideal of truth and firm objectivity above all else, but openly

set as their supreme value themselves, their strength and their creative perspectival 'truths'. Their criterion of creative 'truth' is not a
sense of security but the sense of the expansive growth of life which
the expression of such 'truth' affords them. Whereas the weak are
alienated from life and therefore from their instinctual character, the
strong, who, like Nietzsche, openly glorify and affirm life's perspectival diversity and abundance, are at one with life and their own
creativity and destructiveness; they are like Zarathustra's 'child', who
has won back his lost world and recovered his wholeness.[167] The moral
values of such strong individuals are thus overt expressions and
glorifications of their vigorous selves and are pronounced without
regard to their exact appropriateness or objectivity.

Although Nietzsche is not interested in objective truth, he does not
wish to sink into pure relativism or subjectivism. The values and
interpretations pronounced by the strong whom he champions are
relative to themselves alone, and are not shared by all; however, the
strong will that affirms itself thereby affirms life itself. Similarly, the
weak will that denies and suppresses the vitality of the strong also
denies life itself. The fundamental 'truths' and values of the strong
Nietzschean individuals who are to dominate the future, though consciously partial and expressive of a particular mode of being, are thus
also intrinsic to life, and constitute 'the doctrine preached by life to all
that has life'. Nietzsche may not set up truth as his highest goal, but in
being biased towards the strong he is in fact being 'true' to life as he
sees it.[168]

The 'truths' of Nietzsche's philosophy are thus meant to be epis-
temically superior to those of metaphysics (because they are based on
a more realistic grasp of life), and also symptomatically superior
(because they are the expressions of a stronger, more creative and
interpretative mode of being).[169] Nietzschean strength, therefore, is
measured both by how much reality and life one can endure, *and* by
the extent to which one can give diversified and creative interpretations of that life.[170]

It is Nietzsche's self-appointed task to promote a consciously
perspectival mode of strength and its magisterial, though frequently
cavalier, mode of evaluating and interpreting life. Nietzsche's critique
of modern culture, and in particular of the modern claim to scientific
objectivity and truth, is made in the name of this strength. It is
important to remember, however, that Nietzsche does not advocate
simply returning to the barbarism of the 'blond beasts' embodied in

Scandinavian Vikings or in the Japanese Samurai. If Nietzsche has a historical model for the kind of strength he is affirming, it is the cultivated, sublimated natural energy of the Greeks.[171] But even this model is not an unmediated one, for Nietzsche insists that the two-thousand-year 'tyranny' of Christianity over European civilisation has completely transformed the life of man. This transformation has, of course, also made any thought of a return to naked bestial energy or mere *laisser aller* impossible.[172]

The discipline of the Christian 'denial' of life has turned man's instinctual life against itself and driven it 'inward'. It has thereby trained the strong to be able to exercise power over themselves rather than power over others.[173] As a result they have become more complex within themselves, more interesting, more promising, and more sensitive to that inner complexity.[174] This infection of expressive strength with inward-looking, self-negating weakness is therefore, to a certain extent, irreversible. On the other hand, the struggle against this Christian discipline has created in man a magnificent tension (*Spannung*), a creative antipathy towards Christianity which Nietzsche wishes to unleash in the service of his anti-Platonic, anti-metaphysical crusade.[175]

The strength which Nietzsche advocates is therefore opposed to the repressive inwardness of Christianity and asserts the value of bold self-expression against that of self-denial, self-repression and 'castration' (*Kastratismus*).[176] However, such strength nevertheless profits from the self-discipline and the deepening of human sensitivity that Christianity has brought about and also from the scepticism with regard to truth which the Christian tradition unwittingly produces, and it harnesses these qualities to its own life-affirming purposes. It is consequently able to deepen and refine its vision of life and channel its vitality into a creative role which is at once truly disciplined and self-consciously personal. This Nietzschean ideal of disciplined vitality might appear at first sight to be somewhat contradictory, for Nietzsche insists both that the goal of culture is to produce a man who has great self-control, who can resist reacting to every stimulus and who can hold himself back,[177] and that the true genius is the man who involuntarily overflows with energy, expends himself, 'explodes' and thus, as it were, lacks 'self-control'.[178] However, the contradiction is not as great as it appears since both types of person demonstrate Nietzsche's profound disdain for the impoverished, who are narrowly concerned for their own welfare and comfort and pursue the gratification of their own immediate needs and desires; and both point in different ways to the rich self-confident nature, praised so highly by Nietzsche, which displays that 'higher', creative egoism which has little concern for its own happiness or well-being and which gives of itself and imposes itself without regard to the cost which it may thereby incur.[179] The epitome of Nietzschean strength and self-expression is thus not to be conceived as the crude, material manifestation of physical or political power, but rather as an internalised, spiritualised (*vergeistigt*) form of aesthetic wholeness and creativity. Although Nietzsche did recognise 'superhuman' qualities in Napoleon, Zarathustra's ideal of the *Übermensche* is perhaps approached more by a figure like Goethe, or by Goethe's 'strong, highly cultured human being ... who has reverence for himself', than by anybody else.[180]

What Nietzsche wishes to promote is the courage to be oneself and to respect oneself, to be personal, individual, different, and to be 'true' to one's moral type – and that means having the courage to be openly creative and perspectival in one's evaluations and interpretations, to 'lie' honestly, to be faithful to the inherent injustice of life, and not to deny life by attempting to be just and definitive in one's view of the world.[181] Nietzsche's aim is to be *realistic* and therefore to have the courage to interpret and *falsify* life consciously. The point is thus not to cease judging and predicating altogether – we must judge, distinguish and evaluate as living beings – but to judge out of one's personal strength and exuberance:

We have again *taken back* the predicates of things, or at least remembered that it was we who *lent* them to them: – let us take care that this insight does not deprive us of the *capacity* to lend, and that we have not become at the same time *richer* and *more miserly* [geiziger].[182]

This attitude explains the affected boldness of many of Nietzsche's views.[183] The judgements Nietzsche wishes to combat are those which stem from the pusillanimous desire to run away from personal judgement and be objective, fair or publicly acceptable. Nietzsche's moral evaluations will not therefore pretend to describe an objective moral order and will not appeal to an objective moral capacity in all people, but will emanate from his personal, physiological taste: they will be made from a position 'beyond Good and Evil', beyond moral responsibility, but that of course means that they will *not* be made from a position which is 'beyond Good and Bad'.[184]

Nietzsche's morality of strength is a morality of authentic personal being, of the authentic commitment to the production of fictions and masks. It should be stressed, however, that his moral imperative – 'become who you are' (*werde, der du bist*)[185] – is not a universal imperative directed at all people. Only those who are strong in Nietzsche's sense of the word have the right to the full extent of that personal authenticity. Zarathustra exhorts the people: 'Always do what you will'; but he then adds emphatically, 'but first be such as *can will!*'.[186] Consequently, *pace* J.P. Stern, Nietzsche is able to offer a criterion to distinguish 'the fanaticism that goes with bad faith from his own belief in the unconditioned value of self-realisation and self-becoming'. The criterion he employs is whether or not man is freed from envy and resentment.[187]

Resentment in Nietzsche's view is the characteristic of the weak and the impotent, of those who are obsessed with their own inferiority and slyly envious of the freedom of the strong. Men who have been denied by nature the sense of personal richness and superiority that marks the strong react by begrudging the strong all that they are and by condemning them as evil. Amongst these resentful weak there is

an abundance of the vengeful disguised as judges, who constantly bear the word 'justice' in their mouths like poisonous spittle, always with pursed lips, always ready to spit upon all who are not discontented but go their way in good spirits.[188]

Such resentful, impotent people are fanatics bent on excluding and damning whoever is of a different, more magisterial moral type than themselves. Nietzsche's moral imperative of authenticity is not meant for the ears of such fanatics. For this reason I believe it is wrong to contend that 'no man came closer to the full realisation of self-created "values" than A. Hitler',[189] if one means the full realisation of self-created values in the fullest Nietzschean sense. Hitler may well have espoused the values of heroic, authentic individual effort, but his 'heroism' is vitiated by precisely that resentment (primarily against the Jews) which for Nietzsche disqualified a man from having the right to be 'authentically' himself.[190]

If resentment is characterised by narrowness and the grudging denial and exclusion of what is other, strength manifests itself in the fullness and all-inclusive multiplicity of the self. The strong self is diverse, ever changing, ever responding to new situations, never seeking to reduce life to a stifling norm. The highest man in Nietzsche's view thus contains within himself the greatest number of 'powerfully *conflicting* instincts', disciplined (*gebändigt*) by an overriding will.[191]

Whereas weakness seeks to banish strength, therefore, Nietzsche's strength incorporates and overcomes weakness within itself; the Nietzschean thus needs to recognise and master his own weakness, as well as that of others, in order to prove his own power and virility.[192] Similarly, as we have seen, the Nietzschean has to acknowledge the important role that 'weak' values have played in giving depth and interest to man's life, and must come to exploit those values for his own life-affirming ends.

Strength is further distinguished from resentment, in Nietzsche's view, by having the capacity for genuine magnanimity and generosity towards those whom it favours, that is for 'tolerance ... out of strength'. The weak are capable only of a cloying pity which stems from a depressed self and which matches suffering with more suffering. Nietzsche's generosity, on the other hand, offers to those who suffer, but are nevertheless fundamentally healthy, robust and rich enough to be able to respond to Nietzsche's gift, a vital and dynamic alternative to self-absorbed misery; such generosity is 'mighty', 'overflowing' and 'benevolently spendthrift' (*wohltätig-verschwenderisch*).[193]

It is true that the very exuberance of Nietzsche's strength means that it can just as easily manifest itself in a cavalier attitude towards others as in generosity, and that at times, indeed, Nietzsche's attitude towards others, especially towards the weak, can be positively destructive.[194] However, even when, for example, he actually seems to advocate expunging rather than mastering and overcoming the weak, Nietzsche is never motivated by the cynical contempt for humanity displayed by the National Socialists. Nietzsche's enthusiastic commitment to the principle of life and its diversified particularity often leads him to ride roughshod over the real people who constitute concrete 'life', but this I believe is the product of the blinkered intensity of his personal vision and not of cynical bad faith. Even the excesses of *The Antichrist* are, one feels, perpetrated out of a genuine, if somewhat abstract 'philanthropy' (*Menschenliebe*)[195] and not out of soured resentment. Nietzsche's position is by no means a humane one in the traditional sense – it is radically aristocratic and discriminatory – but it is informed with a passionate concern for man's greatness and vitality which clearly distinguishes it from the *Schadenfreude* and venom of later political developments in Germany.

To recapitulate: Nietzsche undertakes an important reorientation of philosophy as he sees it. His goal is no longer simply to state in propositions what he holds to be true, but rather to promote and embody a strong, expressive mode of being.[196] This mode of being affirms the inconstancy of life and considers that truth in the literal sense is an illusion. Such strength also has the courage to give creative, variegated expression to its deepest insights in a perspectival, hypothetical and metaphorical mode which takes philosophy beyond mere insight to something like art. Nietzsche's philosophical goal – a creative performance that manifests strength – is thus consciously differentiated from what he considers to be the aim of metaphysics.[197]

Nietzsche's anti-metaphysical use of language

We have examined the theoretical basis for Nietzsche's repudiation of truth and for his advocacy of a 'strong' mode of being. In Nietzsche himself, physiological 'strength' is sublimated into the literary activity of writing, into aesthetic style, or rather into a variety of 'styles'.[198] In order better to understand what Nietzschean strength involves, therefore, we must take a brief look at Nietzsche's use of language, and in particular we must examine how his use of language reflects the anti-metaphysical stance we have been expounding so far.

My argument has tried to show that the main thrust of Nietzsche's criticism of metaphysics is directed at its faith in language. In Nietzsche's view the forms of the subject–predicate sentence or judgement impose upon what is in fact a complex, chaotic base an identity that is illegitimate. Not only do the words 'subject' and 'predicate' give the distorted impression that there exist distinct subjects and qualities in the world, but the copula of the judgement implies that these subjects and qualities can in some way be treated as identical. For Nietzsche, there is no justification in our experience for such beliefs.[199]

Due to this radical mismatch between language and life, there is no possibility of language ever expressing the truth of life. All linguistic propositions are falsifications of the life they try to articulate. However, Nietzsche does not believe it is possible to do without language. We think in words and sentences and we cannot escape their forms. The most we can do is realise that linguistic forms are signs and metaphors which refer inadequately to life. For Nietzsche, therefore, language represents 'a suggestive transference, a stammering translation into a completely foreign tongue'.[200]

Nietzsche's philosophy clearly does not consist merely in a negative critique of language, however; Nietzsche employs language in a positive way to give metaphorical expression to his own dynamic, non-metaphysical vision of life: 'All that is intransitory – that is but an image [*Gleichnis*]! . . . But the best images and parables should speak of time and becoming: they should be a eulogy and a justification of all transitoriness!'[201] Yet for all the 'life-affirming' realism in his language, Nietzsche will insist that his own characterisations of life are merely metaphors (*Bilderrede*).[202] He may have realised that life is temporal and fluctuating, and he may use language to give a more appropriate account of life than that given by metaphysics, but he is not able to articulate in language what lies behind the metaphor. Like art, therefore, Nietzsche's language is designed to present 'reality *once more*, only selected, strengthened, corrected. . . '.[203] It is for this reason that Nietzsche develops his frequently tantalising Dionysiac style, which combines direct expression with *Schein* – with dissimulation and concealment. Nietzsche's is a way of writing which provokes the reader and keeps him guessing with its poses, questions and knowing hints and gestures for the 'initiated', a way of writing that constantly invites the reader to see through the masks, to read *properly* and to divine Nietzsche's concealed meaning, but which never lets you be quite sure you know what that meaning is. It is not my purpose, however, to present a full analysis of all these aspects of Nietzsche's texts. All I wish to do in the present section is to draw attention to one or two characteristics of his writing that stamp it as anti-metaphysical.[204]

One of the most obviously anti-metaphysical features of Nietzsche's texts is the way he plays with the very metaphysical terminology he rejects, and uses it as part of his own metaphorical vocabulary.[205] Nietzsche rejects the metaphysician's belief in subjects, causes and things. However, in his writings he retains many of the words which the metaphysicians have used. This is perfectly legitimate, Nietzsche explains, as long as we remember that such terms are merely conventional fictions by means of which we render complex processes manageable, and that they do not refer to objective entities:

One ought not to make 'cause' and 'effect' into *material things* . . . one ought to employ 'cause' and 'effect' only as pure *concepts*, that is to say as conventional fictions for the purpose of designation, mutual understanding, *not* explanation.[206]

Nietzsche uses the word 'subject' as just such a conventional fiction when he puts forward the hypothesis '*that only subjects exist* – that "object" is only a kind of effect produced by a subject upon a subject–a *modus* of *the subject*'.[207] In this passage Nietzsche undermines the idea that there are objects in the world by maintaining that the fiction of an 'object' is created by subjects. But by doing this, of course, Nietzsche also implicitly criticises any attempt to reify or 'objectify' the notion of the subject itself. The impression of stable identity given by the word 'subject' is thus challenged by Nietzsche's rejection of the term 'object', and the word 'subject' is thus implicitly presented as a metaphor for real, unstable, dynamic 'subjects'. There are numerous other examples of Nietzsche's use of metaphysical terms in this metaphorical way in his texts – some of which are indicated by inverted commas, others not – and, of course, Nietzsche's texts can seem hopelessly confused and contradictory if one does not remember what he is doing.[208]

An even more bewildering technique than the one we have just mentioned is Nietzsche's use of the terminology of metaphysics *in the sense intended by metaphysics itself* in order to undermine the values and concepts of metaphysics. We can give an example of this technique by looking briefly at Nietzsche's use of the word 'false'. In Nietzsche's view, what is real is 'becoming'. Metaphysical philosophers, however, have dismissed 'becoming' as ethically evil because they have seen it as inauthentic and deceptive, as 'false'. 'Becoming' is not what it appears to be, but, so the metaphysician argues, conceals a true, authentic world of stable being.[209] Now, when Nietzsche calls temporal reality 'false', he does not mean that he himself considers it to be inauthentic and to conceal another dimension of being; he means that it is 'false' measured against the standard of what counts as true and real for metaphysics. The temporal world is false, therefore, because it is not stable and reliable *in the metaphysical sense*: 'From the standpoint of morality, *the world is false* . . . The concept "the true world" insinuates that this world is untruthful, deceptive, dishonest, inauthentic, inessential.'[210]

Now, as we have seen, the very system of moral values and metaphysical concepts by virtue of which people have considered the temporal sphere to be false is for Nietzsche itself a product and a part of that shifting, insubstantial, 'false' temporal sphere.[211] Actions and attitudes which metaphysics considers to be true and good are thus reduced by Nietzsche to modes of a reality which in metaphysics's own terms is false and evil: 'Can one not reverse *all* values? And is good perhaps evil? And God only an invention and subtlety [*Feinheit*] of the devil? Is everything perhaps ultimately false?'[212] In employing these metaphysical terms, therefore, Nietzsche is actually undermining their ultimate validity, because he is using them to reject the metaphysician's dualistic interpretation and evaluation of the world and to promote his own subversive, anti-metaphysical world-view. Nietzsche is thus attacking the notion that there is a true world wholly distinguished from what is held to be the world of appearance by seeing such a true world as a fiction produced from *within* that world of 'appearance'. He is rejecting metaphysical dualism and positing the world which metaphysics considers false and evil as the only reality.[213] That one reality for Nietzsche 'truly' is chaotic and multiple; it is what it appears to be and does not deceive us by concealing its 'essence', because no such essence exists. From his own point of view, therefore, that temporal world is not false, inauthentic or evil at all. Nietzsche agrees that that world displays the characteristics which for the metaphysician confirm its inauthenticity (i.e. it is insubstantial and shifting), but he himself believes that these very characteristics constitute its authenticity and reality.[214]

Many of Nietzsche's sentences actually employ words used both in their metaphysical sense and in Nietzsche's own sense, a fact which often makes his texts highly confusing:

The antithesis of a true and an apparent world is lacking here: there is only *one* world, and this is false [from the metaphysical point of view], cruel, contradictory, seductive, without meaning ... A world thus constituted is the true world ['true', that is, in Nietzsche's sense of 'real', not in the metaphysical sense of stable or self-identical].[215]

One should remember, however, that, although Nietzsche employs the terminology of metaphysics in order to reject the metaphysician's interpretation and evaluation of the world, this is not all he wishes to do. He also wishes to further a mode of being which overcomes the simple dichotomy between the metaphysical and the non-metaphysical, a mode of being which, though opposed to metaphysics, in a sense almost incorporates it, because it has been interiorised and civilised by it. But Nietzsche never gets beyond that 'almost'; he is never truly able to incorporate the metaphysical in the non-metaphysical because he has no conception of Hegelian *Aufhebung*, of the immanent transformation of one mode of thinking into a moment of a more complex mode. Nietzsche is too closely wedded to polemical antithesis, to the destructive reversal of metaphysics to achieve such an *Aufhebung*; he is too intent on the *difference* between metaphysics and 'strong' thinking to acknowledge metaphysics as a subordinate form of 'strong' thinking itself; metaphysics is always a hurdle for strength to 'overcome' or 'surpass'. Though there is no evidence to suggest that Nietzsche was dissatisfied with his solution, the logic of his attack on metaphysics dictates that he should have been; for his polemical insistence on the difference between metaphysical concepts and life relies on and perpetuates certain oppositions which are themselves metaphysical, as we shall see in the last section of this chapter.

There is one question concerning Nietzsche's use of the word 'false' which we have not yet answered: when Nietzsche says that something is false, does he always mean false by metaphysical standards and authentic by the standards of strength (or indeed false and dishonest by the standards of strength and true by the standards of metaphysics), or are there cases where he means that something is false both in his own terms and in those of metaphysics?

There is one case in which the answer to the second part of this question is yes. The world of our interpretations is characterised by Nietzsche as false in two different senses. It is false in the sense that our interpretations are constantly shifting and changing; but it is also false in the sense that our interpretations are misrepresentations, falsifications of the deeper 'reality' of their own chaotic complexity and of physiological force and instinct. In this first sense, 'false' means 'inauthentic and unreal from the metaphysical point of view'; in the second sense, it means 'incorrect measured against the metaphysical standard of what constitutes linguistic truth'. Whereas Nietzsche's understanding of what counts as 'authentic' and 'real' differs from that of metaphysics, his standard of what would count as formally correct in language is exactly the same as that of metaphysics. Thus, when Nietzsche says that the world of our interpretations is false in the sense of 'incorrect', he means that in a perfectly straightforward way. There are a number of examples in Nietzsche's writings where these two senses of 'false' (one of which Nietzsche shares, the other he doesn't) are joined together – Nietzsche's definition of truth as 'an unconscionable falsification of the false' (*eine gewissenlose Umfälschung des Falschen*) being a case in point.[216]

Here again we see how Nietzsche's philosophy is limited by his polemical reversal of metaphysics. There is a degree of continuity between the distinct perspectives of the weak metaphysician and the strong Nietzschean in that the strong Nietzschean achieves with his 'truths' the 'realistic' insight into the nature of the world which the weak metaphysician in his misguided search for truth is also – at least ostensibly – concerned to achieve. However, paradoxically, the *dif-ference* between the metaphysical and the Nietzschean conceptions of what realism involves reveals that the Nietzschean is actually much more deeply tied to the metaphysical perspective than this continuity suggests. For the fictionalist theory of language which Nietzsche puts forward – his view that linguistic forms are false (i.e. incorrect) and that the most we can achieve are metaphorical 'truths' – derives its force from his retention of the metaphysician's own expectation of what would constitute linguistic truth. Nietzsche never challenges the view that linguistic truth would be adequate reference if it were possible; he never considers that truth might, for example, be found in associative or logical coherence within language and that reference might play a subsidiary role. Nietzsche is thus so obsessed with deny-ing metaphysical truth that he has no awareness of other alternatives to metaphysics that are not predominantly reversals of metaphysics.[217]

We have looked briefly at the way Nietzsche uses metaphysical vocabulary in his texts; but Nietzsche is not of course confined to the use of other philosophers' terms. His philosophy is in many ways a celebration of human creative ingenuity and experimental inventive-ness, and he demonstrates that inventiveness throughout his writ-ings.[218] There are few philosophers who have bequeathed to future generations such a welter of memorable formulations and metaphors: 'God is dead', '*amor fati*', 'the great emancipation' (*die große Loslösung*), 'pathos of distance' – the list is long and well known.[219]

The important thing to note about these formulations is that they derive their value in Nietzsche's eyes as much from the fact that they are *his* formulations as from their appropriateness or expressiveness. Nietzsche frequently draws attention to 'my proposition' (*mein Satz*) or to the 'formula of my happiness' in order to make the reader aware of the fact that he is dealing with Nietzsche's personal interpretations and hypotheses about life.[220]

Now, this strategy seems to serve a dual function in Nietzsche's texts. It seems to testify to Nietzsche's modest recognition of the limitation of his thoughts, but it also seems to highlight his wholly immodest conviction that his personal metaphors have a privileged authority over all others. This contradiction is, however, only an apparent one. In Nietzsche's view all conscious perception is perspec-tival and limited, and his own linguistic formulations are therefore to be regarded as limited points of view. But, as we have seen,

Nietzsche's critical limitation of consciousness rests firmly on the authoritative foundation of his sense of life, and of his own strength. Nietzsche's formulations of life are thus to be seen as limited, perspectival characterisations of his own unassailable personal experience of life. The apparently modest, tentative, critical and exploratory side of Nietzsche, seen, for example, in *Daybreak*, and the emphatic, assertive side of Nietzsche, seen in exaggerated form in *The Antichrist*, but evident throughout Nietzsche's writing, are thus not products of fundamentally different strands of his thinking. Nietzsche's exploratory mode of thinking is thus not quite as modest as it seems, for it is founded on his emphatic assertion of the limitation of human consciousness.

As Nietzsche enters his less analytic, more overtly creative period – *The Gay Science* and after – so it becomes more and more evident that his hypotheses are in fact more the product of bold creative energy than genuine tentativeness or modesty; for Nietzsche's writing becomes 'more richly charged with images, more poetic' (*gleichnisfroher, dichterischer*),[221] more explicitly metaphorical in accordance with his view that language is intrinsically 'metaphorical'. In his later writings, therefore, much of Nietzsche's thinking can be construed as creative extrapolation from his own authoritative sense of life's irrational multiplicity.

The best example of such extrapolation is Nietzsche's idea of the *Übermensch*. In the section 'On the Blissful Islands' in *Thus Spoke Zarathustra*, Zarathustra contrasts the notions of God and the superman. The idea of God, he says, is a supposition (*Mutmaßung*), but it is a supposition that goes beyond the bounds of what man can be expected to conceive. It is too abstract, too other-worldly to be thinkable. Zarathustra, on the other hand, wants our suppositions and ideals to be held within the limits of what is conceivable, and his idea of the *Übermensch* is meant to serve as just such a *thinkable* supposition. But what does it mean for the ideal of the superman to be 'bounded by conceivability'? Surely Nietzsche cannot be limiting our ideals to the forms of thought, when the main thrust of his polemic is directed against the belief that the boundaries of logic and language are the boundaries of life. The clue to what Nietzsche means is given in one simple exhortation: 'You should think your own senses through to the end!' (*Eure eignen Sinne sollt ihr zu Ende denken!*).[222] Our suppositions and ideals should not be limited by our logical forms, but should be creative developments of the content and character of our sensuous (and sensual) life. Our sensations, our fluctuating, shifting, chaotic physiological life should form the basis from which we can construct our new ideals. Whereas the notion of God, therefore, was an ideal created to deny creative life, the notion of the *Übermensch* is an ideal created to affirm and 'deify' the creative life from which it emerged.[223]

Creative hypothesising on the basis of our physiological sense of life, and our relative perceptions of the things and people around us, is, I believe, the key to much of Nietzsche's strategy in the later writings, though it cannot necessarily explain all of his utterances. Such creative hypothesising, which others can follow and develop in their own ways, is evident, for example, in the various typologies which Nietzsche sketched out – typologies of racial and natural differences, of moral character and of history.[224]

Nietzsche's mature position on history is set out in *Daybreak*. Historians, he says, do not deal with what really happened but only with limited perceptions of what happened. History is thus 'a continual generation and pregnancy of phantoms [*Schwangerwerden von Phantomen*] over the impenetrable mists of unfathomable reality'.[225] But in *On the Uses and Disadvantages of History for Life* Nietzsche had already suggested a solution to the historian's dilemma, and it is one with which we should now be familiar. The historian need not attempt to be objective and empirically accurate, but should be openly personal and creative in his interpretation of the past.[226] Such a historian would be an overtly aesthetic man who would impose a pattern on events, who would *create* 'objective' history out of the morass of details available to him; and in his own accounts of history Nietzsche adheres to this principle, creating semi-mythical figures like 'Socrates', 'Wagner' (and even 'Hegel') with often scant regard to the 'facts'.[227]

Nietzsche would have had no time for Hegel's subtle mixture of dialectical analysis and empirical detail even if he had understood what Hegel was attempting to do (which, in my view, he did not). The criteria which Nietzsche would employ to justify his various accounts of the past would be appropriateness to his view of life in general and to his particular perception of certain events (not faithfulness to the 'facts'), together with originality, boldness and 'fruitfulness' of the account. In such accounts fact and fiction could happily be blended together as Nietzsche shows in his playful fusion of the historical Zarathustra and his own fictional creation.[228]

The interpretation of Nietzsche's formulations suggested here also helps us to understand the function of one of the most important of

Nietzsche's ideas: the idea of eternal recurrence. To my mind, this idea is to be understood as a conjecture or hypothesis constructed from Nietzsche's experience of the constantly changing character of life. Nietzsche is not attempting to say 'This is how the world really *is*', but rather 'This is how I must and will see the world'. Nietzsche is thus not concerned with the literal, ontological truth of the teaching, but with its creative, interpretative 'truth'.[229]

Nietzsche bases his theory of eternal recurrence on his view that life has not reached, and cannot reach, a state of equilibrium. He sees that reality is constantly shifting and becoming and he tries to construct 'a conception of the world that does justice to *this* fact'.[230] Although Nietzsche does venture a scientific 'proof' of his theory, the terms in which that proof is couched demonstrate that it, too, results from his commitment to certain assumptions about the world:

wenn die Welt als bestimmte Größe von Kraft . . . gedacht werden *darf* . . .

if it is *permitted* to think of the world as a certain definite quantity of force . . .[231]

Furthermore, the use here of the verb *dürfen*, 'to be permitted', indicates that the doctrine of eternal recurrence is not only a conjecture, but also a test of man's courage. It is as if Nietzsche were saying: 'if you are strong, you will affirm this conjecture as the noblest and most realistic perspective on life yet achieved whether or not it is strictly true'.[232]

The importance of Nietzsche's theory lies not in its truth-value, but in the fact that it is the highest expression of Nietzsche's will to power. In a passage from *The Gay Science*, Nietzsche says that the will to 'eternalise' life, to give it the form of permanence or 'being' can be the product of the resentment and hatred of the weak or of the thankfulness and love of the strong. It can reduce and diminish life or it can spread a Homeric 'light and glory' (*Glorienschein*) over things.[233] (From other passages we know that the same is true of all language for Nietzsche.)[234] It is the strong, affirmative will to 'eternalise' life that underlies Nietzsche's theory of eternal recurrence. Nietzsche is committed to imposing a stable form onto life in the full knowledge that he is *imposing* a form which is not to be taken for the truth. The notion of eternal recurrence is thus the product of Nietzsche's will to make a stable aesthetic phenomenon out of the dynamic aesthetic creativity of life:

To *impose* upon becoming the character of being – that is the *supreme will to power* . . . *That everything recurs*, is the closest *approximation of a world of becoming to a world of being: – high point of the meditation.*[235]

Nietzsche's mode of creative hypothesising is anti-metaphysical because it highlights his conviction that all language in fact consists in the creation of fictions. There is, however, another feature of Nietzsche's writing that is anti-metaphysical for a slightly different reason: that is his technique of writing in short, often aphoristic passages of prose.[236] This technique is based on his belief in the multiple, perspectival character of human consciousness.

Nietzsche's philosophy involves the continual generation of new creative formulations and analytical 'insights'. Nietzsche refuses to rest in, or be confined by, any one total view of the world, but is constantly shifting from one perspective or interpretation to another – and even undermining positions he has defended elsewhere – in order to preserve the 'fascination of the opposing point of view' and indeed to blend 'all opposites . . . into a new unity'.[237] This stylistic feature can of course best be seen in the 'aphoristic' books from *Human, All-too-Human* to *Beyond Good and Evil*, but it runs throughout *Thus Spoke Zarathustra* and other texts as well.

Nietzsche's perspectival way of writing is the consequence of three of his anti-metaphysical concerns, the first of which is his desire for wholeness. We have already seen that Nietzsche conceives of wholeness in terms of multiplicity and variety, rather than identity and continuity.[238] Nietzsche's desire to present a strong, complete philosophy therefore requires him to embrace as many different viewpoints as he can, to experience as many different possibilities of interpretation as he can.[239] However, the limitations and dangers of this desire are great, the major danger being that of the disintegration of the personality – a danger of which Nietzsche was well aware and to which he ultimately succumbed in his madness.[240] Nietzsche embraces a multitude of different perspectives but refuses to integrate them into a unified, definable and articulable whole. Indeed, the emphatic, dogmatic tone in which many of his utterances are couched reinforces their independent, at times even antagonistic, character and is a deliberate strategy to deny continuity and refuse integration.

Nietzsche without doubt valued the single, unique insight more highly than any continuous systematic argument,[241] but he was also acutely aware that the single insight, the isolated judgement or proposition, is only *one* possible perspective and needs to be complemented by a myriad of others. Thus, instead of looking for wholeness in the dynamic continuity and development of thought as Hegel does, Nietzsche seeks it in an assemblage or juxtaposition of different perspectives.[242] The result is that many of Nietzsche's texts resemble a cubist painting – multiple, yes, but angular, jarring, without the coherence of life. Because of the emphatic character of so many of Nietzsche's insights and because there is frequently no evident transition from one thought to another, his texts all too easily give the impression that they are a collection of static positions rather than living, developing thought. What Nietzsche lacks, it seems, is any true sense of

geprägte Form, die lebend sich entwickelt.

minted form which develops as it lives.[243]

The second anti-metaphysical concern which underlies Nietzsche's perspectival style is his wish to remain faithful to the conditions of the genesis of his ideas, to reflect the continually changing, inconstant character of his observations. Nietzsche refuses to order his thoughts according to an explicit guiding logic, but presents them (albeit in general thematic groups) as the products of his illogical, unpredictable impulses. They are (or at least are meant to be) the convictions of the moment which might be felt to be definitive at the time, but are relativised, challenged at another.[244]

The third explanation for Nietzsche's adoption of an 'aphoristic', perspectival style is that he wishes to produce a text which, like that of Horace's *Odes*, is economical and yet powerful, a text, that is, which, in contrast to those of previous philosophers, utilises the minimum of words and signs to the maximum expressive effect. The virtue of such a style, Nietzsche says, is that it is 'compact, severe, with as much substance as possible'.[245] This explanation suggests, of course, that Nietzsche wishes his perspectival style to be seen as the result of supreme self-control and discipline, as well as inspiration, and that consequently a brief dictum may be the fruit and harvest of long reflection, and not just, as was suggested in the last paragraph, of sudden, momentary insight.[246] Such a style encourages the reader to work hard to understand the text because it refuses to present the whole argument supporting a particular point, and it is thus perhaps consciously conceived as an alternative to the allegedly long-winded and ponderous expositions of the classical German Idealists, Kant, Fichte and Hegel.[247]

Zarathustra said of himself: 'All existence here wants to become words, all becoming here wants to learn speech from me', and this could well stand as a motto for Nietzsche's perspectival style as a whole.[248] Nietzsche wants his philosophical style to reflect his ceaselessly shifting view of a ceaselessly shifting world, and thus to be clearly opposed to the metaphysician's timeless, all-embracing Truth. A clear statement to this effect is given in *The Gay Science*: 'We keep changing', Nietzsche says, and as a consequence, 'we are no longer free to do only one particular thing, to *be* only one particular thing.'[249] Nietzsche refuses to be restricted to one perspective. He wants to give the impression that there is no one Nietzschean position or method or style, no one Nietzschean truth, but that there are only Nietzschean 'truths', metaphors, hypotheses.[250] Nietzsche's strength is thus held to lie in affirming that absence of fixity, that presence of continual change, and in forcing that multiplicity under the name 'Nietzsche'.[251]

It has been pointed out that the style (or rather lack of coherent style) in *Thus Spoke Zarathustra* displays features which Nietzsche elsewhere describes as decadent: 'The word becomes sovereign and leaps out of the sentence, the sentence reaches out and obscures the meaning of the page, the page gains life at the expense of the whole – the whole is no longer a whole.'[252] From what has been said in this section, one could extend the parallel and suggest that the very notion of Nietzsche's fragmentary, disintegrated wholeness is from his own point of view decadent. And could one not also add that Nietzsche is as guilty as the 'decadent' Wagner of 'playing hide and seek behind a hundred symbols'?[253]

Yet there is a difference in Nietzsche's eyes between himself and the decadents, and that difference is essential to Nietzsche's whole philosophical project. The source of the difference for Nietzsche lies, as it were, 'behind' the fragmented texts. Decadent fragmentariness is the product of nervous sensibility, 'disgregation of the will' and 'the decline of the power to organise'.[254] Nietzsche's fragmentariness, on the other hand, is the product of energy, substance and power which *is* able to organise, and it is that power which is meant to give Nietzsche's writings their *underlying* wholeness.

To my mind, the dominant concern of Nietzsche's writings is to intimate this fundamental mood of heroic vitality; and it is this intention to abandon truth in favour of the evocation of inner strength which in Nietzsche's eyes marks him out as radically anti-metaphysical. The metaphysician who expects to find a definitive, uncontradicted set of linguistic propositions setting out Nietzsche's view of the world, or who is impatient to 'get on top' of Nietzsche's philosophy, will find his texts very uncongenial and enigmatic.[255] He will be frustrated by the vagueness and elusiveness of many of Nietzsche's metaphors of mood; he will be confused by Nietzsche's employment of the very metaphysical terms Nietzsche rejects; he will often miss continuous argument; he will be tested by Nietzsche's constant shifts of perspective; he will be puzzled by Nietzsche's frequent refusal to answer questions he has raised;[256] he will be baffled by what appear to be blatant contradictions;[257] he will be offended by the aggressive tone of many of Nietzsche's utterances; he will be disturbed by the ironic freedom that Nietzsche wishes to reserve for himself. He will find in Nietzsche what Nietzsche himself wanted to be: 'an *incarnate* declaration of war against, and victory over, all old conceptions of "true" and "untrue" '.[258]

In this sense, Nietzsche is an elitist. His texts are designed not only to be difficult, but actually to be discriminatory and selective. He wants to confuse some readers and be clear to others, and thus does not seek universal intelligibility. One doesn't need any specialised jargon to understand Nietzsche, but one does, it seems, require a non-metaphysical, heroic *vision* of life:

All the nobler spirits and tastes select their audience when they wish to communicate; and choosing that, one at the same time erects barriers against 'the others'. All the more subtle laws of any style have their origin at this point: they at the same time keep away, create a distance, forbid 'entrance', understanding. . . – while they open the ears of those whose ears are related to ours.

Nietzsche's only concession to the unfortunate weak ones is that he does at least state in clear, universally intelligible terms that he doesn't wish to be understood by them.[259]

A critique of Nietzsche's anti-metaphysical philosophy

In this chapter I have tried to show that Nietzsche's philosophy can be understood as a radical alternative to metaphysics as Nietzsche understands it. Nietzsche's hostility to metaphysical thinking rests on his hostility to the conception of permanent, stable identity; in his own anti-metaphysical philosophy, therefore, there is a profound divorce between life or 'becoming' and 'being'.[260]

If we recall that Nietzsche's critique of metaphysics also entails the rejection of fixed divisions or *Gegensätze* between areas of experience, a contradiction emerges in that critique. In order to challenge the validity of fixed conceptual distinctions Nietzsche himself employs an unchallenged conceptual distinction, for he clearly separates life or 'becoming' from the linguistic world of fixed, *seiend* divisions. It is true that Nietzsche bases this distinction on his sense or experience of life and suggests that the linguistic divorce he posits between life and language, between individual and species, is merely a metaphorical approximation to the actual state of affairs.[261] Nevertheless, this distinction between experience and language is itself a linguistic distinction, and, however crude it may be, Nietzsche's experience is moulded by it. Nietzsche's divorce between 'experience' and language is itself informed by the language it seeks to devalue. Furthermore, even if it could be argued that the distinction Nietzsche draws between life and language is not absolute because there is at least a metaphorical representation of life in some kinds of language, the distinction is still enough of a *Gegensatz* to preclude any notion that language and thought can actually articulate the 'form' of life.

Within his own terms, therefore, Nietzsche remains a metaphysical thinker because he employs a metaphysical distinction in order to reject metaphysical categories.[262] Nor can we dismiss this contradiction as peripheral to Nietzsche's main aim: the opposition between 'being' and 'becoming', between articulable form and life, lies at the heart of Nietzsche's philosophy.

The main form in which the opposition of 'being' and 'becoming' appears is, as I have indicated, that of the opposition of life and linguistic consciousness. Nietzsche repeatedly insists that what is changing, what has a history, cannot be formulated or defined accurately. Language and thought can only freeze life in the static form of the judgement; they cannot articulate the process of becoming. He sees 'the character of the world in a state of becoming as *incapable of formulation*, as "false" . . . *Knowledge* and *becoming* exclude one another.'[263] This dogmatic axiom justifies Nietzsche's assertion that life lacks all transcendent form, purpose and meaning; it therefore justifies Nietzsche's atheist view that the world is 'chaos' without divine order.[264] It also justifies Nietzsche's fictionalist epistemology, his belief that language and consciousness impose simplified form onto diversified chaos and are not therefore the element of truth, but of falsification, interpretation, and at best of 'truth'. Nietzsche's reduction of the will to truth to the will to power and the will to create, his vision of man as aesthetic and interpretative rather than straightforwardly cognitive, and his whole project of creative conjecture and experimental typologising rest finally on his belief that reality is 'becoming' and that all consciousness's interpretations of life, however realistic they may be, are characterised by the fictitious form of 'being'.

Nietzsche's critique of metaphysical oppositions fails to challenge the basic dichotomy between being and becoming, and it also fails to challenge another basic dichotomy: that between reality and appearance. Nietzsche abolishes the metaphysical duality between the true world of being and the apparent world of becoming which conceals that true world. However, within his own *one* world he has preserved an opposition between what he sees as the fundamental reality and what he sees as mere appearance. Whether that 'reality' is another person or object, our own instinctual life or even our changing interpretations themselves, it is always fundamentally different from the way it appears to us; it is always falsified by our perception of it.[265] Although Nietzsche treats as real the diversity and flux which metaphysics treats as apparent, and although he gives a performative role to what he considers to be 'appearance' within the dynamic, diversified reality which it falsifies (rather than simply positing each as a separate world), what is real and what is apparent in Nietzsche's world still stand in the same formal relation to one another of opposition and mutual exclusion as being-in-itself (*Ansichsein*) does to appearance (*Erscheinung* or *Schein*) in Nietzsche's view of the metaphysical scheme of things. Nietzsche will thus claim, for example, that the intellect cannot criticise itself because there is no 'true reality' or 'in itself', 'distinct from every perspectival kind of outlook or sensual–spiritual appropriation', with which the intellect could compare itself; at the same time, however, Nietzsche can only claim that the 'in itself' is a pure fiction by comparing it with the fundamental *reality* of those perspectival kinds of outlook and sensual–spiritual appropriation themselves.[266] Nietzsche even employs the metaphysical term 'in itself' (*an sich*) himself in what seems to be a straightforward way in order to criticise the notion of identity: 'what is that function . . . that makes cases identical and similar which are in themselves dissimilar [*an sich ungleich*]?'[267] But if Nietzsche rejects the concept of a reality 'in itself' hidden behind what we experience, how can he be justified in talking of 'cases which are in themselves dissimilar', and how can he claim that identity is therefore a fiction?

Nietzsche fails to acknowledge this problem because the categorial distinction of 'real' flux and 'apparent' identity is his main weapon of attack against the metaphysician's 'true world'. Nietzsche's rhetoric of symptomatic interpretation, by means of which he wishes to unmask the physiological reality behind the metaphysician's apparent moral and logical independence, thus relies on what is basically a metaphysical opposition of superficial form and fundamental under-lying force. In Nietzsche's view, instinctual life always presents itself as what it is not: sexual love, for example, '*desires* to overpower, to take possession, and *appears* as self-surrender'.[268]

Similarly, although Nietzsche criticises the metaphysical separation of subject and object, and dissolves both back into the homogeneity of life by interpreting each as a nexus of desires and instincts, his new understanding of subjectivity as instinctual is still governed by the basic opposition between subjective form (in Nietzsche's case, produced by the action of interpreting forces) and objective matter (in Nietzsche's case, the interpreted force) which characterised Kant's and Schopenhauer's epistemologies. In fact, Nietzsche's basic characterisation of force as that which acts on and interprets other forces is a direct (though psychologised and biologised) legacy of Kant's theory that the forms of sensibility and logic are produced by the activity of the knowing subject.[269] The metaphysical belief that the subject is essentially an agent which acts upon what confronts it is thus not criticised by Nietzsche as profoundly as might appear. All Nietzsche in fact does is replace the traditional notion of the subject as substantial agent with the more physiological notion of the subject as a plurality of interpreting 'affects'. Nietzsche may reject the idea that there is an interpreter behind the interpretation, but he insists in the same breath: 'it is our needs *that interpret the world*'.[270]

Of course, one can claim that these examples are misleading because Nietzsche is merely utilising metaphysical terms in a metaphorical way for his own non-metaphysical purposes. But Nietzsche has to rely on the literal distinction between reality and appearance in order to establish that his terms are merely convenient fictions; he has to use the vocabulary of metaphysics naively in order to be able to claim that he is using it metaphorically.[271]

Nietzsche has set himself the task of overthrowing the traditional conceptions of metaphysics, but the manner in which he undertakes his assault on metaphysics is self-contradictory, for he trades on the metaphysical distinctions between being and becoming, and appearance and reality, in order to dismiss the distinctions of metaphysics as fictions. The question that now comes to mind is this: Do the concepts being and becoming, or appearance and reality have to be understood as opposites? Need the concept of being always be thought of as the denial of becoming? And need appearance always be thought of as the falsification of what is real? Or is not a truly non-metaphysical philosophy one which challenges the fixity of the concepts upon which such oppositions rest? To my mind, it is Hegel's philosophy which issues such a challenge and which resolves the conceptual oppositions to which Nietzsche adheres. Like Nietzsche, Hegel dismisses the idea that there is a realm of being 'behind' or 'beyond' the sphere of becoming which we experience. But unlike Nietzsche, Hegel does not therefore understand the concept of being to be a mere fiction produced within that sphere of becoming. Nor does he treat our dynamic, natural existence as a fundamental reality which is falsified when it 'appears' in language and consciousness. Hegel sees being (at least when it is fully determined as the Idea) as the inherent dynamic form and continuity of becoming itself, and he sees the 'apparent' world of linguistic terms and concepts as revealing rather than concealing the character of the reality they describe. As we shall see in chapter 4 in his discussion of empiricism, Hegel accepts that sensuous experience by itself lacks the unity and continuity of explicit rational form. But this does not lead Hegel to treat life as *an sich ungleich*, nor does it lead him to divorce life and language from one another. In Hegel's view, our explicitly discontinuous sensuous experience does not constitute a *firm* base which may be used to invalidate the determinations of thought and language; rather, it constitutes an immediate level of experience which is only properly determined in the concepts and determinations of language, that is when the empirical qualities and relations of things are specified in language and when that experience is understood in terms of the principles generated by rational thought.

A Hegelian perspective on Nietzsche does not cast doubt on Nietzsche's valuable assertions that we can be dominated by will to power, that we can falsify the diversity of life and deceive ourselves through language, that the conditions of life might include error. However, it maintains that we can only properly determine whether we are falsifying life if we compare our linguistic descriptions of life and our rational arguments with other linguistic descriptions of life and other rational arguments. A Hegelian perspective does, therefore, cast doubt on Nietzsche's belief that we must *always* falsify, that even when our linguistic characterisations of life are apt, concepts and life are known by virtue of some pre-linguistic 'experience' to be fundamentally different in character. Furthermore, if Hegel would challenge the belief that the discontinuous diversity of life constitutes a foundation against which language and thought can be found wanting, he would also challenge the Nietzschean view that the discontinuous diversity of man's selfish instinctual drives constitutes the foundation in terms of which all human activity can be understood. In Hegel's view, human life need not always be dominated by selfish instinctual drives; the will can be brought to exhibit an intersubjective character that reconciles conflicting interests and that is not reducible to the expression of one will's dominance over another.[272]

Although Hegel anticipates Nietzsche's view that a static conception of the categories is not adequate for a proper philosophical understanding of reality, he does not seek to prove this point by asserting that life is ultimately beyond articulation in language as such. Rather, he proves the point by developing a dialectical conception of the categories in which full justice is done to the dynamism of life. In this way Hegel criticises the metaphysical oppositions which Nietzsche criticises and also undermines the metaphysical opposition of life and language which Nietzsche relies on to carry out his own critique. The categories of human thought and language are thus not falsifications of 'unworded' life for Hegel. They are categories which, in their static conception, can yield reliable but limited knowledge of certain areas of experience, and which, in their complex dialectical conception, are perfectly adequate to philosophical knowledge of the world.

Nietzsche's own critique of the categories of metaphysics is far less subtle than that of Hegel. In establishing the one-sided character of those categories, Nietzsche simply espouses the cause of life, the moment which metaphysics neglects. However, he does not see that a philosophical view of life which treats continuity and form as mere abstractions, is itself one-sided, and that he himself therefore is committed to an abstract view of life. Nietzsche does not recognise that, taken by themselves, being and becoming, identity and diversity are both abstractions and that they need to be redefined so as to *include* the other if they are to lose their abstract character. By undertaking just such a redefinition Hegel challenges the dichotomy between these concepts which underlies Nietzsche's whole philosophy of creative falsification.[273]

From Hegel's point of view, Nietzsche is justified in criticising the abstract conception of being which neglects becoming, development and history; but he is not justified in believing uncritically that life is becoming without logical form or identity, without 'being'. In criticising being and *seiend* distinctions, Nietzsche should have gone on to criticise the dichotomy between being and life which turned both into abstractions. This he failed to do; instead of criticising both the abstractions of being and becoming, he simply played one off against the other.[274]

4
Hegel
and
metaphysics

Introduction

The previous chapter set out to show that Nietzsche's philosophy can best be understood as an assault on metaphysics. By metaphysics Nietzsche means a mode of thought which understands the world in terms of discrete entities and conceptual oppositions, the main example of which is the opposition between appearance and reality 'in itself'. In Nietzsche's view, philosophers are tempted into believing in such oppositions by language, particularly by the grammatical and logical distinction between subject and predicate. In chapter 1 it was suggested that Hegel could be seen as an ally of Nietzsche in his critique of metaphysics. The purpose of the present chapter, therefore, is to show to what extent this view of Hegel is appropriate.[1]

The most obvious point of similarity with Nietzsche in Hegel's philosophy is his critique in the *Phenomenology* of the 'unhappy consciousness', the alienated mode of consciousness which is at odds with the world of transience and finitude and which seeks refuge in an ideal 'beyond'.[2] But since a comparison of Hegel's treatment of the 'unhappy consciousness' and Nietzsche's treatment of 'slave morality' has already been undertaken by M. Greene, and was discussed in chapter 1, we will not repeat that discussion here.[3] A more accessible discussion of the phenomenon of the 'unhappy consciousness' is to be found, however, in Hegel's treatment of Judaism in the lectures on the philosophy of history and the philosophy of religion, and it is that which we shall look at briefly first of all.[4]

The main characteristic of dualistic consciousness for Nietzsche is that it separates the sensuous, natural sphere of life from an alleged realm of ideal or 'spiritual' reality. This ideal realm, which includes God and the soul, is conceived, according to Nietzsche, in direct opposition to the natural world, the natural world being viewed as subordinate to the ideal world in terms of value and reality: 'In God a declaration of hostility towards life, nature, the will to life! God the formula for every calumny of "this world", for every lie about "the next world"!'[5] Hegel's view of Judaism, though far less polemical and hostile in tone, presents a strikingly similar opposition of the ideal and the natural. In Judaism 'only the One, spirit, the non-sensuous is the truth'.[6] The ultimate reality and ground of our being is thus the pure subjectivity of God, pure subjectivity which 'has been freed from the natural, and consequently from what is sensuous, whether this is found in the external world of sense or is a sensuous idea [*Vorstellung*]', and by being excluded from God in this way, nature thus loses all its value.[7]

A further characteristic which Nietzsche attributed to the Judaeo-Christian God was the claim to exclusive allegiance and reverence. God, in Nietzsche's eyes, is a jealous God who declares: 'There is *one* God! You shall have no other gods before me!'[8] Nietzsche criticised the exclusivity of the idea of God by insisting that it denies the multiplicity of perspectives which life offers. In Hegel's view, too, the principle of exclusivity is fundamental to the Judaic deity, although it is not fundamental – at least not in its radical form – to the Trinitarian Christian God. Jehovah, for Hegel, is 'the *exclusive* unity . . . Before him all other gods are false: moreover, the distinction between "true" and "false" is quite abstract; for as regards the false gods, not a ray of the divine is supposed to shine into them.'[9] The Christian God, on the other hand, though uniquely revealed in His perfect form in Jesus Christ, is, in Hegel's view, also revealed in an imperfect way in nature and in other forms of historical and religious life (including Judaism). The whole point of Hegel's philosophy, indeed, is to find the Trinitarian God, or in Hegel's terminology, the Idea, in that which is other than God, namely the created world.[10] The close similarity between the criticisms made by Hegel and Nietzsche of the principle of exclusive divinity is seen clearly in the lectures on aesthetics, where Hegel praises the celebration of multiplicity inherent in Greek polytheism in a manner very reminiscent of Nietzsche.[11]

Despite this similarity, however, the positions of Hegel and

Nietzsche are by no means the same, and the difference between them is evident in their treatment of human identity. Nietzsche conceives of human life and personality as an aggregate of competing instincts, controlled by a dominant drive and moulded by various social and psychological masks, but lacking the coherence of continuous selfhood and identity. Hegel, on the other hand, conceives of character as uniting and reconciling the two moments of diversity and identity.[12] Man may have a wide range of differing moods, emotions and perspectives, but he also has a genuine identity defined by his personality, his family and his culture. More importantly, in Hegel's view, man is a self-conscious being and is therefore informed by what Hegel sees as the dynamic structure of self-consciousness. That structure, the 'logic' of self-consciousness, informs all of our behaviour, whether or not we acknowledge it, and constitutes our universal human identity. The pattern of self-conscious activity is the theme of Hegel's philosophy of *Geist* – particularly his philosophy of society and history – and cannot be expounded in detail here. However, the form of that activity can be articulated in general terms. The logic of self-consciousness, Hegel maintains, is that self-consciousness comes to be what it intrinsically is by negating, or 'dying to', partial modes of itself, that is by acknowledging those partial modes to be partial and not to be the whole truth of consciousness. *Geist* is thus

something which necessarily enters into the process of distinguishing itself from itself, of positing its other, and which comes to itself only through this other, and by positively overcoming it – not by abandoning it [*durch die erhaltende Aufhebung – nicht durch Verlassung – desselben*].[13]

In one way or another this general pattern informs all human life, however diversified that may be. It explains how we become aware of ourselves, how man has developed in history, and it also provides the criterion for establishing why consciousness frequently *fails* to become what it intrinsically is. This logic of self-consciousness, in Hegel's view, is fully articulated in tragedy (as we shall see in the last chapter) and also in the Christian religion, particularly in the Christian understanding of God as manifest in and through the Incarnation, Crucifixion and Resurrection. What Christians worship in Jesus Christ, therefore, is the incarnation of man's true character, identity and determination (*Bestimmung*), an identity which brings fulfilment if it is accepted, but which 'damns' man if it is rejected.

Despite similarities in their understanding of the Judaic God,

Hegel's evaluation of the Christian God is, therefore, clearly distinguished from Nietzsche's. Nietzsche sees the Christian God as the fictional essence of man to which man in his self-alienation subordinates himself. The Christian God and the Judaic God are thus for Nietzsche one and the same.[14] This is not true for Hegel. In his view, the Christian God represents the true identity of man which informs in a more or less explicit way all man's manifold manifestations. The Judaic God, on the other hand, represents an abstract – metaphysical – conception of that true identity.[15] Christianity is thus the epitome of metaphysical abstraction for Nietzsche, whereas it presents a critique of metaphysical abstraction for Hegel.

The overall difference between Hegel and Nietzsche can now be brought sharply into focus. Nietzsche's critique of dualism contrasts the *fiction* of spiritual identity with the concrete foundation of 'life'. Instinctual, natural life may well be modified and disciplined during the course of human history, therefore, but it nevertheless remains for Nietzsche the essential locus of human character. Hegel's critique of dualism, on the other hand, involves contrasting an abstract conception of conscious identity, one that is opposed to the diversity of natural, bodily existence, with a concrete conception of conscious identity, one that is inherent in, and lives through, the diversity of natural, bodily existence.[16] Hegel does not therefore see the spiritual identity expressed in the Judaic God as a *fiction*, but as an abstract formulation of the *truth* of man. Man's true identity, for Hegel, is not tied to his instincts; it is *geistig* identity. But it is not disembodied mind. It is a formal identity which emerges within nature and time and which finds its fulfilment in thought and language as a social and historical reality.

Hegel's critique of metaphysical dualism is similar to, but by no means identical with, that of Nietzsche. Hegel does not rely, as Nietzsche does, on the external standard of life to criticise abstract conceptions of identity. From Hegel's perspective, indeed, reliance on such an opposition between life and form merely perpetuates the very metaphysical oppositions which are the object of criticism. Hegel's critique of metaphysics will thus criticise not only the metaphysics which Nietzsche himself is criticising, but also Nietzsche's own critique of it. From Hegel's point of view – and, as we saw at the end of the last chapter, in Nietzsche's own terms – Nietzsche himself appears as a metaphysical thinker. In order to avoid Nietzsche's shortcomings, therefore, Hegel will not employ an external standard to criticise metaphysics, but, as we shall see in chapter 5, he will endeavour to discover the concrete truth inherent in abstraction by means of a process of immanent criticism.

To demonstrate that Hegel's philosophy is in fact equipped to criticise metaphysics and Nietzsche's own philosophical alternative, we must now look in more detail at what Hegel means by metaphysics. In the present chapter we shall thus examine Hegel's understanding of the historical development of philosophy from Scholastic and post-Reformation metaphysics to his own speculative philosophy. In the course of this examination, we shall review Hegel's discussion of metaphysics itself, but we shall also consider his treatment of what he sees as the metaphysical presuppositions behind empiricism and Kantian critical philosophy and indicate how that treatment might bear on Nietzsche. My concern in the present chapter is not, however, with the historical accuracy of Hegel's view of past philosophers, but with the *types* of philosophy which Hegel criticises. I will not, therefore, seek to justify his views by reference to original texts by the figures with which he deals or to other commentators on those figures.

Metaphysics

Metaphysics is characterised in the *Encyclopaedia* first and foremost by the belief that the categories of thought constitute 'the *fundamental determinations of things*'.[17] In Hegel's view, this belief, which runs contrary to Kant's assertion that reality 'in itself' cannot be known in any concrete manner by thought, informs all initial philosophising and all science: 'indeed, even the daily activity of consciousness lives in this faith'.[18] The second important characteristic of metaphysical thought is that the subject-matter with which it deals is absolute and infinite. The objects of metaphysics are 'totalities, which in and for themselves belong to *reason*, to the thought of the universal which is *concrete* in itself – the *soul*, the *world*, *God*'.[19] Metaphysics, in Hegel's eyes, is thus concerned with such issues as the immateriality of the soul, the existence of God and the nature of final causality.[20]

These two characteristics constitute for Hegel what is of lasting value in metaphysics and what is to be taken over (albeit in a revised form) into speculative philosophy. In this respect, therefore, Hegel's evaluation of metaphysics is clearly different from that of Nietzsche, since Nietzsche insists that thought cannot comprehend reality and that infinite objects are pure fictions.

The third characteristic of metaphysics which Hegel identifies is the one which speculative philosophy is intended to overcome and this is what I would call its positivist dimension. The positivism of metaphysics lies in the fact that, although its subject-matter is infinite, metaphysics treats that subject-matter as *gegenständlich*, as comprising the *given* objects (or subjects) of thought: 'Metaphysics took [its objects] from the sphere of *representation* [*Vorstellung*] and considered them to be *complete, given* subjects which form the foundation to which the categories of the understanding are to be applied.'[21] An example of this is seen clearly, Hegel believes, in the fact that metaphysics treats the soul as a 'thing'.[22] Similarly, as we have seen in the case of Judaism, a metaphysical conception of God is one that treats God as a determinate reality distinct from – 'beyond' or 'above' – the world of human and natural relations, rather than as the absolute logical form of human and natural relations themselves. Thus, although in Hegel's view metaphysics considers ultimate reality to be accessible to rational thought, it nevertheless conceives of that ultimate reality as an 'object' fundamentally distinct from the knowing mind. In this latter respect, therefore, Hegel's view of metaphysics corresponds to that of Nietzsche, for both criticise metaphysics for thinking in terms of distinct, ideal entities.

The method of metaphysical philosophy, Hegel maintains, involves attributing predicates to these given subjects, in judgements.[23] Moreover, just as the subject-matter of metaphysics consists of distinct entities, so the qualities to be predicated of those entities are held to be valid by themselves (*für sich geltend*).[24] Of any two opposing predicates, therefore, metaphysics assumes that one must be false if the other is true. Metaphysical philosophy is thus described by Hegel as 'either/or' thinking because it treats predicates or determinations of thought as mutually exclusive, 'as if each of the two terms in an antithesis [*Gegensatz*] has an independent, isolated existence as something substantial and true by itself'.[25] The world either has a beginning and end in time or it does not; matter is either infinitely divisible or it is not; man is either a rigidly determined being or he is not. In this mutual exclusivity, Hegel believes, lies the dogmatism of metaphysics.[26] In spite of the fact that metaphysics deals with infinite objects, therefore, these objects are rendered finite by the employment of mutually exclusive, one-sided determinations – 'categories, the limits of which are believed to be permanently fixed, and not subject to any further negation'.[27]

The major deficiency of the metaphysics criticised by Hegel is thus that it is, in the formulation given in the *Encyclopaedia*, 'the *view which the abstract understanding* takes of the objects of reason' (*die* bloße Verstandesansicht *der Vernunftgegenstände*).[28] Kant, we are told, was the first philosopher to draw the distinction between the two modes of thinking, *Verstand* and *Vernunft*, terms which are usually translated as understanding and reason.[29] Hegel takes over this distinction from Kant, but he does not conceive of the difference between understanding and reason as residing simply in the fact that they have a finite and an infinite content respectively, as Kant himself had done. For Hegel they are significantly different *forms* of thinking. The understanding, Hegel says, 'remains tied to fixed determinations and to their distinction from one another; each of these limited abstractions is believed by the understanding to be and to exist on its own account [*für sich*]'.[30] The understanding thus operates, for example, with an abstract conception of what is universal as that which is distinct from, and opposed to, what is particular. The old metaphysics studied its infinite objects in terms of these abstract determinations of the understanding. As a result, it applied a form of thinking, which was adequate only to finite objects, to 'objects' which, being infinite, require a form of thinking which itself is infinite. This infinite mode of thinking is found in what Hegel calls speculative reason – thinking which does not merely distinguish and separate determinations from one another, but which also conceives of the determinations so distinguished as a unity, that is to say, which is the '*sublation* [*Aufheben*] *of oppositions* as such'.[31] Such speculative reason, as we shall see in chapter 5, is achieved and mediated by philosophical insight into the dialectical dissolution of the fixed determinacy of the categories of the understanding, a dissolution which results when those categories are taken to be the ultimate categories of thought.[32]

Metaphysics considers its infinite objects to be the foundation for its speculation and to provide a firm ground from which to proceed. It views them as the standard by reference to which a certain description is preferred or rejected, rather than things which only come to be understood through description. And yet this is only half the story. For qua *infinite*, the objects of metaphysics cannot be known immediately (as to a certain extent empirical objects can be), but need to be determined by deductive, rational thought. In fact, therefore, they do not provide metaphysics with quite as firm a foundation for predication as metaphysics believes. Metaphysics treats the represen-

tations of religion and the axioms of thought as a determinate foundation, but it does not see them as fully determined. As the activity of
rational clarification in language, metaphysics thus takes it upon itself
to determine a priori out of concepts the specific content of its presupposed notions. In its very procedure, therefore, metaphysics
undermines the firmness of its own presuppositions. What on the one
hand is treated as a firm, self-evident *Vorstellung*, is on the other hand
seen to be in need of specification and determination by deductive
reason. In Hegel's view this contradiction is inherent in the
metaphysical method of seeking actively to determine through
reason infinite objects, such as 'God', which are *given* to thought.[33]

Despite the methodologically equivocal status of its presupposed
conceptions, metaphysics nevertheless considers them to be firm and
reliable. In fact the reliance on, and concern with, what are held to be
firm foundations is a general feature of all metaphysical thought for
Hegel. Hegel distinguishes two main forms of metaphysics – Scholastic
metaphysics and modern, post-Reformation metaphysics – but both
are characterised in his view by the reliance on unanalysed presuppositions. Scholastic metaphysics, Hegel argues, has as its primary
task the proof of theological doctrine; it is therefore subordinated to
the positive authority of the Church.[34] Modern metaphysics, on the
other hand, is more autonomous. In accordance with what he sees as
the Reformation notion that truth is available to all and not the
'property' of an authoritarian institution,[35] Hegel says that modern
metaphysics looks for its content within reason itself, rather than in
the doctrines of the Church.[36] Yet that content is found in the form of
definitions and principles which still serve as the given foundation of
thought.[37] Although modern philosophy seeks a content within itself
which is fully rational and therefore fully its own, that content is not
developed out of thought and thus remains as external to the free process of reasoning as were the religious presuppositions of mediaeval
metaphysics.[38]

Hegel's final criticism of metaphysics is that the metaphysical
method of attributing given predicates and determinations to a given
content can never lead any further than to 'correct' knowledge; it cannot yield insight into the immanent truth and necessary character of
such determinations 'in and for themselves' – the truth which speculative philosophy will endeavour to articulate.[39] This is why Hegel
criticises Anselm's ontological proof of God, for example; the content proven is correct, but the manner of proof is inadequate

(*mangelhaft*).[40] Hegel believes that Anselm's proof convinces us by argument of a particular proposition, namely that God exists, but that it does not allow us to grasp the character of God in the course of that proof:

> In so far as the understanding keeps to the given religious content, it can prove this content; one can demonstrate that it must be so . . . But there still remains something to be desired in order that satisfaction may be complete; the content is proved, but I nevertheless do not comprehend it [*ich begreife es doch nicht*]. Thus Anselm's excellent proposition . . . is a proof, it may be admitted, of the existence of God, but it shows no comprehension of that existence. Though I see the truth of the proposition, I have not attained to the final point, the object of my desire; for there is lacking the I, the inner bond, inwardness as the inwardness of thought. This lies only in the concept, in the unity of the particular and the universal, of being and thought. To comprehend this unity, one would have to recognise that, out of itself, being turns itself into the concept [*daß das Sein aus sich selbst sich zum Begriffe macht*].[41]

As we have seen, Hegel considers it to be the fundamental conviction of metaphysics that thought can reveal to us the nature of things in themselves, but he wishes to show that metaphysics does not actually fulfil its aim. In fact the most that metaphysics can do is scratch the surface of reality and tell us about the nature of things in flat, two-dimensional terms. The reason for this lies in the positivism of metaphysics, the fact that it treats its subject-matter as infinite objects given to thought and that it considers the laws of thought to be no more than the method whereby *we* gain knowledge of those given objects. Metaphysical thought yields many correct propositions and many profound ideas in Hegel's view, but such thought ultimately remains subjective, because the method or structure of metaphysical reasoning is not the dynamic structure or 'logic' of reality itself. The rules of formal logic on which metaphysics is based contain merely

> directions as to how to think correctly . . . laws of our understanding, through which we gain insight, but through a mediation, a movement, which is not the movement of the things themselves. The result is certainly intended to be truth, so that things are constituted as we bring them forth according to the laws of thought; but the manner of this knowledge has merely subjective significance; the judgements and the syllogisms employed are not the forms of the judgement and the syllogism that are in things themselves [*das Urteil, der Schluß ist nicht Urteil, nicht Schluß der Dinge selbst*].[42]

(In the *Science of Logic* Hegel examines this method in abstraction from specific metaphysical systems as the method of 'synthetic' knowledge.)[43]

Empiricism

Like Nietzsche, Hegel criticises metaphysical philosophy for operating with fixed categorial distinctions and oppositions, and for thinking in terms of objective, ideal entities which serve as the given foundations of thought. In the criticisms of metaphysics made by empiricists such as Bacon and Locke, Hegel recognises many of the points he himself makes. However, the empiricists do not criticise metaphysics for making use of abstract, one-sided categories as such, but only for being founded on noumenal or ideal presuppositions. The empiricists object that the foundations of metaphysical knowledge are not firm enough, but are arbitrary and ultimately lacking in concrete determination because they are the products of a priori thought or religious belief alone. Empiricism seeks to put knowledge on a firmer base by replacing the presupposed objects and axioms of philosophy by the immediacy of given sensuous experience. In this way the empiricists believe that they can found knowledge on presuppositions which are concrete in themselves and not in need of concrete determination by rational thought.[44]

Hegel cites Francis Bacon as one of the first thinkers to react against the metaphysical manner of deducing the nature of reality from rational principles. Bacon called the method of the Scholastic metaphysics with which he was familiar *anticipationes naturae* and, according to Hegel, he defined it in the following way: 'men begin with presuppositions, definitions, accepted ideas, with a Scholastic abstraction, and reason further from these without regarding that which is present in actuality'.[45] Against this a priori anticipation of nature, Bacon emphasised the importance of the empirical explanation and interpretation of nature and thereby directed attention to what is empirically given in experience. Empiricism is therefore able to remedy a major deficiency of metaphysics and call men to consciousness of what is present at hand, for, by resting on concrete experience, empiricism seeks to be direct knowledge of objects which are present to the mind, rather than indirect knowledge of what reality rationally ought to be:

In empiricism lies the great principle that whatever is true must be in the actual world and present to perception [*für die Wahrnehmung da*]. This principle is opposed to that 'ought to be' which puffs up reflection to treat what is actually present with scorn and to point to a *beyond* that has no existence or locality except in the understanding of those who talk about it.[46]

This principle, which for Hegel is essential to the development of true philosophical knowledge, is one which has greatly influenced his own speculative philosophy, and indeed is what has enabled speculative philosophy to progress beyond metaphysics. The importance of the empiricist turn for the emergence of speculative philosophy is made clear by Hegel during his discussion of Bacon in the lectures on the history of philosophy. Unlike empiricism, speculative philosophy does not seek to derive all its ideas from perception itself, but rather develops its principal determinations out of pure self-determining reason. But two aspects of speculative philosophy nevertheless show the influence of empiricism: (a) concern for the immediacy and dynamic life of thought, for what thought *is*, rather than for what thought is deduced from presupposed first principles to be, and (b) concern for the manner in which reason is manifested, 'particularised', in the empirical world. No less than empiricism, therefore – and in contrast to metaphysics – 'philosophy recognises only what is, having nothing to do with what merely *ought* to be and thus *is not there before us* [*sie weiß nicht solches, was nur sein* soll *und somit nicht da ist*]'.[47] Hegel's *Realphilosophie* thus shows how the fundamental conceptual determinations of the natural and the human world can be derived from the self-development of reason; but this self-development of reason is at the same time the rational reconstruction of empirical experience. The development of our knowledge of the empirical world 'has thus been an essential condition of the Idea's reaching its full development and determination'.[48] Having said this, however, we must remember that empiricism is not yet speculative philosophy, because what is present to empirical consciousness is still the relatively simple sensuous immediacy of reality and not reality's inherently dialectical character.[49]

Empiricism wishes to base knowledge on sensuous perception, but it also seeks to transform its sensuous perceptions into thoughts in the process which Hegel calls analysis. Analysis, Hegel says, seeks to abstract from perceived objects the different empirical qualities (such as softness and warmth) and pure conceptual determinations (such as identity and diversity) which constitute those perceived objects:

'Analysis is the process from the immediacy of perception to thought; those determinations, which the object analysed unites within itself, receive the form of universality by being separated out.'[50] Since the products of analysis are general determinations or thoughts, empiricism is seen by Hegel to share with metaphysics and speculative philosophy the conviction 'that the truth of things lies in thought'. Like metaphysics, therefore, empiricism distinguishes the objects to be known by consciousness from consciousness itself, and also insists that those objects can be known in terms of the general determinations of consciousness. Empiricism has the great advantage over metaphysics, however, that its analysis proceeds from what is concrete and given in sense experience, rather than from abstract definitions. The products of analysis appear, therefore, to need no explicit deduction or proof, because they are derived directly from the nature of the empirical object analysed.[51]

The philosopher whom Hegel believes most clearly exemplifies this 'metaphysicising empiricism' (*metaphysizierender Empirismus*) is John Locke:[52] 'Locke's philosophy is, if you like, a metaphysics; it is concerned with general determinations, general thoughts, and those general determinations are to be derived from experience and observation.'[53] By starting from sensuous experience rather than from axiomatic definitions, Locke tackled a problem which, Hegel believes, metaphysicians have all too often ignored, namely the problem of the source and the legitimation of our concepts and ideas. In Locke's empiricist view all 'ideas' – including both pure and empirical concepts – are now seen to be empirical in origin, to be 'derived, and no longer oracularly laid down', and as an example of this Hegel points to Locke's rejection of the notion of innate ideas.[54] Hegel's own view on the question of innate ideas, it should be noted, is that, whereas empirical 'concepts' (such as horse or brown) owe their origin, as Locke said, to sensation and perception, necessary, pure concepts (such as identity or causality) are 'essential moments in the nature of thought' and are produced by the mind out of its own reason, rather than derived from experience by analysis as Locke thought. However, Hegel also thinks that these pure, conceptual determinations are only produced in response to empirical experience, as ways of ordering that experience. In this sense, therefore, though for un-Lockean reasons, Hegel also thinks that such pure determinations are not truly innate.[55]

Now, if Hegel appreciates the value of Locke's empiricist attempt to derive ideas from concrete experience, rather than merely assert their validity a priori, he is also highly critical of the residual positivism in that method. Empiricism, Hegel believes, considers ideas to be positive determinations abstracted or separated out from things by an external process of 'comparing, distinguishing and contrasting'.[56] The objects given to immediate sense-experience are thus conceived as the firm standard of concreteness by reference to which all general determinations may be legitimated or rejected.[57] The difference between a priori metaphysics and the a posteriori metaphysics of empiricism therefore resides solely in the nature of the foundation on which knowledge is held to rest. Whereas in a priori metaphysics the presupposed content is infinite and noumenal, and thus not given to sensuous consciousness, in empiricism the presuppositions are finite and sensuous: 'To this extent, then, both modes of philosophising have the same method; both proceed from presuppositions and assumptions which they treat as a firm foundation.'[58]

The empiricist turn in philosophy initiated by such thinkers as Francis Bacon did not therefore revolutionise the method and form of philosophical reasoning: 'In fact it was only to an alteration in the content that, without being aware of it, Bacon was impelled.'[59] In spite of the fact that appeals were constantly made to experience in an attempt to justify empiricist conclusions and to cast doubt on the conclusions of a priori metaphysics, the empiricists still operated with the same categories as the metaphysics they challenged. They considered sensuous particulars to constitute a firm ground distinct from the general ideas which those particulars were to legitimate, and thus showed that they did not question the metaphysical distinction between the categories of particularity and universality, for example. The empiricists therefore based the notion of an empirical foundation for knowledge on unproven metaphysical categories. Similarly, they retained the old apparatus of syllogistic reasoning which the previous metaphysics had employed. All that was really achieved by empiricism, therefore, was to put the syllogistic reasoning of synthetic knowledge onto what appeared to be an immediately concrete base, that is to replace strict deduction by induction:

The delusion that lies at the bottom of scientific empiricism is that it employs the metaphysical categories of matter, force, not to mention those of one, many, generality, infinity, etc.; and that, following the thread provided by such categories, it proceeds to construct *arguments*, and in so doing presupposes and applies syllogistic forms. And all the while it is unaware that it itself contains and engages in metaphysics and makes use of those categories and their combinations in an utterly uncritical and unconscious manner.[60]

Empiricism wishes to avoid the metaphysical error of assuming rational laws and definitions a priori, and thus seeks to derive its necessary laws and definitions from observation of sensuous, empirical phenomena. The conviction of empiricism, therefore, is that such sensuous experience serves as a firm ground for conceptual thought. Hegel believes that there is a serious problem with this position, however, for he holds that empirical perceptions are not able to provide the kind of warrant for scientific laws and definitions that the empiricists hoped for. For the empiricist, in Hegel's view, sensuous experience in its immediate form lacks the universal and necessary determinations of conceptual thought which it is to ground. Things cannot, therefore, simply be *observed* to be subject to necessary, causal relations, for example, but can only be shown to be subject to such relations by means of the process of analysis, abstraction and reflection. But since sensuous particulars in their immediacy lack the conceptual form of necessity, this means that any determinations of necessity of which we are conscious will not have been found in our sensuous perceptions, and thus will not be legitimated by those perceptions. Paradoxically, therefore, because empirical perceptions are treated as the determinate ground of necessary, conceptual thought *prior* to thought, they are treated as irreducibly distinct from thought and thus cannot legitimate it.[61]

Hegel acknowledges David Hume as the thinker who first drew attention to the impossibility of legitimating necessary determinations empirically. Hume, Hegel maintains, begins from the philosophical position of Locke and Bacon, who insist that our concepts are to be derived from sensuous experience. Hume's achievement lay simply in drawing what Hegel sees as the logical conclusion from the empiricist position:

Hume completed the system of Locke by drawing the logical conclusion that, if this point of view be adhered to, experience is indeed the basis of whatever one knows, and perception itself contains everything that happens, but nevertheless the determinations of universality and necessity are not contained in, nor would they be given to us by, experience.[62]

Precisely because the empiricists understand sensuous perception as lacking the determinations of rational necessity and universality, those determinations by definition cannot be justified by being derived from perception. The most we can do, Hume says, is to treat the habitual and customary connections which we recognise in experience as if they were 'necessary' and 'universal', but we must never assume that empirical experience allows us to establish that such connections are in fact *intrinsically* necessary and universal. Contrary to Bertrand Russell's assertion that Hegel had not assimilated Hume's arguments, therefore,[63] Hegel in fact considered Hume's remarks about the attempt to justify necessary determinations empirically to be 'important' and 'acute', and Hume's arguments inform Hegel's own critique of induction in the *Science of Logic*.[64]

Hegel agrees with Hume that no explicit universal and necessary determinations are to be found in particular perceptions if these latter are considered in their immediacy as discrete perceptions. But in contrast to Hume, Hegel does not treat sensuous perception as the ultimate foundation of all our thought about the world, but only as the source of our contingent, empirical concepts. Hegel therefore wishes to claim that reason itself can determine intrinsic, necessary relations between bodies or phenomena in experience, even if perception alone cannot do this. Reason and sensuous perception are clearly distinguished by Hegel, but their difference does not prevent reason from determining and explaining a priori certain general, necessary connections in experience, although Hegel does not, of course, claim that reason has the power to determine a priori the totality of empirical details or facts in the world.[65] Hume is unable to allow reason to determine features of actual experience, however, because he has inherited from metaphysics and empiricism the mode of *verständig* thinking which operates with unreconciled categorial distinctions, and because he has used these distinctions to separate completely the moments of sensuous particularity, on the one hand, and rational necessity and universality, on the other. Hume, therefore – taking up Leibniz's distinction between truths of reason and truths of fact[66] – has set up so sharp an opposition between empirical perception and the necessary determinations of reason that he is led beyond the conclusion that empirical perception cannot itself yield insight into intrinsic rational connections in experience (a view with which Hegel agrees), to the conclusion that reason cannot determine or establish such intrinsic necessary connections in experience either (a view with which Hegel does not agree).

Hume's doubts about the ultimate justification of necessary

rational determinations in experience thus follow directly from his empiricist conception of what the justification of necessary determinations would entail, but both that empiricist conception and Hume's unbridgeable opposition between sensuous particularity and rational necessity are based upon categorial presuppositions which are as limited as those of metaphysics itself. In Hegel's view, Hume does not challenge the empiricist view that the justification of necessary determinations in experience would have to rest on the concrete empirical perception of particulars. He accepts that definition uncritically, for he accepts the absolute primacy of empirical perception; but he correctly demonstrates that, so defined, the justification of necessary determinations in experience is impossible. Hume assumes, however, that no other method of legitimating necessary judgements about experience is possible and takes the fateful step from saying that the empiricist method cannot justify necessary judgements to saying that genuinely necessary judgements about experience are themselves ultimately unjustifiable. The consequence he draws from this is to relapse into scepticism and to abandon the project of the definitive justification of necessary determinations in experience altogether. Necessary connections in experience are thus declared to be ultimately unprovable, and to be in fact mere matters of habit. It is perhaps worth stressing here that what is at issue in this discussion of Hume is whether necessary judgements about what is present to us in *experience* are possible, that is – to follow Kant – whether there are synthetic judgements a priori. Hume does not of course dispute the necessity of formal, analytic truths or 'relations of ideas', but he considers these to be founded on the law of contradiction, and he holds that such truths do not determine what must actually happen in experience, but only what is or is not self-contradictory. Hume does not therefore share Hegel's view that pure reason can determine out of itself not merely what ought to be the case, or what is necessary in the realm of formal possibility regardless of what is given to us in experience, but the necessary determinations of *this* world which is actually present before our eyes.[67]

Here is the point at which Hegel's discussion of the history of philosophy bears directly on the philosophy of Nietzsche. As we have seen, Nietzsche follows Hegel in criticising categorial oppositions and in rejecting the idea that there are ideal entities which are the objects of philosophical knowledge. Furthermore, Nietzsche is also a critic of the empiricists' attempt to ground judgements about the

world on immediate certainty.[68] It appears, therefore, that, like
Hegel, Nietzsche rejects the whole notion of basing philosophical
knowledge upon a foundation. However, the manner in which
Nietzsche criticises empiricism resembles that of Hume, for Nietzsche
casts doubt on the legitimacy of our necessary judgements about the
world by asserting that 'life' does not manifest the determinations and
principles which such judgements express. Hegel's critique of Hume
thus extends to Nietzsche as well. Like Hume, Nietzsche jumps from
asserting that life cannot justify our necessary propositions about the
world, to the view that our necessary propositions about the world are
therefore unjustifiable. But this shows that Nietzsche has accepted
the view that the only way to legitimate such necessary propositions
would be by reference to the foundation of life. Nietzsche shows that
such legitimation is not possible, but he is not thereby led to ask
whether reference to life is the proper way to try to legitimate
necessary propositions about the world; he does not ask, for example,
whether or not reason itself can justify necessary propositions about
the world by a process of dialectical development. For Nietzsche, life
is the standard against which all judgements are shown to be false, but
it is still the standard against which all judgements must ultimately be
tested. This means, therefore, that Nietzsche is not in fact rejecting
the use of life as a foundation to justify judgements after all, for he is
relying on the foundation of life to validate the proposition that
necessary propositions about the world cannot be justified by life.[69]
Like Hume in Hegel's account, therefore, Nietzsche thereby presupposes a sharp categorial distinction between the particularity of
actual existence and the necessity and universality of rational
thought, which for Hegel is by no means clear-cut. Nietzsche thus
trades on the very categorial distinctions which he is meant to be calling into question. Nietzsche is not simply a Humean – he is as disturbed and excited by his epistemological doubts as Hume was
unmoved by his – but the similarity is there. And in Hegel's discussion
of Hume we gain a direct glimpse of what his view of Nietzsche might
have been.[70]

Kant's critical philosophy

Kant's critical philosophy, as Hegel sees it, emerges from the scepticism of Hume. Kant accepts Hume's contention that the universal,

necessary determinations of thought cannot be legitimated by reference to our sense-perceptions. Unlike Hume, however, Kant is not content to consider our concept of necessity to be the product of mere habit. In Kant's view, we judge that there are necessary connections in the world – causal connections, for example – and we have no doubt that such judgements are in fact legitimate and valid for all minds. But how, Kant asks, are those judgements legitimated? Whence is the authority derived to legitimate the concept of necessity with which we, as thinking beings, operate? Kant's answer, Hegel says, is straightforward: 'This element, not being derived from the empirical sphere as such, must belong to the spontaneity of *thought*; in other words, it is a priori.'[71] It is we who bring the categories of causality and necessity to sense-perception, and it is we who construct causal connections out of our sense-perception by means of those categories. With Kant's conclusion, philosophy in Hegel's account appears to have come full circle, for in the critical philosophy, as in post-Reformation, rationalist metaphysics, authority is rooted in rational thought.[72]

Yet, for Kant, since necessity is the a priori product of thought itself and is not abstracted from sense-perception, it can at best be 'subjective' necessity, necessity within the world which the knowing subject constructs. That is to say, the categories by means of which we are able to judge things to be necessary have legitimate application only within the sphere of objects as they *appear* to the mind. These categories have no transcendent ontological application to things as they might be in themselves. Thus, although Kant, in contrast to the empiricists, locates authority within thought itself, he does not simply return to the position of metaphysics, because he conceives of the most pressing task of philosophy as the rational *critique* of the categories employed by metaphysics. Kant's great achievement, in Hegel's eyes, is to recognise that the problem with metaphysics does not lie merely in its not having firm empirical foundations, but in the rationally ascertainable inadequacy of the limited categories which it employs in order to understand reality. With Kant the critique of metaphysics takes on the form of logic and categorial analysis: 'A very important step was undoubtedly made when the determinations of the old metaphysics were subjected to scrutiny ... This is certainly the correct thing to do, since the forms of thought themselves must be made the object of knowledge.'[73]

However, Hegel considers the manner of Kant's categorial critique of metaphysics to be imperfect. For Kant argues that the categories of the understanding are inadequate to the knowledge of reality 'in itself' because they are generated by the mind and therefore subjective, and not, as in Hegel's opinion, because they are logically abstract and one-sided. Hegel is well aware that for Kant the categories give to the multiplicity of sense-perceptions a consistency and objectivity which these otherwise lack. Yet this 'objectivity' remains subjective in Kant's account because it only pertains to reality as our senses perceive it and not to reality as it is in itself. Kant thus rejects the conviction held, but not fulfilled, by metaphysics, and which Hegel himself wishes to retain, that thought can articulate the structure of reality itself.[74] Hegel agrees with Kant that necessary, categorial connections are not explicitly present in perception but are generated by reason. He does not, however, agree that these categorial connections are merely *for us* and not also the logical forms inherent in the real world.[75] In Hegel's view, the world which our senses perceive is in itself structured according to the logical principles with which we operate. Sense-perception, however, is imperfect knowledge of reality and that is why it lacks explicitly universal, necessary, rational determinations. Only in the thoughts rendered explicit and produced by the mind does the logical character of reality become revealed. Since it is merely imperfect knowledge, therefore, sense-perception cannot provide a firm, reliable foundation against which to test the validity of rational thought.

In Hegel's view, Kant treats the a priori products of the mind as subjective because he has inherited the empiricist notion of what would constitute true knowledge of the world.[76] For Kant, therefore, the determinations of thought would be true of the world in itself only if they were derived a posteriori from the world outside us and not from the mind itself. But, as Hume has shown, general determinations drawn by induction from experience ultimately lack the necessity which Kant believes characterises many of our judgements. The conceptual necessity expressed in these judgements must therefore have its source a priori in the mind and consequently cannot belong to reality in itself. By separating reality from the rational determinations of the knowing subject in this way, therefore, Kant is still conceiving of reality in the manner of metaphysics and empiricism – despite his rejection of their claim that thought can know reality – because he is treating reality as an object, as *gegenständlich*, just as they did.

Hegel finds evidence for Kant's reductive, *gegenständlich* view of reality and for his employment of finite metaphysical categories in a variety of areas of the critical philosophy, two examples of which I will mention here, namely Kant's treatment of the antinomies of reason and his critique of the ontological proof of God.

The old metaphysics, Hegel contends, treated contradictions in philosophical speculation as 'an accidental aberration', resting on mistakes made by the subject in his reasoning. The contradictions were in no sense objective or in the world, since only propositions and not the world itself could be considered contradictory.[77] Kant made a great contribution to philosophy by maintaining (though not proving) that the formal logic employed in the natural sciences necessarily resulted in contradictions when employed metaphysically, that is when applied to 'objects' which transcend our sense-experience.[78] Kant argued, for example, that we could prove both that the universe had a beginning in time and that it did not, or both that there exists a being which is necessary and that there does not exist such a being. Kant thereby undermined the confidence which metaphysics had that it could attain to unequivocal rational knowledge of reality, and opened the way to a dialectical conception of the nature of thought. But Hegel believes that Kant only drew the negative conclusion from the antinomies that the categories of formal logic are not applicable to reality as it is in itself. He did not draw the affirmative conclusion that reality is contradictory in itself,

that everything actual [*alles Wirkliche*] contains contrary determinations within itself, and that, consequently, to know, or rather to comprehend [*begreifen*], an object means precisely being conscious of it as a concrete unity of contrary determinations.[79]

If Kant's assertion that reason when applied beyond its empirical bounds necessarily produces antinomies was profound, his solution of those antinomies, Hegel says, is trivial: 'The blemish of contradiction should not be allowed to mar the real world [*das weltliche Wesen*], but should *only* taint thinking reason, the *essence of mind.*' It is in this exclusion of contradiction and negation from his concept of reality that Kant betrays that he is employing the metaphysician's simple, *gegenständlich* concept of identity in order to conceive of reality.[80]

Similarly, Hegel believes that Kant's critique of the ontological proof of God rests on the employment of finite categories, in particular the abstract distinction between what is universal (*Allgemeines*) and what is determinate or particular (*Bestimmtes*).[81] Kant's assertion,

Hegel tells us, is simply that thought and being are different and that therefore one cannot deduce the existence of God from the concept of God. Kant seeks to prove this by reference to the example of one hundred dollars. He maintains that 'being' is not a real predicate of anything, not a determination which belongs to the concept of a thing in addition to the thing's many qualities. The *concept* of one hundred actual dollars thus differs in no way whatsoever from the *concept* of one hundred possible dollars. Both have the same content. What differentiates one hundred *actual* dollars from the mere *concept* of one hundred (actual or possible) dollars is not a quality predicated of the latter, but existence itself: 'The one is the concept, or rather the representation [*Vorstellung*], the other is the object . . . or to my concept the real hundred dollars are synthetically added.' For this reason, Kant argues, one cannot deduce from the concept of something that it exists, but one must actually go and look: 'We must go out beyond the concept to reach existence . . . Our consciousness of all existence [i.e. *that* something exists] belongs entirely to experience.'[82]

Hegel in no way disagrees with this analysis as it applies to finite objects such as one hundred dollars; indeed everything finite for him is characterised by the fact that the concept of the thing does not necessarily imply that the thing actually exists.[83] Hegel is in fact quite indignant about those of his critics who fail to see that speculative philosophy incorporates so obvious an insight: 'Those who constantly remind philosophical reason that *thought and being are different* should finally recognise that philosophers are not wholly ignorant of this fact either; indeed can there be any more trivial insight than this?'[84] Hegel insists, however, that God is not such a finite object, the question of whose existence or non-existence is separate from the question of how it is to be conceived. God is indeed the sole reality whose existence is by definition entailed by the determination of its concept, because for Hegel God is the absolute form or Idea of existence itself.[85] When thought thinks God, therefore, it thinks the absolute character of existence, and this absolute character cannot be thought of as that which might or might not exist. It can only be conceived as that which *does* exist, as the truth of existence itself. Furthermore, although pure thought for Hegel may not be able to determine a priori which specific finite objects actually exist, or what contingent properties they have, such thought is able, by determining the particular forms that the Idea of existence must take, to determine the general forms of rational necessity to which finite existing things must be subject. By showing that the Idea necessarily manifests itself as mechanism and chemism, for example, Hegel can thus give philosophical legitimation to the view that causal relations are an intrinsic feature of existence as such. Hegel believes that Kant is unable to comprehend such a synthesis of thought and being, however,[86] because, despite his claim that the categories of finite experience are not applicable to infinite realities, he actually treats the Idea or God in the same way he treats the one hundred dollars, namely as a 'finite' object whose existence is in no sense entailed by its conceptual determination. On the one hand, therefore, Kant anticipates Hegel and resolves the opposition of thought and being by claiming that thought can determine a priori the categories or logical determinations which inform the objects that are known through empirical experience to exist. On the other hand, however, Kant preserves the opposition of thought and being which Hegel wishes to overcome since, by claiming that something can only be known to exist through empirical experience, he is asserting that there is no way of coming to know of the existence of the objects of pure thought. This means, as we have just seen, that we cannot conclude from our a priori 'idea' of God or the soul alone that such a thing actually exists. But, equally, it means that we cannot conclude from the fact that we order the objects of empirical experience through a priori categories, such as causality and substance, that such categories actually 'exist' in reality either. Indeed, Kant goes so far as to assert that the whole empirical world, whose structure and form are constituted by those a priori categories, cannot be said to exist in reality independently of its being experienced by a rational mind. Paradoxically, therefore, Kant wants to argue that the world which contains the only objects of whose independent existence we can actually be assured – the empirical world – cannot itself be known to exist independently of the knowing mind, because it is constructed a priori and can thus only be said to constitute the world of our own phenomenal human experience.

Kant's conviction that ultimate reality is wholly distinct from the rational determinations of the knowing mind prevents him, Hegel believes, from drawing ontological conclusions from the valuable insights of his epistemology, insights which Hegel sees as anticipating his own speculative philosophy of *Geist*. Kant's view that thought is the spontaneous synthesis of the manifold of sense-perceptions is acknowledged by Hegel to be profoundly important, and he sees in Kant's notion of synthetic judgements a priori 'nothing other than a connection of opposites through themselves, or the absolute concept [*der absolute Begriff*], i.e. the relations of different determinations such as those of cause and effect which are not given by experience but are determinations of thought'.[87] Similarly, Hegel praises Kant's notion of Schematism as 'one of the most attractive sides of the Kantian philosophy, whereby pure sensuousness and pure understanding, which were formerly expressed as absolute opposites, are now united'.[88] In Hegel's view all these features indicate that Kant has developed a notion of the subject as a concrete unity of opposing determinations. But for Kant this concreteness belongs only to the subject which is the condition of our knowledge; it is not concreteness which may be said to inhere in the subject, or indeed any reality, 'in itself'. This concreteness cannot be the nature of reality itself because, Hegel argues, Kant has already assumed reality to be *gegenständlich*, to be simple being-in-itself. Kant, therefore, fails to see 'that the I, as this universal or as self-thinking, has in itself the essence, the true reality and the moment of actuality which he requires in an objective [*gegenständlich*] mode'.[89]

Since he believes that Kant's critical philosophy depends upon a *verständig* conception of reality as that which is distinct from the determinations of reason, Hegel sees Kant's criticism of the categories of the understanding as entailing a glaring unresolved contradiction. For, on the one hand, Kant limits the categories of the understanding to the sphere of sense-experience and denies their transcendent application to things as they are in themselves; but, on the other hand, Kant implicitly relies upon those categories to make that very distinction between reality 'in itself' and reality as it appears to us. Kant employs, for example, the category of negation to say of reality 'in itself' that it is not the sphere in which the categories (including negation) can legitimately be applied.[90] Hegel's solution to this problem is not to reject out of hand Kant's assertion that the categories of the understanding are inadequate to the genuine knowledge of reality, but on the contrary to seek to pursue that assertion to its logical conclusion. Just because they are not adequate to determine the true nature of reality, they cannot be used to produce the abstract notion of reality 'in itself' against which to establish their inadequacy. The categories for Hegel are not inadequate because, measured against the external standard of a purely objective reality, they are merely subjective, but because they are logically one-sided or abstract in themselves. That is to say that they do not give appropriate logical form to their implied logical content.

Conclusion

This chapter has attempted to show what Hegel means by metaphysical thinking. In the course of the chapter we have examined Hegel's view of metaphysics proper, but we have also examined the metaphysical presuppositions which Hegel believes underlie empiricism and Kantian critical philosophy. The most important characteristic of metaphysical thinking for Hegel is that it operates with mutually exclusive categories; what is infinite is thus opposed to what is finite, mediation is opposed to immediacy, and subject is opposed to predicate. Metaphysical thinking thus treats the subject or object to be known as a given foundation for philosophical knowledge, as the standard to which our thoughts must correspond if they are to be true. As a result of treating its content as a foundation in this way, however, Hegel believes metaphysical thinking falls into contradictions in all three of its modes.

In metaphysics proper the status of the infinite objects, such as God or the soul, which comprise the content of knowledge is problematic. On the one hand, the object – for example, the representation (*Vorstellung*) of God – is held to be the firm standard against which to measure whether or not the predicates suggested by thought actually characterise the object. On the other hand, however, the object qua infinite *Vorstellung* is itself held to be in need of firm specification by deductive, rational thought. The infinite content of metaphysics does not therefore provide metaphysics with quite as firm a foundation as it first appears. A solution to this problem is sought in empiricism, in the attempt to base knowledge on an empirical foundation that is concrete and immediate. The empiricists thus sought to legitimate our concepts and the necessary connections which we discover in the world by deriving them from empirical experience. However, the problem with this method was that the necessity which was to be legitimated by empirical experience was actually absent from that experience itself. Empirical foundations to knowledge may thus be concrete, but they cannot ground our universal, necessary judgements.

A solution to the problem raised by empiricism was suggested by Kant. Kant accepted Hume's view that necessary judgements could not be legitimated by reference to empirical experience, and he thus sought to legitimate those judgements by claiming that the knowing mind itself constructed the necessary connections in its experience. These connections are not arbitrary, but are constructed according to rules which are intrinsic to rational subjectivity itself and therefore

universal. The consequence of Kant's solution, however, was that the
necessary judgements we make only apply within the world as it
appears to us; they do not apply to things as they may be in themselves. In Kant's critical philosophy, therefore, the metaphysical
separation of thought and reality is so sharpened that knowledge of
reality 'in itself' is no longer held to be possible.

The criticisms of metaphysics made by empiricism and the critical
philosophy are considered to be inadequate by Hegel because they
fail to address the heart of the matter, that is to say they fail to criticise
the metaphysician's reliance on conceptual oppositions and his desire
to base knowledge on a firm foundation. Kant comes closest to the
kind of critique of metaphysical categories envisaged by Hegel
through his argument that the categories of the understanding are not
applicable to things as they may be in themselves. But Kant's critique
fails to satisfy Hegel because it merely removes forms of objective
thought from reality; it does not, however, criticise the abstract way
in which those categories are conceived by the understanding.[91]

In spite of much that he holds to be valuable in metaphysics,
empiricism and the critical philosophy, therefore, Hegel believes that
these three modes of philosophy are vitiated by their reliance on conceptual distinctions which they never fundamentally challenge.
Indeed, Hegel's objection to all non-speculative philosophies is that
they fail to examine and question the categories and presuppositions
underlying their own arguments.[92] All rational reflection on man and
nature – in whatever language or culture it occurs – presupposes certain universal categories or forms of thought, and it is the task of
philosophy in Hegel's view to examine those categories and to
understand them properly.

Like that of Kant, Nietzsche's critique of metaphysics entails the
comparison of metaphysical categories with an external standard to
which they are held to be alien. However, the use of an external standard distinct from metaphysical categories relies on a categorial distinction between thought and reality which itself is metaphysical.
Hegel avoids this contradiction by undertaking an immanent critique
of the categories of metaphysics, a critique, that is, in which the
categories 'must examine themselves, determine their intrinsic limits
and show up the defects in their very nature'.[93] It is only through such
an immanent critique, Hegel believes, that the true character of the
categories can be revealed, since it is only through an immanent critique
that thought displays '*the dialectic which it possesses within itself*'.[94] In the

course of this immanent critique Hegel will criticise the straight-forward one-sided conception of the categories by revealing the dialectical complexity inherent in each category. He will thus come to a conception of the categories in which the categories are seen to unite opposing determinations in themselves and thus to be develop-ing logical forms. By conceiving of the categories in this complex, dialectical way, Hegel believes he can reveal the concreteness, the 'life-pulse',[95] within reason itself, a concreteness which the two-dimensional understanding cannot encompass and which philosophers like Nietzsche look for outside reason.[96]

In Hegel's view the categories in their finite, static conception will be seen to be too abstract – not too subjective – to be adequate to proper philosophical knowledge, whereas the categories in their dialectical conception will be seen to be quite capable of yielding definitive philosophical knowledge of reality. In this way Hegel conceives of his speculative logic both as offering the true critique of the abstract categories of metaphysics and as recovering the important convic-tion, which Kant and Nietzsche in varying ways contested, that reality can be known determinately in conceptual thought.[97]

Hegel's dissatisfaction with the distinctions of the understanding will not therefore lead him to reject determinate knowledge of the subject-matter of metaphysics altogether, but rather to conceive of that subject-matter in a new and reformed way. He will no longer con-ceive of the absolute ultimately as a transcendent object or *Gegenstand*, but rather as the dynamic logical form of natural and human activity. The task of the next chapter will be to show how this speculative, non-metaphysical account of the absolute is derived.[98]

5

Speculative thought and language in Hegel's philosophy

In his argument against Kant's transcendental idealism, Hegel rejects the idea that there is a dimension of reality – what reality is 'in itself' – which cannot be comprehended by the categories and concepts of thought. His reason for doing so is simple, namely that our formulation of the idea of a level of reality which is not accessible to our thought, itself relies (at the very least) on the use of the concept of negation.[1] The concepts with which we think thus constitute for Hegel the determinations of *any* level of reality we may conceive. We can articulate our perceptions of the empirical world in terms of those concepts; we formulate laws of nature by means of those concepts; and we understand the realm of consciousness and freedom through the use of those concepts. The structure of our thought and language is therefore the structure of our world, and we have no standard of reference by which to judge the truth of the ontology to which our concepts commit us which does not itself rely on those concepts or which cannot at least itself be adequately stated in terms of those concepts.[2]

How, therefore, can we ever hope to achieve true philosophical knowledge of the world? The answer, in Hegel's view, is that we can only achieve such knowledge by employing the right categories; and we can only establish what they are by coming to understand the inherent logical structure of our thought. Consequently, Hegel replaces the traditional metaphysical science of ontology with

122

speculative logic, the study of the categories of thought which are laid down in language and which structure our world.[3]

In this chapter we shall examine the mode of speculative philosophy which Hegel develops through his dialectical exposition and critique of the abstract categories of metaphysics. We shall look first at his conception of a philosophy 'without foundations', and then we shall consider the form of 'speculative' sentence which he uses in that philosophy and the redefinition of the subject which that sentence form enacts. At the end of the chapter I shall conclude by briefly comparing the non-metaphysical conception of thought and language put forward by Hegel with that offered by Nietzsche. This chapter will inevitably have to concentrate on the general character of Hegel's philosophy and will not be able to examine the details of Hegel's treatment of any particular concept or area of experience. I hope, however, that something of the complexity of Hegel's project might nevertheless become clear.

Hegel's philosophy 'without foundations'

Speculative philosophy is not merely an alternative to metaphysics, but is, as it were, 'reformed' metaphysics,[4] for it fulfils the task which in Hegel's view metaphysics tried, but failed, to fulfil: namely to achieve conceptual knowledge of reality. The significant difference between speculative philosophy and metaphysics is that speculative philosophy challenges certain of the basic assumptions on which metaphysics is founded. It challenges the absolute distinctions between categories; it challenges the notion of a discrete subject distinct from its predicates and relations; and it even challenges the very notion of a foundation to philosophy itself. And perhaps the best way to understand what Hegel means by speculative philosophy is to examine what this critique of the notion of a foundation to philosophy involves.

The problem with basing philosophy on a foundation, Hegel argues, is that it conflicts with the freedom and self-determination which he sees as an essential feature of thought. Thought based on a foundation is tied to axiomatic principles, to an empirical content, or to relative presuppositions which operate as the given standard against which all ideas and propositions are (and are to be) tested. The content with which thought deals is therefore determined by something other than thought's own free activity. This is an important reason why Hegel is critical of empiricism. As we saw in the last chapter, Hegel praises empiricism for calling us to consciousness of what is present at hand and for directing our attention towards the world of actual experience, and he acknowledges that his own speculative philosophy, which is concerned with the living rationality active in the world rather than with formal metaphysical abstractions removed from concrete experience, has been greatly influenced by empiricism. However, Hegel also believes that empiricism is severely limited since its positivist reliance on the primacy of given fact prevents any critical scrutiny, by reason, of the legitimacy of what is given to consciousness, and stops us seeking to transform what is given into what is explicitly rational and actual (*wirklich*). Despite being of great value for the development of speculative philosophy, therefore, empiricism in fact makes us slaves to the given situation in which we find ourselves, for if criticism is undertaken, it can only be undertaken for pragmatic reasons or on the basis of *given* standards of value, not on the basis of freely self-determining reason which itself establishes what is of value:

Since this sensuous content is and remains for empiricism something given, so empiricism is a doctrine of unfreedom, for freedom consists precisely in the fact that I have no absolute other over against me, but depend upon a content which I myself am. Furthermore, reason and unreason on this view are only subjective, that is to say we have to accept what is given just as it is, and we have no right to ask whether, and to what extent, what is given is in itself rational.[5]

As this quotation implies, Hegel's own philosophical commitment to look for the rationality of reality entails asking the critical questions: To what extent can any given reality be said to be rational and *wirklich* rather than just to exist? And to what extent must any given reality be criticised in order to be made explicitly rational?[6] Hegel thus does not simply give the stamp of authority to what happens to exist and thereby justify the imperfections of the present as, for example, Nietzsche claims.[7]

Hegel's speculative philosophy is not therefore based on a given foundation. It does not entail strict deduction from first principles, nor does it conceive of truth as residing primarily in correspondence with given experience. This is not to say, however, that Hegel rejects these two conceptions of knowledge out of hand, but rather that he considers them to be inappropriate for philosophy. Hegel in fact holds the synthetic method of deduction from first principles to be appropriate, for example, for geometry, and he holds the analytic or inductive method of basing knowledge on experience to be appropriate for the natural sciences.[8] Indeed, as far as the natural sciences are concerned, Hegel's position at times seems close to that of his twentieth-century adversary, Karl Popper. In his discussion of synthetic knowledge in the *Science of Logic*, for example, Hegel argues against the tailoring of empirical observation to fit presupposed theories and hypotheses on the grounds that such a practice violates the requirement that scientific theories must be open to falsification by experience, and thus 'obviates any empirical refutation'.[9] Moreover, although speculative philosophy is to be self-determining reason, the conception of rationality which it generates must also, Hegel argues, correspond to our ordinary experience if that rationality is to be anything other than mere abstraction:

Indeed, this correspondence [of philosophy with actuality and experience] can be seen as at least an external test of the truth of a philosophy, just as it is to be seen as the highest purpose of philosophical science to bring about, through the recognition of this correspondence, the reconciliation of self-conscious reason with reason *in existence* [*mit der* seienden *Vernunft*] and with actuality.[10]

Despite being a form of rationalism, therefore, Hegel's philosophy must be understood as responsive to the empirical investigation of nature and man. The conclusions of speculative philosophy, as we have just seen, must accord with those of common experience, and Hegel also thinks that the emergence of speculative philosophy in history presupposes the development of empirical science and research.[11] Indeed, Hegel's overwhelming concern to be faithful to empirical experience is evident in his most frequent criticism of the natural scientists of his day, namely that they do not stick closely enough to empirical experience, but rely on metaphysical categories or mathematical determinations to invent certain invisible 'realities' (such as 'forces' or 'pores') which appear to explain natural phenomena, but which run counter to both experience and dialectical logic.[12] (The terms in which Hegel dismisses what he sees as the contemporary idea of centrifugal force – he calls it a 'metaphysical chimera' (*metaphysisches Unding*) and a 'fiction of the understanding' (*Verstandesfiktion*) – are, incidentally, remarkably Nietzschean in tone.)[13]

Hegel's own speculative philosophy will thus attempt to give a philosophical account of the world which remains true to our ordinary experience of that world and which has no need to resort to non-observable metaphysical or mathematical 'entities'. However, although speculative philosophy must correspond with experience, it will not be *based* on experience, as Hegel's comments in the philosophy of nature show. Hegel's philosophical method is rather to develop the concepts of particular areas of the experienced world by deriving pure, a priori conceptual determinations immanently from the logical structure of reason, and by then looking to experience to find the particular empirical phenomena which manifest those determinations and which provide us with the contingent details that extend and fill out our understanding of those determinations. Such a procedure thus combines straightforward empirical investigation of the world with an unashamedly a priori dialectical derivation of the fundamental logical determinations which are recognised in the empirical phenomena. [14]

The truth of Hegel's philosophical account of the world depends, therefore, both upon the proper logical derivation of the conceptual determinations and upon the correct identification of the empirical phenomena which correspond to them. If an empirical phenomenon does not appear to us to manifest the conceptual determination which Hegel claims it manifests, and if that determination has been shown to be rationally necessary, then either the logic is telling us something about the empirical phenomena which we have not yet seen, or Hegel has matched up the wrong empirical phenomenon with the logical determination. In neither case, however, do we have any proof that the logical determination concerned has been falsely derived or that it is not manifested in the empirical world at all. Empirical experience, therefore, can confirm the truth of logical determinations, but it cannot definitively falsify them. Experience can, of course, alert the philosopher to possible logical errors, but only reason itself can show the speculative derivation of logical determinations to be false. [15]

Now, this does not, of course, mean that Hegel can never be wrong. Due to the great range of his philosophy, Hegel has plenty of opportunities for empirical and logical errors, and, indeed, he makes many assertions which we would now consider to be simply mistaken or to be products of the limited scientific knowledge of his day. [16] But if we accept the above account of the relation of a priori reasoning to empirical experience, we are committed to the view that where experience does not as yet appear to confirm the applicability of a logical determination, and where that determination is understood to be rationally necessary, experience will at some time to come be seen to confirm that determination. In this way, philosophical reason must – indeed *will* – be confirmed by experience if it is true reasoning, but it may also offer a critique of our present understanding of the empirical world in the process. The only way to tell if the speculative philosopher is simply wrong about some feature of the world (which is always a possibility we must take serious account of), or if his philosophy is offering a critique of the way in which we see the world at present, is to establish precisely what in speculative philosophy is strictly necessary. Such a procedure will also be able to determine where speculative philosophy can show us the way beyond the limits of present empirical knowledge and where empirical science itself must make the important advances.[17]

Anyone who studies the historical development of Hegel's philosophy throughout his career will be struck by the extent to which Hegel takes note of the empirical research of his day and changes the details and the systematic presentation of his philosophy in the light of new discoveries and of his own revisions to his logic. However, Hegel's aim – at least from the beginning of the Jena period, in 1801, onwards – is always to produce a system of logical determinations which is strictly a priori. The path whereby speculative philosophy emerged, therefore, may have entailed certain changes and revisions right up until Hegel's death, but that path is quite different from the *system* of philosophical legitimation and dialectical development which Hegel aims to produce; and that system was intended to be unequivocally immanent and a priori.[18]

Though correspondence with experience is important for philosophy, therefore, essential even, philosophy cannot be *founded* on experience, because the philosopher's task is not merely to observe what appears to be the case at the moment; it is rather to derive a conception of what the living rationality of the world actually is and thereby to obtain a standard by which to legitimate or criticise our ordinary understanding of experience, and indeed to legitimate or criticise forms of natural and human existence themselves. Furthermore, as we saw in the last chapter, Hegel believes that empirical experience itself, though articulable in terms of concepts, cannot legitimate those concepts or ground our conception of rationality. The final arbiter of truth and validity in philosophy is therefore rational coherence, which is to say that philosophical concepts are ultimately 'legitimated by its being shown that they are implicit in the essential nature of thought'.[19]

Since Hegel's speculative philosophy is not to base itself on unquestioned assumptions, however, it finds itself in the strange and difficult position of not being able to presuppose the precise subject-matter or the method of its own reflection.[20] Other sciences are clearly concerned with a given area of research – history, nature, the human mind or whatever – and they proceed on the basis of certain established, though not always explicit, methodological presuppositions. But if speculative philosophy is to be a thorough critical study of our categorial presuppositions, it cannot itself uncritically presuppose the rules of logical procedure.[21] Hegel's speculative examination of the categories of thought must therefore itself determine the nature of its subject-matter and method as it proceeds, 'for what this subject-matter is . . . will be explicated only in the development of the science and cannot be presupposed by it as known beforehand'.[22]

What, then, does speculative philosophy actually involve? And how can it possibly proceed without basing itself on some presupposition or other? To answer this question we must specify more closely what Hegel is actually claiming for speculative philosophy. Hegel is not claiming that the speculative philosopher should try to begin philosophy with a completely blank mind. His own philosophy of history shows that every philosophy is situated in its own time and culture, and the lectures on the history of philosophy make clear that speculative philosophy itself is a distinctive product of post-Reformation Europe.[23] The speculative philosopher, like any other, thus brings with him to the study of philosophy a certain level of education and a certain range of understanding that are conditioned by his personality and the age in which he lives. These factors constitute the conditions of the speculative philosopher's ability to pursue his philosophical task, for without a certain level of intellectual discipline and without the ability to think abstractly, and indeed, in the *Realphilosophie*, without a great deal of empirical knowledge, the philosopher would clearly be unable to embark on the study of philosophy at all.[24] However, these cultural conditions do not form the foundation of philosophical reasoning itself; they do not constitute any principle from which speculative reason is derived. Similarly, the broader cultural presuppositions of Hegel's time – such as the contemporary interest in development, wholeness and identity

– may facilitate our understanding of what Hegel is doing, but they do not by themselves allow us to understand what speculative reason is. Indeed, the insistence that Hegel is to be understood primarily as a product of his time, rather than primarily as a rational thinker, often leads to the mistaken approximation of his philosophical views to those of his contemporaries such as Fichte. The implication of this remark, clearly, is not that we should ignore Hegel's historical situation, but that we should be seeking ultimately to understand the distinctive *point* of Hegel's own philosophy; or to follow Hegel himself, and of course in opposition to Nietzsche's genetic method, we should be concerned primarily with whether speculative philosophy is true 'in and for itself' (*an und für sich*), rather than with where it comes from.[25]

Hegel's demand that speculative philosophy should not presuppose its method or content is not therefore an exhortation to the philosopher to forget his language and his historical position; such an exhortation would be an absurdity. What Hegel is demanding is that speculative philosophy should have no *systematic* foundation. This is a claim not about the situation and character of the philosopher, but about the logical nature of the systematic starting-point of philosophical reasoning itself.[26] In Hegel's view, speculative philosophy can claim to be non-metaphysical because its starting-point does not constitute an axiomatic principle from which propositions are deduced; the starting-point is not therefore a determinate conception which is presupposed at the start of philosophy as an anticipation of the result of philosophy. The beginning of speculative philosophy for Hegel, the beginning of the rational determination of the true character of thought, is thus nothing more than a beginning.[27]

The systematic foundationlessness or presuppositionlessness of speculative philosophy itself seems to be called into question, however, by Hegel's claim that speculative philosophy logically presupposes the arguments of the *Phenomenology*. Speculative philosophy begins with the science of logic, the science of pure self-determining thought, and this discipline, Hegel says, presupposes the phenomenological demonstration that self-determining thought or 'pure knowing' is the fulfilment of consciousness and the full manifestation of its intrinsic nature.[28] The task of the *Phenomenology*, therefore, is to show that consciousness fulfils its inherent nature as consciousness when it is freely self-determining thought, and also to show that such thought is actually possible, that is that consciousness can know itself as pure thought. The enterprise of speculative logic is thus justified by, and therefore presupposes, the *Phenomenology*. But does not this invalidate Hegel's claim to begin speculative philosophy without a determinate presupposition or foundation? In fact this is not the case, for what the *Phenomenology* provides is merely the *element* in which speculative reasoning is to take place. The work culminates in 'pure knowing', but leaves philosophy with the task of determining precisely what that pure, conceptual self-knowledge is. The *Phenomenology*, in Hegel's view, frees the mind from the opposition (*Gegensatz*) of consciousness, that is the belief that the objects of consciousness are alien to consciousness, by showing that all objects of consciousness are in fact informed by the determinations of consciousness itself and are therefore knowable by consciousness. The depth of perception of things achieved by a particular level of consciousness is thus determined by the constitution of the particular mode of consciousness concerned. The *Phenomenology* ends with the mode of consciousness which has achieved full self-knowledge by understanding the determinations of its own free reason as the fundamental determinations of objects as such, that is by understanding that nothing can lie beyond thought,

daß das an und für sich Seiende gewußter Begriff, der Begriff als solcher aber das an und für sich Seiende ist.

that the absolute truth of being is the known concept and the concept as such is the absolute truth of being.

This unity of thought and being in pure thought constitutes the element which the *Logic* is to determine. The *Science of Logic* presupposes the *Phenomenology*, therefore, not by inheriting from it any determinate conclusion or premises, but rather by inheriting a task.[29]

The beginning of the *Logic* only constitutes a determinate foundation to the extent that the element of logic is known to be pure thought rather than imagination, representation or natural existence. However, at the beginning of the *Logic* that element remains indeterminate in itself. It is merely the presence of abstract self-consciousness which knows its absolute form to be the truth of being, but which is still without any determinate content; and it is the task of the *Logic* to determine the nature of that element concretely, that is to spell out what pure self-determining thought actually is. Hegel's project of pure categorial analysis is bound to appear strange to the modern philosopher, however, since the dominant principle today seems to be the Kantian one that 'we can attach sense to a concept only in terms of the conditions of its empirical employment'.[30] But it should be remembered that Hegel also believes that concepts are initially determined and formulated in judgements in response to a given empirical content.[31] Hegel thus in fact begins from the Kantian point of view. Where he differs from the Kantian position, however, is in maintaining that the concepts which constitute the form of experience have their own 'unschematised' logical content or meaning which can be determined by speculative philosophy. The truth that speculative philosophy seeks, therefore, is the proper understanding of the logical determinations which constitute our world. It is not merely the truth which empirical science looks for, namely the correspondence of judgements with given or transcendentally constructed experience; nor, indeed, is it the correspondence of judgements with transcendent metaphysical entities.[32]

Hegel's project in the *Logic* is to determine the immanent character of thought, to articulate the true nature of the categories which all of us employ in our language and which constitute the objective determinations of things in the world. Now, as I have said, Hegel does not wish to presuppose that thinking follows any particular laws; he does not want to presuppose that thought exhibits any particular structure. He may not therefore begin by considering a category which has a determinate meaning. The solution which Hegel finds to this problem is simple and straightforward, although it has caused later commentators considerable intellectual concern. That solution is simply to begin speculative logic with the one category which has no concrete determination, which presupposes no determinate logical form, and which is the most primitive and indeterminate category with which we operate, the category of pure immediacy or pure being.[33] There is nothing sinister or mystificatory about beginning with the category of pure being, however. Hegel chooses that category because thinking in terms of it represents the mere beginning of thought: 'it is . . . essential that it [pure being] be taken only in the one-sided character in which it is pure immediacy, *precisely because* here it is the beginning'.[34] In Hegel's view, therefore, we are just beginning to think conceptually when we say that something *is*, though we nevertheless are beginning to *think*. Such thinking merely signals the beginning of thought because it is quite indeterminate and yields no concrete information; it commits us to no determinate understanding of what constitutes the content of thought.

The objection will of course be made by those of a Nietzschean persuasion that, by beginning with the category of pure being, Hegel's
Logic is merely dealing with a linguistic fiction to which nothing in life
corresponds. However, Hegel can retort that the category of pure
being is nevertheless one that we actually operate with in our
language. When we speak, we frequently appeal to the immediacy of
evidence, we frequently insist that 'surely A *is* B'; we do so, indeed,
when we assert that pure being *is* merely a fiction, and the psychological
assertion involved in such statements relies on the category of 'being'.
The meaning of that category may well be indeterminate, therefore,
but we cannot simply dismiss it, for we *intend* at least to establish
something by using it.

Since, in Hegel's view, pure being is a category with which we
actually operate, we cannot avoid considering it. However, when we
try to think pure being, when we try to determine precisely what pure
being is, Hegel maintains that we in fact think nothing at all. All we are
left with is an empty word.[35] Because of its indeterminacy, therefore,
the category of pure being is revealed to be equivalent to the category
of nothing. However, this does not imply that that is all there is to say
about pure being. The meaning of the category is indeed indeterminate, but the logical character of that indeterminacy can itself be
specified. What we in fact think when we try to think pure being can
thus be determined further. The character of the indeterminacy of
pure being is revealed in the disappearance of the category of pure
being into mere nothingness. When we think pure being, therefore,
we do not think a determinate content; but we do not think *absolutely*
nothing at all either, for we think the disappearance of an intended
meaning. Pure being or pure immediacy is thus shown to entail the
logical tension between being and nothingness. And that logical tension is thereby revealed to constitute the logical character of pure
being itself; it is what pure being is. Being in its sheer immediacy is
tension and instability because it constantly wavers between being
and being nothing at all. By thinking pure being we have thus seen our
contentless thought begin to reveal and determine its own inherent
content. Our initial category of pure being has therefore been
redefined by the revelation that the logical tension between being and
nothing is inherent in pure being, and pure being has been recast as a
unity of opposing moments, that is, as 'becoming'.[36] When we simply
say that something *is*, therefore, we may intend to establish the
irreducible reality of that something, but we in fact unwittingly dis-

solve that something into total logical indeterminacy and instability.

Pure being is indeterminate and unstable because it disappears into pure nothingness. But pure, indeterminate being is therefore determined as that disappearance and instability. As long as being is meant to be *pure* immediacy, it remains wholly unstable in this way and constantly undermines itself. However, the instability inherent in the notion of pure being reveals that pure being is not in fact as pure as we first thought. We are thus forced to give up our insistence on the purity of being, to render explicit what the instability reveals about the category and to redefine being as 'a being which includes nothing within itself'.[37] Such redefined being is no longer simply being which disappears into nothingness, but being which now has the negative moment in itself and is thus also intrinsically not-being. This being, Hegel says, is determinate being. Determinate being is thus not pure but always the negation of some other determinate being; it is inherently relational. Any attempt to determine what something *is* must thus always show that it is not this or that or the other, if it is to yield determinate information whose meaning we can specify.[38] The notion of pure being may be indeterminate in itself, therefore, but that does not make consideration of it a pointless exercise, because hidden in its very indeterminacy is the key to the determinacy that is lacking.

It should be noted, therefore, that Hegel makes a distinction in the *Logic* between pure being and determinate being. Both are somewhat bare as categories, but there is nevertheless a difference between them. Determinate being for Hegel is being which is the explicit negation of something else; it is what it is by virtue of what it is not. Pure being, however, lacks this moment of distinctness from anything else which could give it a determinate meaning. Pure being is what we ordinarily mean by being, but thought as *pure*, without any further determination. Pure being is therefore not even to be thought as the negation of determinate being; rather it is 'the immediacy of indeterminateness, indeterminateness prior to all determinacy, the indeterminate which is before all else'.[39] The various determinate words that Hegel uses in the opening chapter of the *Logic* to describe pure being are not therefore designed to give us a determinate conception of pure being, but to show that pure being lacks all determination. When Hegel says that being is 'indeterminate immediacy' without 'variety' or 'diversity' (*Verschiedenheit*), or 'content' (*Inhalt*), he thus does not mean that we are to conceive of pure being as the definite 'negation' of determinacy or mediation, or as having the logical structure of 'identity' or 'form'. He means that pure being is 'without any further determination'.[40] The initial category of the *Logic* is thus intended to be *pure* being. But precisely because of its purity and lack of determination, pure being is in fact indistinguishable from pure nothingness. Or, rather, there is a distinction between the categories, but it is a distinction only in the *intended* meanings of the categories. Pure being is thus meant to be pure *being*, but, due to the absence of any determination which would distinguish it from nothing, it is thought as pure *nothingness*.[41]

Now, this point may seem somewhat academic, but it is important since, if the logical development of categories in the *Logic* is to proceed immanently from the character of the initial determinations of being and nothing, the speculative philosopher cannot import into the initial determinations the determinate logical structure of more complex categories in order to generate the dialectical redefinition of those initial determinations. The speculative philosopher can employ more complex categories such as 'diversity', 'determination' or 'immediacy' in order to determine that the initial categories lack all determination; in fact he must use such categories (and of course ordinary words like 'without' and 'further') because he is thinking in language. But he must use those determinate words to conceive an initially indeterminate category and to expound the inherent logical character of that indeterminate category alone. The subsequent development and speculative derivation of the categories of the *Logic* must thus be understood to follow solely from the immediate indeterminacy of *pure being* itself and not from the logical structure of the more complex categories which may be used to conceive pure being. As we proceed in the *Logic* through the categories of 'becoming', 'determinate being' (*Dasein*) and so on, this problem of distinguishing the character of the categories themselves from the meanings of the terms used to conceive them fortunately becomes less acute, since the categories under consideration generate their own, more complex, intrinsic determinations. Categories such as 'diversity' which were used descriptively earlier in the *Logic* will then come to be considered in their own right, and their own structure will actually generate further logical development.

In this abridged account of the beginning of the *Logic* we can see the bare bones of Hegel's dialectical method. Hegel takes an initial categorial determination and thinks through what is involved in thinking that determination. The process of thinking a determination reveals contradictions in the category which are not immediately evident. By rendering these intrinsic contradictions explicit, however, Hegel effectively redefines the initial determination, that is to say the category itself implies its own redefinition by being contradictory in itself, by concealing in its immediate form determinations which undermine and transform that immediate form.[42] The further development of the *Logic* entails the further determination of the initial category of being by means of the revelation of contradictions in the notion of determinate being and in subsequent categories. Being comes to be defined as determinate being, quality, quantity, specificity and so on, until a final determination is reached in which the full complexity of the initial category is rendered explicit and the form of the category is no longer at odds with its content.[43]

The *Logic* proceeds by a process of conceptual redefinition. An initial category is seen to entail greater complexity than at first appears and its determination is thus revised so as better to articulate the form of the category. The difficulty involved in understanding this process is that it is actually going in two different directions, and doing two different things, at the same time. By redefining an initial determination, thought is both advancing to new determinations, to new categories, and it is also intensifying our understanding of the nature of thought itself. The sequence of categories in the *Logic* thus forms a continuous, ever more complex determination of what thought is:

> It must be admitted that it is an important consideration – one which will be found in more detail in the logic itself – that the advance is a *retreat into the ground*, to what is *primary* and *true*, on which depends and, in fact, from which originates, that with which the beginning is made.[44]

This quotation should not be taken to imply, however, that the justification for the whole process comes only at the end of the *Logic*. The logical development is rigorously *ex ante*, but only at the end of the *Logic* is the truth rendered explicit that the initial category of 'being' is really an abstract mode of dialectical reason and not merely pure immediacy.[45]

In the course of the *Logic*, therefore, Hegel is thinking through the categories as separate categories and also as various 'definitions of the absolute',[46] various definitions of what thought as such is, which are revealed to be implicit in the initial category of pure being. By beginning with the category of pure being, the *Logic* is starting out by saying that thought is mere immediacy, the immediate presence of abstract form. But by revealing the contradictions in that initial conception, the *Logic* shows that thought in its very immediacy is also inherently dynamic. In this way the initial characterisation of thought as immediacy is challenged and thought is revealed to be determinate immediacy, qualitative immediacy, quantitative immediacy and so on. In the more advanced stages of the *Logic*, Hegel then exposes what he sees as the contradictions in the *verständig* conceptions of thought as reflection, as judgement and as syllogistic inference, until he reaches the conception of thought which he believes to be final and self-consistent, namely thought as self-determining, dialectical reason or 'Idea'.

In Hegel's view, all conceptions of thought which determine thought to be less than self-determining, dialectical reason are therefore inadequate and reductive. Attempts to understand the nature of thought as immediacy thus reduce thoughts to qualitative or quantitative units whose determination is immediate and therefore 'indifferent' to that of other categories. (Attempts to conceive of thought on the model of mathematical logic are thus criticised by Hegel.)[47] Similarly, attempts to conceive of thought as reflection reduce thought to that which is reflectively opposed to whatever it informs. Thought conceived reflectively, therefore, is understood as the mere form of a given content, the mere essence behind appearance or the mere necessity underlying and governing reality. Hegel does not deny that thought does take on such forms, that thought can be mathematical, reflective or syllogistic, and that these forms can yield valid knowledge within a restricted range of experience.[48] Indeed, the *Logic* can be seen as explaining why thought *must* assume these finite forms. But the *Logic* also criticises these finite forms and shows that they do not exhaust the possibilities of thought. They do not constitute what philosophy recognises to be the most important and essential character of thought, and they are not therefore the main forms of thought which philosophy itself employs in its study of thought or in its study of nature and human life. Thought as such, therefore, cannot be reduced to these forms, and any attempt to criticise or limit thought as such (if one is to be undertaken) misses its target if it is only addressed to these forms.[49] Whilst sharing Nietzsche's view that metaphysical thought operates with conceptual oppositions, Hegel thus shows that Nietzsche's belief that *all* thought operates with such oppositions is in fact only true of a subordinate, reflective mode of thought and not of thought as such.

Conceived properly, Hegel argues, thought is self-determining, dialectical reason. But that is to say that, conceived properly, the less complex forms of thought mentioned in the last paragraph must be seen by philosophy to be implicitly self-determining and dialectical, too. They must be seen as entailing contradictions which challenge the definitiveness of their own self-understanding and cause them to be redefined into something more complex. In Hegel's speculative, dialectical logic, therefore, the immediacy of thought is understood not merely as simple, 'indifferent' qualitative or quantitative determination, but also as the unintended transition from one determination to another (*Übergehen in Anderes*). Reflection is understood not merely as the external positing of form in opposition to content, of essence in opposition to appearance, but also as the active mediation of one determination by another (*Scheinen in Anderes*). Finally, traditional logical thought or reasoning is understood not simply as judgement or syllogistic inference, but also as the mode of thought in which the articulated, continuous self-development (*Entwicklung*) of thought first begins to become explicit.[50] The final conception of thought as 'the absolute Idea' is the culmination of the conceptual development in the *Logic* precisely because it fully articulates the logic of dialectical self-determination and self-redefinition which has been shown to be implicit in the lower forms. The idea of dialectical self-determination, which is the final concept of the *Logic* and thus different from the other concepts and categories, is at the same time, therefore, revealed to be the absolute method within all thought, the method which is only employed and rendered fully explicit, however, by philosophy itself.[51]

The process of development in the *Logic* does not consist in a series of external reflections on the categories and is not therefore infinitely extendable. Rather, it consists in the deepening and intensification of an initial determination by the dialectic immanent in that determination. The process is therefore one of self-revelation and is completed when the dialectical self-determination which in fact redefines all the categories, but which in the more primitive categories is only implicit and is not yet stated to be the true character of thought, is at last fully articulated as the true character of thought. In this way, the whole process of thought's self-redefinition and self-determination is 'a circle in which the first is also the last and the last is also the first'.[52] This method of the *Logic* is not set up by Hegel as the only legitimate method of knowledge; it is not the approach adopted in the natural sciences, nor in geometry. Nor do we explicitly follow dialectical logic in most of our ordinary reflection on the world. But dialectical, speculative method, Hegel argues, is the only method for determining the inherent character of thought. As such, it provides a thorough critique and explication of the categories with which all of us in fact think.

This critique reveals various ways in which each category and each form of thought can be conceived. It shows, for example, that reflective terms such as 'essence' or 'appearance' can have either a purely reflective or a dialectical form, that they can be opposed to one another or understood as moments of one unity. The notion of being 'in itself', therefore, can be understood as Nietzsche understands it, that is as implying a level of reality *behind* what we experience, or it can be understood as Hegel understands it, that is as implying (in an abstract and insufficiently determinate way) the inherent form of the reality we experience. The extent to which one feels that the notion of being 'in itself' detracts from the dynamism of life or constitutes the dynamism of life depends upon one's conception of the term. Nietzsche, as I have argued in chapter 3, has a reflective conception of being 'in itself' as the unity allegedly 'underlying' life, and a correspondingly fragmented, discontinuous notion of life; whereas Hegel has a dialectical conception of being 'in itself' as the dialectical, unified form of life itself. The implication of Hegel's argument, of course, is that, whereas the reflective conception of being 'in itself' might be valid in certain specific cases where what is real is in fact obscured by what is apparent, such a conception is not adequate for the philosophical understanding of being or reality as such. Nietzsche's rejection of the idea that there is any 'being' at all is thus, from Hegel's point of view, based on a misconception of the term.

However, Hegel's critique of the categories not only reveals various ways in which the categories and forms of thought can be conceived; it also places the categories in a hierarchy and thus delimits the range of complexity with which each category can deal, *however that category is conceived*. By implication, therefore, certain categories are suitable for understanding certain levels of experience but not others. The categories of quantity and specificity, for example, may well be able to reveal features of inorganic nature but do not reveal the true character of life or self-consciousness.[53] Similarly, different categories are suited to different levels of resolution within their allotted areas.

The notion of mechanism, for example, thus reveals more of the structure of inorganic matter than does quantitative analysis, though both are suited to it. The failure of a thinker like Nietzsche, therefore, is not only that he has a reflective conception of immediate or reflective categories such as 'being' or 'essence' which is inadequate for philosophy, but that he applies the wrong categories to human life and self-consciousness; that is he applies categories which even in their dialectical form do not reveal the degree of complexity in man's life, but which reduce it to a lower level of determination. Heinz Röttges argues, for example, that in his early essay, *On the Uses and Disadvantages of History for Life*, Nietzsche misconstrues self-consciousness by measuring it against the category of 'measure' (*Maß*).[54] One could also argue that Nietzsche misconstrues the relation between life and thought by understanding that relation in terms of the category of 'positing' (*Setzen*), rather than Hegel's notion of self-development. Thought is thus held by Nietzsche to be posited by, and therefore to be subordinate to, natural life, rather than to be the mode of natural life which itself develops into conscious self-determination.[55]

The great difficulty in understanding the *Logic* is that one must see it as doing two different things. On the one hand, it is a study of various *forms* of thought – reflection, judgement, syllogism – which culminates in the conception of thought as self-determining, dialectical reason. Hegel is thus saying that in philosophy thought must be self-determining and dialectical rather than merely reflective. On the other hand, Hegel's *Logic* is also a study of the *categories* of thought which are to constitute the principal determinations of his *Realphilosophie*. This study shows, similarly, that these categories are only to be employed in philosophy in their dialectical conception and also that different categories are to be employed to understand different levels of reality. The *Logic* thus delimits the range of complexity which the various ordinary forms of thought are able to understand, and it also delimits the range of complexity that the various dialectical categories of philosophical reason are appropriate to. The possibilities for thought left open by the *Logic* therefore include the ordinary understanding of the determinations of finite things, the dialectical understanding of the determinations of finite things, and the dialectical understanding of the determinations of 'infinite' universals such as *Geist*, 'history' or reason itself. What is ruled out is merely the metaphysical attempt to understand those 'infinite' universals in ordinary, finite terms.

Before ending this section on Hegel's philosophy 'without foundations', a few words should be said about the relation of Hegel's dialectical logic to the freedom and contingency of the real world. This is a large and difficult topic, but one that needs to be addressed here – however inadequately – in order to counter any impression that may be gained that Hegel's absolute Idea subjects life to an all-embracing, all-consuming deterministic necessity. Hegel's *Logic* articulates the absolute logical determinations of the natural and the human world. It determines what that world essentially is, and it spells out the general form of its activity. Now since the *Logic* determines what the world is, it must determine what it means for anything to be a finite quantum or object. Significantly, the *Logic* determines such objects to be determined by a complex interchange between themselves and the other objects around them. Here, therefore, is the point at which the absolute determinations of reason and the complex finitude of objects intermesh – because philosophy's absolute dialectical understanding of the determinations of finite things reveals those things to be subject to the laws and empirical contingencies of nature.[56] Philosophical understanding also shows that there is a genuine dialectical propensity in nature towards the generation of increasingly unified and complex forms, and that life and consciousness are the logical goal of that propensity.[57] However, philosophical reason determines life and consciousness as that which can only emerge and develop if natural conditions are right. Dialectical reason in nature is thus not something which overrides the natural finitude of finite things, but rather both grounds, and is mediated by, that finitude. Dialectical reason can only be said to become a potent force 'overriding' natural laws when consciousness itself begins to develop according to the explicitly dialectical logic of self-consciousness. Even then, however, the logic of self-consciousness determines that consciousness pass through various levels of development before it reaches full self-awareness and self-determination. Even in the case of self-consciousness, therefore, dialectical rationality gives rise to forms of conscious life which fail to conform to dialectical reason completely. The absolute determinations of reason do not therefore guarantee that all aspects of reality will be fully rational; rather they ground multiple forms of existence and determination which it is up to science and other forms of enquiry to discover and which only come to manifest a fully dialectical, rational character late in the day.[58]

What is true of the objective world is also true of human thought about that world. Hegel claims that the determinations of the *Logic* are the absolute categories of all human thought. But this does not mean for Hegel that thought is always explicitly and uniformly rational. The logical determinations which Hegel sets out in the *Logic* make possible a wide variety of human responses to experience and do not stifle the openness, freedom and exploratory tentativeness of consciousness. Indeed, it is only because we operate with the categories of possibility and contingency that we can be open or tentative in our everyday experience at all.[59] Hegel's own dialectical philosophy claims to be the definitive articulation of the general categories with which we operate; but that claim to definitiveness betrays no disdain for caution or self-criticism on Hegel's part; rather, it grounds the possibility of such caution in experience and establishes its proper character.[60]

These remarks are brief and inevitably limited. However, they may serve to indicate, I hope, the subtle way in which Hegel understands the logical determinations with which he deals.

Hegel's theory of the speculative sentence

It is to be the task of the *Science of Logic* to undertake a critique of the categories of metaphysics and thereby to make available to philosophy a thoroughly self-critical understanding of thought. Since Hegel's death, however, there has occurred in philosophy what has been referred to as the 'linguistic turn'.[61] This shift in interest amongst philosophers towards a more self-conscious concern with language presents a challenge to Hegel's project of categorial analysis because of the methodological nominalism with which that shift in interest is associated. Such nominalism, according to Richard Rorty, entails the view

that all the questions which philosophers have asked about concepts, subsistent universals, or 'natures' which (a) cannot be answered by empirical enquiry concerning the behaviour or properties of particulars subsumed under such concepts, universals, or natures, and which (b) can be answered in *some* way, can be answered by answering questions about the use of linguistic expressions, and in no other way.[62]

If Hegel's critique of the categories of metaphysics were intended to be a direct study of concepts, perhaps by means of introspection and without due attention to observable linguistic usage, then it is clear that his whole philosophical project would be viewed with great suspicion by linguistic philosophers. But is this what Hegel intends? Does his categorial critique by-pass language in this way? In my view this cannot be the case, for it is one of Hegel's fundamental beliefs that it is only in language that we can think and understand concepts at all.

The intimate connection between thought and language is made clear in Hegel's discussion of theoretical mind in the *Encyclopaedia*. Representations for Hegel are internalised and generalised images which are connected by the imagination with names, but which can be pictured without them.[63] Thoughts on the other hand are formal determinations of the mind which cannot exist for the subject without words. Language, he says, is absolutely necessary for our thoughts: 'we *think* in names'.[64] We only know our thoughts when they are conceived in a determinate, differentiated and objective form, but a form which nevertheless bears the stamp of inwardness; such a form, Hegel says, is the word. Hegel does not mean by this that thoughts are reducible to words; he was well aware that words can be used without clear awareness of the thoughts they express, and he warned against confusing conceptual and linguistic distinctions. But he insists nevertheless that conceptual distinctions can only be made in language.[65]

Similarly, Hegel believes that there can be no language without thought, since it is thought which provides the mind with the grammar of language. The element of language – the sign – is the product, Hegel says, of the imagination which creates signs (*die Zeichen machende Phantasie*), but the form or grammar of language is the product of thought or *Verstand*.[66] Grammar for Hegel thus involves relating words to one another according to the relations between logical categories, rather than according to the meanings signified, or representations referred to, by the individual words. Words may well designate various representations, but they also perform various logical functions within a language. Understanding a language therefore always entails grasping abstract, formal relations between words.[67] As I have indicated, however, grammatical, linguistic relations and logical relations are not identical for Hegel. Grammatical relations are merely relations between the signs and words of a language which determine the specific function of words with respect to each other. They are distinct from logical relations, which obtain in what is 'sensed, intuited, presented' by consciousness.[68] Language may well express a content in which no claim to logical consistency or to objectivity is made, for example when it gives expression to the subjective associations of the imagination. But, nevertheless, when such a content is expressed, language will give that content a grammatical structure which renders it communicable to others and which is based on universal categorial functions.[69] There can even be a distinction between grammatical and logical relations when the content expressed is intended to be objective. In the section on judgement in the *Science of Logic*, for example, Hegel shows that the simple form of the proposition-type, 'S is P', can conceal differences between what he calls positive, singular, categorical and assertoric judgements.[70] In this case, similarities of grammatical structure seem to obscure logical differences in the thoughts expressed.[71] On the other hand, grammar may make rigid distinctions, for example between subject and predicate, where Hegel's dialectical logic seeks to dissolve those distinctions.[72] In both these examples, Hegel suggests, '*language* . . . is exposed to the fate of serving just as much to conceal as to reveal human thought'[73] – though on no account should this be taken to mean that the grammar of language *always* obscures our thoughts. For Hegel, we can only argue that one mode of language obscures our thinking if we contrast it with another mode of language in which our thoughts are adequately formulated, because, as we have seen, thoughts can only exist in language.[74]

The study of the categories of thought cannot therefore by-pass the question of language in Hegel's view. But it should be said at the outset that Hegel's *Logic* is not an empirical study of the way in which certain words and expressions are used (and are to be used) in specific situations in a given language. In the *Logic*, Hegel thus does not undertake a Wittgensteinian examination of the specific linguistic activities of commanding, reporting, guessing, requesting, thanking and so on.[75] Hegel insists, however, that people can express a wide variety of states of mind in language, and he is thus well aware that words can have a great many differing meanings and uses.[76] Hegel also sees that words are arbitrary signs whose meaning does not suggest itself but has to be learnt.[77] Furthermore, since he emphasises that language is an essentially social phenomenon intended to meet man's need for 'theoretical communication' (*theoretische Mitteilung*),[78] one might say that Hegel sees words as signs which only acquire a regular meaning for a community when it is understood by that specific community that these words are to be used in a particular way.[79] The social character of language is emphasised particularly in §197 of the *Philosophy of*

Right, where Hegel argues that the development of the linguistic capacities of individuals forms part of the theoretical education of those individuals and is brought about by engaging in various types of labour and activity within what he calls the system of needs. Becoming competent in one's use of language and engaging in social life and work are thus closely related for Hegel.[80]

Hegel is thus well aware that to use language is to live in a specific community at a specific time and place and to speak a specific language, and his acute sense of the specific individuality of languages is well illustrated by his remarks regarding the possibility of translation in his end of year speech at the Nuremberg Ägidiengymnasium in 1809. The richness of a culture is bound up with the language of that culture, Hegel says, and only by learning languages do we attain to that richness 'in its full particularity' (*in seiner ganzen Eigentümlichkeit*). Translations may well put across the content of a particular passage, but they can never accurately reproduce the form. They are like imitation roses which can resemble the original closely, but lack the 'loveliness, delicacy and softness of life'.[81] Hegel is thus quite clear that words which seem to express the same concepts can have very different meanings and roles to play in different communities. The distinctions he draws in the lectures on aesthetics between the Greek αρετη and the Latin *virtus*,[82] or between the Greek παθος and the German *Leidenschaft*,[83] bear witness to his sensitivity to cultural differences in this respect.

On the other hand, it must be remembered that Hegel considers different languages to be specific instances of *language*: 'although *individual* languages are throughout conventional, their respective structures are anchored in the same universal activity of knowing, expressing consciousness'.[84] Hegel believes, therefore, that the meaning of all words in whatever particular context they are used depends upon certain logical categories, such as quality, negation, necessity, possibility, which may be expressed by different words in different languages, and which may be understood by different communities in radically different ways, but which are the universal categories of thought which all languages do in fact employ. Speaking a specific language does not therefore prevent one's expressing and becoming aware of the universal categories of thought; it is rather the condition of any such awareness.

Hegel's *Logic* is a study of those universal categories and attempts to spell out how they should properly be conceived. Thus, even though

Hegel's *Logic* does not quite meet Rorty's criterion of what philosophy should be doing, Hegel is nevertheless studying language, since on his own admission 'the forms of thought are, in the first instance, displayed and stored in human *language*'.[85] Furthermore, Hegel's study of thought is not based on introspection as it is for Descartes or Fichte; nor is his the romantic path of following the 'inner way'. Hegel rejects any attempt to found philosophical knowledge on 'inner intuition' (*innere Anschauung*) – including, therefore, Nietzsche's reliance on pre-linguistic 'experience' – as merely another form of unmediated positivism, just as he rejects the attempt to found it on personal feeling.[86] If the imagination does not wish to communicate, it can wilfully pursue its own fantasies within the privacy of the mind, though it cannot actually have any determinate conception of anything that is purely private or totally unintelligible to others. Thought, on the other hand, because of its claim to objectivity, always requires a public medium. Thinking for Hegel cannot therefore lie in private cogitation and certainty behind the words of the public language, but must be a publicly accessible and publicly criticisable activity. Even if we think something 'to ourselves', we can only claim to be *thinking* if we make linguistic and logical connections whose criterion of validity can be made available for all to see and criticise.[87]

Hegel thus analyses the categories of thought by studying the public medium of thought, by studying sentences of language. However, this study of categories does not concentrate on ordinary sentences in which the categories are employed, although Hegel does of course consider some examples of such sentences.[88] Rather, it is a study of those sentences which directly articulate what the categories *are*. The *Logic* is specifically intended to determine the nature of the logical categories; the sentences which Hegel examines are thus those in which the nature of the categories is directly expressed. Such sentences take the form 'being is the indeterminate immediate' (*das Sein ist das unbestimmte Unmittelbare*) or 'real necessity is *determinate* necessity' (*die reale Notwendigkeit ist* bestimmte *Notwendigkeit*), and are called philosophical or speculative sentences.[89]

Hegel does not write much about the speculative sentence; indeed, what he has to say on the subject is confined to the preface of the *Phenomenology*, and one must therefore be cautious in interpreting the idea. Yet it is clearly an important idea because it is the kernel of his theory of what constitutes non-metaphysical philosophical language, the mode of language appropriate to dialectical method. Thus, if we are to understand what Hegel means by speculative philosophy, an attempt must be made, however inadequately, to understand his theory of the speculative sentence.

The main characteristic which we have to recognise in a speculative sentence is that the subject- and the predicate-terms are both logical categories or universal concepts. Speculative sentences are thus clearly distinguished from propositions or judgements with a sensuous, representational content. A statement such as 'the rose is red' is not therefore a speculative sentence, whereas 'the *actual* is the *universal*' (*das* Wirkliche *ist das* Allgemeine) is.[90] The concepts in a speculative sentence may of course be 'infinite' determinations of nature or of the human world, such as 'time', 'space', 'history', 'language' or indeed *Geist*. But any such universal determinations are always to be understood first and foremost in terms of the relations of logical categories to one another from which they are derived, and not merely as given, pictorial representations. It is for this reason that, although Hegel gives as an example of a speculative sentence the sentence 'God is being', he also thinks it is advisable not to use the word 'God' in philosophy, since that word is usually understood in terms of a given representational content.[91]

A further important characteristic of a speculative sentence is that it is a statement of identity between subject and predicate. It therefore states one category to be identical with another. A speculative sentence is not, however, to be confused with a simple tautology, or what Hegel calls a positive, infinite judgement, such as 'the universal is universal' (*das Allgemeine ist allgemein*).[92]   The identity involved in a speculative sentence is *speculative* because it incorporates the moment of difference as well. That is to say, although subject and predicate are held to be identical, they are also recognised to be conceptually differentiated.[93] Yet that difference-in-identity is not the same as the distinctness-in-identity that one finds in a judgement. In the speculative sentence no clear distinction between subject and predicate can be made, since subject and predicate are not presented as 'independent' (*selbständig*) entities or qualities.[94]

But how then are we to understand what is involved in a speculative sentence? How is it that subject and predicate can be identical yet different? And how is it that they can be different yet not distinct? The answer lies in the manner in which the predicate of a speculative sentence is conceived. In an ordinary judgement the subject-term refers to a given subject – say, a rose – and the predicate characterises that given subject in one way or another – say, as red, small, pretty and so on. There is a tension between the fact that the subject is distinct from the predicate and therefore given prior to the enunciation of the predicate, and the fact that we only fully understand what the subject is meant to be once the predicate is enunciated; but the explicit form of the judgement nevertheless presents the subject as 'a passive subject [*ein ruhendes Subjekt*] inertly supporting the accidents', and thus holds the subject and predicate apart.[95]   In a sentence such as 'the rose is red', therefore, we begin with a given subject to which predicates can be referred and which the sentence is 'about'. Having uttered one predicate, we are thus free to proceed to any further – possibly wholly unrelated – predicates which can also be referred to the same subject. In the speculative sentence, however, the distance between the subject and the predicate disappears. What is expressed in the grammatical predicate is thus no longer one of the many given qualities of a given subject, but rather 'the substance, the essence and the concept of what is under discussion'.[96]   The subject and predicate are thus *absolutely* identical because the predicate states what the essence of the subject is. The difference between them, therefore, is not that they are distinguished conceptually as particular and universal terms, but that one universal term – the predicate – identifies and constitutes the intrinsic character of another universal term – the subject – which that subject-term itself does not express and which is not stated until the predicate is uttered. In the speculative sentence, 'the *actual* is the *universal*', for example, 'the universal is not meant to have merely the significance of a predicate, as if the proposition asserted only that the actual is universal; on the contrary, the universal is meant to express the essence of the actual'.[97]

What is most important about the speculative sentence is that the subject and predicate are conceived in a radically new way. In the ordinary judgement, the given subject is presented as 'the *objective*, fixed self' (*das* gegenständliche *fixe Selbst*) which serves as a firm point of reference for the attribution of predicates.[98] In the speculative sentence the subject-term – 'the actual', for example – seems perhaps to serve as a similar firm point of reference; after all, we have already derived our understanding of the concept 'the actual' from the earlier categories of the *Logic* and we think we know what it means. However, in the speculative sentence the predicate is itself a subject, in fact it is a statement of the substance of the initial subject-term. It is the predicate, therefore, which states what the subject intrinsically *is*. But this means that the subject-term loses the substantial determinacy that it initially appears to have. The subject-term is not the firm point of reference for the sentence because it is only the predicate which tells us what the subject in fact is. What we understood by the word 'God' is now stated to be 'being' and what we understood to be 'the actual' is now stated to be 'the universal'. The substance of the subject thus seems to have disappeared from the subject-term as we understood it into the strange new predicate. The predicate itself, therefore, 'has the significance of something substantial in which the subject is dissolved'.[99]

The predicate of a speculative sentence does not specify a given subject through the enunciation of a quality of that subject. On the contrary, by stating what the essence of the subject is, the predicate has, as it were, usurped the position of the subject and has taken away our immediate certainty that we know what the subject-term refers to: '*Being* is here [in the proposition "God is being"] meant not to be a predicate, but rather the essence; it seems, consequently, that God ceases to be what he is from his position in the proposition, viz. a fixed subject.'[100] Rather than feeling that the predicate has added to our already firm understanding of the subject, therefore, we feel 'thrown back', as Hegel puts it, to the subject, and we are caused to think again about what the subject-term itself means: 'Thinking, instead of making progress in the transition from subject to predicate, in reality feels itself checked by the loss of the subject, and, missing it, is thrown back on to the thought of the subject.'[101]

But the speculative sentence also offers a way out of this dilemma, since it states in the predicate what the subject essentially is; the predicate states the subject to be 'being', 'the essence' or 'the universal', for example. Although the mind has lost the firm foundation which it thought it had in the subject, therefore, it can recover a definition of the subject by looking to the predicate. But in order to understand the full implications of what the sentence is revealing the subject to be, we have to change our expectations and read the sentence in the right way. We have to realise that the speculative sentence does not refer a particular given quality to a fixed subject, as does the judgement, but rather takes us via the predicate more deeply into the logical complexity of the subject itself and therefore unfixes the subject which we considered so firm by expanding or intensifying our conception of the logical nature of that subject: 'Thinking therefore loses the firm objective [*gegenständlich*] basis it had in the subject when, in the predicate, it is thrown back on to the subject, and when, in the predicate, it does not return into itself, but into the subject of the content.'[102] If we are prepared to read the sentence properly, therefore, the sentence does not in fact cause us to lose our initial understanding of the subject altogether as we think; it causes us rather to revise and redefine that understanding. That is to say, the sentence 'the *actual* is the *universal*' does not destroy our initial concept of 'the actual' – a concept that has been built up like all the others in the course of the *Logic* – but it forces us to understand how that concept can be intrinsically 'the universal'. All we lose, therefore, is the definitiveness of the initial conception. What we initially take to be the total disappearance of the subject into the predicate is in fact the dynamic transformation of the subject into the unity of the subject and predicate. It is the emergence of a determinate grasp of the actual as exhibiting the logical structure of actuality *and* universality – a determinate grasp that comes about through the recognition that one category is inherent in the other, through the dialectical transformation of one category into the other, and through the redefinition of both in terms of their identity with the other.[103] In this way, speculative sentences do not talk 'about' a fixed, given subject; they continually generate a new conception of the subject by redefining the terms in the sentence in the light of one another.[104]

The speculative sentence thus effects an important transformation of the subject; what is thought to be a fixed concept is in fact revealed to be a developing logical form.[105] The transformation of the subject is only evident, however, if one reads the sentence as explicitly speculative. If the sentence is read as an ordinary sentence the reader will either import into the sentence representations of the terms concerned to give them meaning, or, like Schopenhauer, he will be frustrated by the absence of an obvious sense to the sentence and will dismiss it as empty nonsense. In order to ensure that the transformation of the subject is grasped by the reader, that, therefore, the reader's expectations are changed and his or her attention is focused on the dialectical form of the categories in the sentence, the speculative character of the sentence must be expounded in further sentences: 'this return of the concept into itself must be *set forth* [*dargestellt*] ... The dialectical movement of the proposition itself ... alone is the speculative *in act* [*das* wirkliche *Spekulative*], and only the expression of this movement is a speculative exposition.'[106] The speculative sentence can only be recognised as truly speculative when it is seen as one sentence in a whole speculative discourse, that is in a continuity of speculative sentences which renders explicit what is exhibited in the initial sentence of the discourse.[107]

Hegel's speculative exposition involves a process of continued attention to, and explicit statement of, the implications inherent in the initial speculative sentences in which the abstract conceptual identity of 'being' is expressed. This means that, for Hegel, the structure of, for example, the *Logic* cannot be expressed by one speculative sentence alone, even if that sentence is the most concrete definition of reason as dialectical self-determination. By itself, therefore, a single speculative sentence is inadequate to the articulation of philosophical truth. The philosophical truth which Hegel seeks to express in his writing is not contained in a single principle or *Grundsatz*,[108] indeed it cannot be contained in a simple sequence or collection of principles either, and the *Logic* must not be read in this way. Hegel's view is that a philosophical sentence cannot be true by itself, in the way that a proposition such as 'the rose is red' can be quite definitively correct or incorrect as it stands, because the philosophical sentence is not simply describing a given state of affairs.[109] Philosophical language is, rather, articulating the inherent structure of thought. Since that structure, Hegel believes, is dialectical and developmental, it cannot be adequately revealed in one straightforward utterance or articulation of it, but requires a systematic *continuity* of utterances which gradually brings that structure to full self-manifestation and self-articulation. Hegel's philosophy should not therefore be read simply as a set of propositions or beliefs which might or might not be true. Hegel's philosophical statements about the world must at least be true in the ordinary sense of 'correct', and his philosophy is not valid if, as Russell believes, 'almost all Hegel's doctrines are false'.[110] But the point is that even if all his doctrines were seen to be correct, we would still have missed the whole point of his philosophy if we understood no more than this and failed to grasp the method or process of dialectical analysis and logical 'movement' by which those beliefs are derived.

Hegel's analysis of the speculative sentence contains the essence of his whole critique of metaphysical philosophy. It presents a critique of the distinct categories employed by metaphysics and thus challenges the adequacy of the understanding of language which underlies metaphysics. In his speculative philosophy Hegel redefines the traditional conception of categories. Categories are no longer thought of as units – as mental elements or as existing realities – which are identified by names as firm points of reference and which are then talked 'about' or described in sentences. Thought is conceived, rather, as that which fully determines and develops itself in the activity of speaking and thinking speculatively. This shift in understanding on Hegel's part has profound consequences for his view of human subjectivity. The subject of the ordinary sentence is presented as the foundation of predication; in the speculative sentence, however, the subject is constituted in the uttering of the sentence. This means, therefore, that the subjectivity which metaphysics previously conceived as distinct from human language, as 'transcendent', is now conceived by Hegel as constituted in human thought and language.[111] The subject for Hegel thus has no other-worldly connotations; it does not reside beyond the activity of man in history, but is immanent in that history. Like Nietzsche, Hegel is critical of the view that there is any subjectivity which transcends the historical specificity of human existence. He is critical of the view that presents the human subject as a soul independent of social and historical conditions, and he is critical of the view that makes human existence depend on an all-powerful cosmic subjectivity. However, unlike Nietzsche, Hegel does not simply invert the hierarchy and construe the notion of man's unified subjectivity as a fiction produced by human existence. Hegel does not therefore reject the notions of subject and identity as such and reduce human existence to natural life or 'will'. Rather, he retains the notion of subjectivity and redefines it as the conscious identity which man develops in language and linguistic communities, that is to say in society and history.[112]

It is not possible to go into the details of Hegel's philosophy of history in this book. All I wish to point out is that Hegel's redefinition of subjectivity which is carried out in the *Logic* commits him to the view that subjectivity has an intrinsically dialectical structure and that such dialectical subjectivity is by definition social and historical. The words 'reason' and 'Idea' in Hegel's philosophy do not therefore refer to metaphysical entities to which human life is subordinate. They do not constitute a manageable ideal pattern under which the flux of human experience is forced, as Nietzsche maintains. Rather, they refer to the immanent dialectical rationality within nature and human self-consciousness; they refer to the dialectical form of human experience and activity which leads man to mature self-understanding. They refer to the self-imposed fate of man, the fact that he drives himself to maturity through the unintended consequences of his actions.

Hegel endeavours as much as possible to avoid giving the impression that 'the Idea' is a transcendent entity, rather than the immanent dialectical structure of linguistic and non-linguistic practice, by his use of at times impossibly contorted sentences. A sentence from the preface to the *Phenomenology* may serve as an example of what is meant by this. Hegel writes at one point:

Die lebendige Substanz ist ferner das Sein, welches in Wahrheit *Subjekt* oder, was dasselbe heißt, welches in Wahrheit wirklich ist, nur insofern sie die Bewegung des Sichselbstsetzens oder die Vermittlung des Sichanderswerdens mit sich selbst ist.

Further, the living substance is being which is in truth *subject*, or, what is the same, is in truth actual only insofar as it is the movement of positing itself, or is the mediation of its self-othering with itself.[113]

This sentence is literally an unfolding of what it states substance to be: first of all, substance is stated to be being, but being itself is immediately redefined by being stated to be 'in truth *subject*'; the sentence then concludes by saying that substance is only revealed to be subject insofar as we reflect on the movement of 'self-positing' displayed by the sentence itself. Substance is thus stated and shown to be identical with the process of its own emergence; it is not something which enters into a process and which can therefore be distinguished from its process. The purpose of Hegel's convoluted sentence structure is to bring out the continuity and identity of the subject-term and the speculative exposition. Seen in this way, Hegel's notorious linguistic 'obscurity' results from a deliberate attempt to avoid the very thing more positivist-minded critics accuse him of, namely being a metaphysical word-monger who talks unclearly and uncritically about mythical, mystical entities.

Hegel is of course aware that when first approaching speculative discourse the reader expects to find ordinary sentences in which subject and predicate are related in the conventional manner. And he is also aware that speculative sentences can appear at first sight to involve ordinary predication: 'The philosophical proposition, since it is a proposition, leads one to believe that the usual subject–predicate relation obtains, as well as the usual attitude towards knowing.'[114] Sentences, for example in the philosophy of history, which refer to *der Weltgeist* or to God can thus give rise to the hypostatisation of the subject. But Hegel insists that the expectation that speculative sentences will conform to the model of ordinary sentences ignores their philosophical, speculative content and entails a radical misreading of his texts. The contradiction between our ordinary expectation of what speculative discourse involves and the dialectical content of speculative discourse will, however, eventually lead to confusion on the part of the reader. The reader will thus be forced to revise his expectation of what speculative sentences mean and re-read the sentences properly in the light of the speculative exposition. In order as much as possible to avoid misleading the reader, therefore, the speculative philosopher, Hegel says, should not write in a way that confuses the speculative and the ordinary relation of subject and predicate.[115] This does not mean, however, that philosophy should never employ ordinary sentences or literary devices such as metaphor; one can open any page of Hegel's and find perfectly conventional sentences. But it does mean that in those statements in which philosophical concepts are expounded directly, the predicates of the sentences should be seen genuinely to express the essence rather than a quality of the subject, and that the subject should be shown to be clearly and unequivocally dialectical.[116] Those interpretations of Hegel, such as Charles Taylor's, which see him as describing some kind of cosmic spirit which enters into or posits the world and governs it with reason and necessity, must therefore be misinterpretations, for the whole structure of Hegel's language is aimed explicitly at refuting them.[117]

Hegel's notorious style is not therefore the result of mystificatory intent (as Schopenhauer believed)[118] nor of expository clumsiness (as one might say, for example, of Kant). It emerges necessarily from his critique of metaphysical categories and of the conventional expectation of how language should operate. Like Nietzsche, therefore, 'Hegel gives precision . . . to his criticism of metaphysics by uncovering and questioning the linguistic and predicative relations which underlie metaphysics.'[119] The character of the respective styles adopted by Hegel and Nietzsche is of course very different. Nietzsche's is much more metaphorical and allusive; Hegel's, on the other hand, is severely conceptual (though not without some striking metaphors and even at times a certain Nietzschean quality).[120] However, the intention behind the styles of these two very different philosophers is similar; it is to expose as a fiction and therefore effectively destroy (in Nietzsche's case), or transform and redefine (in Hegel's case) the simple identity entailed by the substantive or noun. Both Hegel and

Nietzsche want their style to reflect the shift they make from understanding the world in terms of things to understanding the world in terms of processes and activities. One of the ways in which their styles reflect this shift is the fact that simple substantives are often replaced by verbal nouns as (in Nietzsche's case) the medium for evoking the dynamic character of life or (in Hegel's case) the linguistic element in which the dialectical form of reality is articulated. Examples of this are not hard to find. In the passage from the *Phenomenology* quoted earlier Hegel describes substance as

die Bewegung des Sichselbstsetzens oder die Vermittlung des Sichanderswerdens mit sich selbst.

the movement of positing itself, or . . . the mediation of its self-othering with itself.[121]

Or in another example, chosen at random, Hegel describes the positive and negative moments in contradiction each as

das Übergehen oder vielmehr das sich Übersetzen seiner in sein Gegenteil.

the transition or the self-transposition of itself into its opposite.[122]

Nietzsche's texts also abound with such verbal nouns, as, for example, in *The Genealogy of Morals*, where he writes:

es gibt kein 'Sein' hinter dem Tun, Wirken, Werden . . . das Tun ist alles.

there is no 'being' behind the doing, effecting, becoming . . . the doing is everything.[123]

Or in the famous section from the *Nachlaß* in which he describes the world as

diese meine *dionysische* Welt des Ewig-sich-selber-Schaffens, des Ewig-sichselber-Zerstörens.

this, my *Dionysiac* world of the eternally self-creating, the eternally self-destroying.[124]

Neither philosopher, of course, ceases to understand the world in terms of nouns since even verbal nouns remain nouns. However, both focus attention onto the dynamism implied by the words they use rather than any implied static identity. Nietzsche achieves this by maintaining that the substantiality invested in processes, even by his own dynamic words, is merely a fiction produced by all words, that is that even verbal nouns do not fully express the dynamism they point to.[125] Hegel, on the other hand, regards the substantial identity of verbal nouns such as *Sichanderswerden* as *itself* dynamic, and he attempts in his speculative discourse to articulate that dynamism inherent in identity.

Both Hegel and Nietzsche want the language they use to embody the fundamental activity they believe in. Neither is content for his text merely to present a series of propositions and arguments about the world in the manner of Leibniz's *Monadology* or Wittgenstein's *Tractatus*, and both attempt to enable the reader to experience the very activity that is the object of philosophical interest for them. There is, however, a great difference in how this is achieved by each philosopher. Nietzsche is obsessed with the fact that language cannot articulate the character of reality. His own words thus ultimately refer the reader to an experience which is pre-linguistic. Language cannot therefore describe flux; and yet in the very play of metaphors and in the swift changes of perspective which characterise many of his texts, Nietzsche wants his words to manifest that activity that they can never describe. Sometimes this dynamic quality is concentrated into one passage of writing as in the *Nachlaß* passage already mentioned, in which Nietzsche evokes the seething, shifting character of the world in a long sentence containing a succession of metaphors for activity. The world is seen as

ein Ungeheuer von Kraft . . . als Spiel von Kräften und Kraftwellen zugleich Eins und Vieles . . . ein Meer in sich selber stürmender und flutender Kräfte, ewig sich wandelnd, ewig zurücklaufend . . . mit einer Ebbe und Flut seiner Gestaltungen, aus den einfachsten in die vielfältigsten hinaustreibend, aus dem Stillsten, Starrsten, Kältesten hinaus in das Glühendste, Wildeste, Sich-selber-Widersprechendste, und dann wieder aus der Fülle heimkehrend zum Einfachen, aus dem Spiel der Widersprüche zurück bis zur Lust des Einklangs.

a monster of energy . . . as a play of forces and waves of forces, at the same time one and many . . . a sea of forces flowing and rushing together, eternally changing, eternally flooding back . . . with an ebb and a flood of its forms; out of the simplest forms striving toward the most complex, out of the stillest, most rigid, coldest forms toward the hottest, most turbulent, most self-contradictory, and then again returning home to the simple out of this abundance, out of the play of contradictions back to the joy of concord .[126]

Dynamic this passage certainly is, but its dynamism resides only in the restless succession of metaphors Nietzsche calls upon. The dynamism of a Hegelian text such as the *Logic* is very different. First of all, it is articulated, logical and determinate. It is the sober dialectical movement of thought generated by definite contradictions and which yield a definite redefinition of a category.[127] It is not the protean restless-ness and excitement of Nietzsche's passage. Secondly, the dynamism of Hegel's texts does not merely reside in a *succession* of metaphors which are either unconnected or whose connections are largely associative.[128] It is a developing continuity of thought in which a category is intensified and redefined as we articulate it. Hegel's dynamism is thus not 'without goal',[129] but is developing towards the immanent goal of full self-explication.

The difference between Nietzsche's aggregate of metaphors and Hegel's developing logic reflects the fundamental difference in their philosophies and their critique of metaphysics.[130] Nietzsche bases his critique of metaphysics, and his critique of the subject–predicate distinction enshrined in the judgement, on the *judgement* that life cannot be captured in language. For Nietzsche, the locus of concreteness lies outside language and thought in life. His task as a philosopher, therefore, is to circle around life viewing it from as many different perspectives as he can. Hegel, on the other hand, bases his critique of the metaphysical subject and metaphysical language on an immanent critique of the categories of metaphysics themselves. Hegel's task as a philosopher, therefore, is not to circle around a locus of concreteness given to the philosopher outside thought, but to uncover and render explicit the concreteness or dialectical complexity inherent within thought.[131] Hegel does not therefore confront metaphysics and language with a pre-linguistic, non-metaphysical 'experience' as Nietzsche does; rather, he develops a dialectical, non-metaphysical conception of thought as the inherent form of life out of the categories employed by metaphysics itself.

6

Hegel's conception of the judgement

So far I have examined the criticisms made by Hegel and Nietzsche of the mode of oppositional thinking which both call 'metaphysical', and I have also examined the alternatives to such metaphysics which the two philosophers propose. In the course of this exposition I have indicated what I believe is the most important difference between Hegel and Nietzsche: the fact that Nietzsche bases his critique of metaphysical distinctions on the *distinction* between life and thought, whereas Hegel subjects *all* such distinctions to an immanent, dialectical critique, in which the speculative, dialectical character of reason is seen to inhere in the categories and forms of thought themselves. In chapter 8 I will try to highlight this general difference by looking at the treatment which Hegel and Nietzsche give to a specific area of philosophical interest, namely tragedy. Before that, however, the idea that Hegel's speculative rationality is immanent in the forms of human thought and consciousness and does not, as Nietzsche maintains, transcend those forms, needs to be developed further. Chapters 6 and 7 will therefore attempt to reinforce this 'immanent' interpretation of speculative thought by looking at two areas of Hegel's philosophy: his treatment of the speculative character of the judgement in the *Science of Logic*, and his understanding of context and the immanence of rationality in the *Phenomenology*. The present chapter – chapter 6 – will consider the first of these areas.

Hegel's *Logic* and his analysis of the categories in speculative sentences entails the redefinition of what is traditionally thought of as the subject. The subject is no longer conceived as the firm point of reference for predication, but as dialectical self-determination constituted in the act of speaking and thinking. Language and thought thus come to be seen, not simply as the tool of an underlying subject or force, but as the *element* of conscious subjectivity. This is not, of course, to say that a conscious subject cannot have desires or form images and representations without words, but that the subject can only have a clear understanding of its own unity as a subject – can only *be* a unified, self-conscious subject – in thought and language. The task of the present chapter is to show that this redefinition of the subject, which is enacted by the sentences of speculative thought, is also to a certain extent enacted by the form of judgement – the form of language in which we ordinarily think about things in the world, and of course the form of language which, in Hegel's view, underlies metaphysics.[1] In the course of this chapter it will become clear that, though different from speculative sentences, judgements, like the other forms of thought considered in the *Logic*, themselves contain a dialectical core which is only properly articulable in speculative sentences.

Hegel's study of the judgement anticipates Nietzsche's view that the distinction between subject and predicate in ordinary language gives rise to the conception, with which metaphysical thought operates, that the subject is an 'entity' or 'thing'.[2] In Hegel's view, therefore, we posit an independent or self-subsistent (*selbständig*) metaphysical subject every time we begin to utter a sentence of the type 'John is...' or 'the tree is...'.[3] But Hegel's study also shows that the form of the judgement undermines that conception of the subject by implying that the subject is only properly identified when the predicate is stated.[4] Judgement transforms the subject from a simple unit into a unity of subject and predicate every time we complete a sentence or even imply that a sentence requires completion. In predicative utterance, therefore, we implictly redefine the subject into one that is only fully determined in the act of predication, and thus, to that extent, into one that is speculative. Hegel's analysis thus shows what Nietzsche fails to show, namely that a redefinition of the subject is implied by the very sentence form which produces the metaphysical subject in the first place.

In showing this, however, Hegel has to challenge what he sees as the traditional conception of the judgement form. In Hegel's understanding, the judgement both separates the subject and the predicate from one another and posits an identity between them.[5] The traditional conception of the judgement, on the other hand, emphasises, according to Hegel, the separation and distinctness of the terms and overlooks their underlying identity. The subject-term, on this traditional view, is taken to denote a real object and the predicate a quality or general determination of objects which we conceive in our minds. The judgement as a whole is brought about by an act of external synthesis by the mind in which the subject-term and the predicate are connected with one another. The copula is thus taken to express the connection of these two elements which are treated as wholly independent or *selbständig*.[6] This conception of the judgement as the *connection* of subject and predicate is also understood as traditional by Ernst Tugendhat, for example,[7] and indeed a number of commentators have argued that it is in fact Hegel's own view. David Bell, for example, names Hegel along with Aristotle, Kant and Lotze as a philosopher for whom 'the elements which comprise a proposition are terms' and who believes that 'one cannot understand a proposition without first understanding the terms of which it is composed'.[8]

It is true that Hegel divides formal logic into three parts – the doctrine of concepts, the doctrine of judgements and the doctrine of syllogisms – and this might give rise to the belief that he begins with certain basic elements, or concepts, and proceeds to construct judgements and syllogisms out of them. However, as we saw in the last chapter, Hegel's method does not build on foundations in this way. The starting-point of a Hegelian analysis is always abstract in itself and thus can only be fully understood as a moment of a whole. That whole is not composed of elements which are complete in themselves 'outside' or 'before' it, but is the context within which things are properly understood and from which they must be abstracted if they are to be considered as separate elements. Hegel treats concepts before judgements in order to show that it lies within their nature as concepts to be moments of judgements rather than separate units. Judgement is thus 'this positing of determinate concepts by the concept itself', or 'the proximate [*nächste*] *realisation* of the concept, inasmuch as reality denotes in general entry into *existence* as a *determinate* being'. For Hegel, therefore, the meaning of a concept is in fact initially determined within the judgement.[9]

In Hegel's account, concepts and categories are not merely combined to form judgements; they are first determined and formulated in judgements as the determinate logical forms of those judgements.

In considering concepts by themselves the philosopher is thus abstracting them from their real logical context: 'the concept's determinations, or . . . the determinate concepts, have already been considered on their own', Hegel says at the beginning of his treatment of the judgement in the *Logic*, 'but this consideration was more a subjective reflection or subjective abstraction'.[10] A judgement, for Hegel, is thus not the *connection* of pre-existing determinate concepts, but rather determines and conveys a single thought in which the complex unity of a thing is conceived.[11] In the subject and the predicate, therefore, the same thing is determined in two distinct ways. Thus 'the relationship between a subject and a predicate is not a strictly arbitrary, external one. The possibility of a meaningful proposition resulting depends upon an underlying "identity" between them.'[12] This identity is central to the judgement in Hegel's view and is expressed in the copula of the judgement. It is important to note, however, that for Hegel, as for many modern logicians, the copula 'is' does not denote a separate element in the judgement. The judgement consists of subject and predicate and the copula merely marks the formal identity of these terms: 'the copula expresses that *the subject is the predicate*'. For this reason judgements can have copulative form even when they do not explicitly contain the word 'is'.[13]

Hegel's view that a judgement identifies subject and predicate has drawn sharp criticism from a number of commentators. Bertrand Russell, for example, accuses Hegel of 'confusing the "is" of predication, as in "Socrates is mortal", with the "is" of identity, as in "Socrates is the philosopher who drank the hemlock" '. Russell then goes on to say that this confusion underlies Hegel's whole conception of identity in difference:

Owing to this confusion he [Hegel] thinks that 'Socrates' and 'mortal' must be identical. Seeing that they are different, he does not infer, as others would, that there is a mistake somewhere, but that they exhibit 'identity in difference'. Again, Socrates is particular, 'mortal' is universal. Therefore, he says, since Socrates is mortal, it follows that the particular is the universal – taking the 'is' to be throughout expressive of identity. But to say 'the particular is the universal' is self-contradictory. Again Hegel does not suspect a mistake, but proceeds to synthesise particular and universal in the individual, or concrete universal.[14]

To my mind, however, there is nothing confused in Hegel's theory provided it is properly understood.

Russell's charge is that Hegel is claiming to see an 'identity' between the subject 'Socrates' and the predicate 'mortal' which in fact only obtains between two subject-terms such as 'Socrates' and 'the philosopher who drank the hemlock', that is identity in the strong sense of total interchangeability. From this perspective, Hegel's claim that the subject and predicate are 'identical' thus shows that he must have misconstrued the nature of a predicate by confusing it with the name of a subject or thing. In fact, however, what Hegel means by saying that the subject and predicate in the judgement are 'identical' is not that they are interchangeable, but that they overlap and are inseparable. Hegel's may be an unconventional understanding of the term 'identity' here, but his meaning is nevertheless quite clear. In the speculative sentence, on the other hand, subject and predicate do not merely overlap, but are completely congruent, since the predicate expresses the *essence* of the subject-term. However, it is doubtful whether even in the speculative sentence the subject and predicate are simply 'interchangeable' for Hegel; for to say such would be to reduce both to the status of merely equivalent descriptions of the same thing, and thus to abstract from the fact that the predicate expresses the essence of the subject which the subject-term does not express. A speculative sentence, therefore, does not merely posit the interchangeability of two given names or descriptions, any more than a judgement does, but is rather a dialectical moment in the immanent development and determination of an initial – purely conceptual – subject-term, an immanent development which, of course, a series of mere judgements could not articulate.

Terms in a judgement such as 'the rose' and 'red', or 'Socrates' and 'mortal', are, in Hegel's view, to be seen as logically distinct, since 'Socrates' refers to a particular individual and 'mortal' denotes a general quality of a man. However, although a quality may not exhaust the subject's being and may not be equivalent to the essence of the subject's character, it cannot be divorced from that subject either, since it constitutes a determinate feature of the subject's general character.[15] There has therefore to be 'identity' between the subject 'Socrates' and the predicate 'mortal', since the subject's quality is part of what the subject is. To deny this, in Hegel's opinion, is to assume that there is a subject 'in itself' which perhaps possesses certain determinate characteristics but is not *in itself* constituted by those determinate characteristics. But to do that, Hegel believes, is to posit a metaphysical abstraction.[16] 'Identity' is thus necessarily involved in predication for Hegel, since a quality in his view constitutes a determination of whatever it qualifies.

From his analysis of the judgement it is clear that Hegel does not confuse a logical predicate or general quality such as 'red' with the name of a subject or thing. Hegel keeps nouns and adjectives distinct. Indeed, the reason there is 'identity' between 'the rose' and 'red' is precisely because 'red' is a *quality* of the rose, an empirical determination of the rose that has no existence apart from its instantiation in the rose (or some other subject); it has nothing to do with the predicate's naming some existing 'thing' which could be identical with another existing 'thing' denoted by the word 'rose'. Far from proving that Hegel confuses a predicate with the name of a thing, therefore, Hegel's conception of the relation between subject and predicate proves that he clearly understands what differentiates a predicate from the name of a thing. It is just because a predicate does not refer to a thing, but to a determination of a thing, that the subject and predicate overlap or are inseparable, and to this extent are 'identical'.

True predicative identity is that between a subject and a quality for Hegel. The predicate is held to be identical with the subject because it is held to be true of the subject, because it is held to be the subject's '*posited* determinateness' (gesetzte *Bestimmtheit*), or what the subject is determined by the sentence to be.[17] If we take the subject as our basis, therefore, the predicate can have no 'self-subsistence of its own' (*selbständiges Bestehen für sich*), but is merely a quality inherent in the subject or a mode of being of that subject. The predicate cannot stand alone because it does not denote an independent entity.[18] If we abstract the predicate from its role in the sentence and consider it as a universal entity – a 'Predicate' or 'Quality' – then we are merely producing what is in Hegel's view a subjective abstraction.[19] According to this view, therefore, a word like 'red' is either the name for a subjective abstraction or it is a predicate in a sentence and denotes a quality instantiated in objects. Either way, it cannot denote an objective universal entity 'redness'. Hegel's theory of predication in judgements thus contains a direct criticism of any metaphysics which wishes to talk about universal, abstract 'entities'.[20]

There is a certain similarity between Hegel's view of the predicate and that put forward later in the nineteenth century by Gottlob Frege. A predicate for Frege cannot stand alone either, but is 'unsaturated' or 'in need of supplementation' in the sense that it is an incomplete function which requires the name of a subject to complete its meaning. The predicate – 'is now alive', for example – requires a name such as 'The Queen of England' to produce a sentence which has what Frege considers to be 'a meaning that is complete in itself'.[21] Frege, therefore, shares Hegel's view that judgements are units of meaning 'prior' to concepts and that concepts and predicates properly conceived are moments of those prior units.[22] As far as I know, however, Frege does not take a further step suggested by Hegel and argue that, just as the predicate can be seen as incomplete with respect to the subject, so the subject, which is also a moment of the whole judgement, can itself be seen as incomplete with respect to the predicate. For Frege the subject-term is simply the name of the given subject of the judgement as it is in the traditional metaphysical or empirical conception of judgement. The revolutionary element entailed in Hegel's thesis of the primacy of the judgement over the concept – namely the redefinition of what has traditionally been held to be the subject – is missed by Frege.

For Hegel the predicate is incomplete because it denotes merely a specific characteristic or determination of the subject, but equally the subject is incomplete because it is only properly determined once the predicate is stated. It is the predicate which completes what we mean by the subject: 'the subject is determined only in its predicate, or, only in the predicate is it a subject'.[23] This calls into question the neatness of the distinction between subject and predicate drawn by such philosophers as John Searle. Searle has suggested that 'the subject serves to identify an object, the predicate . . . serves to describe or characterise the object which has been identified'.[24] The implication of Hegel's theory, however, is that the predicate, by characterising the subject, actually participates in identifying that subject properly. In the judgement, the given subject is *presented* as a firm point of reference for predication, but without the predicate the subject can in fact only be identified in an approximate way. For Hegel the subject-term by itself is a name which at most denotes 'the mere *general idea* [*Vorstellung*] that constitutes the presupposed meaning of the subject';[25] it is the predicate which, if true of the subject, thereby specifies what we mean by the subject. Predication does not therefore simply involve the application of a predicate to a subject which we have already concretely identified; rather, it involves the proper identification or determination of that subject, since the subject can only be properly determined through the use of predicates. Judgement thus implicitly redefines the subject from something that is sufficient in itself into something that is only fully constituted in the act of predication. Ordinary language, therefore, provides a perpetual challenge to the metaphysical assumptions which it itself entails, for although subject and predicate in the judgement are presented as logically distinct, the judgement redefines each as united with the other. The various forms of the judgement – positive, negative, reflective, categorical, and so on – obscure this redefinition, however, to a greater or lesser degree.

Hegel clearly distinguishes the judgement from the speculative sentence. Speculative discourse presupposes no *given* meanings for its terms, but derives its concepts from the dialectical transitions in the sentences in which initially abstract categories are expressed. Judgement or ordinary predication, on the other hand, presupposes a given subject-term and a given predicate-term, although the subject is speculative to the extent that it is only fully determined when the predicate is uttered, that is to say although subject and predicate 'dovetail deeply into each other's being'.[26] Since subject and predicate in the judgement are logically distinct, therefore, the judgement appears not to assert any essential, truly dialectical identity of subject and predicate such as is asserted by the speculative sentence, but only the partial identity entailed by the 'overlapping' or the 'dovetailing into one another' of given elements. Nevertheless, this essential identity is in fact also present in the judgement, in Hegel's view, and in this sense one can say that every judgement conceals a speculative sentence within itself. The judgement form 'the individual is universal' (*das Einzelne ist allgemein*) can thus be read as the speculative sentence 'the individual is the universal' (*das Einzelne ist das Allgemeine*), as Hegel's habit of changing from one form to the other shows.[27]

Hegel is justified in reading the judgement as a speculative sentence, since he undermines the firm distinction between subject and predicate in the judgement not only by showing that the one entails, and participates in, the other, but also by showing that the logical determination of the one turns dialectically into that of the other, that is to say that the relationship of subject and predicate to one another is that of reciprocal determination or dialectical *Wechselbestimmung*.[28] Briefly, Hegel's argument runs as follows. In the immediate or positive judgement (such as 'the rose is red') the subject is a singular or individual term and the predicate is a universal term. Since, however, the subject is posited by the judgement as continuous with itself in that universal, the subject is itself posited as that universal, but now conceived as a concretely realised or instantiated universal. The predicate, on the other hand, which is initially determined as the universal *vis-à-vis* the individual subject, is now to be conceived as more abstract than that concrete subject, since it is only *one* of the many universals that can be instantiated in the subject. The predicate, therefore, which was the universal term, now comes to be conceived as the individual term *vis-à-vis* the concretely instantiated universal which is the subject. The sentence 'the individual is universal', therefore, has transformed itself into the sentence 'the universal is individual', and has thus shown that the subject which is initially determined as the individual is just as much the universal, whereas the predicate which is initially determined as the universal is just as much the individual.[29]

The judgement which states that the individual is universal at the same time implies that the individual is *the* universal, and can therefore be read as a speculative sentence. Thus, the predicate of the judgement must be conceived in two ways. Considered as a distinct moment of the judgement 'the individual is universal', the predicate expresses a quality of the individual subject of the judgement. However, considered as a dialectical moment of the speculative sentence 'the individual is the universal' at the heart of the judgement, the predicate expresses not merely a quality of the individual subject, but rather the *essential* or *necessary* moment of universality in that individual subject. That is to say, the predicate states that an individual subject which is contingently asserted to have a certain universal quality is thereby at the same time necessarily transformed by the judgement into the concrete manifestation or instantiation of that universal quality.

The speculative sentence is therefore clearly different from the judgement, but nevertheless is immanent in its structure. Hegel does not import the speculative sentence into his analysis of the judgement as a methodological tool; he is treating judgement as a speculative sentence as soon as he takes seriously the consequences of the moment of identity that he believes is stated in the form of the judgement itself. The positive judgement 'the rose is red', therefore, asserts the identity, in the sense of overlapping or inseparability, of subject and predicate by treating the predicate as an inherent quality of the subject. But, qua judgement, this sentence also entails a speculative sentence in which the logical determinations of the subject and predicate turn dialectically into one another and are redefined by the dialectical movement of the sentence. Equally, however, qua judgement, the sentence does not present the subject as *purely* speculative, as *purely* constituted by the dialectical movement of the sentence, since it still treats the subject as something *given*.[30]

Like the other forms of thought discussed in the *Logic*, the judgement, in Hegel's analysis, must be read in more than one way. We must challenge the traditional view of the judgement which sees the judgement as simply connecting two elements that are basically independent of one another, and we must recognise the fundamental inseparability of the subject and the predicate. But, equally, we must look more deeply into the structure of the judgement than that and recognise that the logical determinations of the subject and the predicate actually pass dialectically into one another. If we do not recognise in the judgement the structure of a different kind of sentence, namely the speculative sentence, we shall not be able to study the dialectical development of the judgement through its various forms. Ordinary perception of the nature of the judgement can be compared to the vision of the naked eye; if we do not focus our eyes on the hidden structure by means of a speculative lens and see the explicit and hidden structure together as one, we overlook, in Hegel's view, what is philosophically most significant. Speculative discourse is therefore the *Aufhebung* of ordinary discourse, not merely an alternative to it, because it is discourse which brings out the immanent structure of ordinary discourse, which is inaccessible to ordinary consciousness itself.[31]

7

Context and the immanence of rationality in Hegel's *Phenomenology*

In the previous three chapters I have presented my arguments for considering Hegel to be a non-metaphysical philosopher. By claiming this, of course, I am maintaining neither that Hegel's philosophy has nothing to say about the real world, nor that it is merely a collection of provisional empirical conjectures. Hegel's is a non-metaphysical philosophy because it does not conceive of the subject as a foundational entity or as a simple substance in the manner of a Leibnizian monad. The subject for Hegel is constituted in the activity of thinking and speaking; it is not merely a spiritual 'thing' which underlies that activity. Hegel is not denying that each human subject is a unique individual, conscious of himself as distinct from all other selves, but he is insisting that such unique individuality, and the freedom of self-determination which individuals can enjoy, is itself made possible by social relations and by the public medium of language that constitutes the element of consciousness. Consciousness, therefore, is 'the *I* that is *We* and the *We* that is *I*'.[1] The purpose of the present chapter is first of all to bring out this public, social and contextual character of Hegel's notion of subjectivity, and then to reinforce the idea that Hegel conceives of the form of dialectical rationality as immanent within consciousness.

The inherently public, contextual character of consciousness is brought out by Hegel in his treatment of sense-certainty in the *Phenomenology*. Sense-certainty, Hegel says, seems to be the most rich and immediate mode of knowledge. It appears to have direct and immediate knowledge of objects and thus to be the standpoint of pure sensory realism.[2] At this level of consciousness, knowledge of objects is not mediated by an awareness of its being the product of my thinking or my language, nor is it mediated by an awareness of the manifold relations into which objects enter with other objects. It is immediate certainty of the presence of objects in their own unalloyed specificity. Sense-certainty thus has as its content *this* particular thing and feels no need to determine the nature of this content beyond the sense of its being *this*. Since the object is known immediately, this immediate sensuous consciousness believes itself to rest on an unshakeable foundation of real fact, namely on the knowledge of what is objective and completely independent of its being known by a subject. But, Hegel argues, sense-certainty contradicts itself. On the one hand, it claims to know *this* specific thing and it prides itself on cutting through all the relational properties of the thing to get right to the heart of the thing itself. On the other hand, by not being explicitly aware of the mediations and negations which distinguish objects from one another, sense-certainty deprives itself of any criterion for determining what the content of its consciousness – this specific thing – really is. Sense-certainty is in fact only aware of the immediacy or bare presence of objects, of the universal form of specificity or 'thisness', which fails to bring out what is specific about any given content of consciousness.[3]

Hegel exposes this contradiction in the sensory realist's position by asking him to specify precisely what he means by 'this'. What is the 'this' of which he is conscious? The realist might answer, for example, 'now is night' (*das Jetzt ist die Nacht*).[4] The certainty that it is night will be immediate; it is because it *is* night for me that I *know* that it is. But if we try to fix the meaning of 'this' by writing down that it is nighttime and then look later at what we have written, we will see that our previous certainty or 'truth' has become 'stale' (*schal*), for now we are certain that it is daytime. We have indeed the same immediate certainty of *this* being day as we had previously of *this* being night. In both cases what we mean is this particular thing – night or day – but in being aware of this particular thing only as *this*, we are merely aware of a universal form which is continuous throughout, and compatible with, any particular content. 'This' does not therefore mean what we want it to mean. Thus, although sense-certainty considers itself to be immediate consciousness of something definite, it cannot determine what its content is merely by saying it knows 'this'.[5]

In the *Encyclopaedia* Hegel appears to blame language for this difficulty by saying that it is because of the intrinsic generality of words that consciousness is unable to specify the pure immediacy that it wants to identify: 'what I only *mean* [*meine*] is *mine* [*mein*]; it belongs to me as a particular individual. But language expresses nothing but universality; and so I cannot say what I only *mean*.'⁶ However, consciousness's failure to refer to what is immediately present for it by means of the word 'this' is not due to any limitation of language as such. Hegel's discussion of pointing (*Aufzeigen*) in the section on sense-certainty shows that sub-linguistic consciousness cannot make a pure reference to something either.⁷ Language cannot express 'what I only *mean*', because I cannot actually have any determinate conception of 'what I only *mean*'. Hegel does not say, therefore, that language frustrates consciousness's attempts to refer to pure immediacy, but that the attempt to give linguistic expression to that pure immediacy reveals the impossibility of actually pointing to pure immediacy even at the sub-linguistic level: 'language, as we see, is the more truthful; in it, we ourselves directly refute what we *mean* to say'.⁸

This is not to say, however, that consciousness is incapable of knowing particulars altogether. Consciousness cannot form any determinate conception of 'pure' particularity in Hegel's view, indeed 'pure' particularity as such cannot exist; but consciousness can identify particulars by relating its universal terms to one another. The words 'this' and 'here' are terms which serve a general grammatical and logical function and by themselves indicate nothing specific, but when set in different relations to one another, they can be used to indicate different specific things: 'The *here pointed out*, to which I hold fast, is similarly a *this* here which, in fact, is *not this* here, but a before and behind, an above and below, a right and left.'⁹ An important conclusion of Hegel's analysis of sense-certainty, therefore, is that it is the contextual relations between words such as 'this' and 'here' which give those words their specific meanings.

Not all critics have been entirely happy with Hegel's analysis of sense-certainty, however. The suspicion is that Hegel is generating the dialectic of sense-certainty by means of his confused use of words. Hegel, so the criticism goes, is creating the problem of what words like 'here' and 'now' refer to by turning into a substantive what is actually an adverb, by making a thing out of a relation. J.N. Findlay makes a similar point with regard to the word 'this' when he says that 'Wittgenstein would regard Hegel's treatment as resting on a misunderstanding of demonstratives, which are unique linguistic instruments, and neither name nor describe.'¹⁰ In fact, it is not Hegel but sense-certainty which is responsible for this misunderstanding. The sensory realist believes that in being conscious of immediate presence, of 'this', 'here', 'now', he is thereby conscious of something specific. The implication of Hegel's argument, however, is that these words indicate only the general form of presence and that they can only be used to designate something specific when used in conjunction with other terms, i.e. when we say 'this, not that' or 'this red book on the table'. These words thus require a context in order to have a specific meaning. The realist, however, believes that a demonstrative such as 'this' can refer to something by itself. He therefore misuses the demonstrative to refer to something specific and thereby nominalises that term. For the realist, 'this' is '*the* this', and indeed the German text has '*the* now is night' (das *Jetzt ist die Nacht*), rather than just 'now is night' as cited above.

Although Hegel is critical of this misuse of words, there is a sense in which he does himself treat the adverb 'now' or the demonstrative 'this' as a noun. As we have seen, Hegel believes that 'now' only means something specific when used adverbially in conjunction with other terms. Hegel also believes, however, that when we use 'now' adverbially at specific moments, we are conscious of a continuity of such moments. He would say that consciousness of this continuity is consciousness of 'nowness'. From this point of view, therefore, it is legitimate for Hegel to treat the adverb 'now' as a noun, as long as he is using the word to designate the continuity of the moments at which the word would be used adverbially in conjunction with other terms, and as long as he is not abstracting 'now' from its adverbial function and treating it simply as a noun or as a name for a simple thing.[11]

Hegel does not therefore turn an adverb into a substantive or a relation into a thing; rather, he understands things as configurations of empirical and conceptual relations.[12] Insofar as we nevertheless conceive of things as units and give them names, we are using these names to designate complex units or continuities of different moments, not isolated atomic elements or aggregates of such elements. (Hegel's criticism of hieroglyphic scripts is that they lead us to lose sight of this point and cause us to believe that our complex conceptions and representations are all reducible to simple units, thereby giving rise to a simplified notion of philosophical analysis.)[13] Hegel sees philosophical knowledge of pure *conceptual* relations as the true goal of consciousness, but he does not thereby reject other levels of consciousness. He insists that all levels of consciousness are important.[14] He believes, however, that, through our language, all levels of consciousness and all forms of knowledge – including even empirical perception, which by itself lacks any explicitly necessary rational determinations – are informed to some extent by the concepts of reason.[15] Philosophical knowledge thus has priority over other levels of consciousness for Hegel because it renders explicit the concepts which the other levels of consciousness are aware of only implicitly. It is therefore more true to the inherently logical character of the world which we experience.

Through his analysis of sense-certainty Hegel shows that reference, if it is not to be indeterminate and directionless, must situate what is referred to in the context of publicly understood terms. As David Lamb has pointed out, this conclusion is remarkably similar to that reached more recently by the later Wittgenstein. Both philosophers, Lamb maintains, are alert to 'the difficulty involved in making a determinate reference, in the absence of the system of conventions'.[16] Wittgenstein's point, briefly, is that we cannot know the meaning of a word or sign merely by pointing to something. By itself, ostensive definition does not single out anything in particular, because it 'can be variously interpreted in *every* case'.[17] We have, therefore, to know in advance what sort of thing is being referred to; indeed, for us to understand what a sign points to, we have to understand that it is being used to point with at all: 'unless we share a number of conventions and have many interests in common, the mere stretching of an arm is meaningless'.[18] Understanding a sign thus involves understanding how it is being used, and only when this is grasped can we know *if* it is being used to refer to something, and if so, what to.[19]

For this reason Wittgenstein argues that the meaning of a sign cannot merely be its bearer or an object referred to by it, but – at least in most cases – has to be the way the sign is to be used in a particular context.[20] Wittgenstein points out that words can have a variety of different functions and meanings; what words mean is determined by how they are related to other words within a sentence,[21] how sentences are related to one another,[22] how sentences are used in different language-games[23] and how language-games are related to various forms of life.[24] Words, therefore, have no fixed meanings which transcend specific contexts and practices, but are always relative to those practices.[25]

This insight has a radical effect on Wittgenstein's later philosophical method. Like Nietzsche, Wittgenstein is critical of that metaphysical mode of philosophy and logic which is concerned with the 'a priori order of the world', with what *must* be common to all experiences, that is to say with transcendent or transcendental necessity.[26] What is necessary in Wittgenstein's view is necessary only within and for a certain system of discourse, and within such systems all necessary rules are flexible rather than rigid.[27] Wittgenstein denies that we must always be drawn into a system of absolute rational necessity,[28] for such a notion rests for him upon a metaphysical use of words, that is on the assumption that there is such a thing as 'Necessity'. Wittgenstein's philosophical method is thus designed to bring our attention down from such ostensible universal meanings of words to the multiplicity of specific meanings which words have in the specific contexts of ordinary usage. His interest is in examining and describing the ways in which we actually use words in specific language-games, rather than setting up and proceeding from theory.[29]

This method does not, however, involve mere passive description; Wittgenstein is not simply recording what we say. His purpose in showing how we use words in ordinary life is to dissolve philosophical problems.[30] By uncovering the specific context in which a word is rooted he hopes to expose the ground from which the philosopher has taken off in search of universal meanings.[31] Wittgenstein would therefore agree with Austin that linguistic philosophy is concerned not merely with recording how we do speak, but also with saying '*what we should say when*'.[32] Wittgenstein presents his treatment of language-games in a particular manner in order to make us aware of features of our ordinary language which are otherwise hidden, that is the differences in ordinary usage which the superficial form of our language obscures from view. He is therefore concerned with what is profound and not apparent, but 'he saw the profound as an extra dimension of things which in themselves are very simple'.[33] He thus tries to discover what is hidden in our ordinary linguistic practices by studying closely what he sees rather than by looking through it.[34]

Does Hegel develop a method of philosophising which is any way similar to that of Wittgenstein? Our analysis of Hegel's critique of metaphysics and Kant's critical philosophy in chapter 4 certainly suggested that, like Wittgenstein, Hegel also rejects the idea that there is a 'permanent neutral framework'[35] behind experience – a timeless, transcendent world of things in themselves – which philosophy can discover. But the speculative analysis of logical categories which we discussed in chapter 5 is hardly comparable with Wittgenstein's examination of language-games. Hegel's speculative logic is not concerned with any atemporal, non-spatial 'phantasm' (*Unding*)[36] behind the phenomena which we see about us, but articulates the logical nature of the categories of our language, categories which are also the logical determinations of things in the world. Speculative logic, therefore, is concerned with the concepts which form part of the context of any utterance we may make. But the analysis explicates the intrinsic logical form of those concepts; it does not deal with the particular ways in which they are formulated by people in given situations. And because of this, Hegel's speculative project is unlikely to appeal to the committed Wittgensteinian. Indeed, the level of abstraction achieved in the *Science of Logic* would probably have seemed to Wittgenstein to be mere playing with words. In §67 of the *Philosophical Investigations*, for example, he dismisses any suggestion that 'the disjunction of all their common properties' might itself constitute a common feature of differentiated elements; 'one might as well say: "something [*ein Etwas*] runs through the whole thread – namely the continuous overlapping of those fibres" '. These comments suggest that Wittgenstein would have considered Hegel's treatment of identity in difference or of the category of 'something' (*Etwas*) to be empty abstraction.[37]

It is not therefore to Hegel's *Logic* that we must turn to find a method of philosophy similar to that of Wittgenstein, but rather to Hegel's *Phenomenology*. Phenomenology for Hegel is the study of modes of consciousness or forms of life. It sets out to examine and describe these modes of consciousness – individual, social, historical, aesthetic, religious and philosophical – in their own terms and not against a standard which is external to them. Hegel, like Wittgenstein, thus develops a mode of philosophy which (as its name suggests) analyses contexts of consciousness which are apparent in human life, and he does not look for any timeless, transcendent essence *behind* those contexts. Since many of these contexts are modes of linguistic consciousness they can perhaps be compared with Wittgenstein's language-games. Hegel's criticism of Kantianism in the introduction to the *Phenomenology*, for example, which involves an argument about the misuse of concepts and representations, also involves an argument about the misuse of words. What Hegel rejects in such philosophy are the 'adventitious and arbitrary [ideas], and the words associated with them like "absolute", "cognition", "objective" and "subjective", and countless others whose meaning is assumed to be generally familiar'.[38]

But the parallel between Hegel's phenomenological method and Wittgenstein's later philosophy should not be pushed too far. Hegel is not only interested in how we use words; he is also interested in other modes of human behaviour where words can, but need not, be used. Phenomenology is thus more than linguistic philosophy for the simple reason that 'the study of language . . . gains its importance only when it is seen in the context of the dynamic experience of the consciousness (whether individual or collective) uttering it'.[39]

The other, much more obvious, difference between Hegel and Wittgenstein lies in their attitude to necessity. Wittgenstein insists that there is no transcendent necessity since all necessity is necessity *for* a system of discourse. Hegel, on the other hand, insists that there is no transcendent necessity since necessity is always immanent in natural and human activity; in Wittgensteinian terms, therefore, necessity for Hegel is the necessary form *of* systems of human discourse. Hegel realises that our ability to understand the varying meaning of words depends upon a shared grasp of the rules of usage within a common system of discourse; but that awareness does not prevent him from reflecting on the necessary limitations of individual systems, nor on the intrinsic logical form of the categories which figure in all such systems. The phenomenological study of modes of consciousness and the speculative study of categories are thus themselves considered by Hegel to be perfectly legitimate 'systems of discourse'. Hegel's understanding of the contextual nature of human consciousness is quite compatible with his philosophy's claim to 'absolute knowledge', therefore, since the aim of that philosophy is to articulate the absolute form of human self-consciousness.

Phenomenological method reveals the absolute dialectical necessity within the free activity of consciousness. Such necessity for Hegel is not an a priori form imposed upon human practice, but 'a disporting [*Spielen*] of love with itself'.[40] And in this idea of dialectical form as the form of 'play' is a notion of absolute necessity which, it might be argued, Wittgenstein himself described in his arguments about private reference, that is to say the game of trying to refer to something without a system of acknowledged coordinates has, in Wittgenstein's view, necessary limitations.[41]

The method of phenomenology is broadly this: it involves comparing the form which a particular mode of consciousness believes its content to have with the form that that content actually has for consciousness.[42] In terms of language, therefore, it compares the way consciousness actually uses words with the way it thinks it is using words. This method involves no reference to a presupposed standard of judgement. Phenomenological knowledge of consciousness is relative to a specific mode of consciousness (or, in Nietzsche's terms, 'perspective'). We are not concerned with the question as to whether, in the abstract, consciousness is 'right' about the world. We are merely to accept the conception of reality that a particular mode of consciousness believes it has and compare that with the manner in which it conceives of reality in its practice. We can thus examine how internally consistent each mode of consciousness is, that is whether each mode of consciousness is determined as it believes itself to be.

It is important to stress at the outset that Hegel's concern with the 'self-consistency' of modes of consciousness is not based on the dubious premise that all modes of consciousness should be explicitly logical and systematic. Such a claim would overlook the distinctive value of unsystematic, associative, sceptical consciousness, and would indeed be reductive. What Hegel is concerned with is whether a mode of consciousness is consistent in the sense that it has the character that it thinks it has, that it is what it thinks it is. Does a mode of consciousness understand itself properly and live within the limits of its nature? Or does a mode of consciousness attribute to itself characteristics which it does not have, and thereby live at odds with itself? This question can be put to any mode of consciousness. Even a mode of consciousness such as Nietzsche's, in which no claim to explicit consistency is made, can still be examined to see whether it understands its character and limits properly. And where its self-understanding and its character conflict, consciousness can be said to contradict itself at a fundamental level. In a case such as Nietzsche's the contradictions that are uncovered will not necessarily be the ones that he himself is proud to admit to.

In Hegel's view, each mode of consciousness assumes its own identity and 'absolute independence' (*Selbständigkeit*), and needs to be shown where its intrinsic limits lie. This certainty of self is present in all forms of consciousness: 'in every phase of his knowledge . . . whatever the content may be, the individual is the absolute form, i.e. he is the *immediate certainty* of himself and . . . therefore unconditioned *being'.*[43] Here, therefore, despite the multiplicity of different conscious views and perspectives on reality, and despite the absence of any external frame of reference by means of which we might compare the 'correctness' of those views, we do after all have an immanent universal standard by which to compare modes of consciousness. Different modes of consciousness are commensurable, insofar as we can examine the degree to which they are what they claim to be. Different modes of consciousness can thus be seen as different forms of the claim of consciousness to self-certainty.

The analysis in the *Phenomenology* proceeds as follows. A particular mode of consciousness perceives its objects in a particular way. However, as we saw in the discussion of sense-certainty, consciousness does not always perceive its objects in quite the way it believes it does. When consciousness is brought face to face with the public fact that its self-understanding is misconceived, it changes the way in which it claims to perceive its objects in order to make its own understanding of its perception consistent with its actual perception. Consciousness now believes it perceives its objects in the proper way, but in doing so it has generated new possibilities for contradiction. It has acquired a new standard for judging whether it actually perceives its objects as it believes it does. This process of gradually redefining the objects and character of perception is described by Hegel as 'experience' (*Erfahrung*).[44]

As in the *Logic*, therefore, Hegel's method in the *Phenomenology* is that of immanent criticism. Consciousness itself is able to compare its perception of its objects with its own understanding of that perception, since consciousness in Hegel's view is itself able to make that distinction. Consciousness thus contains both the criterion (*der Maßstab*) and that which is to be tested within its own experience. Our task as philosophers is merely descriptive – 'simply to look on' (*das reine Zusehen*). Hegel insists that we, as observers of the dialectic of consciousness, must not import standards of judgement of our own which are not intrinsic to the mode of consciousness observed:

the essential point to bear in mind . . . is that . . . we do not need to import criteria, or to make use of our own bright ideas and thoughts during the course of our inquiry; it is precisely when we leave these aside that we succeed in contemplating the matter in hand [*die Sache*], as it is *in and for itself.*[45]

Our standard of judgement is set up by the mode of consciousness we examine; it is the standard it itself employs. There is only one dimension which we as philosophers add to this examination, and that is an explicit awareness of the developmental continuity generated by this transformation of consciousness and its objects. We have to make this continuity explicit because, although the modes of consciousness change the way they perceive themselves and their objects, they cannot encompass an awareness of the *development* which they as modes of consciousness form. It is only with the last mode of consciousness reached in the *Phenomenology* – philosophical consciousness itself – that consciousness becomes fully aware of the inherent continuity of its subordinate modes.[46]

But why must the forms of consciousness necessarily constitute a developing continuity? After all, in ordinary experience consciousness does not always proceed from one form to a higher one in this way, so why does this occur in the *Phenomenology*? The answer to this question is that the *Phenomenology* is not simply an empirical study of the ways in which people change their minds in given situations. It is a systematic study of *types* of consciousness which sets out to reveal what it makes sense for consciousness to do given the characteristics it has. Hegel believes that when consciousness runs up against features of its character that it has overlooked, when it realises that it is more complex than it first thought, it is rational for consciousness to redefine itself, for it to take account of this new insight into itself and understand itself as a new mode of consciousness. Consciousness may see itself as 'strong', 'sceptical', 'tentative', 'absolute' or 'self-alienated', or as a fusion of many different modes; but however it is constituted, it lays claim to a sense of what it is. Now if consciousness is really to claim that it is tentative or sceptical, if it is to claim that it knows what those words mean, it must take account of the complexity which it discovers in those characteristics. Since consciousness claims to be consciousness of itself and its objects, therefore, it must acknowledge what it becomes conscious of in itself and its objects; it must in other words *learn* about its world. This drive towards greater knowledge and understanding is inherent in consciousness's claim to be *consciousness*. The fact that individuals do not always develop in this way, that they often do not realise things about themselves or that they often resist such realisation, simply shows that people do not always behave in accordance with their intrinsic character as conscious beings. But it does not disprove Hegel's understanding that consciousness is actually born to learn and develop; nor does it disprove Hegel's wider claim that in general consciousness does develop

in this way, that history, for example, in its general form, is the product of such changes and developments in human self-understanding
and behaviour.

Hegel's *Phenomenology* systematically thinks through and redefines
various modes of consciousness until it reaches the point at which
consciousness becomes explicitly aware of its intrinsic character as
self-knowledge and self-certainty.[47] Phenomenology thus retains the
critical moment which characterises Kant's philosophy, for it reveals
the intrinsic limits of all modes of consciousness in which the content
of consciousness and consciousness's perception of that content are
not identical; however, 'the emphasis of criticism falls not on the
structure of the cognitive faculties, but rather on the action of
knowledge as it expresses itself in the world'.[48] Phenomenology offers
not a transcendental critique, but an immanent critique of consciousness.

Despite all their obvious differences, therefore, the important
similarity between Hegel and the later Wittgenstein is that neither
'*operated without a standard, yet they had no standard of their own*'.[49] And here
is a major difference between these two philosophers and Nietzsche.
Nietzsche's rejection of the idea of a neutral realm of things 'in themselves' and his emphasis on the individuality of human perspectives
might have led him to adopt a similar method to that of Hegel and
Wittgenstein. One could almost consider his method of philosophising 'with a hammer' to be a way of allowing specific modes of consciousness to criticise themselves by their own standards. The
philosopher, Nietzsche says, does not destroy false idols by smashing
them, but taps lightly on the outside in order to expose the hollow-
ness within.[50] However, Nietzsche's critical attention to individual
specificity always leads back to his conviction that all specificity is
fundamentally will to power. The individuality of the specific case is
lost – both in Nietzsche's philosophical theory and in his cavalier
practice – beneath the generality of the power-drive.[51] Furthermore,
by placing things outside the reach of language in order to safeguard
their particularity from our falsifying activity, Nietzsche actually renders that particularity inaccessible to us. Nietzsche is unperturbed by
his failure to do justice to individual cases because in his view all interpretation and evaluation – all life indeed – involves doing 'violence' to
what is being considered.[52] We are thus condemned to remain within
our own perspectives and not to share in the perspectives of others. In
his essay, *On the Uses and Disadvantages of History for Life*, for example,

Nietzsche criticises the idea of historical neutrality, that is the idea that there is for the historian only one, objective, way of viewing things. Such an idea, Nietzsche says, leaves the observer a 'passive sounding board' (*ein nachtönendes Passivum*) and ignores the multiplicity of self-interested perspectives behind so-called 'objective' judgement.[53] But Nietzsche's appreciation of the distinctiveness of individual perspectives does not lead him to a self-critical openness to the perspectives of others, nor does it encourage him to enter sympathetically into those other ways of looking at things. Unlike Hegel, therefore, Nietzsche does not 'penetrate the opponent's stronghold and meet him on his own ground',[54] but, as his deliberate falsification of historical figures such as Socrates shows, he remains as closed off to others as the 'objectivity' he rejects. Nietzsche's creative alternative to that neutral 'objectivity' is distinguished merely by its 'superior strength' (*überlegene Kraft*),[55] by its self-conscious, open, rather than concealed, partiality. Like the 'genuine' artist, therefore, Nietzsche achieves 'true' objectivity by informing the past with a unity which expresses *his* personality and which does not necessarily lie in the material itself.[56] In contrast to Hegel's procedure of entering into the strength of his opponents' terms, Nietzsche's critical method is thus not that of immanent criticism, but involves confronting the target of his attack with his own 'intimations . . . of something better' (*Ahnung eines Besseren*).[57]

In Nietzsche's own view, of course, Hegel's is a philosophy which completely ignores the variety of individual perspectives in the world and is motivated rather by the 'desire for brilliant, boneless generalities'.[58] This view of Hegel is, however, a misinterpretation, as this chapter has attempted to show. Hegel is fully aware of the differences between modes of human life and does not impose any a priori pattern of rationality onto human actions out of a craving for a unified view of man. To say that consciousness is rational for Hegel is not to say that consciousness conforms to a presupposed notion of reason. Rather, it is to say that when we describe and test the definitiveness of any mode of consciousness and its own *specific* self-understanding – with the exception of speculative philosophy, in which consciousness achieves full self-awareness – we observe the breakdown of that self-understanding and a consequent dialectical transformation in the way that mode of consciousness perceives itself, and we call the form of that transformation 'reason'.[59] The rationality of consciousness is therefore the structure of consciousness's own activity; the systematic structure which emerges in the *Phenomenology* is the product of the immanent self-redefinition and self-systematising of consciousness itself. Consciousness is not drawn towards its goal of full self-knowledge by an uncritically presupposed conception of what the 'unity' or 'maturity' of consciousness must involve; rather, it moves towards full self-knowledge because of the inability of its partial modes to preserve and sustain their own self-image. The project of systematisation is thus not undertaken from a single external point of reference. There is no given 'absolute' point of reference for Hegel, but only the claims of consciousness itself and the experience which consciousness makes about itself. Phenomenology, Hegel says, is

the cunning which, while seeming to abstain from activity, looks on and watches how determinateness, with its concrete life, just where it fancies it is pursuing its own self-preservation and particular interest, is in fact doing the very opposite, is an activity that results in its own dissolution, and makes itself a moment of the whole.[60]

Phenomenological description does not presuppose a conception of reason as its own standard of judgement, but *produces* such a conception by treating modes of consciousness in their own terms. Phenomenology thus shows the gradual unfolding of the dialectical character of consciousness – and the emergence of a consciousness of that dialectical character – out of consciousness itself, and is therefore the 'exposition of how knowledge makes its appearance' (*die Darstellung des erscheinenden Wissens*).[61] (Consciousness finally determines the character of dialectical reason in purely formal terms by developing it out of the category of being in the *Science of Logic*.)[62]

Properly conceived, thought or reason for Hegel is not a separate reality which lies outside the systems of consciousness or the things which we see around us. The Idea is not something which lies 'beyond' ordinary experience, accessible only to privileged thought. The Idea is the conceptual, dialectical form of our categories and the conceptual, dialectical form of our world, a form which all levels of consciousness are aware of, and manifest, to a greater or lesser degree. Hegel emphasises over and over again that the 'absolute' categories of reason are the immanent determinations of things in the world. In fact he stresses the immanence of all universal forms, whether they be logical categories or empirical qualities and species. In the *Encyclopaedia*, for example, Hegel says:

The *animal as such* cannot be shown; nothing can be pointed out except a specific animal. The animal *in general* [das *Tier*] does not exist; it is merely the universal nature of individuals, whilst each existing animal is a more concretely defined and particularised thing.[63]

And in the lectures on aesthetics he comments:

So, for example, the species is actual only as a free concrete individual; *life* exists only as a *single living thing*, the *good* is actualised by *individual* people, and all truth exists only as *knowing* consciousness, as spirit *for itself as spirit* [für sich seiender *Geist*]. For only concrete individuality is true and actual; abstract universality and particularity are not.[64]

Hegel thus clearly rejects the notion that there are metaphysical entities – 'universals' – distinct from particular things. However, he studies particulars in the light of the universal relations and principles of organisation which make those particulars what they are.

The difficulty with Hegel's philosophy is that his attitude to what is universal embraces both the poles of nominalism and realism. Hegel considers universality to be real insofar as he understands conceptual determinations and empirical qualities to be the constitutive determinations of natural objects. But equally he insists that such determinations and qualities only exist as the determinations and qualities of the *particular* objects which they constitute. Universal determinations exist, therefore, as the forms of particular things, not as independent universals. The *Logic* is thus not to be understood as articulating the nature of an independently existing Idea or cosmic spirit. Dialectical rationality constitutes, rather, the general conceptual form of the natural and the human world.[65] Like the laws of nature, the dialectical form of activity in the world is not written up on the heavens.[66] It is only conscious human beings who give that rationality and those laws explicitly abstract form in language; and in the case of certain manifestations of reason such as 'art' or 'history', it is only the conscious activity of human beings which brings them into being at all. There are many critics who insist on seeing in Hegel the archetypal philosopher of the transcendent Idea or cosmic spirit, and Nietzsche was undoubtedly one of these. But it is evident that this is a misreading of Hegel's philosophy:

Common opinion puts the absolute far away in a world beyond. But the absolute is rather the ever-present [*das ganz Gegenwärtige*], which, so long as we can think, we must – though without always being explicitly conscious of it – always carry with us and always use. Language is the main depository of these determinations of thought.[67]

8

Hegel
and Nietzsche
on tragedy

Introduction

The argument of this book has tried to demonstrate two points. The first is that for all the undeniable differences that separate them temperamentally and stylistically, Hegel and Nietzsche share a common aim: to criticise the lifeless abstractions that in their view have formed too prominent a part of European religious and philosophical thinking since the Greek period, and to develop a new mode of philosophising which does justice to the multiple and dynamic quality of life. The second point is that although Nietzsche is superficially much more critical of abstraction than Hegel, he nevertheless remains caught up in the abstract oppositions which he claims to reject, whereas Hegel, for many the arch-metaphysical system-builder, is the one who subjects those oppositions to their most thoroughgoing criticism.

Nietzsche criticises traditional metaphysical concepts, particularly that of the subject or soul, by reference to the external standard of 'life'. Metaphysical thinking, which is held to be characterised by naive faith in the truth of linguistic form, is confronted by Nietzsche with the *wirklich* nature of life and with the physiological conditions of its own genesis, and it is accused of obscuring or denying both. Qualities of life extrinsic to metaphysical thought – 'before' or 'behind' it, as it were – are adduced by Nietzsche in order to challenge the authority of such thought. In doing so, however, Nietzsche falls

182

into a contradiction, for he sets up a radical opposition between language and life in order to reject the radical metaphysical oppositions to which language gives rise.

Hegel, on the other hand, employs no such external standard in order to criticise metaphysics. The source of Hegel's critique of the metaphysical subject, for example, does not therefore lie outside language in 'life', but resides within the very language which produced the metaphysical conception of the subject in the first place. Hegel argues that the superficial form of the judgement 'S is P' gives rise to the concept of the subject which is distinct from its predicates; but at the same time he maintains that the dialectical form inherent in the judgement and the categories of thought, and rendered fully explicit in speculative sentences, redefines the subject as one that is constituted in the act of predication. Hegel's critique thus undermines the oppositions and distinctions of metaphysics from within and avoids the contradiction into which Nietzsche falls.

Hegel's virtue, of course, is not simply that he avoids a contradiction to which Nietzsche succumbs; it is rather that he is led by his consideration of the speculative character of language and thought to a much richer conception of reason and subjectivity than Nietzsche. As we saw in chapter 5, Hegel's immanent critique of the categories of the understanding yields a dialectical conception of the subject, that is a conception of the subject as constituted in the activity of speaking and thinking. Such a dialectical subject is a social, developmental subject for Hegel; it is one that comes to be a true subject only when it recognises the inadequacy of trying to understand itself as an independent individual, and instead explicitly acknowledges and manifests its social character.

Nietzsche's critique of the categories goes hand in hand with a very different conception of subjectivity. Just as life is opposed by Nietzsche to the categories of metaphysical thinking, so authentic subjectivity is understood by him as the antithesis of what he sees as the traditional conception of the soul. The authentic subject for Nietzsche is natural and instinctual, rather than spiritual; it is multiple and ever-changing, rather than unified and continuous; it pursues its own egoistical ends, rather than seeking conformity with reason or the will of God. Like that of Hegel, Nietzsche's 'subject' is dynamic; but, unlike that of Hegel, its dynamism is rooted in its instinctual 'life', rather than in its social and historical character. Such a subject is the embodiment of chaotic, pulsating reality, and is considered to be a 'true' subject when it manifests the vigour and abundant energy of life. Ideal human subjectivity for Nietzsche is therefore a strong, vigorous self which demonstrates its heroic nobility by defiantly confronting whatever opposes it. The 'true' Nietzschean thus *confronts* the darker side of life, *confronts* the weak mode of being, and of course *confronts* the metaphysical conception of the subject. This heroic subject recognises that it is a member of a community of 'higher' beings, but its predominant posture is antagonistic and individualistic. And in this respect there is a similarity between Nietzsche's notion of the subject and the metaphysical conception of the subject which he endeavours to overthrow. Nietzsche may reject what he sees as the monadic atomism of the traditional 'soul', and he may replace it with the notion of subjectivity as a nexus of competing desires and instincts, deeply embedded in the flux of 'life'; but by conceiving of 'true' subjectivity as heroic and individualistically self-assertive, he preserves, and indeed exceeds, the very 'atomism' he is attacking.

Nietzsche fails to free philosophy from the metaphysical conception of the subject as something isolated and independent because he fails to free philosophy from the *form* of oppositional thinking, and thus conceives of the 'true' subject as confronting and asserting itself against – that is, in opposition to – the metaphysical subject. In Nietzsche's philosophy there is no dialectical resolution of conceptual oppositions, and there is no dialectical redefinition of the subject from something independent into something essentially constituted by social relations and historical development. The overall difference between Hegel and Nietzsche can thus be put like this: Nietzsche opposes the metaphysical subject with 'life' and with the heroic subject, and thereby restricts heroic, Dionysiac subjectivity to the forms of opposition and independence which are features of the very subject he opposes. Hegel, on the other hand, resolves the oppositions of metaphysical thinking through his dialectical critique of the categories, and thus challenges both the metaphysical and the heroic conceptions of the subject through his dialectical redefinition of subjectivity.

In this final chapter I wish to bring this difference between Hegel and Nietzsche into sharper focus by looking at their theories of tragedy. One could, of course, conclude a comparative study of Hegel and Nietzsche by considering their treatment of other areas of mutual concern, such as Christianity or history, but neither area in my view allows us to highlight the differences between the positive conceptions of life offered by the two philosophers quite as clearly and concisely as does the question of tragedy. A discussion of Christianity, for example, would allow us to consider Hegel's positive conception of man, since he views Christianity as consciousness, in the form of pictorial representation (*Vorstellung*), of the very same dialectical character of life that philosophy knows as the speculative Idea. But since Nietzsche sees Christianity in a primarily negative light, as an example of other-worldly – metaphysical – consciousness, we would be forced to repeat much of what has been said in previous chapters about Nietzsche's critique of metaphysics. A discussion of the question of history, on the other hand, would provide a good opportunity to compare Hegel's dialectical conception of man with Nietzsche's Dionysiac conception, but this question, I believe, would require much more extensive consideration than it is possible to provide within the confines of a concluding chapter. Furthermore, although the question of history is extremely important for Nietzsche, it is possible to argue that the question of tragedy is even more important since Nietzsche equates the Dionysiac mode of being – both in his early, romantic conception of it, and in his later, heroic conception of it – specifically with the *tragic* attitude to life.

In one way or another Nietzsche is always preoccupied with the question of tragedy. The nature, origin and promise of tragedy form the central concerns of Nietzsche's first book, *The Birth of Tragedy* (1872), and it is in that book, as he himself was keen to emphasise in later years, that we encounter the antithesis between the Dionysiac or tragic mood and the theoretical, rationalistic spirit of Socrates, which was to be of lasting importance throughout Nietzsche's life.[1] This antithesis may not form the centre of the book, as Nietzsche later wishes to claim, but it is an important theme nevertheless, and it prefigures what will become the central preoccupation of his later writings. Indeed, if Nietzsche's later philosophy has one identifiable aim, it is surely to give variegated expression and stylistic embodiment to the Dionysiac, tragic mood (now considered in a more heroic, less romantic way than in *The Birth of Tragedy*), and from within that mood to pass judgement on Christianity, metaphysics and traditional morality.[2] To understand what Nietzsche wants to achieve throughout his philosophical career, therefore, we must examine his theory, or rather his frequently ill-defined sense, of what tragedy is.

In *Ecce Homo* Nietzsche claims that, with the possible exception of Heraclitus, no other philosopher before him has understood what the terms 'Dionysiac' or 'tragic' mean. No philosopher, therefore, has been able to grasp the tragic character of human life. Tragic sensibility informed the culture of the ancient Greeks, but it was never adequately transformed into philosophical 'pathos' or tragic *wisdom*. 'In this sense', Nietzsche argues, 'I have the right to understand myself as the first *tragic philosopher*.'[3] This is a large claim, and we must remember that it is not merely a claim about aesthetics. It is a claim to be the first philosopher to have discovered and embodied the 'truth'.[4] If we are to pursue a Hegelian critique of Nietzsche, therefore, we must take Nietzsche on on his own terms, and that means that we must eventually confront Hegel with Nietzsche's theory of tragedy.

Nietzsche on tragedy

Like the rest of his philosophy, Nietzsche's understanding of tragedy undergoes a decisive change as his romantic devotion to Schopenhauer and Wagner gives way to a more 'scientific', more 'critical' mode of thinking in the mid-1870s. The early theory is set out in vivid, alluring, though frequently confusing, terms in *The Birth of Tragedy*.[5] Nietzsche's view of tragedy in that work rests on his distinction between two forms of aesthetic, psychological and metaphysical drive: the Apolline and the Dionysiac.[6] The Apolline drive, manifest in an unconscious form in dreams and in a consciously artistic form in the arts of sculpture and epic poetry, serves to conceal the horrific character of life from our view by transforming that life into images of delightful, idealised individuality. The images thus produced entrance us through their freedom from 'the wilder emotions', through their proportion and balance, through what is traditionally referred to as their serenity. This is not to say that they are by any means bland or insipid: 'the serious, the troubled, the sad, the gloomy, the sudden restraints, the tricks of accident, anxious expectations, in short the whole divine comedy of life, including the *Inferno*, also pass before [the aesthetically sensitive man]'; but the overall impression is still one of light and delight.[7]

An important aspect of our enjoyment of Apolline art is the fleeting sense we have that what we are seeing is illusion or mere appearance (*Schein*).[8] We delight in illusion which we know to be illusion: 'I see Apollo as the transfiguring genius of the *principium individuationis* through which alone redemption in illusion [*Erlösung im Scheine*] is truly to be obtained.'[9] In Apolline art, therefore, we knowingly protect ourselves from 'the terrors of nature' through the use of illusion, just as our eyes protect themselves from the glare of the sun by forming dark spots.[10] Apolline art thus involves consciously and creatively falsifying a life which we know to be terrible; it does not involve trying to convince ourselves that life is essentially rational and subject to critical improvement as, so Nietzsche claims, Socrates and 'theoretical man' have done.

The effect of Dionysiac art is more difficult to explain. Dionysiac art does not so much conceal life as rather reveal and express life. As individuals we are horrified by the wild, destructive character of life, and in Dionysiac art we are confronted with its untameable energy. However, Dionysiac art is also a form of illusion which enables us to bear the life with which we are confronted. Dionysiac art achieves this, not by concealing life from view and thus abolishing the sense of horror we feel, but by swathing our horror in a deep feeling of rapturous bliss. At the same time as we are faced with life, there is engendered within us a mysterious sense that we have lost our individuality in the wash of cosmic oneness. Life is thus no longer felt to be simply something which threatens our individuality, but also something into which we dissolve and in which we participate. The illusion produced by the Dionysiac drive, therefore, is not pictorial, but one of ecstatic rapture. If the Apolline drive is manifest in dreams, the Dionysiac drive is thus manifest in intoxication or *Rausch*.[11]

Dionysiac art puts us in contact with, and expresses, the darkness and horror of life; and yet at the same time it delights and redeems us. But the connection between revelation and illusion in Dionysiac art is in fact even closer than I have indicated here. The illusion or rapture produced by Dionysiac art does not simply save us from the chaos with which Dionysiac art confronts us; that illusion itself reveals a further dimension of reality which otherwise remains inaccessible to us and which we find comforting rather than horrifying: life's aesthetic creativity. This point is not developed systematically by Nietzsche, but it is suggested in various passages. In the course of his discussion of lyric poetry (a predominantly Dionysiac art), Nietzsche argues that man can only know about the eternal essence of art by melting into, and becoming one with, the 'primordial artist of the world' (*Urkünstler der Welt*) in the act of artistic creation.[12] The insight gained into the nature of art is also, it seems, insight into the aesthetic, creative character of being, awareness that art has its source not merely in human psychology, but in metaphysical, cosmic reality itself. This point is echoed towards the end of the book in the course of a discussion of tragedy. Here Nietzsche's point is less concerned with the artist and more with the audience. Tragic art, whose Dionysiac effect is to give us a sense of oneness with being, has also, we are told, to convince us 'that even the ugly and disharmonic are part of an artistic game that the will in the eternal amplitude of its pleasure plays with itself'.[13] As well as bewitching us, therefore, Dionysiac illusion reveals to us the aesthetic character of being.

The ambiguity involved in the notion of a form of *illusion* which is also the only means whereby the creative dimension of metaphysical *reality* can be made known to us occasionally causes Nietzsche to forget that the Dionysiac sense of unmediated oneness with being is in fact a form of illusion. In §17, for example, Nietzsche describes the effect of Dionysiac rapture in highly 'realistic' terms: 'we are really for a brief moment primordial being itself, feeling its raging desire for existence and joy in existence'.[14] However, in other passages Nietzsche uses words like *Zauber* (charm or magic) and *mystisch* (mystical) to describe the Dionysiac state of intoxication.[15] Moreover, the conditional tone of some passages serves to remind us that, although the Dionysiac sense of oneness with 'the primordial unity' (*das Ur-eine*) reveals to us an otherwise inaccessible dimension of reality, Dionysiac rapture is nevertheless itself artistic illusion.[16] The point is made explicit in §25; referring to the Dionysiac art of music and to the mainly Dionysiac art of tragedy, Nietzsche explains that 'both transfigure a region in whose joyous chords dissonance as well as the terrible image of the world fade away charmingly; both play with the sting of displeasure, trusting in their exceedingly powerful magic arts'.[17]

In two different ways, therefore, art fulfils a 'metaphysical intention to transfigure' (*metaphysische Verklärungsabsicht*) in Nietzsche's view.[18] Apolline art transforms life into an Olympian spectacle of majestic, free individuals; Dionysiac art, on the other hand, bewitches us into feeling one with nature and thereby grants us insight into the ultimate aesthetic creativity of reality. These two features of aesthetic experience suggest two possible meanings for Nietzsche's intractable phrase: 'it is only as an *aesthetic phenomenon* that existence and the world are eternally *justified*'.[19] Life for Nietzsche is painful, horrifying, without an intrinsic moral structure; but it is justified and held to be worthy of affirmation when it is given a beautiful though false form, or when we realise that it is in itself a creative artistic reality.

Tragedy is the highest art in Nietzsche's view because it combines both the Apolline and Dionysiac perspectives in one art-form.[20] It is generated out of a 'musical' sense of the world's Dionysiac character and by the Apolline, pictorial representation of that 'musical' mood. Tragedy is therefore able to justify our experience in both the above-mentioned ways.[21] It offers us the delightful Apolline vision of heroic individuals – idealised men and women – acting nobly and majestically, and consequently it terrifies us when we see such splendid individuals suffering or destroyed. And yet the tragic destruction of the heroes also thrills us, fills us with 'a higher, much more overpowering joy', because it excites in us a profound Dionysiac sense of oneness and identity with the metaphysical forces that destroy the heroes, and thereby allows us to glimpse 'the highest artistic primal joy in the bosom of the primordially One'.[22] These two aesthetic moments are not simply wedged clumsily together in Nietzsche's view, but are fully integrated with one another. We see a world of Apolline individuals and yet that Apolline world itself intimates the Dionysiac primordial unity behind it in the destruction of those individuals. The sense of oneness we feel, the 'metaphysical comfort' of tragedy, is thus something we enjoy at the same time as we see the individuals on stage. We do not, therefore, lapse into completely blind rapture; rather we *see* and also dissolve into what lies beyond what we see. In Schacht's words, tragedy 'enthralls' us.[23]

Nietzsche's dualistic aesthetic theory of the Apolline and the Dionysiac drives provides an intriguing answer to the problem of tragic effect: why are we both horrified and satisfied, pleased even, by the spectacle of tragedy? Nietzsche claims to be able to answer the problem by reference to purely *aesthetic* criteria, by drawing on his insight into two modes of distinctively aesthetic experience: the delight we take in images, in *Schein*, and the mystical bewitchment of music. Nietzsche thus need not have recourse to moral criteria as Hegel is indirectly alleged to do, nor to 'pathological' criteria like Aristotle (though it must be said that Nietzsche's talk of redemption (*Erlösung*) through the loss of self has a suspiciously 'pathological' ring to it).[24]

Nietzsche's early theory of tragedy is rooted in his Schopenhauerian metaphysics. The distinction which Schopenhauer drew between the world of appearance – the spatio-temporal realm of objects and living things – and the sphere of the will informs the whole of Nietzsche's book. Nietzsche is by no means uncritical of Schopenhauer, however.

He disagrees with Schopenhauer's account of lyric poetry;[25] he locates the source of aesthetic production in artistic 'impulses' (*Kunsttriebe*) rather than in the contemplative, knowing subject;[26] and his evaluation of the will, despite his view of it as horrifying and painful, is predominantly affirmative and 'joyful', rather than merely negative and gloom-ridden[27] (an attitude reflected in his belief that exhilaration and metaphysical comfort, and not renunciation and resignation, are the true effects of tragedy).[28] Yet Schopenhauer's metaphysical subordination of man to the will remains an essential feature of Nietzsche's scheme. This, I believe, has important consequences for Nietzsche's view of tragic downfall. Like Schopenhauer, and in contrast to Aristotle, Nietzsche sees the tragic hero as destroyed by supra-personal cosmic forces. That is not to say that man is merely a victim for Nietzsche – Nietzsche recognises that the hero 'commits sacrilege' (*frevelt*) by overstepping the limits of individual action – but the final cause of the hero's destruction, that with which the heroic individual comes into conflict, is a supra-personal, metaphysical force 'behind' the actions of men. The tragic hero 'suffers in his own person the primordial contradiction that is concealed in things'.[29]

Tragedy in Nietzsche's view does not therefore have any moral dimension. There is no sense that the hero, having infringed the moral order, gets his just deserts; there is no 'triumph of the moral world order' (*Sieg der sittlichen Weltordnung*).[30] The tragic outcome is not the result of the conflict between individuality and the moral structure of the world, but between individuality and 'the misfortune in the nature of things' which destroys individuality. Consequently, even though he revels in the hero's destruction, the artist does not point an accusing finger at the tragic hero and does not blame him for his 'sin'. The moral notion of sin, Nietzsche believes, denigrates and condemns the sinner; the tragic concept of 'sacrilege' (*Frevel*), on the other hand, celebrates and 'justifies' the hero in his noble conflict with the all-powerful elemental forces. Tragedy therefore affirms both the hero's nobility and his destruction.[31]

Nietzsche does not banish justice from tragedy altogether, however. He does not see the outcome of tragedy simply as the breakthrough of Dionysiac reality into the realm of Apolline individuals. In Aeschylus's dramas in particular, Nietzsche praises 'the profound . . . demand for *justice*'.[32] Aeschylean tragedy contrasts the immeasurable suffering of the bold individual with the distress of the gods, and also presents 'the power of these two worlds of suffering to compel reconciliation'.[33] The individual who oversteps the limits of individuality is thus apparently returned to those limits and reconciled with what he opposed, through the workings of eternal justice. Yet these tones of reconciliation and the sense of justice which informs Aeschylean tragedy do not serve any moral function; their rationale is purely aesthetic. The presence of justice in tragedy is the product of the Apolline drive, of the 'cheerfulness [*Heiterkeit*] of artistic creation that defies all misfortune'. Aeschylean justice is therefore an Apolline illusion which conceals the awful Dionysiac reality behind a surface of 'measured' (*maßvoll*) restraint.[34] On one level, therefore, it appears as if the individual is restored to the limits he has transgressed by Apolline justice, but at a deeper level, the power which confronts the individual is known to be Dionysiac. The core of tragedy thus remains the spectacle of human nobility and heroism crushed by cosmic forces. This spectacle is profoundly painful for us, but it also delights us because we gain through it a consoling feeling that we are essentially one with those cosmic forces.

As we have said, Nietzsche does not treat tragic heroes as mere victims. Their fate is to a certain extent a consequence of their own action. Nevertheless, the sense that hubris brings its own downfall is diminished by the fact that supra-personal, cosmic force is what ultimately destroys the hero. The emphasis in Nietzsche's early theory of tragedy is therefore less on the dire consequences of human action and more on the *vision* of Dionysiac reality.[35] This is seen clearly in the emphasis Nietzsche places on the origins of tragedy in the spirit of music. Tragedy, like lyric poetry, has its source for Nietzsche in 'a *musical mood*', a deep feeling of oneness with the 'primordial contradiction' and 'primordial pain' of reality.[36] The lyrical images or tragic plot mediate that musical mood and allow us to see a pictorial reflection of it. Such art-forms centre on the *vision* of truth in two senses, therefore: in the sense of intuitive feeling and of contemplative imaging. Nietzsche's theory of tragedy is thus mainly concerned with the subjective side of tragedy – the author's state of mind in producing it and the audience's response to it – and only to a lesser extent with the objective problem of what constitutes tragic action.[37]

In Nietzsche's later post-Schopenhauerian and post-Wagnerian phase, his theory of tragedy undergoes some important changes. Not only is there much less emphasis on the theatrical and dramatic expression of the tragic mood and much more on the tragic attitude in general, but the character of that attitude changes, too. The nature of these changes is best demonstrated by reference to Nietzsche's own later comments on *The Birth of Tragedy* in the 1886 preface, 'Attempt at a Self-Criticism', and in *Ecce Homo* (1888).[38] In Nietzsche's later theory the Dionysiac moment remains central to tragedy; tragedy is still thought of as essentially a vision of a terrible, horrifying reality. However, the quality of tragic pleasure and satisfaction is now different. In *The Birth of Tragedy* satisfaction lay in the mystical sense of oneness with being which tragedy was held to evoke in us, that is in the metaphysical consolation brought about by the bewitching feeling that we have cast off our burdensome individuality and submerged ourselves in the whole. In the 1886 preface this consolation is repudiated as romantic;[39] indeed, in *The Gay Science* (1882) the whole notion of 'redemption from oneself' – so prominent in *The Birth of Tragedy* and of distinctly Schopenhauerian and Wagnerian heritage – is criticised for being a sign of a form of life which lacks inner strength.[40] In the preface Nietzsche quotes a passage from *The Birth of Tragedy* in which he had talked enthusiastically of a new heroism dawning in the nineteenth century, a heroism critical of the value of the science and 'optimistic' rationalism which had dominated Western thought since Socrates and which, he thought, was stultifying modern German culture. Nietzsche had said that such an attitude of heroism, heralded by Kant and Schopenhauer, was gradually replacing science with Dionysiac wisdom, and he had described a new generation, 'with this heroic passion for the tremendous', resolutely confronting a pessimistic reality. But he had added that such an attitude needed at times the metaphysical consolation which tragedy – especially Wagnerian tragedy – affords.[41] Commenting on that passage in the preface, however, Nietzsche now insists that heroic individuals should not need metaphysical consolation; they should rather make do with 'this-sided' consolation. This involves no longer seeking to flee into a beyond, no longer yearning for the delight of forgetting the confrontation with terrible reality, but learning to find joy in that confrontation itself. The tragic attitude has now been redefined by Nietzsche; it is now equated with the heroism which revels in its own heroic strength, which 'laughs' in its confrontation with Dionysus because it has a sovereign sense that it is powerful enough to bear the god. The tragic attitude now involves what Nietzsche calls 'pessimism of *strength*' and is opposed to the romantic mood which permeated *The Birth of Tragedy*.[42]

The total identification of the tragic and the heroic mood forms the dominant theme of Nietzsche's later theory of tragedy. The tragic spirit now combines heroic effort and heroic wholeness or self-possession. It is a spirit which, like Zarathustra's, boldly confronts the inevitability of destruction, and indeed which vehemently affirms that destruction as the means to further heroic creativity.[43] The clearest statement of this tragic feeling is to be found in *Twilight of the Idols*:

Affirmation of life even in its strangest and sternest problems, the will to life rejoicing in its own inexhaustibility through the *sacrifice* of its highest types – *that* is what I called Dionysiac, *that* is what I recognised as the bridge to the psychology of the *tragic* poet. *Not* so as to get rid of pity and terror . . . but, beyond pity and terror, *to realise in oneself* the eternal joy of becoming – that joy which also encompasses *joy in destruction* . . .[44]

When discussing tragedy in his later writings, Nietzsche continues to concentrate on the tragic vision or feeling. However, there is a shift away from the vision of the chorus, in which the individual self is submerged in undifferentiated communion with others, to the vision of the isolated heroic individual. Tragic feeling still entails being one with the eternal joy in becoming, but that does not diminish the sense that our individuality is irreducible. Tragic feeling does not now involve the loss of self, but the conviction that the creativity and destructiveness of life itself is expressed in the very heroic individuality which is confronted by life. In his later writings, therefore, Nietzsche comes more and more to identify with the subject of tragedy himself: the heroic individual. This is why Nietzsche does not simply describe himself as the first philosopher to understand tragedy, but as the first tragic philosopher.[45] Nietzsche sees his own position as a philosopher as itself tragic. He must confront and affirm 'the most detested and notorious sides of existence',[46] and he must also joyfully affirm the suffering and the sacrifice of his personality which that philosophical heroism entails. His philosophical task forces him, so he feels, into depths of isolation, hostility and self-fragmentation which constitute the tragic price he has to pay for his heroic affirmation of truth. The tragic twist, of course, is that he can only prove his heroism by showing that he can bear that price. Suffering is thus a value in itself in Nietzsche's philosophy because it proves the worth of the tragic soul that bears it.[47]

Nietzsche's later theory of tragedy is an important manifestation of his affirmation of life and of the self. The early Nietzsche had shared Schopenhauer's positive evaluation of self-negation, although of course he understood it in terms of the magic of intoxicated rapture and not in terms of pure selfless contemplation or asceticism. Nietzsche's hostility in his early phase towards the idealistic morality of self-denial was thus counterbalanced by his retention of an aesthetic form of ecstatic self-abandonment. As Nietzsche began to break with Schopenhauer, however, he began to shun all such self-negation as romantic or metaphysical, and he sought rather to stress the irreducibility and omnipresence of selfish interest. In his later philosophy, Nietzsche's attack on traditional, altruistic morality consists in exposing the self-oriented basis on which that morality is founded. Human life is selfish, Nietzsche maintained, and that cannot be avoided. The only proper course for man to take, therefore, is to affirm that selfishness in its strongest, richest and most powerful form. In a world where 'transcendent' value is lacking, where nothing compensates for death, Nietzsche located true value in the heroic nobility of spirit which confronts death and life without debilitating trepidation or rancour. The tragic mood which affirms life is thus seen by Nietzsche as the only hope for the qualitative revival and perfection of man, as the only defence against what he sees as the Christian, romantic and metaphysical denial and denigration of life.[48]

The contrast between the tragic and the moral views of life, which we saw in *The Birth of Tragedy*, comes into full prominence in the later philosophy. The point is made forcibly by Nietzsche in *Daybreak*. Tragedy, he says, is not concerned with 'guilt and its dire outcome'; it does not present us with a moral condemnation of man's sinful deeds. *Macbeth*, for example, is not intended to warn us of the evil of ambition, any more than Wagner's *Tristan und Isolde* is meant as a tract against adultery. These tragedies do not condemn passion, but celebrate it, even in its destructive consequences. The tragic poet, Nietzsche writes, is proclaiming his joy at life, and declaring: 'it is the stimulant of stimulants, this exciting, changing, dangerous, gloomy and often sun-drenched existence! It is an *adventure* to live'.[49]

This is not to say that Nietzsche completely denies the notion of tragic guilt.[50] As we saw in *The Birth of Tragedy*, however, Nietzsche wants us to come to a positive, tragic evaluation of guilt, rather than a negative, moral one. To accuse someone of sin in a moral sense, Nietzsche believes, is to burden them with bad conscience, to make them feel that they are deeply in the wrong. The tragic poet, on the other hand, wants to achieve the opposite effect. His aim is, 'through poetry, to imbue sacrilege with dignity' (*dem Frevel Würde anzudichten und einzuverleiben*), to celebrate human power, audacity and independence, and thereby to banish bad conscience.[51]

The tragic philosopher affirms what is terrible in life, and he also affirms the heroic freedom which itself proudly celebrates man's 'sinful' deeds. In affirming what is terrible, therefore, the tragic spirit affirms *itself* as a source of that terror; and this bring us to the most problematic area of Nietzsche's theory. An essential condition of the tragic spirit is the ability to bear suffering; but equally essential is the ability and willingness to inflict suffering, the readiness to destroy or sacrifice others when necessary.[52] This idea was suggested in *The Birth of Tragedy*,[53] but it comes fully to the fore in the later texts. Nietzsche is quite clear that he does not mean to confuse this heroic willingness to destroy with the destructiveness which stems from impoverished, resentful and therefore malicious life; he only praises the destructiveness which is an expression of 'an overflowing power that is pregnant with future', of creative, life-enhancing energy;[54] but the problem is not thereby removed.

A concrete example of what Nietzsche means is to be found in the character of Brutus in *Julius Caesar*. Nietzsche sees Shakespeare's portrayal of Brutus as a celebration of the independence and sovereign freedom of the human soul. But a condition of that greatness is the readiness to sacrifice even one's dearest friend to one's ambition: 'Independence of the soul! – that is at stake here. No sacrifice can be too great for that: one must be capable of sacrificing one's dearest friend for it, even if he should also be the most glorious human being, an ornament of the world, a genius without peer.'[55] The problem here is not that Nietzsche is legitimating disloyalty or treachery, but that his justification of the destructiveness associated with the tragic mood has a disturbingly cavalier ring to it. There is a criterion for distinguishing 'valid' from 'invalid' destruction in Nietzsche's philosophy, namely whether or not the destruction leads to further creativity. But this criterion – Nietzsche's notion of creativity – is itself only really understandable in subjective terms, as a mood. Such creativity remains unhelpfully vague and difficult to conceive as an objective process, since not all productive action is truly *creative* in Nietzsche's sense. The ultimate criterion for deciding the legitimacy or illegitimacy of destruction is therefore a subjective one. Nietzsche affirms destruction not so much because of the objective forms of human action and organisation that it may lead to, but because of the creative strength of spirit from which it emanates and which it will in its turn further. This strength of spirit is, however, only known to those who 'know' they have it, and is not ascertainable by everyone. It is therefore also not attainable by everyone. The right to create and to destroy 'creatively' is thus the privilege of the noble, heroic few. When we recall that Nietzsche wishes to reform the whole of modern culture (and therefore society) on the basis of this noble, tragic heroism, then the disturbing consequence of Nietzsche's view becomes apparent; for the fate of the many is to be in the frequently unjust and unpredictable hands of the noble few.

It should be said, of course, that Nietzsche is mainly concerned with the 'spiritual' and cultural domination of the weak by the strong. He is advocating an attitude of mind, a way perhaps of writing and thinking about the weak; he is not developing a sinister blueprint for political life. And yet he is a philosopher who does away with the distinction between the body and the soul. His cultural hierarchy is not, therefore, to be divorced from political and social hierarchy. The furtherance of Nietzsche's mode of being will have physical and political consequences; and that is where we are most disturbed, because Nietzsche's ideas about what an aristocratic, tragic society might actually look like are very rudimentary and by no means clearly thought through. The problem is not that we have incontrovertible evidence of inhuman intentions on Nietzsche's part – we do not have such evidence – but that we are just not sure how cavalier the treatment of political and social injustice and suffering would be in a Nietzschean society. After all, we remember that according to Nietzsche's interpretation Brutus had to be prepared actually to kill Caesar in order to preserve the independence of his soul. But on the other hand, of course, *Julius Caesar* is 'only' a play.

Having discussed the major feature of the later Nietzsche's tragic view of life – the affirmation of all that is questionable and terrible in life – and having briefly mentioned a problem that that raises for an understanding of what a *tragic* culture might look like, we should mention finally an important aesthetic moment in that affirmation which we have so far neglected; for Nietzsche's later conception of the tragic mood does not simply involve confronting the world of pain and suffering heroically, it also involves transfiguring it. This transfiguration appears to have two senses, although Nietzsche does not distinguish them systematically. The first entails having the strength to see 'the terrifying and questionable character of things' *as* beautiful. The transfiguration in this case is the product of our healthy, powerful attitude to life. We do not alter the 'ugly' things themselves, but see them through 'pleasure' (*Lust*) and *amor fati*, and thereby transfigure their ugliness into beauty for us. Similarly, we experience ourselves through the warm glow of Dionysiac fullness – 'from that height of joy where man feels himself to be altogether a deified form and a self-justification of nature'.[56] The second sense of transfiguration, on the other hand, involves idealising life itself, giving it a quasi-Apolline aesthetic form. The true artist actually idealises the sinner, perfects and 'deifies' his existence.[57] Here the victorious, heroic will does not simply affirm things as beautiful for itself; it issues in the concrete act of imposing beauty and simplicity onto things: 'Artists should see nothing as it is, but fuller, simpler, stronger.'[58] Whereas in the earlier theory, therefore, Apollo and Dionysus were the two antithetical artistic drives of the cosmic artist, Apollo has now become a moment of Dionysus himself.

The tragic, Dionysiac mode of being which Nietzsche celebrates in his later philosophy is opposed in two important ways to the alleged asceticism of the moral (including the Christian) view of the world. It boldly confronts the harsh reality which the moral view wishes to repress, and it transfigures the harsh reality which the moral view sees as 'sinful' and 'fallen'. It thus combines the realistic and the aesthetic instincts which the moral view is said to lack. It is in terms of this contrast that Nietzsche seems to see the theory of tragedy put forward by Hegel. Hegel's theory of tragedy is not mentioned by name in Nietzsche's work, but it is discussed indirectly. The belief that tragedy presents the 'triumph of the moral world order' is lined up alongside the theories of Schopenhauer and Aristotle as a suspect, life-denying, *moral* interpretation of tragedy, an interpretation generated by a weak mode of being.[59] The question that now concerns us is therefore this: Is Hegel's theory of tragedy really a moral one in Nietzsche's sense? Or might it not be that Hegel's view of tragedy can be turned against Nietzsche's to show up the lack of realism and the metaphysical inadequacies in Nietzsche's whole conception of tragic philosophy? In the next section we shall examine Hegel's theory of tragedy with this question in mind, and since Hegel's theory is much more closely rooted in his study of particular tragic dramas than Nietzsche's, we will need to refer to specific plays more frequently than was the case with Nietzsche.

Hegel on tragedy

Before we proceed we should briefly point out the limits and intentions of Hegel's theory of tragedy. Although he refers directly to many more plays than Nietzsche, Hegel is still a philosopher and not a literary critic. This means that like Aristotle, Schopenhauer and Nietzsche, he is interested above all else in the meaning of the terms 'tragic' and 'tragedy'. He is not attempting to give an exhaustive analysis of the plays he discusses, but only to explain why they might or might not be considered tragic. His task is not therefore merely expository and descriptive, but also critical. He wants to offer us a criterion by which we can decide whether all the plays (and experiences) which we call tragic truly live up to their name, or whether some are simply sad. This point should be borne in mind in case the impression is gained that Hegel's treatment of the various dramas he discusses is somewhat cursory.

Hegel distinguishes two different conceptions of tragedy: the Greek conception, which he finds represented in its greatest form in the plays of Aeschylus and Sophocles, and the modern conception, represented supremely in the plays of Shakespeare. Hegel, of course, makes wide reference to other dramatists, including Euripides, Racine, Schiller and Goethe, but Aeschylus, Sophocles and Shakespeare clearly command his greatest admiration. The broad difference between the Greek and the modern conceptions of tragedy in Hegel's view can be put quite simply: Greek tragedy is the tragedy of man's justified, substantial interests, whereas modern tragedy, on the other hand, is simply the tragedy of human character. In Greek tragedy, therefore, we witness the fate of individuals who, in the main, insist on certain principles of ethical, religious or political *right*; whereas in modern tragedy we see conflicts produced by human ambitions, desires and passions.[60] As Hegel himself devotes most of his time to Greek tragedy, we shall begin with that.

It is well known that Hegel saw Greek tragedy as a conflict of competing forces that are both in themselves rightful and justified. Yet the point is not always stressed that Hegel actually distinguishes two main types of Greek tragedy.[61] The first presents the conflict of rights in its pure form; it is that found in plays like *Antigone* or the *Oresteia*, in which legitimate principles of ethical, religious or political right clash in different individuals.[62] The second, however, deviates somewhat from that pure form; it is that found in *Oedipus Rex*, in which the conflict is between, on the one hand, the right of consciousness only to acknowledge as its own what man knows he has done, and, on the other hand, the course of actions which have been ordained by the gods and which man has unknowingly carried out.[63] Hegel does in fact recognise other forms of tragic conflict in Greek drama, but he considers them to be less important than the two just mentioned. In the lectures on aesthetics, for example, we learn no more than that such subordinate forms of tragic conflict are concerned partly with the individual's general relation to fate and partly with more particular relationships.[64] In the lectures on the philosophy of religion, on the other hand, Hegel gives us a concrete example of one such subordinate form of conflict, namely the *Hippolytus* of Euripides. Here, Hegel suggests, the conflict is brought about by Hippolytus's devotion to Artemis and to the ideal of chastity, and by the consequent desire of Aphrodite to take revenge on Hippolytus for ignoring the rights of sensual love.[65] Even though the subordinate forms of tragic conflict which Hegel has in mind need not always be primarily concerned with ethical, religious or political matters, therefore, or with the fundamental antagonism between man's conscious awareness and his unconscious deeds, they are still considered by Hegel to involve forces which have some degree of *right* to command assent. It should be said, however, that the plays of Euripides, in Hegel's view, tend frequently to locate the source of conflict in mere subjective emotion and passion (as is the case in most modern tragedy) and thus tend to diminish the rightfulness and justness of the character's motivation.

The main form of conflict which Hegel discusses is the first of those mentioned in the preceding paragraph, that is the straightforward clash of substantial rights which are embodied in different individuals. In such conflicts the tragic heroes are motivated not by jealousy or greed, but by ethical, religious and political interests that are legitimate and justified. Such interests include, for example, the familial bonds between parent and child, brother and sister, or husband and wife; the interests of the state or community as a whole, the patriotism of the state's citizens and the will of the ruler; and man's holy allegiance towards gods or a religious community.[66] These interests are justified and rightful in Hegel's view because they are *sittlich*, essential to the healthy organisation and life of the community. The term *sittlich*, of course, refers to duties which are enshrined in social practices and customs, rather than personal conscience.[67] In its fullest sense, indeed, *sittlich* means simply what is of substantial importance to the coherent, organised life of man;[68] and this means that it includes social ethics and family piety, but also that it includes state interests which may conflict with what society and the family demand.

The essence of the tragic conflict in the first form of Greek tragedy that Hegel discusses – say in *Antigone* or in *The Libation Bearers* – is this: an individual (Antigone or Orestes) is moved by a *sittlich*, substantial principle to act in order to safeguard or realise that principle. Antigone, for example, feels impelled to uphold the rights of family piety and respect for the dead, and give to her brother Polynices an honourable burial. Orestes is moved to avenge the murder of his father Agamemnon by his mother Clytemnestra. By pursuing their own particular justified interest, however, these characters are caused to violate another justified, rightful principle which they ought to re-spect. Antigone defies the legitimate authority of Creon, and Orestes denies his mother's right to avenge the sacrifice of her daughter Iphigenia for which Agamemnon was responsible. The tragedy of both Antigone and Orestes, therefore, is that they assert their own rights by committing a wrong against another. Although the charac-ters represent what is of the highest value, they – tragically – can only carry through their rightful interest in a one-sided, wrongful way.[69]

Hegel's account is famous, but it is not without its critics. It is acknowledged, for example by M.S. Silk and J.P. Stern, that this account admirably explains the conflict of the *Oresteia*, but they claim that it does not fairly represent the conflict in *Antigone*. Silk and Stern recognise that Creon and Antigone both represent *legitimate* interests, but they argue that the balance within Sophocles' play is nevertheless tilted in favour of Antigone and against Creon. 'Notwithstanding the legitimacy of his rule', they maintain, 'Creon was wrong – in breach of Greek ethics – to produce his edict proscribing the burial of Polynices's body and to punish Antigone as he did.' Hegel, in their view, overlooks this ethical wrong of Creon and reduces the play to an all-too-simple conflict of rights.[70] However, Silk and Stern have them-selves oversimplified Hegel's position. Hegel does indeed maintain that tragedy involves the conflict of rights; in the case of *Antigone* this conflict is between the legitimate interests of public welfare and state security, and Antigone's legitimate ethical duty to her dead brother.[71] But Hegel does not say that the conflict leaves these rights pure and uncompromised. His point, as I have already suggested, is that the conflict which ensues when principles of right are asserted in opposition to one another turns each right into a wrong. Indeed, it is the fact that principles, which are in themselves rightful, become wrong when asserted by inflexible individuals that makes the situation in plays like *Antigone* or the *Oresteia* so profoundly *tragic*.

Despite what Silk and Stern claim, therefore, Hegel is fully aware that from the perspective of Antigone's ethic of family piety Creon is in the wrong. Creon's tragedy for Hegel is precisely that in safeguarding the interests of his state he violates the ethical holiness of blood which he ought to have respected. But Hegel also insists at the same time that from the perspective of the welfare of the whole community Creon is justified in issuing his edict. After all, though Hegel himself does not cite these lines, Polynices was a man

who came
to burn their pillared temples and their wealth,
even their land, and break apart their laws.[72]

Antigone, whose devotion to the cause of her brother's honour is wholly justified and rightful, is thus herself in the wrong in not respecting the right of Creon to govern and the right of the state in which she lives to protect itself against its enemies.[73]

The second main form of conflict in Greek tragedy which Hegel discusses is that in *Oedipus Rex*. Here the tragedy is not one of deliberately chosen action. Oedipus does not knowingly bring himself into conflict with another legitimate right through his deeds. In what Oedipus has done – in killing his father and marrying his mother – he has not committed any deliberate wrong; he is not directly responsible for what he has carried out, but has simply been the victim of the gods. The tragedy of Oedipus for Hegel is therefore the tragedy of his assumed wisdom and innocence. As the wise, all-seeing king, as the one who solved the riddle of the Sphinx, Oedipus insists that it is his right and duty to discover how Laius was killed and also that it is his right to safeguard his innocence against the accusations of Tiresias; but in so doing, Oedipus tragically brings himself face to face with the terrible deeds he himself has actually committed. On the one hand, Oedipus is justified in assuming that he himself is not guilty of killing Laius, since he has no knowledge of carrying out the act; on the other hand, it is precisely this initial assurance that he is innocent which makes his consciousness tragically one-sided, for in laying claim to certain knowledge of his own condition he neglects the 'power of the unconscious'. By pursuing the legitimate desire to bring truth into the light, therefore, Oedipus brings himself into tragic conflict with the 'sins' of which he has remained ignorant, but which are nevertheless his own. (As Hegel points out, the Oedipus story parallels the story of Adam's Fall. Man who sets his right to *know* above all else, thereby gains knowledge of his sinfulness and tragically destroys his happiness.)[74]

These two examples, in Hegel's view, reveal the essential character of tragic conflict in Greek drama: individuals pursue what is a legitimate, rightful interest, and yet through pursuing that interest in an insistent manner, they commit a wrong or come to consciousness of a wrong that they have already committed.

And yet tragedy is not only a matter of conflict, it is also a matter of the result or *resolution* of that conflict. In Hegel's view what is essential to the resolution of tragic conflict is that the absoluteness of each side's claim to right is denied. The claims are not completely invalidated but recognised to have only the relative legitimacy of one-sided, partial purposes. The exclusive one-sidedness of each principle is, in Hegel's words, *abgestreift*, stripped away or negated, and a certain harmony is established.[75] This resolution may, however, take many forms. One form is found, for example, in *The Eumenides*, where the resolution is effected by the external or objective agency of Athene. The votes of the Areopagite court are equal for Orestes and the Furies; however, Athene resolves the conflict by allowing Orestes to go free and by giving the Furies a place of honour in Athenian life. Resolution may also take a more subjective form, however, in the sense that the acting individuals themselves give up their one-sided insistence on their right. This happens, Hegel says, in the case of Philoctetes, although Philoctetes only changes his mind on the advice and order of Heracles. An external *deus ex machina* is required, therefore, to effect the change of heart. A more beautiful form of resolution is seen, in Hegel's view, in *Oedipus at Colonus*. Although Oedipus is not brought to acknowledge any relative legitimacy in the claims of Creon and Polynices, he does come to dissolve the divisions within his own soul and to purify himself. As E.F. Watling writes, Oedipus is brought to a sense of 'his symbolic sacredness, as a person set apart, a sufferer in whom others may find redemption'.[76] Oedipus is, as it were, transfigured; once the source of the curse on Thebes, he now in his death becomes the source of strength for Athens.[77]

One should note here that, unlike George Steiner, for example, Hegel does not believe that a play must necessarily have an unhappy ending to count as a tragic play.[78] In the lectures on aesthetics, Hegel points out that certain plays unite aspects of tragedy and comedy in such a way that

the individual [*die Subjektivität*], instead of acting with comical perversity, is filled with the seriousness characteristic of solid [*gediegen*] concerns and stable characters, while the tragic fixity of the will is so far softened, and the depth of the collisions involved so far reduced, that there can emerge a reconciliation of interests and a harmonious unification of the individuals and their aims.[79]

Now, one might think that this fusion of the tragic and the comic modes might disqualify all such plays from counting as tragic in Hegel's view, but this is not in fact the case. It is true that Hegel refers to modern examples of this fusion of modes, such as Goethe's *Iphigenie auf Tauris*, simply as 'plays' (*Schauspiele*) or 'dramas' (*Dramen*); however, he still refers to the ancient Greek examples of this fusion of modes, such as *The Eumenides* and *Philoctetes*, as 'tragedies' (*Tragödien*). Furthermore, he also clearly identifies the peaceful resolution of the dramatic conflict in *The Eumenides, Philoctetes*, and *Oedipus at Colonus* as examples of 'tragic dénouement'.[80]

What is the difference, therefore, between an ancient Greek 'tragedy' with a peaceful resolution and a modern dramatic 'play' which ends peacefully? The decisive difference, it seems, lies in the fact that in a modern dramatic play the protagonists, in Hegel's view, are able *of their own accord* to relinquish their antagonistic purposes and reach a harmonious reconciliation with one another; whereas in the Greek examples of the hybrid mode which Hegel cites this is not the case.[81] In *The Eumenides* and *Philoctetes*, for example, a peaceful resolution to the conflict is only achieved with the help of an external mediator, whereas in *Oedipus at Colonus* the conflicts between Oedipus and Polynices, and Oedipus and Creon, are not in fact properly resolved, although Oedipus does achieve harmony and purity within himself and is called to the gods. For Hegel, therefore, it is the heroic single-mindedness and inflexibility of the conflicting sides involved, their unwillingness to come by themselves to any compromise with their antagonists, which distinguishes a tragedy from a simple dramatic play. A conflict between powerful opposing interests is thus already tragic in Hegel's view – even in a play which ends happily – if that conflict is so sharp that neither side will give way to the other before the intervention of some kind of external mediator or before one side is lifted out of the sphere of active conflict altogether by the gods and transfigured.[82] Such tragic inflexibility may of course lead to a disastrous, bloody conclusion, but it does not necessarily have to. Even in a play such as *Oedipus at Colonus*, therefore, which ends with the hero's glorious transfiguration, rather than his downfall, the conflict can still be considered tragic from a Hegelian perspective, since Oedipus does not seek reconciliation with either Creon or Polynices, or revoke his curse upon them, despite finding peace within his own soul.

The three Greek plays mentioned by Hegel in his discussion of the fusion of the tragic and the comic modes confront us with conflicts that are clearly sharp and 'tragic'; but they also hold out the hope that despite the presence of such sharp conflict in human life, peace, reconciliation and harmony can be attained. The conclusions of *The Eumenides* and *Philoctetes*, for example, present us with the vision of a civilised, 'harmonious actuality' (*einklangsvolle Wirklichkeit*), and the conclusion of *Oedipus at Colonus* presents us with the vision of an 'inner reconciliation' (*innerliche Aussöhnung*) which approaches, but does not quite attain, the depth of Christian inner blessedness.[83] These plays, therefore, show us harmony emerging peacefully out of difference and discord – an achievement which modern dramatic plays also show us (though there, of course, the differences and conflicts are not tragic, because not as acute) and an achievement which Hegel sees as the goal of man's historical development.[84]

Having said all this, however, it should be stressed that these particular Greek plays are not considered by Hegel to be the fullest or most complete tragedies, since they are the product of the fusion of the tragic with the comic mode. The most genuinely *tragic* form of resolution does not yield an obviously comforting result for Hegel – rather, it takes the form of catastrophe. When the individuals involved are so intimately bound up with the rights they assert that they cannot willingly give them up and bring about a reconciliation with their antagonists (as in a modern dramatic 'play'), or leave behind the sphere of active conflict by finding the inner peace achieved by Oedipus at Colonus, and when no external mediator (such as Athene or Heracles) is present, then the resolution of the conflict, the negation of the one-sidedness of the claims involved, necessitates the spiritual desolation, or even the physical destruction of the heroes.[85] Antigone and Creon clash and each violates the right of the other. Unbending as they are, the clash culminates in disaster. Antigone loses her life and Creon loses his son and wife. It is true that Creon eventually relents and rushes desperately to save Antigone, but only after Tiresias has warned him of the catastrophic price he has to pay for the life 'you sent ... to settle in a tomb'.[86] In such a resolution the conflicting rights of Antigone and Creon are reconciled with one another through the violent downfall of each.

A similarly violent end occurs of course in *Oedipus Rex*. There Oedipus's ostensibly all-seeing, but in fact tragically limited, consciousness is reconciled with the unwitting wrong he has committed, since Oedipus accepts that wrong as his own deed; and yet at the same time that reconciliation can only be effected through the destruction of Oedipus's vision and the loss of his innocence.

Violent though such endings are, Hegel believes they bring about an important sense of harmony and satisfaction in the audience. The source of that satisfaction is our sense that we have witnessed the workings of eternal justice.[87] Individuals, who through the pursuit of their own legitimate claims have tragically overstepped the bounds of legitimate action, or ignored the possibility of their own unwitting guilt, are destroyed. This justice is no external, cosmic power but the immanent dialectic of man's own action. Painful though it is, it makes profound sense to us, in Hegel's view, that proud, insistent, self-assured individuality eventually brings itself down. This justice is what in Hegel's understanding makes tragedy profoundly rational.

It is important to note that, *pace* Nietzsche, Hegel is not putting forward a simplistic theory of moral justice here. He is not proclaiming the victory of Good over Evil; the tragic heroes who suffer their catastrophic fate are not simply condemned for lack of virtue.[88] As both Aristotle and A.C. Bradley point out, there is nothing tragic about seeing an evil man fall.[89] What is it then that makes the eternal justice or fate which brings down Greek heroes and heroines so profoundly *tragic* for Hegel? Hegel's answer lies in his discussion of guilt and innocence. Greek heroes in Hegel's view are neither simply innocent nor simply guilty but both innocent and guilty at the same time. The characters are innocent insofar as they do not simply choose to pursue their justified claim. They act because as characters they are wholly identified with what Hegel calls their legitimate 'pathos'. They do not merely decide to act, but are motivated ineluctably by what they hold to be right. They are thus brought into conflict with another individual because of what they are and affirm. And yet they are not simple victims of their pathos either. They exercise freedom insofar as they freely stand by, and assent to, the pathos that moves them.

They consciously identify with it and assume responsibility or guilt for what they do. Although they do not choose the pathos that moves them, therefore, their one-sided insistence on their rights, which can often degenerate into childish stubbornness (as in Creon's case) or treachery (as in Clytemnestra's), is something they themselves wish to be, and are, responsible for. The tragedy of their actions is thus that in legitimately, but unbendingly, pursuing their own rights they incur the guilt of neglecting, and conflicting with, other rights. In this way they bring themselves to destruction through their own justified, but guilty actions.[90]

The tragic prospect with which we are confronted in those plays which end in catastrophe is, in Hegel's view, profoundly shattering; but it also makes sense.[91] It follows directly from the character of unbending human individuality. If right is to be realised in action, it must initially be given heroic individual embodiment.[92] But unbending heroic individuals persist in asserting their rights in a one-sided way until they are restrained by an external mediator, broken by the consequences of their deeds, or, perhaps, achieve inner peace and harmony. Until that point of transformation, desolation or destruction, such individuals stand by the pathos through which they collide with others and thereby incur guilt. The tragedy of the unbending hero, therefore, is that, without the staying hand of an Athene or the inner peace which Oedipus finds at Colonus, the hero will not relent before he is desolated or destroyed by what he does. This, for Hegel, is the inherent law of heroic human action. Indeed, tragedy is even more deeply rooted in human life than I have indicated; for not only must man be brought to suffering and pain by the consequences of the unrestrained and unrelenting pursuit of his right; in the absence of external mediation or inner self-purification, it is only through suffering and pain that man can ever free himself from his uncompromising self-assertion and learn to be truly – that is, not merely one-sidedly – *sittlich*.[93] It is thus only through 'dying' to his proud, insistent individuality that the hero can come to that full awareness of his *sittlich* communion with others which Hegel sees as the mark of true humanity and as the historical goal of man. As the chorus in the *Agamemnon* proclaim, therefore, Zeus 'has laid it down that wisdom comes alone through suffering'.[94]

In Greek tragedy for Hegel, conflict, suffering and pain are not imposed upon hapless victims by irrational forces or by chance. They emanate from man's own actions, indeed from man's own justified actions; and they are the gateway through which unchecked and unbending heroic individuals must pass if they are to achieve full self-understanding. And the fact that painful compromise or even destruction is seen to be the inherent rational consequence of heroic action is what reconciles us to the fate we see enacted on stage; it is what satisfies us. Here I think is the nub of Hegel's theory of Greek tragedy. For Hegel sees the satisfaction afforded by tragic catastrophe as stemming from the very same understanding that makes that catastrophe so deeply shattering. In Hegel's view, tragedy does not present suffering as the consequence of an irrational nature or cosmic will. Even in the case of a hero so ill-fated by the gods as Oedipus, suffering is something which man himself is responsible for, since Oedipus's suffering is not a direct result of the actions themselves which he has been fated to carry out, but stems rather from *his* wanting to discover the truth.[95] True tragedians thus do not push responsibility out onto the harsh and hostile world, but understand the noble hero's suffering as the result of his own activity. Even though the hero is justified in acting as he does, even though he feels compelled to act as he does, the responsibility for his fate is his. This insight into the noble hero's responsibility fills us with terror when we see him destroyed; but that very same insight also gives us a deep sense of the justice of his destruction. And it is that sense of justice which constitutes our tragic satisfaction. The essence of full tragic effect in Hegel's interpretation, therefore, is that the destruction of the tragic hero is understood to be shattering and just at the same time. We feel profound pain at the sight of human nobility or dignity destroying itself, but we feel consoled by the justice of the hero's fate. In Hegel's words, we are 'shattered by the fate of the heroes, but reconciled fundamentally [*versöhnt in der Sache*]'.[96] Hegel's position is thus not as different from Bradley's as Bradley thinks, therefore, when the latter says:

even the perception or belief that it must needs be that offences come would not abolish our feeling that the necessity is terrible, or our pain in the woe of the guilty and the innocent. Nay, one may conjecture, the feeling and the pain would not vanish if we fully understood that the conflict and catastrophe were by a rational necessity involved in the divine and eternally accomplished purpose of the world.[97]

Insofar as Hegel sees the spectacle of tragic destruction as itself satisfying, his theory is, of course, close to that of the early Nietzsche.[98] The difference between the two philosophers, however, is that whereas Nietzsche sees in the destruction of the hero the expression of man's irrational Dionysiac nature in which man can joyously lose himself, Hegel sees in that destruction the manifestation of reason and justice in human life.

It is the sober recognition that tragic conflict and suffering is the inherent rational consequence of the justified actions of individuals which Hegel believes purifies the feelings of fear and pity aroused by Greek tragedy. Tragic fear for Hegel is not, therefore, mere terror of external force, but fear of the eternal law within man which is called into being by man's own free action and which man brings down upon himself by infringing it. And tragic pity is no ordinary sense of being saddened or moved by another's misery, but involves being shattered by the fate of the hero and at the same time recognising the justification and positive worth of the tragic pathos which leads the hero to that fate. Tragic pity does not therefore merely mean feeling sorry for someone in their misfortune; rather it is profound sympathy, understanding and admiration for the nobility and stature which assumes responsibility for, and bears, pain.[99]

In Greek tragedy, according to Hegel, individuals are motivated by substantial, *sittlich* interests; in modern tragedy, on the other hand, he says individuals are motivated simply by human characteristics, by the wealth of their subjective passions.[100] Almost anything from the range of human emotions and interests can be the subject of modern tragedy because we, as moderns, are interested in human character as such. The modern hero may be motivated by 'universal' interests like honour or loyalty, or like Goethe's Faust, by the desire for the ultimate experience of life. Ethical motives may also play a part. But the modern hero may also be motivated by greed, ambition and jealousy.[101]

Modern tragedy does not therefore essentially deal with the clash of *rights*; it presents the clash between an individual's personality and the external circumstances and characters around him. Hegel exemplifies the difference by contrasting the cases of Orestes and Hamlet.[102] Orestes is justified in wanting to take revenge on Clytemnestra for the murder of his father Agamemnon. But Clytemnestra herself was justified in taking revenge on Agamemnon for the sacrifice of Iphigenia. Though both violate another's legitimate right, they do so out of their own legitimate concern for vengeance. Hamlet's cause is different, Hegel says. Hamlet is confronted by a crime: Claudius has murdered his brother, Hamlet's father, and married Gertrude, Hamlet's mother. There is no legitimate, *sittlich* justification for the murder, and Hamlet holds no respect for the king. He is not therefore confronted by a right he should acknowledge. As Bradley writes: 'what engrosses our attention is the whole personality of Hamlet in his conflict, not with an opposing spiritual power, but with circumstances and, still more, with difficulties in his own nature'.[103]

In Hegel's view modern tragedy does not necessarily result from the pursuit of *sittlich* interests – though it may do[104] – but rather from the multiplicity of human characteristics. Nor is Hegel arguing that modern tragedy necessarily stems from the exaggeration of human qualities (such as ambition) which are in themselves praiseworthy. For Hegel, the fate of Lear, for example, is rooted not in any valuable human quality but in Lear's initial foolishness in trusting to the flattery of two daughters and in mistrusting the silent, loyal Cordelia.[105] However, even though the conflict need not be *produced* by laudable human characteristics or by ethical or social principles, Hegel prefigures Bradley in arguing that modern characters have to arouse our interest and a degree of admiration to be tragic. Shakespeare's tragic characters achieve this because of their imagination and expressive power, because of the immediacy and richness of their individuality, because of what Hegel calls their strength of purpose or the greatness of their soul. Modern tragic heroes must have qualities on which we place spiritual value and cannot therefore be purely evil, though they can approach depths of evil and criminality not approached by the Greeks.[106]

Modern tragedy, therefore, is rooted in character. Individuals act out of character; their fate results from what they are and what they decide and do.[107] They have greater room for decision and intention than Greek characters – their inner world is altogether more complex and subtle – but they still combine both innocence and guilt as the Greeks did. They possess the character and passions given to them by nature and society, and they may even – like Macbeth – be tempted into action by external circumstances; but nevertheless *they* are ultimately the ones who take the decision to act and who carry out the act which leads to their downfall (or, as in the case of Hamlet, it is *they* who are ultimately responsible for the initial hesitancy and subsequent incaution which leads to their downfall). The fate of the hero is therefore a self-imposed ruin (*ein selbstbereitetes Verderben*), that is to say a ruin which follows from the one-sidedness of passion or character

for which the characters themselves must bear the final responsibility. [108]

The two main forms of modern tragedy Hegel discusses are differentiated by the kind of character involved. Due to the manifold
richness of purpose in modern tragic characters, Hegel recognises
that it is difficult to generalise about them, but he does identify two
main types. The first kind of character, exemplified by Macbeth,
Othello or Richard III, is distinguished by what Hegel calls 'firmness'
and 'consistency'. By this Hegel does not mean that these characters
never waver, nor that they never change or develop; but that their
character is dominated by the determined pursuit of an emotion, a
suspicion or an ambition which they intend to satisfy. Hegel thinks in
fact that modern characters develop much more than Greek characters, but that within that development they remain true to the passion
that motivates them. The changes in the internal condition of the
character are thus the consistent consequence of the force of the
character's motivation and of the conflict to which that gives rise. In
Hegel's eyes, therefore, Lear's 'madness' is as it were latent in his
original foolishness, and Macbeth's criminality follows directly from
his initial ambition. Such characters, Hegel says, bring ruin upon their
own heads through persistently clinging to themselves and their
purposes. [109]

The second kind of character Hegel discusses is directly opposed to
this one. Hamlet is not internally weak; he has a definite sense of purpose and identity, but his character is distinguished by a noble inwardness which is unwilling and unable to act decisively. When he learns
that his father was murdered, he thus knows well enough *what* he has
to do (i.e. avenge his father), but he is unsure *how* to do it, and he has
not got that vigorous sense of life which will carry him into action. He
does not rush into murder like Macbeth, but remains caught in the
inactivity of his melancholy, noble soul, reluctant and unable to
advance to real action and to engage with the present circumstances.
Hamlet waits and seeks for greater certainty about his father's death,
but even when he is certain of Claudius's guilt he comes to no firm
decision to act and lets himself be led by external circumstances:

In this unreality Hamlet now makes a mistake, even in what confronts him,
and kills old Polonius instead of the king; he acts too hastily when he should
have investigated prudently, while when the right energy was needed he
remains sunk into himself – until without his action, in this broad course of
circumstances and chances, the fate of the whole realm and of Hamlet's own
constantly withdrawing inner life has been unfolded. [110]

Hamlet is not therefore merely an innocent victim of external circumstances. Though circumstance and accident play a part in his death, they are depicted, as Bradley expresses it, so that they are felt to coincide with something in the hero himself, so that he is not simply destroyed by outward force: ' "This bank and shoal of time" is too narrow for his soul, and the death that seems to fall on him by chance is also within him.'[111] In this respect, therefore, although Hamlet's death may be brought about by chance and circumstance, it is nevertheless ultimately the result of, and in tune with, his own inwardness and his own hesitation (*das eigene Zaudern*), and as such it makes sense.[112] In fact in spite of the role that chance plays in many modern tragedies, Hegel thinks it is necessary that the destruction of the hero should make sense if it is to be *tragic*. However, the justice at work in modern tragedy is more abstract than in Greek tragedy in Hegel's view. Since the parties involved in the conflict are not themselves *sittlich*, there is no sense that *sittlich* interests are reconciled or brought into harmony at the end. We simply see the downfall of individuals at odds with their being-in-the-world. Often, indeed, modern justice appears to take the form of cold punishment; Macbeth and Richard III, for example, though not simply evil, deserve, according to Hegel, no better than they get.[113] I should add, however, that even in a case such as that of Macbeth, Hegel does not reduce the fate of the hero to a matter of *mere* punishment or retribution. Macbeth may deserve his fate in Hegel's view, but there is nevertheless genuine tragedy in the shattering spectacle of his greatness plunging itself into destruction. In the case of Hamlet, of course, though we may feel that it is rational that his noble inwardness should lead him into disaster, it would be absurd to talk of his being 'punished' for his hesitancy and, indeed, Hegel employs no such notion in his discussion of Hamlet.

One further element of modern tragedy which in Hegel's view distinguishes it from most Greek tragedy is the requirement that the individual himself be reconciled with his fate. What shape this will take depends of course, as Bradley points out, on the story and the character of the hero. It may appear in a religious form, as the feeling that one is exchanging earthly being for an indestructible happiness (as, for example, in Schiller's *Maria Stuart*); or, again, in the hero's recognition of the justice of his fall (as in *Othello* or *King Lear*); or at least the hero may show us that, in face of the forces that crush him to death, he maintains the tenacity and strength of his own will (as in *Macbeth*).[114]

Modern tragedy is very different from Greek tragedy in Hegel's account, but nevertheless retains important similarities with it. The main thing to note is that both Greek and modern tragedy present, for Hegel, the self-destructive fate of *one-sided* passion and character. Whether the characters are motivated by justified concerns or by the interests of ambition or whether, like Hamlet, they are too inward for this world, they suffer because *their* individuality conflicts with other individuals who make up their world or, indeed, with neglected aspects of their own being. Fearful and shattering though tragic catastrophe may be, in Hegel's view it is rational. Tragedy is rooted in a heroic age, an age of individuals acting largely by themselves or for themselves, and tragedy reveals the self-destruction inherent in that age.[115] As such it has a lesson for us, and the lesson is an extremely harsh one, above all in modern tragedy. The tragic consequences of man's actions often seem needlessly cruel and wasteful – Cordelia's death being perhaps the most frequently cited example – but, if Hegel is right, it is we, through our self-oriented and self-absorbed action (or inaction), who ultimately determine the sequence of events which culminates in that waste and who must ultimately bear responsibility for it. We are not simply the victims of blind fate or chance.[116] We are the tragic victims of the conflicts with people and circumstance that our own one-sidedly individual actions and character initiate.

In conclusion, therefore, three points seem to be important in Hegel's theory of tragedy. (a) Conflict and suffering are tragic when they derive from a character's *own* action or inaction. Circumstance and chance may play their part, but the tragic hero's destruction must be seen to follow ultimately from what he himself does, or at least from his own innermost moods and emotions. (b) Conflict is tragic when we see rightful action turn into wrong, or the legitimate pursuit of enlightenment confront individuals with unsuspected but shattering truths about themselves; or, alternatively, when we simply see the powerful human passions or the noble inwardness of great or worthy individuals lead to harm and destruction. (c) Conflict and suffering are tragic when they stem neither from mere villainy nor from external forces, but when they result from what one might call *innocent guilt*. Truly tragic conflict arises when we act out of what we respect or what we are, but fail to take account of our limitations. Our tragic fate, for Hegel, is to be reminded of those limitations by one means or another.[117] Tragedy, therefore, shows us not the pitiable sight of innocence crushed or weakness destroyed, but rather the *self-destruction* of man's uncompromising heroic freedom and greatness.

Such a view of tragedy should not leave us resigned, nor does it justify any Nietzschean intoxication or Bradleyian exultation; but it is profoundly sobering.

Concluding comparison of Hegel and Nietzsche

There are important differences between Hegel's and Nietzsche's theory of tragedy. Nietzsche's theory must be understood in the light of his rejection of what he sees as traditional metaphysical morality. To counter the 'moral' view of the world, Nietzsche emphasises two points. Firstly, insofar as man is guilty and sinful, tragedy idealises and glorifies that guilt as a noble virtue; it does not condemn the tragic hero as evil. Secondly, tragedy does not locate *ultimate* responsibility with the hero, since his fate is that he is to be destroyed by elemental, natural forces; we do not therefore witness the justified downfall of immoral men.

The striking feature of Nietzsche's theory of tragedy – especially the later theory, which is what primarily concerns us in these concluding pages – is how eager he is to avoid the negative connotations of human guilt. He does not wish to see in tragedy anything of a critique of heroic individuality. Although Nietzsche acknowledges that human 'sacrilege' itself leads to suffering and destruction, he exonerates man from blame by subtly shifting the ultimate responsibility away from him onto the eternally creative–destructive character of the world. The hero may overstep the limits of his individuality, but it is the natural *forces* at work within him and outside him – the Dionysiac character of life – which destroy him. The tragedy of human existence for Nietzsche – exemplified by the myth of Prometheus – is that man's greatest and most noble achievements lead him into conflict with the contradiction at the heart of things. Heroism must therefore accept the tragic fate that it is faced with a hostile world. The glory of man's existence, in Nietzsche's view, is that the heroic posture cannot ultimately be defeated by that hostile world, for man proves his heroic superiority precisely by affirming the inevitability of his downfall. The ineluctable destruction of the tragic hero is thus the source of tragic pain, but also the test and condition of victorious heroic nobility.

Hegel's view is somewhat different, although he agrees that tragedy affirms the nobility of the tragic hero. Hegel's discussion of tragic pity makes it quite clear that we are not merely to feel sorry for the hero's misfortune, but to appreciate the worth and the stature of the pathos or passion which leads to the hero's suffering. We are to acknowledge either the hero's personal greatness or the *sittlich* justification for what he does, or indeed both. Moreover, Hegel's explicit rejection of the moralistic view of tragic fate – his rejection, that is, of the view that tragedy merely shows Evil defeated by Good – also demonstrates that his attitude to the hero is by no means negative.

However, in contrast to Nietzsche, Hegel insists that tragedy presents a *critique* of the hero as well as affirming his stature. In *Antigone*, for example, both Antigone and Creon violate rights which they clearly ought to respect. Antigone is the daughter of a king and betrothed to a king's son, and so should respect the demands of kingly rule; Creon is a father and a husband and so should respect the holiness of family ties: 'There is thus immanent in both of them themselves that which each protests against, so that they are gripped and shattered by something intrinsic to their own being.'[118]

Although tragic heroes are led into conflict by their rightful interests or their character, and although they are actually brought down by other people, it is they, through their one-sided insistence on their own interests, who carry the conflict to its tragic end, and it is they who must bear ultimate responsibility for it.[119] The final cause of the hero's destruction is thus not a hostile world, but the self-contradiction at the heart of the hero's own heroism, the fact that the character's heroic self-assertion and persistence is at odds with his own best interests. Tragedy does not therefore simply express the vision of the condition into which man is cast; it enacts the immanent dialectic, the intrinsic rationale of self-destruction, within man's own self-oriented actions. The eternal justice which Hegel sees in tragedy is nothing other than this immanent dialectic of human action. It is not therefore merely an Apolline veneer over a Dionysiac reality, but the core of tragedy itself. Nor does it have anything other-worldly about it; it does not ultimately come upon man from the outside, but is initiated by what men themselves do: 'it is the deed itself which has created a law that now comes to dominate' (*erst die Tat hat ein Gesetz erschaffen, dessen Herrschaft nun eintritt*).[120]

The Nietzschean encounters the moment of tragic destruction as a *force* over against himself. He affirms it, but keeps it at a distance at the same time; it is always at one remove from the heroic spirit which confronts it. In Hegel's view, on the other hand, the moment of tragic destruction is inherent in man's own unbending heroic individuality; it is the self-contradiction within man's self-assertion and thus his own self-imposed fate.

If the spectacle of suffering is to be tragic, rather than merely sad or miserable, the hero must have the stature and dignity to engage a degree of sympathy and admiration, and so cannot be weak or merely evil; but his fate must also be seen to be the just consequence of his own action. The tragic hero need not necessarily intend to destroy himself, but tragically he will be responsible for his own fate. Now, to say that the tragic hero is responsible for his fate is not to maintain that he simply chose to act as he did, nor is it to imply glibly that he could or should have chosen to act differently. Such a claim would abstract from the concrete situation in which the hero finds himself. As I have shown, Hegel does not consider tragic characters to be completely and utterly responsible for what happens to them; but he does consider them to be ultimately responsible. Although the Greek hero is impelled to act by his substantial convictions, he nevertheless assents to what he does; and although the modern hero may be drawn near to conflict by circumstance, he nevertheless acts out of his own character and intentions. To say that the tragic hero is responsible for his fate, therefore, is to say that conflict flows from the actions of human beings and that man is not condemned by nature to eternal conflict and antagonism. Although human beings cannot simply decide to act differently, their situation is not one of irredeemable conflict; men can be brought to reconciliation. This, indeed, can be seen as the purpose of tragedy for Hegel: to lead men through an understanding of the dire consequences of heroic individualism to a true sense of reconciliation with one another.[121] The tragedian does not say that conflict ought never to arise; he shows how conflict does arise. But by revealing that conflict and contradiction are inherent in the heroic posture, he points the way forward to a non-heroic conception of life in which conflict and contradiction can be resolved. In tragedy, therefore, our sense of what man can and should be is transformed and redefined by the tragic fate of individuals which one sees acted out before one's eyes. Our initially heroic conception of man thus gives way to a consciousness which, like that of the Eumenides, has become truly conciliatory and *sittlich*, or, like that of Othello or Lear, has become fully self-aware.

No such transformation occurs in Nietzsche's philosophy. The heroic mood, the magisterial will to power, remains individualistic and heroic. The Nietzschean spectator of tragedy does not witness the self-contradiction produced by man's own heroism; rather, he sees the contradictions of the world into which man is cast, the inevitable contradiction between man and the world. Since man is not responsible for his tragic fate in Nietzsche's view, no change in man's life could mitigate his suffering. Tragedy does not therefore cause man to transform his heroic individualism into communion and reconciliation with others. Rather, it confirms the heroic pose as the only one able to confront and bear man's inevitable fate.

Here, I think, lies the fundamental difference between the two philosophers. For Hegel the moment of tragic negation or destruction in life comes from man's own hubris. In tragedy, therefore, man is brought to a sober awareness of the limits of his heroism, and he is directed towards a new life of reconciliation. For Nietzsche, however, tragedy does not primarily reveal the limits of man's heroism; rather, the forces of tragic destruction lie outside man as the catalyst or stimulant to man's own heroic affirmation, as a hurdle over which man may test his individualistic, gymnastic soul.[122]

For all Nietzsche's emphasis on the affirmation of tragic suffering, therefore, it is Hegel who is in fact touched more deeply by it, because Hegelian consciousness is actually transformed by that suffering. Nietzsche does not tie tragic suffering directly to human responsibility, so the individual does not feel the tragic destructiveness of life as essentially his own, but always 'overcomes' it, covers it up or pushes it away in the very act of affirming it. Nietzsche will say 'yes' to the tragic world, but only to defy it by giving it an aesthetic, fictional form. His heroic conception of man is not, however, altered by the pain and death which he sees confronting and flowing from the heroic life. And this I believe is the reason for Nietzsche's often cavalier attitude to the suffering of others. It is as if the other does not fully impinge upon Nietzsche's consciousness, but merely provides Nietzsche with the opportunity to demonstrate his strength. Indeed, Nietzsche perhaps says as much in *Beyond Good and Evil* when he exclaims: 'there are heights of the soul seen from which even tragedy ceases to be tragic'.[123] This emphasis on joyful energy and exhilaration suggests a mind which is neither touched deeply enough, nor sobered enough by the horrors he sees acted out before him. This is not to say, of course, that in Nietzsche's personal life his attitude towards the suffering he encountered was necessarily cavalier. He did after all volunteer to serve in the German army as a medical orderly in the 1870 war with France and saw the horrors of war at first hand.[124] But in his writings Nietzsche does seem to treat suffering – that of others and of himself – more as a stimulus for him to test his ability to overcome that suffering, than as a cause for genuine, and perhaps humbling, compassion and concern.[125]

In the light of what we have said about his keeping reality at a distance – and *distance* is of course essential to all nobility for Nietzsche[126] – Nietzsche's position does not seem so radically different from that of the pietistic Jesus whom he describes in *The Antichrist*.[127] Jesus is depicted by Nietzsche as the epitome of pietistic inwardness – sensitive to such an extent that he cannot resist or confront reality,[128] and at the end of *Ecce Homo* Nietzsche declares that he and his view of man are opposed to that of this Jesus: *'Dionysus versus the Crucified'*.[129] However, if Jesus is alleged to be an inward soul who denies the outside world and dissolves it into a mere symbol of an inner state of mind, Nietzsche is merely an inward soul who affirms that outside world. The terms in which Nietzsche's affirmation of the world is couched always refer us back to the effort of the inward soul in its commitment to reality; and that effort and emphatic insistence itself belies his openness to the world. As his continual emphasis on mood and his frequent use of modal verbs to describe and evaluate people show – the Gospels, for example, as products of 'weakness', are characterised by 'the blessedness . . . of not *being able* to be an enemy' (*die Seligkeit . . . im Nicht-feind-sein*-können)[130] – Nietzsche remains caught up in an inner world of psychological and physiological 'perspectives'. Nietzsche lacks a clear sense of how the self is objectified in concrete social situations because concrete social situations are invariably dissolved back into states of subjectivity.[131] His emphasis in the theory of tragedy is consequently on the heroic state of mind, not on the dramatic situation or plot, and he seems to have no true understanding of the objective dialectic of heroic individuality which Hegel sees enacted in tragedy.[132]

Nietzsche is a philosopher who prides himself on bringing to an end the tradition of other-worldly metaphysics; but he remains trapped within the subjective moods and perspectives to which he wishes to reduce human life, perspectives which are also at one remove from the world. Nietzsche thus fails to reflect on the objective character of subjectivity itself: he does not give adequate attention to the social forms which the heroic mode of being will generate, nor does he grasp the dialectical nature of the subject. In both these respects his philosophy lags far behind that of Hegel.

At the heart of the philosophies of Hegel and Nietzsche lies the question of tragedy, and through the consideration of that question the differences between the philosophers become clear. In Hegel's view tragedy reveals in an aesthetic mode the dialectical truth of man and nature, most fully revealed in the Christian religion and in speculative philosophy. The 'tragic' character of Hegel's *Logic*, for example, is evident from the fact that it is only through the 'death' of the categories, through the negation of their simple, one-sided determinacy, that the true complexity of thought can be understood.[133] And essentially the same thought, that man must be shown the limits of his finitude and his individuality if he is to be brought to true life in communion with others, forms the core of the Christian religion for Hegel.[134]

In Nietzsche's view the relation of tragic art to Christianity and speculative philosophy is quite different. For Nietzsche the self is essentially natural, instinctual and individual rather than social. Communion and association with others do not therefore constitute true human freedom for Nietzsche as they do for Hegel. This is not to say that Nietzsche is wholly insensitive to the value of communion and association, but that he only appreciates it insofar as it mediates the natural self in an external way and helps to produce sovereign, autonomous individuals.[135] Man's aesthetic creativity thus stems ultimately from his self-assertive individuality in Nietzsche's view, and tragedy is the expression of that natural human vitality in two senses. Tragedy glorifies the individual hero and his strength, and the aesthetic energy of the tragic artist transfigures that heroism into idealised beauty. Christianity and Hegelian speculative philosophy, as Nietzsche understands them, subject the self to a life-denying moral condemnation or logical negation and are thus opposed to tragic art.[136]

For Nietzsche, therefore, tragedy celebrates the heroism of confrontation. The tragic hero nobly confronts and affirms his tragic fate, and the tragic artist or philosopher nobly confronts and affirms the destruction of the tragic hero. Such 'heroism' lies at the heart of the later Nietzsche's critique of metaphysics, for Nietzsche criticises what he sees as the fiction of the discrete metaphysical subject by confronting it with 'heroic' physiological strength and life. Nietzsche's critique of that subject is not, however, radical enough, for since his

heroism itself remains individualistic, it retains a formal similarity
with the very metaphysical self which is the object of criticism. For all
his interest in tragedy, therefore, Nietzsche does not seem fully to
understand the dialectic of tragic hubris, and does not allow his
individualistic sense of selfhood to be transformed by it. Individual,
natural life remains the foundation of selfhood for Nietzsche, and the
'inauthentic' forms of community and social identity, such as
language, shared belief and rational institutions, can never do more
than merely mediate that natural life. In Hegel's view, on the other
hand, the dialectic of tragic hubris is all-important. Tragedy for Hegel
enacts in an aesthetic medium the immanent redefinition of the
individual subject which his own philosophy fulfils. From this
perspective, therefore, tragedy presents a critical challenge to the
metaphysical subject; but, equally, it presents a critical challenge to
the Nietzschean misconception of man. Individuality and instinctual,
natural life do not constitute the *foundation* of human freedom for
Hegel, but only the *beginning* of freedom, for freedom finds its fulfilment in the conscious unity and community of social existence. *Pace*
Nietzsche, therefore, man's need for community is not rooted in any
desire to deny individuality and seek refuge in the security of the herd;
it is rooted in a realistic understanding of the limits of individuality.
For Hegel man's individuality should neither be suppressed nor
privileged, but should be brought to fulfilment by being situated in
the context of communal interest and concern. However refined or
'sublimated' Nietzsche's ideal of individual strength and energy may
be, insofar as it fails to equate freedom with social harmony or *Sittlichkeit*, it remains the limited vision of a philosopher who has missed
the lesson of tragedy.

The final Hegelian charge against Nietzsche's tragic, aesthetic
philosophy is thus twofold: on the one hand, that Nietzsche has misrepresented the nature of tragic art by presenting it as the product of
man's creative energy, as the expression of man's individual, natural,
falsifying genius, rather than as the revelation of truths which point
man beyond heroic individualism to the value of community; and on
the other hand, that Nietzsche has misrepresented the character of
the Christian religion and speculative philosophy as other-worldly
and life-denying, whereas in fact, in their understanding of the tragic
limitations of heroic life, they are much more realistic than
Nietzsche. By means of these misrepresentations Nietzsche has been
able to present his own ideal of emphatic, exuberant individual

wholeness as the sole hope for mankind's future, and he has been able to denigrate the Hegelian and the Christian notion of communally constituted wholeness as weak and abstract. Hegel and Nietzsche are actually allies against metaphysical abstraction and against the fragmented weakness and 'decadence' of the modern age, but Nietzsche's failure to realise this prevented him from taking account of Hegelian objections to his own project.

Notes

1 *The Hegel–Nietzsche debate*

1 B. F. Beerling, 'Hegel und Nietzsche', *Hegel-Studien*, 1–2 (1961), 231.
2 See, for example, R. Schacht, *Nietzsche* (London, 1983), p. 1.
3 Beerling, p. 231.
4 It is not of course possible to discuss all the commentators who have ever mentioned Hegel and Nietzsche in one breath, but I have attempted to give a representative survey of the kinds of direct comparison that have been made. Reviews of some of the texts that I have not discussed or mentioned in the notes are contained in Beerling's article, in D. Tchijewsky, 'Hegel et Nietzsche', *Revue d'histoire de la philosophie*, 3 (1929), 321–47; and in D. Breazeale, 'The Hegel–Nietzsche Problem', *Nietzsche-Studien*, 4 (1975), 146–64.
5 G. Deleuze, *Nietzsche et la philosophie* (Paris, 1962), pp. 9, 223 (Tomlinson trans., pp. 8, 195).
6 W. Kaufmann, *Nietzsche: Philosopher, Psychologist, Antichrist* (Princeton, 1950), p. 206.
7 W. Kaufmann, *Hegel: Re-interpretation, Texts and Commentary* (London, 1965), p. 290.
8 Breazeale, p. 147.
9 Breazeale, p. 147.
10 Heinz Röttges' book, *Nietzsche und die Dialektik der Aufklärung* (Berlin, 1972), is perhaps an exception to this insofar as he employs Hegelian concepts throughout his discussion of Nietzsche (p. vi). However, Röttges does not offer a detailed comparison of the two philosophers, and the Hegelian concepts only form the background to what is primarily an interpretation of Nietzsche alone. Although I agree with many of Röttges' conclusions, his treatment of the material is quite different from mine. He concentrates much more on the question of history and includes no extended analyses of Hegel's own arguments.
11 J. Günther, 'Nietzsche und der Nationalsozialismus', in 'Hegel und Nietzsche', *Nationalsozialistische Monatshefte*, 21 (December 1931), 563.
12 H. Rimke, 'Was bedeutet uns Hegel?', in 'Hegel und Nietzsche', *Nationalsozialistische Monatshefte*, 21, 559. The view that Hegel's dialectic is rooted in the German language in particular, rather than in language in general, is not of course a Nazi prejudice, but has been advanced by H.

Gadamer, *Hegels Dialektik* (Tübingen, 1971), p. 93. For a critique of this view, see D. Cook, *Language in the Philosophy of Hegel* (The Hague, 1973), p. 170.

13 Rimke, p. 560. See also G. Hennemann, *Von der Kraft des deutschen Geistes: Fichte–Hegel–Nietzsche* (Cologne, 1940). Hennemann stresses the importance of Hegel and Nietzsche for the process of cultural renewal which he saw as the main task of the National Socialists in Germany. Despite its obvious political bias, however, Hennemann's book contains some important ideas (particularly on Hegel's 'concrete' notion of thought) and should not be dismissed out of hand.

14 H. C. Graef, 'From Hegel to Hitler', *Contemporary Review*, 158 (July–December 1940), 550–1. See also K. Popper, *The Open Society and its Enemies* (London, 1945). For a criticism of the view that Hegel ignores the rights of the individual, see S. Avineri, *Hegel's Theory of the Modern State* (Cambridge, 1972), pp. 167–8.

15 Graef, pp. 554, 556. For a criticism of the view that Nietzsche's individualism is 'unfettered', see Kaufmann, *Nietzsche*, pp. 220–1.

16 Graef, p. 556.

17 For a study which reaches similar conclusions to those of Graef, but which was written after the Second World War by a German, see A. von Martin, *Geistige Wegbereiter des deutschen Zusammenbruchs: Hegel–Nietzsche–Spengler* (Recklinghausen, 1948). A rather more discerning view of the problem, particularly regarding Nietzsche's relation to National Socialism, is to be found in H. W. Brann, 'Hegel, Nietzsche and the Nazi Lesson', *Humanist*, 12 (1952), 111–15 and 179–82. However, even though Brann recognises that Hegel (like Nietzsche) had 'humanistic tendencies' (p. 112), he still talks, unfortunately, of 'the Hegelian ideas of the preponderance of the state over the individual . . . and of the rationality of any reality whatsoever' (p. 114).

18 R. J. Hollingdale, *Nietzsche* (London, 1973), p. 37.

19 Hollingdale, pp. 37–40.

20 See J. N. Findlay, *Hegel: A Re-examination* (London, 1958), pp. 348–9.

21 Deleuze, *Nietzsche et la philosophie*, p. 223 (Tomlinson trans., p. 195). For a fuller discussion of Deleuze, see Breazeale, pp. 153–62.

22 Deleuze, *Nietzsche* ([Paris], 1965), p. 27.

23 Deleuze, *Nietzsche et la philosophie*, pp. 60–1 (Tomlinson trans., pp. 53–4); and *Nietzsche*, p. 25. All bodies, in Deleuze's view, contain active and reactive forces, but a body will nevertheless tend to exhibit one quality more than another and can thus be characterised as a master or a slave; see *Nietzsche et la philosophie*, p. 166 (Tomlinson trans., p. 146, column headed 'Type').

24 Deleuze, *Nietzsche et la philosophie*, pp. 64–5 (Tomlinson trans., pp. 56–8), 72–3 (Tomlinson trans., pp. 64–5, 'on the contrary, they triumph . . .').

25 Deleuze, *Nietzsche et la philosophie*, p. 137 (Tomlinson trans., p. 120) and F. Nietzsche, *Werke*, edited by K. Schlechta, 3 Vols. and Index (Munich, 1954–) (cited below as *Werke*), II, 750 (*JGB*, §287).

26 Deleuze, *Nietzsche et la philosophie*, pp. 136–8 (Tomlinson trans., pp. 119–20).

27 Deleuze, *Nietzsche et la philosophie*, pp. 9–10 (Tomlinson trans., pp. 8–9).

28 Deleuze, *Nietzsche et la philosophie*, pp. 136, 138–9 (Tomlinson trans., pp. 119, 121).

29 Deleuze, *Nietzsche et la philosophie*, pp. 139, 206 (Tomlinson trans., 121, 179–80).

30 Deleuze, *Nietzsche et la philosophie*, p. 181 (Tomlinson trans., p. 157, 'It is unaware of the real element . . .').

31 Deleuze, *Nietzsche et la philosophie*, p. 21 (Tomlinson trans., p. 18).

32 Deleuze, *Nietzsche et la philosophie*, p. 200 (Tomlinson trans., p. 174).

33 See Breazeale, pp. 159–61.

34 See G. W. F. Hegel, *Theorie Werkausgabe*, edited by E. Moldenhauer and K. Michel, 20 Vols. and Index (Frankfurt, 1969–) (cited below as *TWA*), V, 122 (*WL*, Miller trans., p. 115, 'Reality itself contains negation . . .'); and G. R. G. Mure, *The Philosophy of Hegel* (London, 1965), p. 115, note 1.

35 Deleuze, *Nietzsche et la philosophie*, p. 45 (Tomlinson trans., p. 40, 'a plurality of irreducible forces . . .', 'Active and reactive are precisely the original qualities . . .').

36 Deleuze, *Nietzsche*, p. 25.

37 Deleuze, *Nietzsche et la philosophie*, p. 203 (Tomlinson trans., p. 176); but see also p. 216 (Tomlinson trans., p. 188, 'Negation is *opposed* to affirmation, but affirmation *differs* from negation . . .').

38 It should be stressed that this account of Deleuze's argument is simplified. As I have said, Deleuze distinguishes negation as the secondary consequence of affirmation from negation as the product of negative will to power. However, he also thinks that this latter, wholly negative negation can be harnessed to the affirmative will to power as a weapon with which to destroy reactive forces (*Nietzsche et la philosophie*, pp. 200–7 (Tomlinson trans., pp. 174–80) and *Nietzsche*, pp. 32–3). It remains true, though, that Deleuze in no sense acknowledges affirmation to be inherently mediated by negation.

39 Deleuze, *Nietzsche et la philosophie*, p. 137 (Tomlinson trans., p. 119).

40 Deleuze, *Nietzsche et la philosophie*, p. 11 (Tomlinson trans., p. 10). For a discussion of a contradiction in Deleuze's treatment of recognition, see Breazeale, p. 160, note 15.

41 W. Schulz, *Der Gott der neuzeitlichen Metaphysik* (Pfullingen, 1957, seventh edition 1982), pp. 102–6. A number of commentators have, of course, pointed to the importance of movement or 'becoming' in the philosophies of Hegel and Nietzsche without necessarily stressing the circularity of that movement. See, for example, Tchijewsky, pp. 326–8; and A. Kremer-Marietti, 'Hegel et Nietzsche', *La revue des lettres modernes*, 76–7 (Winter 1962–3), 22.

42 Schulz, pp. 105–10. For a critique of the view that Hegel conceives of being in a metaphysical way as thing-like or object-like (*gegenständlich*), see M. Theunissen, *Sein und Schein: die kritische Funktion der Hegelschen Logik*

(Frankfurt, 1980), p. 24; and chapters 4 and 5 below. Might it not be that Hegel's dialectical logic is precisely an articulation of what Heidegger ought to mean by Being?

43 For Brose's discussion of what Hegel and Nietzsche themselves mean by 'critical history', see K. Brose, *Kritische Geschichte: Studien zur Geschichtsphilosophie Nietzsches und Hegels* (Frankfurt, 1978), pp. 12–13.

44 Brose, *Kritische Geschichte*, pp. 27–8, 36.

45 Brose, *Kritische Geschichte*, pp. 27–8, 30.

46 Brose, *Geschichtsphilosophische Strukturen im Werke Nietzsches* (Bern/Frankfurt, 1973), pp. 14–27; and *Kritische Geschichte*, p. 30. See also Beerling, who says that 'no-one has philosophised [about the affairs of the world] in such grand style and at the same time so relentlessly "beyond Good and Evil" as precisely Hegel' (p. 238). G. O'Brien raises the point that Hegel and Nietzsche are both grappling with a problem bequeathed to them by Kantian ethics: 'how can the highest value for man fail to include his peculiarity as an individual self-consciousness'. Both Hegel and Nietzsche, in O'Brien's view, place the right of self-consciousness to fulfil itself above that of morality. O'Brien points out, however, that whereas Nietzsche finds self-fulfilment in the superman, Hegel finds it in social and historical self-consciousness (G. O'Brien, *Hegel on Reason and History* (Chicago, 1975), pp. 119–20).

47 Brose, *Kritische Geschichte*, pp. 9–10.

48 Brose, *Kritische Geschichte*, p. 29.

49 Brose, *Kritische Geschichte*, pp. 28–9; and *Geschichtsphilosophische Strukturen*, p. 30. See also K. Jaspers, *Nietzsche: Einführung in das Verständnis seines Philosophierens* (Berlin, 1936, second edition 1947), p. 236; and Kremer-Marietti, pp. 21–2.

50 Brose, *Kritische Geschichte*, p. 40; and *Geschichtsphilosophische Strukturen*, pp. 16, 27.

51 Brose, *Kritische Geschichte*, pp. 30–1, 35.

52 Brose, *Kritische Geschichte*, p. 35.

53 Brose, *Kritische Geschichte*, p. 31.

54 Brose, *Kritische Geschichte*, pp. 35–6. For a critique of the view that Hegel subordinates the individual to the universal, see chapter 1, note 14. For a critique of the view that Nietzsche's 'will to power' is to be understood as an abstract, universal 'essence', see A. Lingis, 'The Will to Power', in *The New Nietzsche*, edited by D. Allison (New York, 1977), pp. 37–8.

55 Breazeale, p. 151.

56 Kaufmann, *Nietzsche*, pp. 206, 211.

57 R. Zimmermann, 'On Nietzsche', *Philosophy and Phenomenological Research*, 29, 2 (December 1968), 274.

58 Zimmermann, p. 275.

59 Zimmermann, p. 277.

60 Zimmermann, p. 280.

61 Mark 8:34–5; Luke 17:33.

62 See Deleuze, *Nietzsche et la philosophie*, p. 205 (Tomlinson trans., pp. 178–9); and chapter 1, note 38.

63 Zimmermann, p. 277.
64 Zimmermann, p. 280, note 10.
65 Kaufmann, *Nietzsche*, pp. 206–7.
66 Kaufmann, *Nietzsche*, pp. 192–3.
67 Kaufmann, *Nietzsche*, p. 193.
68 Hegel, *TWA*, V, 113–14 (*WL*, Miller trans., pp. 106–7).
69 Kaufmann, *Nietzsche*, p. 195. Kaufmann does not distinguish these two senses of sublimation explicitly, but they are nevertheless present in his account.
70 Kaufmann, *Nietzsche*, pp. 200–1.
71 Kaufmann, *Nietzsche*, p. 208.
72 Hegel, *TWA*, VII, 340 (*PRecht*, §183).
73 Breazeale, p. 151.
74 Theunissen, p. 284.
75 Beerling, p. 234, 'das Denken Hegels gibt dem Nietzsches an "Anti-Jenseitigkeit" kaum etwas nach'.
76 Beerling, p. 241; and Nietzsche, *Werke*, II, 782 (*GM*, I, §10). See also M. Greene, 'Hegel's "Unhappy Consciousness" and Nietzsche's "Slave Morality" ', in *Hegel and the Philosophy of Religion*, edited by D. Christensen (The Hague, 1970), pp. 125–41; and I. Soll, *An Introduction to Hegel's Metaphysics* (Chicago, 1969), p. 41. In his book on Hegel Kaufmann draws attention to the similarity between the criticisms of other-worldliness made by Nietzsche and the young Hegel (p. 185), and Tchijewsky even goes as far as to speak of 'the "Nietzscheanism" of the young Hegel' (p. 338).
77 Breazeale, p. 162. The similarity between the criticisms levelled by Hegel and Nietzsche against epistemological dualism has been pointed out by Jaspers (p. 292), by D. Lamb, in *Hegel: From Foundation to System* (The Hague, 1980), pp. 26–8, and by J. Habermas, in *Erkenntnis und Interesse* (Frankfurt, 1968), pp. 353–4. The parallels between the Hegelian and Nietzschean critiques of Kant's alleged moral dualism are discussed in detail by Tchijewsky (pp. 333–8, 345–7).
78 Beerling, p. 246.
79 Beerling, p. 239.
80 Beerling, pp. 244–5.
81 S. Rosen, *G. W. F. Hegel: An Introduction to the Science of Wisdom* (Yale, 1974), pp. 195–6.
82 S. Rosen, p. 197.
83 S. Rosen, p. 195.
84 S. Rosen, p. 265. See E. Fackenheim, *The Religious Dimension in Hegel's Thought* (Bloomington, 1967), pp. 13–14. In his book, *Von Hegel zu Nietzsche* (Stuttgart, 1941, third edition 1953), Karl Löwith suggests a general contrast between Hegelian unity and post-Hegelian fragmentation: 'Hegel's pupils and successors put asunder what he had so skillfully joined together, and demanded decisions in place of his mediations. While Hegel everywhere sought the mean, the Young Hegelians became radical and extreme' (p. 264 (Green trans. p. 244)); see also p. 58

(Green trans., p. 45). Moreover, it is clear that Löwith sees Nietzsche in this sense as one of a kind with the Young Hegelians: 'For Hegel, the incarnation of God means a once and for all reconciliation between human and divine nature; for Nietzsche and Bauer, it means that man in his true nature was broken' (pp. 205–6 (Green trans., p. 188)). Interestingly, Löwith also points out that 'Hegel's reconciliation with "what is" itself developed out of the same thing which it gave rise to: a fundamental estrangement from the existing order' (p. 179 (Green trans., p. 162)) – a suggestion, perhaps, that Löwith believed that something of that reconciliation, if not precisely in Hegel's sense, might be resurrected. On the close parallels between Nietzsche and the Young Hegelians, particularly Bruno Bauer, see Tchijewsky, pp. 330–3, 339–45; and E. Benz, *Nietzsches Ideen zur Geschichte des Christentums und der Kirche* (Leiden, 1956), pp. 104–21.

85 Greene, p. 127, 'In Nietzsche . . .'.

86 Greene, pp. 130–1. For Hegel the negation of natural desire does not, however, mean its abolition, but, as I suggested in my discussion of Kaufmann, its transformation into a moment of social consciousness.

87 Greene, pp. 127–8.

88 Greene, p. 128.

89 Greene, pp. 131–2.

90 Greene, pp. 129, 137.

91 Greene, p. 138. Greene's point is not contradicted by Zimmermann's argument as may appear to be the case. Zimmermann maintains that for Nietzsche the master's true freedom is mediated by the slave's negation of the instincts (p. 277). But the slave's role is only to modify the master in an external manner. The bearer and ultimate source of freedom remains the master. Human fulfilment does not, therefore, lie immanent in the slave's self-negation as it does for Hegel.

92 W. Seeberger, *Hegel und die Entwicklung des Geistes zur Freiheit* (Stuttgart, 1961), p. 288.

93 Seeberger, p. 85.

94 A similar point, though from a non-Hegelian background, is made by J. P. Stern, in *A Study of Nietzsche* (Cambridge, 1979), p. 106.

95 See Hegel, *TWA*, IX, 339 (*E*, II, §337, Addition, 'Life is . . . the resolution of oppositions in general [*die Vereinigung von Gegensätzen überhaupt*]'); XI, 250 (*BS*, 'true thinking, as the *sublation of oppositions* as such [Aufheben der Gegensätze *überhaupt*]'); and Nietzsche, *Werke*, III, 541 (*WM*, §552, 'Es gibt keine Gegensätze', 'There are no opposites'). See also chapter 3, note 37.

96 This book makes no attempt to determine whether the accounts which Nietzsche and Hegel give of 'metaphysics' in any way do justice to the philosophers of the Western tradition – such as Plato, Spinoza or Kant – who might perhaps ordinarily be called 'metaphysical'; nor is the book concerned with the question of whether those accounts necessarily coincide with other philosophers' understanding of the word 'metaphysics'. It is concerned simply with the phenomenon which Nietzsche and Hegel

themselves describe as metaphysics and with how consistent they are in their critique of that phenomenon.

97 In the account of Hegel's philosophy given in this book the terms 'dialectical' and 'speculative' are used virtually interchangeably, though Hegel does in fact distinguish between the two terms; see *TWA*, VIII, 172–7 (*E*, I, §§81, 82).

98 See chapter 8, pp. 199–200, 206. Human interest is *sittlich*, therefore, when it is concerned with the substantial interests of society rather than mere personal advancement; but such interest only becomes truly and fully *sittlich* when it is pursued in such a way that it is reconciled, rather than in conflict, with other substantial interests.

2 *Nietzsche's view of Hegel*

1 Deleuze, *Nietzsche et la philosophie*, pp. 9, 187, 210 (Tomlinson trans., pp. 8, 162–3, 183, 'Hegelian being is pure and simple nothingness').

2 See C. P. Janz, *Friedrich Nietzsche: Biographie*, 3 Vols. (Munich, 1978–9), I, 404. Janz points out, however, that there were great gaps even in Nietzsche's knowledge of Greek philosophy. Nietzsche's knowledge of Kant, Janz maintains, was derived mainly from Kuno Fischer, *Geschichte der neueren Philosophie* (Mannheim, 1854–), Vols. III and IV, 'I. Kant: Entwicklungsgeschichte und System der kritischen Philosophie', though he did read Kant's *Critique of Judgement* (*Kritik der Urteilskraft*) for himself during the winter of 1867–8 (Janz, I, 199, 404).

3 Nietzsche, *Werke und Briefe: Historisch-kritische Gesamtausgabe*, edited by H. J. Mette, W. Hoppe and others, 9 Vols. (Munich, 1933–) (cited below as *HKG*), *Briefe*, II, 9. Paragraph 190 in *Daybreak* perhaps suggests that Nietzsche might also have read some of Hegel's letters, but the passage by no means establishes that he actually did; see *Werke*, I, 1137.

4 Nietzsche misquotes the title of Strauß's book, which is *The Halves and the Wholes* (*Die Halben und die Ganzen*).

5 Both Schopenhauer's and Nietzsche's views of Hegel's style are discussed later in this chapter.

6 Nietzsche, *Werke*, I, 1014 (*M*, Preface, §3, 'alle Dinge sind sich selbst widersprechend'). Nietzsche might have had in mind Hegel's discussion of contradiction in the *Science of Logic*, but his quotation differs slightly from Hegel's exact wording, which is 'alle Dinge sind an sich selbst widersprechend' (*TWA*, VI, 74 (*WL*, Miller trans., p. 439, 'all things are inherently contradictory')).

7 That Nietzsche was acquainted with the writings of Strauß is of course clear from the first of his *Untimely Meditations*; see *Werke*, I, 137–207. It is not so clear, however, how much he had read of Feuerbach. He requested Feuerbach's *The Essence of Christianity* (*Das Wesen des Christentums*) for his birthday in 1861 (*HKG Werke*, I, 251; see also Janz, I, 23), and he refers in *The Genealogy of Morals* to 'Feuerbach's cry of "healthy sensuality" ' (*Werke*, II, 842 (*GM*, III, §3)). But, as far as I know, he does not state

explicitly that he has studied Feuerbach's writings in detail. K. Schlechta's *Nietzsche-Chronik* (Munich, 1975) does not mention Feuerbach at all, though Janz is of the opinion that Nietzsche did in fact study Feuerbach quite closely; see Janz, I, 404.

8 See Schlechta, *Nietzsche-Chronik*, p. 75; and Nietzsche, *Werke*, II, 1114 (*EH*, III, UB, §2), and III, 1259 (letter to H. Taine, 4 July 1887).

9 Nietzsche, *Werke*, III, 1278 (letter to G. Brandes, 19 February 1888). See Schlechta, *Nietzsche-Chronik*, p. 109; and Janz, II, 266.

10 See Janz, III, 212–13, 343–5. Schlechta claims that in 1874 Nietzsche recommended writings by Max Stirner to Adolf Baumgartner (*Nietzsche-Chronik*, p. 49). This information is probably taken from C. A. Bernoulli, *Franz Overbeck und Friedrich Nietzsche: eine Freundschaft*, 2 Vols. (Jena, 1908), I, 135–7.

11 Bernoulli, I, 144–5.

12 Nietzsche, *HKG Werke*, III, 297–8, 313, 'I become acquainted with Schopenhauer'. See Schlechta, *Nietzsche-Chronik*, p. 24.

13 Nietzsche, *HKG Briefe*, II, 63 (letter to H. Mushacke, presumed to have been written on 12 July 1866). The connection between Hegel and historical optimism is made explicit in a note written in 1875; see Nietzsche, *Werke: Kritische Gesamtausgabe*, edited by C. Colli and M. Montinari (Berlin, 1967–) (cited below as *KG*), IV$_1$, 133.

14 Nietzsche, *HKG Briefe*, II, 46 (letter of 7 April 1866). See also Nietzsche's letter to his mother of 31 January 1866 (*HKG Briefe*, II, 32, 'Dieser Philosoph...'); and his letter to von Gersdorff written in August 1866 (*HKG Briefe*, II, 83, 'wenn die Philosophie erbauen soll...').

15 See Nietzsche, *HKG Briefe*, III, 84 (letter to von Gersdorff, 7 November 1870). Nietzsche attended the weekly seminars on 'the study of history' which Burckhardt held in the winter of 1870–1, and he also went to one of the three lectures Burckhardt gave on 'historical greatness' in November 1870. For information about the dates of these seminars and lectures (which were edited into the collection entitled *Weltgeschichtliche Betrachtungen* and published in 1905 by J. Oeri), see J. Burckhardt, *Weltgeschichtliche Betrachtungen*, edited with Afterword by W. Kaegi (Basle, 1970), pp. 198–9.

16 Nietzsche, *KG* IV$_1$, 132–3.

17 Nietzsche, *HKG Briefe*, II, 108. See also *HKG Briefe*, II, 83 (letter to von Gersdorff, August 1866); and *HKG Briefe*, II, 182–3 (letter to von Gersdorff, 16 February 1868).

18 For Überweg, see Nietzsche, *HKG Briefe*, II, 219–20 (letter to mother and sister, 1 July 1868); Schlechta, *Nietzsche-Chronik*, p. 29. For Dühring, see *KG* IV$_1$, 205; IV$_4$, 386; Schlechta, *Nietzsche-Chronik*, pp. 76, 93. For Hartmann, see *HKG Briefe*, II, 348 (letter to von Gersdorff, 4 August 1869); *HKG Briefe*, III, 7 (letter to E. Rohde, 11 November 1869); Schlechta, *Nietzsche-Chronik*, pp. 33–4, 103.

19 Nietzsche, *HKG Briefe*, II, 255 (letter to P. Deussen, October 1868, 'überverwegne Überwege', 'over-audacious Überwegs'), though see also *HKG Werke*, III, 354, where Nietzsche seems to see some justice in Über-

weg's critique of Schopenhauer; *KG* IV,, 207, 'In [Dühring's] language there is something illogical . . .'; *HKG Briefe*, IV, 182 (letter to R. Wagner, 24 May 1875, 'Sickness of Hartmannianism . . .').

20 G. Teichmüller, *Die wirkliche und die scheinbare Welt : neue Grundlegung der Metaphysik* (Breslau, 1882); see Schlechta, *Nietzsche-Chronik*, p. 86. E. de Roberty, *L'ancienne et la nouvelle philosophie: essai sur les lois générales du développement de la philosophie* (Paris, 1887); see Schlechta, *Nietzsche-Chronik*, p. 109. H. Martensen, *Grundriß des Systems der Moralphilosophie* (Kiel, 1845); see Schlechta, *Nietzsche-Chronik*, p. 70.

21 In contrast to Schopenhauer, for example, who thinks that Hegel is more concerned with mystifying and bemusing his audience and with serving the ends of the state than with philosophical truth and intellectual honesty, Martensen sees in Hegel's philosophy an expression of ethical dignity and freedom: 'Whoever has studied the philosophy of religion and the aesthetics attentively will have had ample opportunity to convince himself that Hegel was aware of a higher form of morality than one whose purpose is fulfilled in the state [*deren Zweck in den Staat aufgeht*]' (p. viii); 'the more one weans oneself away from seeing [Hegel's] philosophy as a completed, finished result – as it has often been misunderstood by friends and foes alike, who thereby fall into a mode of thought which is dead and fatalistic– . . . the more will it become evident that the principle of this philosophy is freedom, the more abundantly will that philosophy reveal its great ethical insights, and the more clearly will it point to the idea of personality as the central concern [*Schwerpunkt*] of thought' (p. ix).

22 Nietzsche, *HKG Briefe*, II, 83 (letter to von Gersdorff, August 1866).

23 Nietzsche, *HKG Briefe*, III, 88 (letter to Rohde, 23 or 27 November 1870). Amongst Nietzsche's friends in the late 1860s and early 1870s the dominant philosophical influence was also Schopenhauer. Richard Wagner, for example, got to know Schopenhauer's *The World as Will and Representation* in the autumn of 1854, and was impressed by 'the great clarity and manly precision' with which Schopenhauer dealt with metaphysical problems. Wagner's enthusiasm for Schopenhauer contrasts sharply with his earlier frustration at trying to read Hegel and Schelling, and, since he admits to having been persuaded by an English critic that Hegel's lack of clarity was the product of 'the intentionally bombastic style [*der absichtliche Schwulst*] in which this philosopher has clothed his problems', it is likely that he would have reinforced Nietzsche's early, Schopenhauerian prejudice against Hegel; see R. Wagner, *Mein Leben*, edited by M. Gregor-Dellin (Munich, 1963, second edition 1976), pp. 442–3, 521–3 (authorised trans., pp. 521–2, 614–16). Similarly, the majority of Nietzsche's other friends at the time were admirers of Schopenhauer: 'By the way Rohde belongs to those who have been enticed to see the centre of their spiritual life in Schopenhauer' (*HKG Briefe*, II, 209 (letter to P. Deussen, 2 June 1868)); 'a number of admirers of Schopenhauer . . . amongst whom was my friend Gersdorff' (*HKG Briefe*, II, 302 (letters to E. Rohde, 22 and 28 February 1869)); 'my

old companion Deussen has gone over to Schopenhauer with body and soul, as the last and the oldest of my friends'; 'Romundt has brought a Schopenhauer society into being' (both *HKG Briefe*, III, 28–9 (letter to E. Rohde, end of January and 15 February 1870)); 'a very thoughtful and talented person, a Schopenhauerian, by the name of Rée' (*HKG Briefe*, IV, 4 (letter to E. Rohde, 5 May 1873)). This overwhelming concurrence of opinion in support of Schopenhauer amongst Nietzsche's friends makes it seem likely that the philosophical atmosphere which Nietzsche breathed during his time at Leipzig and his first years at Basle was largely anti-Hegelian.

24 See W. Abendroth, *Schopenhauer* (Hamburg, 1967), p. 66; and Schopenhauer, *Sämtliche Werke*, edited by J. Frauenstädt, 6 Vols. (Leipzig, 1873–4), IV, Part 2, vi–vii, xvii–xxv (*GPE*, Preface to first edition, Payne trans., pp. 4, 13–20).

25 Schopenhauer, *Sämtliche Werke*, II, 48 (*WWV*, I, Book 1, §9, Payne trans., I, 40, 'Now although concepts are fundamentally different from representations of perception [*von den anschaulichen Vorstellungen*] . . .'); II, 78 (*WWV*, I, Book 1, §14, Payne trans., I, 65, 'Every concept has its value and its existence only in reference to a representation from perception . . .'). Schopenhauer does not of course adhere strictly to his 'Kantian' principle himself because he is willing to formulate concepts and judgements about a content which, he insists, cannot be perceived, intuited or represented, namely the 'thing-in-itself' or 'will'. Since, however, Schopenhauer's comments about the will 'in itself' are based on extrapolation from what he sees as our immediate consciousness or 'feeling' of our own personal will, Schopenhauer may still be said to adhere to the broad 'Kantian' principle that concepts require some kind of given, non-conceptual content to be meaningful and that they have no purely logical content of their own; see II, 122–3 (*WWV*, I, Book 2, §18, Payne trans., I, 102–3) and II, 130 (*WWV*, I, Book 2, §21, Payne trans., I, 109).

26 Schopenhauer, *Sämtliche Werke*, III, 69 (*WWV*, II, Book 1, chapter 6, Payne trans., II, 64, 'those modern philosophemes that constantly move in nothing but very broad abstractions'); II, xxv (*WWV*, I, Preface to second edition, Payne trans., I, xxiv, 'minds strained and ruined in the freshness of youth by the nonsense of Hegelism', 'frantic word-combinations in which the mind torments and exhausts itself in vain to conceive something'); III, 47 (*WWV*, II, Book 1, chapter 4, Payne trans., II, 40, 'a mere *display of words*'); II, 508 (*WWV*, I, 'Criticism of the Kantian Philosophy', Payne trans., I, 429, 'senseless and maddening webs of words'); III, 92 (*WWV*, II, Book 1, chapter 7, Payne trans., II, 84, 'the most sickening and loathsome tediousness').

27 Schopenhauer, *Sämtliche Werke*, II, 508 (*WWV*, I, 'Criticism of the Kantian Philosophy', Payne trans., I, 429, 'the most ponderous and general mystification'); IV, Part 2, 147 (*GPE*, 'On the Basis of Morality', §6, Payne trans., p. 80, 'not to instruct, but to fool'); V, 164 (*PP*, I, 'On Philosophy at the Universities', Payne trans., I, 151, 'I find them all . . .

bent on ... producing effect'); III, 15 (*WWV*, II, Book 1, chapter 1, Payne trans., II, 12–13, 'Fichte is the father of *sham philosophy*, of the *underhand* method that by ambiguity in the use of words, incomprehensible talk, and sophisms, tries to deceive, to impress by an air of importance, and thus to befool those eager to learn. After this method had been applied by Schelling, it reached its height, as is well known, in Hegel, with whom it ripened into real charlatanism').

28 Schopenhauer, *Sämtliche Werke*, III, 505–6 (*WWV*, II, Book 3, chapter 38, 'On History', Payne trans., II, 442, 'a crude and shallow realism', 'shallow optimism', 'a comfortable, substantial, fat state'); III, 507–8 ('On History', Payne trans., II, 444, 'raising the temporal aims of men to eternal and absolute aims', 'that, in spite of all these endless changes ... we yet always have before us only the same, identical, unchangeable essence'); V, 159 (*PP*, I, 'On Philosophy at the Universities', Payne trans., I, 147, 'But it was these constitutional aims [*Staatszwecke*] ...').

29 See chapter 3, pp. 67–77.

30 Burckhardt, p. 2 (M. D. H. trans., p. 16). '(*sic!*)' is in Burckhardt's own text.

31 Burckhardt, p. 3 (M. D. H. trans., p. 16).

32 F. A. Lange, *Geschichte des Materialismus und Kritik seiner Bedeutung in der Gegenwart* (Iserlohn, 1866), p. v. The preface to the first edition is not included in the Thomas translation, which is a translation of the second edition of Lange's book.

33 Lange, pp. 285–6 (Thomas trans., ii, 249). As I shall argue in chapters 4 to 7, it is true that Hegel rejects the idea of a reality beyond human understanding, but it is wrong to see him as in any way an uncritical thinker. Hegel is well aware that human consciousness can be severely limited in its understanding of the world and of itself, but he believes it is self-contradictory for philosophy to claim that *all* consciousness is limited, because philosophy transcends those 'limits' in making that claim.

34 Lange, p. 290 (Thomas trans., ii, 254). This comment is actually made about Feuerbach, but Feuerbach is said by Lange to believe in 'sensationless thought' 'quite in the spirit of Hegel'. See also p. 284 (Thomas trans., ii, 247, 'A "consequently" in Feuerbach does not ... carry the force of a real, or at least intended, inference of the understanding, but it means, as with Schelling and Hegel, a leap to be taken in thought').

35 Lange, p. 550 (Thomas trans., iii, 352, 'As in politics. ...').

36 Lange, p. 281 (Thomas trans., ii, 238).

37 Lange, p. 330 (Thomas trans., ii, 346). Although I agree with Lange that Hegel did not intend to put an end to scientific enquiry, I think he did believe he had brought philosophy – at least in principle – to definitive self-understanding.

38 Lange, p. 21 (Thomas trans., i, 93). The Thomas translation does not exactly match the wording of the first edition of Lange's book in this passage since it follows the second edition.

39 Lange, p. 281 (Thomas trans., ii, 239). Lange is particularly keen to

praise the contribution that Hegel and his 'school' have made to a proper understanding of the Sophists; see p. 14 (Thomas trans., i, 40).

40 Nietzsche, *Werke*, II, 226 (*FW*, §357).

41 On the importance of Lange for Nietzsche's philosophical development, see J. Salaquarda, 'Nietzsche und Lange', *Nietzsche-Studien*, 7 (1978), 236–53; and G. Stack, *Lange and Nietzsche* (Berlin, 1983).

42 Nietzsche, *HKG Briefe*, II, 9. Hegel is in fact first mentioned by Nietzsche in his 'Letter to my friend, in which I recommend him to read my favourite poet', but he is mentioned only in passing as part of the biographical background to Hölderlin's poetry (*HKG Werke*, II, 4).

43 Nietzsche, *Werke*, I, 164 (*UB*, I, §6). Nietzsche talks of *gröblichster Realismus*, whereas Schopenhauer talks of *roher und platter Realismus*; see chapter 2, note 28.

44 Nietzsche, *KG* IV₁, 357. See also *Werke*, I, 196–7 (*UB*, I, §12, 'the most infamous of all corrupters of German, the Hegelians', 'Hegelian mud').

45 Nietzsche, *HKG Werke*, III, 342.

46 Nietzsche, *KG* IV₁, 132–3.

47 Nietzsche, *Werke*, I, 262 (*UB*, II, §8, 'I believe there has been no dangerous vacillation. . .').

48 Nietzsche, *Werke*, I, 262–4 (*UB*, II, §8). See Burckhardt, pp. 2–3 (M. D. H. trans., pp. 16–17).

49 Nietzsche, *Werke*, III, 226 (*ÜZBA*, III, Kennedy trans., p. 87, 'apotheosis of the state'); *HKG Werke*, V, 193 ('Persönlichkeit nur als Reflex des Zeitgeistes. . .', 'Personality only as the reflection of the spirit of the times. . .').

50 Nietzsche voices some criticisms of Schopenhauer as early as 1868 (see *HKG Werke*, III, 354–61), but it is the year 1876 which marks the close of his 'Schopenhauerian' period and the turn towards his 'mature' philosophy. In the winter of that year he dictated thoughts to Peter Gast which were initially intended for a fifth 'untimely' meditation, but which in fact prepared the ground for *Human, All-too Human* (see Janz, I, 713–14 and Nietzsche, *Werke*, II, 764 (*GM*, Preface, §2)), and in that year also he started to make many, more serious criticisms of Schopenhauer. In the summer of 1875 he could still write: 'I want to add Schopenhauer, Wagner and ancient Greece together: that offers a glimpse of a magnificent culture' (*KG* IV₁, 179). But towards the end of 1876 he would write, for example: 'love is not at all explained by Schopenhauer' (*KG* IV₂, 453), or: 'Schopenhauer is to the world as a blind man to a written text' (*KG* IV₂, 465). See also *KG* IV₂, 506 ('eine solche Tatsache . . .').

51 Nietzsche, *Werke*, II, 664 (*JGB*, §204).

52 Nietzsche, *Werke*, III, 481 (*WM*, §366).

53 Nietzsche, *Werke*, II, 718 (*JGB*, §252).

54 Nietzsche, *Werke*, III, 593 (*WM*, §382).

55 Nietzsche, *Werke*, II, 986 (*GD*, 'What the Germans lack', §4); II, 1002 (*GD*, 'Expeditions', §21).

56 Nietzsche, *Werke*, II, 924 (*FWag*, §10).

57 Nietzsche, *Werke*, II, 226–7 (*FW*, §357). See chapter 2, p. 31.
58 Nietzsche, *Werke*, I, 1014 (*M*, Preface, §3).
59 Nietzsche, *Werke*, III, 447 (*WM*, §422).
60 Nietzsche, *Werke*, I, 1140–1 (*M*, §193); II, 1159 (*EH*, IV, §8).
61 Nietzsche, *Werke*, I, 146 (*UB*, I, §2).
62 Nietzsche, *Werke*, III, 512 (*WM*, §95).
63 Nietzsche, *Werke*, III, 511 (*WM*, §95).
64 Nietzsche, *Werke*, III, 496 (*WM*, §416).
65 Nietzsche, *Werke*, II, 227–8 (*FW*, §357).
66 Nietzsche, *Werke*, III, 486 (*WM*, §410).
67 Nietzsche, *Werke*, III, 479, 903 (*WM*, §§415, 412).
68 Nietzsche, *Werke*, III, 881 (*WM*, §1.3).
69 Nietzsche, *Werke*, III, 496 (*WM*, §416). See Burckhardt, p. 2 (M. D. H. trans., p. 16, 'recognition of the affirmative in which the negative (in popular parlance, evil) vanishes, subjected and overcome').
70 Nietzsche, *Werke*, II, 676 (*JGB*, §211).
71 Nietzsche, *Werke*, I, 1140–1 (*M*, §193).
72 Nietzsche, *Werke*, II, 1149 (*EH*, III, FWag, §3).
73 Nietzsche, *Werke*, II, 924 (*FWag*, §10). Nietzsche's remark in *Ecce Homo* that *The Birth of Tragedy* 'smells offensively Hegelian' might thus equally mean that it 'smells offensively Wagnerian'; see *Werke*, II, 1108 (*EH*, III, GT, §1).
74 Nietzsche, *Werke*, III, 729 (*WM*, §515).
75 Nietzsche, *Werke*, III, 484 (*WM*, §253, 'God is demonstrable but as something in process of becoming, and we are a part of it. . .').
76 In pursuing the comparison between Hegel and Nietzsche I reverse the historical order and treat Nietzsche first. The reason for so doing is that it allows me to present a critique that is *Nietzsche-immanent* first of all, and then to reveal the Hegelian arguments which inform that critique.

3   *Nietzsche and metaphysics*

1 Nietzsche, *Werke*, III, 1435, Afterword by K. Schlechta.
2 For a full discussion of Nietzsche's understanding of metaphysics, see Schacht, pp. 118–86.
3 Nietzsche, *Werke*, III, 883 (*WM*, §579); II, 957 (*GD*, ' "Reason" in Philosophy', §1); III, 438 (*WM*, §407). The passages on II, 957 and III, 438 do not refer to metaphysics by name but only to 'the philosophers'. However, several passages suggest that Nietzsche considers all past philosophers to a certain extent to be metaphysicians; see, for example, I, 451 (*MA*, §6, 'For this reason there is so much high-flying metaphysics in all philosophies. . .').
4 Nietzsche, *Werke*, III, 883 (*WM*, §579).
5 Nietzsche, *Werke*, I, 448 (*MA*, §2).
6 Nietzsche, *Werke*, II, 957 (*GD*, ' "Reason" in Philosophy', §1). See E. Fink, *Nietzsches Philosophie* (Stuttgart, 1960, fourth edition 1979), p. 140.

7 Nietzsche, *Werke*, II, 567–8 (*JGB*, §2).

8 M. Heidegger, 'Wer ist Nietzsches Zarathustra?', in *Vorträge und Aufsätze* (Pfullingen, 1954), p. 112 (Magnus trans., p. 70).

9 Nietzsche, *Werke*, III, 883 (*WM*, §579). See also II, 958 (*GD*, ' "Reason" in Philosophy', §2); and II, 1171 (*A*, §10, 'One had made of reality an "appearance" '). Examples of Nietzsche's use of the term 'metaphysical world' (rather than just 'true world') are to be found on I, 452 (*MA*, §9); and I, 462 (*MA*, §21).

10 Nietzsche, *Werke*, I, 461 (*MA*, §18, 'But inasmuch as all metaphysics. . .'); III, 883 (*WM*, §579); III, 540–1 (*WM*, §552c, 'Duration, identity with itself, being. . .').

11 Nietzsche, *Werke*, III, 895 (*WM*, §617).

12 Nietzsche, *Werke*, II, 344 (*ASZ*, II, 'On the Blissful Islands'); II, 1178 (*A*, §18). See Stern, *A Study of Nietzsche*, p. 145. The warrant for implying that Nietzsche sees Christianity as having a 'metaphysical' conception of God is provided by a passage from the *Nachlaß* headed 'Psychology of metaphysics: the influence of timidity'; see III, 912 (*WM*, §576, 'God as the antithesis of evil. . .').

13 Nietzsche, *Werke*, II, 1170 (*A*, §9). See also II, 431 (*ASZ*, III, 'Of the Apostates', §2, 'There is *one* God! . . .').

14 Nietzsche, *Werke*, II, 134–5 (*FW*, §143). Hans Küng argues, however, that Christians claim unique, but not exclusive authority for their religion; see *Christ sein* (Munich, 1974, fifth edition 1980), pp. 125–7.

15 Nietzsche, *Werke*, II, 577 (*JGB*, §12).

16 Nietzsche, *Werke*, I, 749 (*VMS*, §17).

17 Nietzsche, *Werke*, III, 821–2 (*WM*, §765, 'Christianity has accustomed us to the superstitious concept of the "soul". . .').

18 Nietzsche, *Werke*, II, 1175 (*A*, §15).

19 Nietzsche, *Werke*, I, 1096 (*M*, §120); I, 481 (*MA*, §39, 'Nobody is responsible for his actions'); I, 512 (*MA*, §106). See Schacht, p. 312, 'What we do . . .'.

20 Nietzsche, *Werke*, III, 767 (*WM*, §551, 'We have absolutely no experience of a cause').

21 Nietzsche, *Werke*, II, 790 (*GM*, I, §13, 'das Tun ist alles', 'the doing is everything'). (Kaufmann and Hollingdale translate *das Tun* rather inappropriately as 'the deed' and thus lose the sense of dynamism conveyed by Nietzsche's verbal noun.)

22 See Nietzsche, *Werke*, II, 1015 (*GD*, 'Expeditions', §38, 'Freedom means. . .'); III, 913 (*WM*, §705); III, 696 (*WM*, §46).

23 Nietzsche, *Werke*, III, 729 (*WM*, §515, 'No pre-existing "Idea" was here at work').

24 Nietzsche, *Werke*, III, 502–3 (*WM*, §557); III, 752 (*WM*, §625).

25 Nietzsche, *Werke*, II, 115–16 (*FW*, §109).

26 Nietzsche, *Werke*, II, 977–8 (*GD*, 'The Four Great Errors', §8).

27 Nietzsche, *Werke*, III, 685 (*WM*, §715, ' "multiplicities" in any case; but "units" are nowhere present in the nature of becoming').

28 Nietzsche, *Werke*, II, 978 (*GD*, 'The Four Great Errors', §8).

29 Nietzsche, *Werke*, III, 678 (*WM*, §12a).

30 Even the 'monistic' Spinoza, who sometimes earns Nietzsche's highest praise for his denial of evil and of the freedom of the will (see *Werke*, III, 1171, letter to Franz Overbeck, franked 30 July 1881), is associated by Nietzsche with the hatred of transience, which he holds to be characteristic of dualistic thinking; see, for example, III, 518 (*WM*, §578, 'Descartes' contempt for everything that changes; also that of Spinoza').

31 Nietzsche, *Werke*, II, 957 (*GD*, ' "Reason" in Philosophy', §1, 'Moral: escape from sense-perception. . .').

32 Nietzsche, *Werke*, II, 978 (*GD*, 'The Four Great Errors', §8).

33 Nietzsche, *Werke*, I, 450 (*MA*, §5).

34 Nietzsche, *Werke*, III, 883–4 (*WM*, §579).

35 Nietzsche, *Werke*, II, 568 (*JGB*, §2).

36 The idea that selfishness and selflessness are wholly opposed to one another is, of course, an important principle of Schopenhauerian metaphysics in particular. On the incompatibility of self-interested will and pure aesthetic contemplation, for example, see Schopenhauer, *Sämtliche Werke*, II, 209–13 (*WWV*, I, Book 3, §34, Payne trans., I, 178–81). Schopenhauer differs slightly from Nietzsche's model of traditional metaphysics, however, in that he locates the source of selfless contemplation in the transcendental 'subject of knowing' (*Subjekt des Erkennens*), rather than in the transcendent 'thing-in-itself', which he determines as 'will'.

37 Nietzsche, *Werke*, I, 907 (*WS*, §67). See III, 615 (*WM*, §786, 'One must therefore attack determinism. . .'); III, 763 (*WM*, §583, 'We possess no categories. . .'); III, 531 (*WM*, §124, 'To remove *antitheses* [*Gegensätze*] from things. . .'); III, 541 (*WM*, §552, 'There are no opposites [*Gegensätze*] . . .').

38 Nietzsche, *Werke*, II, 963. See also Stern's remarks on Nietzsche's criticism of metaphysical and grammatical antitheses (*A Study of Nietzsche*, pp. 61, 67, 201). Nietzsche is in fact not only critical of metaphysical and grammatical antitheses, but also of cultural divisions; see I, 237 (*UB*, II, §4, '*the unity of German spirit and life*').

39 Nietzsche, *Werke*, III, 875 (*WM*, §562, 'Root of the idea of substance in language. . .'); II, 581 (*JGB*, §19, 'a unity only as a word. . .'); I, 893 (*WS*, §33, 'never wearied of scenting a similar unity in the word "value". . .'). See also II, 584 (*JGB*, §20).

40 Nietzsche, *Werke*, III, 476 (*WM*, §532, 'There could be no judgements at all. . .'); III, 498–9 (*WM*, §500, 'Our sense-perceptions. . .'); III, 526 (*WM*, §521, 'This same compulsion. . .').

41 Nietzsche, *Werke*, II, 959 (*GD*, ' "Reason" in Philosophy', §5); I, 878–9 (*WS*, §11).

42 Nietzsche, *Werke*, III, 675 (*WM*, §704, 'The fact of a millionfold growth. . .'); III, 795 (*WM*, §536, 'Whatever is real. . .'); II, 221 (*FW*, §354, 'Fundamentally, all our actions. . .'); III, 313 (*ÜWL*, Breazeale trans., p. 83, 'We obtain the concept. . .'). See also J. T. Wilcox, *Truth and Value in Nietzsche* (Michigan, 1974), p. 128. In this chapter I have quoted

from Nietzsche's early essay *On Truth and Lie in an Extra-moral sense* (1873) alongside much later texts of Nietzsche because I believe that Nietzsche's views on language expressed in that essay, though refined and developed, do not change fundamentally throughout his philosophical career. See also such early passages as I, 43–4 (*GT*, §6) and III, 365 (*PTZG*, §3), where Nietzsche talks of the divorce between language and philosophical or 'musical' intuition, a divorce which parallels the distinction between language and life and which clearly has its roots in Schopenhauer's distinction between 'representation' (*Vorstellung*) and 'will'.

43 Nietzsche, *Werke*, III, 685 (*WM*, §715). See also III, 543 (*WM*, §517, 'The character of the world in a state of becoming as incapable of formulation').

44 Nietzsche, *Werke*, II, 579–80 (*JGB*, §16); III, 501 (*WM*, §550, 'fundamental belief . . . that there are subjects, that everything that happens is related attributively [*prädikativ*] to some subject'); III, 577 (*WM*, §484, 'a formulation of our grammatical custom that adds a doer to every deed [*Tun*]'). See chapter 3, note 199.

45 Nietzsche, *Werke*, II, 222 (*FW*, §354); II, 960 (*GD*, ' "Reason" in Philosophy', §5, 'I fear we are not getting rid of God because we still believe in grammar. . .'); I, 878 (*WS*, §11, 'We do not merely thereby *designate* [*bezeichnen*] things; the thought at the back of our minds is that by the word and the concept we can grasp their *essence* [*das* Wahre *desselben*]'). See also I, 453 (*MA*, §11).

46 Nietzsche, *Werke*, III, 862 (*WM*, §522, '*We cease to think*. . .'); III, 751 (*WM*, §625, 'We cannot change our means of expression at will. . .'); II, 600 (*JGB*, §34 'Ought the philosopher not to rise above the belief in grammar?').

47 Nietzsche, *Werke*, III, 685 (*WM*,§715, 'Linguistic means of expression. . .').

48 Nietzsche, *Werke*, II, 1170 (*A*, §8, 'Pure spirit is pure lie. . .'); II, 1175 (*A*, §15, 'This purely *fictitious world*. . .').

49 Nietzsche, *Werke*, I, 448 (*MA*, §2); III, 917 (*WM*, §1067).

50 Nietzsche, *Werke*, III, 313–14 (*ÜWL*, Breazeale trans., pp. 83–4). For a longer discussion of this essay, see Stern, *A Study of Nietzsche*, pp. 182–6.

51 The relativity of all human knowledge seems to be twofold for Nietzsche; it is both individual and social. When a person thinks he knows something, therefore, he is really conscious of 'his own relationship to many other things (or the relationship of the species [*oder die Relation der Art*])' (Nietzsche, *Werke*, III, 440 (*WM*, §496)).

52 Nietzsche, *Werke*, I, 479 (*MA*, §39); III, 390 (*PTZG*, §11, 'Words are but symbols for the relations of things to one another and to us'); III, 751 (*WM*, §625, 'it is of the essence of a language . . . to express a mere relationship').

53 Nietzsche, *Werke*, III, 751 (*WM*, §625, 'The demand for an *adequate mode of expression* is *senseless*').

54 Nietzsche, *Werke*, II, 119 (*FW*, §112).

55 Nietzsche, *Werke*, II, 586 (*JGB*, §22, 'Granted this too is only interpretation. . .'). See Wilcox, pp. 158–9; and Schacht, pp. 95–6.

56 Nietzsche, *Werke*, II, 600 (*JGB*, §34). See also III, 915 (*WM*, §535); and J. Derrida, *Éperons* (Paris/Chicago, 1979), p. 107.

57 Nietzsche, *Werke*, II, 382 (*ASZ*, II, 'Of Poets', 'But Zarathustra too is a poet'); II, 379 (*ASZ*, II, 'Of Immaculate Perception', 'Yet with them I can still – tell the truth to hypocrites!'); II, 394 (*ASZ*, II, 'Of Redemption', 'Is he a poet? Or a truthful man [*ein Wahrhaftiger*]?'); II, 526 (*ASZ*, IV, 'Of the Higher Man', §9, 'He who cannot lie does not know what truth is'); II, 1152 (*EH*, IV, §1, 'Perhaps I am a buffoon. . .'). I shall use inverted commas in this chapter to distinguish Nietzsche's metaphorical and creative 'truth' from the metaphysical ideal of literal or definitive truth. My usage of inverted commas in this way does not, however, exactly parallel Nietzsche's own, but is intended to introduce some systematic clarity into Nietzsche's often bewildering discussion.

58 Hegel, *TWA*, XIII, 516–39 (*Ä*, Knox trans., I, 402–21); X, 269 (*E*, III, §457, Addition).

59 Nietzsche, *Werke*, I, 903 (*WS*, §55); II, 752 (*JGB*, §289).

60 Nietzsche, *Werke*, II, 1066 (*EH*, Preface, §3). See M. Pasley, 'Nietzsche's Use of Medical Terms', in *Nietzsche: Imagery and Thought*, edited by M. Pasley (Cambridge, 1978), pp. 134–6.

61 T. J. Reed has pointed to the dangers inherent in Nietzsche's 'confusion between literal and metaphorical statement', particularly in his frequent reduction of harsh realities such as war to the status of 'exhortatory and excitatory cyphers' or metaphors of mood; see 'Nietzsche's Animals: Idea, Image and Influence', in *Nietzsche: Imagery and Thought*, edited by M. Pasley, p. 178.

62 Nietzsche, *Werke*, I, 1096 (*M*, §121).

63 Nietzsche, *Werke*, III, 769 (*WM*, §568).

64 Nietzsche, *Werke*, II, 365 (*ASZ*, II, 'The Dance Song').

65 See Derrida, p. 55.

66 Nietzsche, *Werke*, I, 651 (*MA*, §405); II, 946 (*GD*, 'Maxims and Arrows', §27). The 'mystery' of life or 'woman' for Nietzsche is precisely that it (she) seduces us into searching for a hidden ideal form or essence which is in fact no more than a fiction; see II, 79–80 (*FW*, §60); III, 870 (*WM*, §806, 'Woman, conscious of man's feelings concerning women. . .').

67 Nietzsche, *Werke*, I, 32 (*GT*, §4, 'primal unity'); I, 282 (*UB*, II, §10, 'life'); II, 118 (*FW*, §110, 'life'); III, 681 (*WM*, §674, 'occurring'); II, 115 (*FW*, §109, 'chaos'); II, 120 (*FW*, §112, 'continuum'); III, 769 (*WM*, §568, 'the world'); III, 776 (*WM*, §689, 'the only reality'); II, 1175 (*A*, §15, 'actuality'); III, 503 (*WM*, §604, 'everything is fluid'). See also M. Haar, 'Nietzsche and Metaphysical Language', in *The New Nietzsche*, edited by D. Allison, p. 11.

68 Nietzsche, *Werke*, II, 196 (*FW*, §335, 'every action that has ever been done. . .'); II, 221 (*FW*, §354, 'Fundamentally, all our actions. . .'). See also II, 208 (*FW*, §344), where Nietzsche contrasts faith in 'morality' and 'science' with belief in *this* world of 'life, nature and history'.

69 See, for example, Nietzsche, *Werke*, II, 117–18 (*FW*, §110, 'This subtler honesty and scepticism. . .').

70 Nietzsche, *Werke*, III, 730 (*WM*, §539).

71 Nietzsche, *Werke*, III, 475 (*WM*, §492).

72 Examples of the use of negative definition are found on Nietzsche, *Werke*, II, 211 (*FW*, §346, 'ungodly, immoral, "inhuman". . .'); II, 572–3 (*JGB*, §9, 'without mercy or justice. . .'). Examples of the use of the word 'something' are found on III, 440 (*WM*, §686, 'something flows on *underneath* individuals. . .'); 489 (*WM*, §643, 'ein wachsenwollendes Etwas', 'something that wants to grow' – note that in this passage Nietzsche actually writes '*a* something', not just 'something'); and 537 (*WM*, §488, 'rather something that in itself. . .').

73 Nietzsche, *Werke*, III, 486 (*WM*, §410); 499 (*WM*, §486). See Habermas, pp. 353–4.

74 Nietzsche, *Werke*, I, 110 (*GT*, §19). Similarly, perhaps, one could suggest that Nietzsche treats natural science as a means to clarify and underscore his basic convictions, rather than as a source of genuine discovery.

75 Nietzsche, *Werke*, III, 321 (*ÜWL*, Breazeale trans., p. 90); III, 534 (*WM*, §569, 'the formless unformulable world. . .'); III, 540 (*WM*, §552, 'Sensationen-Wirrwarr', 'medley of sensations'); I, 1095 (*M*, §119). See also II, 859–60 (*GM*, III, §12, 'what is felt most certainly to be real and actual . . . where the instinct of life most unconditionally posits truth'). It will be noted that in Nietzsche's view the senses are responsible for producing fictional form and yet also serve as a chaotic foundation against which fictions are judged to be false.

76 Stern, *A Study of Nietzsche*, p. 95.

77 Nietzsche, *Werke*, I, 1106, (*M*, §133, 'how coarsely does language assault . . . so polyphonous a being'). This passage refers specifically to the complexity of the feeling of pity.

78 See Fink, p. 165. What distinguishes Nietzsche from the metaphysician is actually both a cognitive and a 'moral' capacity. Nietzsche claims to have a more vivid experience or feeling of life than the metaphysician and is therefore unable to accept linguistic forms as true; see *Werke*, III, 627 (*WM*, §485, 'The degree to which we feel life and power. . .'). However, he also claims to have a greater will to confront and affirm life than the metaphysician, and is therefore unwilling to accept linguistic forms as true; see II, 1032 (*GD*, 'What I Owe to the Ancients', §5, 'Affirmation of life. . .').

79 Nietzsche, *Werke*, II, 958 (*GD*, ' "Reason" in Philosophy', §2).

80 Nietzsche, *Werke*, III, 534 (*WM*, §569).

81 Nietzsche, *Werke*, II, 766 (*GM*, Preface, §4).

82 Nietzsche, *Werke*, II, 600 (*JGB*, §36).

83 Nietzsche, *Werke*, III, 476 (*WM*, §532, 'the *body* . . . is the much richer phenomenon. . .'); III, 500 (*WM*, §518, 'it is allowable . . . to employ the more easily studied, much richer phenomenon as evidence for the understanding of the poorer'); III, 860 (*WM*, §489).

84 Nietzsche, *Werke*, II, 196 (*FW*, §335, 'Anyone who still judges. . .').

85 Nietzsche, *Werke*, III, 751 (*WM*, §480, 'There exists neither "spirit" . . .

nor truth'); II, 1152 (*EH*, IV, §1, 'I was the first to *discover* the truth. . .').
For a fuller discussion of Nietzsche's views on truth, see Schacht, pp. 52–
117.

86 Nietzsche, *Werke*, II, 585 (*JGB*, §21, 'for the purpose of designation'); I,
471 (*MA*, §32, 'We are from the beginning illogical, and therefore unjust
beings, and *can recognise this*'). Evidence for the fact that it is indeed the
accurate or adequate articulation of the character of life that Nietzsche
rejects when he rejects truth, is to be found in the essay *On Truth and Lie in
an Extra-moral Sense*, where the term 'adequate expression' stands in
apposition to the word 'truth'; see III, 312 (*ÜWL*, Breazeale trans., p. 82,
'with words it is never a question of truth, never a question of
adequate expression').

87 Nietzsche, *Werke*, III, 321 (*ÜWL*, Breazeale trans., p. 90). See also II, 379
(*ASZ*, II, 'Of Immaculate Perception', '*my* words are poor, despised, halt-
ing words . . . Yet with them I can still – tell the truth to hypocrites!').

88 Nietzsche, *Werke*, III, 271 (*ÜPW*, Breazeale trans., p. 65).

89 See *The New Nietzsche*, edited by D. Allison, pp. xv–xvi (Introduction by
D. Allison). In her essay 'Nietzsche's Conception of Truth', in *Nietzsche:
Imagery and Thought*, edited by M. Pasley, pp. 33–63, Mary Warnock has
also suggested that there is a difference between the literal truth that
Nietzsche rejects and the hypothetical 'truth' of his own statements.
However, Warnock associates this distinction with another alleged distinction in Nietzsche's writings between particular (literal) statements
of fact and general (hypothetical) scientific theories (pp. 61–2). To my
mind this latter distinction is not one Nietzsche actually draws. What he
is concerned to show is that no linguistic statement – whether general or
particular – does full justice to the complexity of the 'facts', and that
therefore all linguistic statements, including everyday statements, scientific hypotheses and his own metaphorical 'truths' involve a creative
falsification and simplification of whatever is referred to or expressed by
the utterance.

90 See, for example, Nietzsche, *Werke*, II, 1156 (*EH*, IV, §5, 'conceives
reality *as it is*'). See also Schacht, p. 108. This ambiguity is perhaps most
evident in Nietzsche's notion of 'joyful science', which incorporates a
creative, fiction-producing moment and an element of feeling-based or
sensuous 'positivism'. (What is meant by talking of the 'realism' of
Nietzsche's philosophy is that his general metaphorical characterisations of life are based on his 'realistic' grasp of what human life is, and
that his interpretations of particular people and cultures are made in the
light of those general characterisations. It does not of course mean that
Nietzsche claims unmediated knowledge of those particular people and
cultures themselves.)

91 Nietzsche, *Werke*, II, 12 (*FW*, Preface, §3, 'constantly, we have to give
birth to our thoughts. . .').

92 Nietzsche, *Werke*, II, 302 (*ASZ*, I, 'Of Joys and Passions', 'Unutterable
and nameless. . .'); III, 444 (*WM*, §943, 'Our doubts as to the com-
municability of the heart. . .').

93 Nietzsche, *Werke*, II, 167 (*FW*, §286); II, 697 (*JGB*, §231); II, 740 (*JGB*,

§268); II, 1100 (*EH*, III, §1, 'For what one lacks access to from experience. . .').

94 See Stern, *A Study of Nietzsche*, pp. 36, 107.

95 See Stern, *A Study of Nietzsche*, p. 106.

96 The term 'anti-metaphysical' is not merely my characterisation of Nietzsche's thought, but is one that he himself uses to describe his own philosophy; see *Werke*, III, 481 (*WM*, §1048, 'an anti-metaphysical view of the world – yes, but an artistic one').

97 Nietzsche, *Werke*, II, 300 (*ASZ*, I, 'Of the Despisers of the Body'). See Schacht, p. 317.

98 Nietzsche, *Werke*, I, 1093–6 (*M*, §119); III, 903 (*WM*, §481, 'It is our needs *that interpret the world*. . .').

99 Nietzsche, *Werke*, III, 707 (*WM*, §314). See also II, 600 (*JGB*, §36, 'Thinking is only the relationship of these drives. . .'); III, 673–4 (*WM*, §477, 'Between two thoughts. . .').

100 Nietzsche, *Werke*, II, 222 (*FW*, §354, 'We simply lack any organ for knowledge. . .'); III, 475 (*WM*, §492, 'We gain the correct idea. . .').

101 Nietzsche, *Werke*, II, 600 (*JGB*, §34). Precisely how physiological life becomes conscious and linguistic is to my mind never adequately explained by Nietzsche. Whether the notion of 'sublimation' is sufficient to explain this development is a matter for debate. (For the earlier passage referred to, see chapter 3, pp. 51–3).

102 Nietzsche, *Werke*, III, 461 (*WM*, §362, 'the false valuation is aimed at the interests. . .').

103 Nietzsche, *Werke*, I, 48 (*GT*, §7). See also I, 212–13 (*UB*, II, §1, 'Imagine the extremest possible example. . .').

104 Nietzsche, *Werke*, II, 119 (*FW*, §111, 'every sceptical tendency. . .'); II, 113–14 (*FW*, §107); II, 569 (*JGB*, §4); II, 589 (*JGB*, §24).

105 Nietzsche, *Werke*, I, 22–3 (*GT*, §1, 'It is a dream!. . .'); I, 34 (*GT*, §4, 'Apollo could not live without Dionysus!').

106 Nietzsche, *Werke*, II, 208 (*FW*, §344, 'that it is still a *metaphysical faith*. . .'); II, 888–91 (*GM*, III, §24).

107 See Stern, *A Study of Nietzsche*, p. 124.

108 Nietzsche, *Werke*, I, 447–8 (*MA*, §§1–2, 'Historical philosophy. . .'). See R. Hayman, *Nietzsche: A Critical Life* (London, 1980), p. 1.

109 Nietzsche, *Werke*, II, 130 (*FW*, §132, 'taste'); II, 146 (*FW*, §184, 'taste'); II, 1152 (*EH*, IV, §1, 'My genius is in my nostrils. . .'); II, 12 (*FW*, Preface, §3, 'this art of transfiguration. . .').

110 Nietzsche, *Werke*, I, 1092–3 (*M*, §117); II, 249–50 (*FW*, §374); II, 861 (*GM*, III, §12); III, 440 (*WM*, §496).

111 Schopenhauer, *Sämtliche Werke*, II, 118 (*WWV*, I, Book 2, §18, Payne trans., I, 99, 'his knowledge . . . is . . . given entirely through the medium of a body').

112 Nietzsche, *Werke*, II, 860–1 (*GM*, III, §12). See Schopenhauer, *Sämtliche Werke*, II, 210–11 (*WWV*, I, Book 3, §34, Payne trans., I, 179, '*pure*, will-less, painless, timeless *subject of knowledge*').

113 Nietzsche, *Werke*, I, 1093 (*M*, §118). Examples of how we fashion the

other into our own creation are found on I, 647–8 (*MA*, §§380, 385). Nietzsche can of course only justify his claim that we falsify the other on the basis of his general conviction that we are falsifying beings, not because he can in any way directly compare the other with his perception of the other.

114 Nietzsche, *Werke*, III, 455 (*WM*, §619); II, 600–1 (*JGB*, §36); III, 835 (*WM*, §320, 'We read something else into the heart of things. . .'). Here again is a parallel with Schopenhauer, who tried to understand natural objects distinct from our own body 'according to the analogy of this body', and who consequently conceived of those objects as objectifications of will; see *Sämtliche Werke*, II, 125 (*WWV*, I, Book 2, §19, Payne trans., I, 105). Schopenhauer, however, was much less conscious than Nietzsche of the fact that he was merely employing an analogy.

115 Fink talks of Nietzsche's fictionalist epistemology committing him to a 'negative ontology of the thing' (p. 165).

116 Nietzsche, *Werke*, III, 685 (*WM*, §715).

117 Nietzsche, *Werke*, III, 495 (*WM*, §600). See chapter 3, pp. 42–3.

118 Nietzsche, *Werke*, III, 778 (*WM*, §635); III, 502–3 (*WM*, §557); III, 752 (*WM*, §625); III, 706 (*WM*, §567, 'totality of these actions'). See Schacht, pp. 202, 209, 265.

119 Nietzsche, *Werke*, III, 534 (*WM*, §569).

120 Nietzsche, *Werke*, III, 487 (*WM*, §556).

121 Nietzsche, *Werke*, III, 489 (*WM*, §643).

122 Nietzsche, *Werke*, III, 858 (*WM*, §501, 'All thought, judgement, perception. . .'). The pride of place Nietzsche gives to interpreting texts, as opposed to labour or to intersubjective communication, is evidence, I think, of his aestheticised and highly literary view of life. Two examples of Nietzsche's use of the metaphor of reading a text to talk about other human activities are to be found on I, 1094–5 (*M*, §119) and II, 602 (*JGB*, §38), where the metaphor is used to describe how we produce dreams and how we view history.

123 Nietzsche, *Werke*, III, 489 (*WM*, §643).

124 Nietzsche, *Werke*, III, 769 (*WM*, §568). It is true that Nietzsche sometimes talks of language and consciousness as mere epiphenomena of the body without any positive role to play at all. This view is contradicted, however, by his theory that Western man's natural energies have been disciplined and internalised by his rationality. In general, I think, Nietzsche sees language as a potent product of human physiology; see Schacht, pp. 302–4, 312–15; and Wilcox, pp. 17–26.

125 Nietzsche, *Werke*, I, 131 (*GT*, §24, 'an artistic game. . .'); III, 425 (*WM*, §1046, 'das *künstlerische* Grundphänomen', 'the *artistic* basic phenomenon'); II, 113–14 (*FW*, §107, 'as an aesthetic phenomenon existence is still *bearable* for us'); II, 514 (*ASZ*, IV, 'At Noontide', 'What? Has the world not just become perfect? Round and ripe?'); II, 473–6 (*ASZ*, III, 'The Seven Seals', '*For I love you, o Eternity!*').

126 See chapter 3, pp. 42–3.

127 Nietzsche, *Werke*, III, 706 (*WM*, §567, 'The *specific mode of reacting*').

128 Nietzsche, *Werke*, III, 767–8 (*WM*, §551, 'A necessary sequence of states. . .'). On the similarity between Nietzsche and Hume in this respect, see A. Danto, *Nietzsche as Philosopher* (Columbia, 1965), p. 94. For a conception of causality such as that criticised by Nietzsche, see Schopenhauer, *Sämtliche Werke*, I, 34–6 (*VWSG*, §20, Payne trans., pp. 52–5).

129 Nietzsche, *Werke*, III, 542 (*WM*, §552, 'All occurring. . .'); III, 768–9 (*WM*, §633, 'Two successive states. . .'); III, 896 (*WM*, §617, 'Instead of "cause and effect" . . .'). The idea that nature is a constant process of struggle or *Kampf* is also a Schopenhauerian one; see *Sämtliche Werke*, II, 173–8 (*WWV*, I, Book 2, §27, Payne trans., I, 145–9). For an account of Nietzsche's relation to Darwin, who of course also conceived of life in terms of struggle, see Stern, *A Study of Nietzsche*, pp. 111–13.

130 Nietzsche, *Werke*, I, 512 (*MA*, §106). See III, 377 (*PTZG*, §7, 'Man is necessity down to his last fibre, and totally "unfree", that is if one means by freedom the foolish demand to be able to change one's *essentia* arbitrarily, like a garment').

131 Nietzsche, *Werke*, III, 684 (*WM*, §708); II, 115–16 (*FW*, §109, 'in the sense not of a lack of necessity. . .'). See III, 615 (*WM*, §786, 'Determinism. . .').

132 Nietzsche, *Werke*, III, 586 (*WM*, §639).

133 Nietzsche, *Werke*, II, 161 (*FW*, §276); II, 1156 (*EH*, IV, §5, 'reality *as it is*. . .').

134 Fink, pp. 102–3, 'To give to the thisness [*Diesheit*] and facticity of existence an in-finite depth'. See Nietzsche, *Werke*, III, 680 (*WM*, §1065, 'I seek an eternity for everything').

135 Nietzsche, *Werke*, III, 705 (*WM*, §636).

136 Nietzsche, *Werke*, III, 487 (*WM*, §556, 'the "*it is deemed to be*" is the real "*it is*", the sole "this is" '). Nietzsche's own use of 'is' in this passage is meant to register the fact that the metaphysical 'it is' is a relative assertion or '*opinion* about the "thing" ' (III, 487 (*WM*, §556)); it is not itself meant to commit Nietzsche to any such 'opinion' (although it does indirectly commit him to a negative ontology).

137 Nietzsche, *Werke*, II, 1090 (*M*, §115, *'we are none of us*. . .'). See chapter 3, note 72.

138 Nietzsche, *Werke*, III, 775–6 (*WM*, §689); II, 601 (*JGB*, §36). This attempt to understand the world in terms of will to power alone is not an arbitrary whim of Nietzsche's, but is dictated to him by his 'conscience of method' which demands that we must not resort to a variety of types of causality until the attempt to get by with one type of causality has been taken to its extreme – perhaps absurd – limit. Nietzsche's theory is therefore a conscious experiment in the simplified interpretation of life; see II, 601 (*JGB*, §36).

139 Heidegger, 'Wer ist Nietzsches Zarathustra?', p. 121 (Magnus trans., p. 76).

140 Nietzsche, *Werke*, III, 690 (*WM*, §690).

141 Nietzsche, *Werke*, II, 581 (*JGB*, §19, 'Willing seems to me. . .'); III, 750

(*WM*, §692, 'that this will *does not exist at all...*'); III, 685 (*WM*, §715, 'There is no will...'); III, 913 (*WM*, §671, 'There is no such thing as "will"...').

142 Nietzsche, *Werke*, II, 601 (*JGB*, §36); III, 917 (*WM*, §1067, '*and nothing besides...*').
143 See chapter 3, pp. 42–3.
144 Nietzsche, *Werke*, III, 527 (*WM*, §308, 'the homogeneity [*Einartigkeit*] in all occurring'); III, 582 (*WM*, §272, 'the absolute homogeneity [*Homogeneität*]...').
145 Nietzsche, *Werke*, III, 679 (*WM*, §675).
146 Nietzsche, *Werke*, III, 778 (*WM*, §635).
147 Nietzsche, *Werke*, III, 455 (*WM*, §619, 'an inner will...'). See Haar, 'Nietzsche and Metaphysical Language', p. 10. Nietzsche is hostile to the idea of an overriding moral teleology guiding life to the goal of peace or 'goodness', but he does not object to the metaphorical conception, drawn from his own experience, that chaos has its own inner – 'teleological' – orientation striving towards greater growth and power.
148 Nietzsche, *Werke*, III, 778 (*WM*, §635).
149 Nietzsche, *Werke*, III, 917 (*WM*, §1067, 'Do you want a *name* for this world?'); III, 896 (*WM*, §617, 'verkleinerte Formel', 'diminutive formula'); and Haar, 'Nietzsche and Metaphysical Language', p. 11.
150 Nietzsche, *Werke*, III, 461 (*WM*, §362); III, 428 (*WM*, §364); III, 439 (*WM*, §873); II, 1008 (*GD*, 'Expeditions', §33).
151 Nietzsche, *Werke*, III, 456 (*WM*, §549); III, 627 (*WM*, §485).
152 Nietzsche, *Werke*, II, 729–33 (*JGB*, §260). People are categorised by Nietzsche as masters or slaves, but he also acknowledges that strength and weakness can be found together in one individual (II, 730).
153 Nietzsche, *Werke*, II, 968 (*GD*, 'Morality as Anti-Nature', §5, 'When we speak of values...').
154 Nietzsche, *Werke*, I, 468 (*MA*, §28); II, 631 (*JGB*, §108); II, 644–5 (*JGB*, §187); II, 979 (*GD*, 'The "Improvers" of Mankind', §1).
155 Nietzsche, *Werke*, II, 1180–1 (*A*, §21).
156 Nietzsche, *Werke*, II, 789–90 (*GM*, I, §13). For an alternative account of the origins of the notion of free will, see II, 810 (*GM*, II, §7).
157 Nietzsche, *Werke*, II, 779 (*GM*, I, §7, 'an act of the *most spiritual revenge*'); II, 865 (*GM*, III, §14, '*poisoning the consciences* of the fortunate...'); II, 815–16 (*GM*, II, §11, 'conversely, one can see...'). In §§16–25 of *The Genealogy of Morals*, however, Nietzsche suggests that it is social pressures which infect the strong with bad conscience, and that the weak (through religion) act essentially to intensify that bad conscience but do not actually bring it about.
158 Nietzsche, *Werke*, II, 859 (*GM*, III, §11, 'here physiological well-being itself is viewed askance...'); II, 1178 (*A*, §18).
159 Nietzsche, *Werke*, I, 1073–4 (*M*, §95); III, 897 (*WM*, §588). See Fink, pp. 46–7.
160 See, for example, Nietzsche, *Werke*, III, 481 (*WM*, §70), where Nietzsche says that the force within man is infinitely superior to the influence of

milieu. Although the strong and healthy can be weakened by the weak and sick in Nietzsche's view, the weak, at least according to *Ecce Homo*, cannot be made strong; see II, 1020–1 (*GD*, 'Expeditions', §45, 'a strong human being made sick'); II, 1072 (*EH*, II, §2, 'a typically morbid being. . .'). On this interpretation, strength and health can never be acquired, but can only be released from the shackles of the slaves' fictions; see II, 750 (*JGB*, §287, 'something which may not be sought or found and perhaps may not be lost either'). Although Nietzsche does talk at times of 'breeding' a new race of strong men, therefore (III, 810 (*WM*, §398); III, 521 (*WM*, §898)), it seems that he views the weak themselves as irredeemably weak and beyond conversion, and that such breeding must be understood as a process of selecting and strengthening those who are already fundamentally strong. (Deleuze points out that the weak come to dominate the strong, not by becoming strong themselves, but by separating the strong from their strength through the fiction of bad conscience; see *Nietzsche*, pp. 26–7; and Nietzsche, *Werke*, II, 789 (*GM*, I, §13, 'so popular morality also separates. . .').)

161 See chapter 3, pp. 58–9.
162 Nietzsche, *Werke*, III, 827 (*WM*, §54, 'I teach the Yes. . .').
163 Nietzsche, *Werke*, II, 208 (*FW*, §344, 'a *metaphysical faith* . . . that truth is divine. . .'); II, 889 (*GM*, III, §24, '*they still believe in truth*. . .').
164 Nietzsche, *Werke*, I, 1031 (*M*, §26, 'Even the sense for truth. . .').
165 Nietzsche, *Werke*, II, 12 (*FW*, Preface, §2, 'what was at stake in all philosophising hitherto. . .'); II, 371 (*ASZ*, II, 'Of Self-Overcoming', 'Truly, my will to power walks. . .').
166 Nietzsche, *Werke*, III, 919 (*WM*, §534).
167 Nietzsche, *Werke*, II, 294 (*ASZ*, I, 'Of the Three Metamorphoses').
168 Nietzsche, *Werke*, III, 470 (*WM*, §125). In this sense, therefore, Nietzsche can speak of 'the actual order of rank and differences in the value of men' (*die tatsächliche Rangordnung und Wert-Verschiedenheit der Menschen*) (III, 458 (*WM*, §988)), the 'objective' moral superiority of the strong over the weak.
169 See Schacht, pp. 96–7.
170 Nietzsche, *Werke*, II, 602 (*JGB*, §39, 'the strength of a spirit. . .'); III, 575 (*WM*, §852, 'It is a sign of one's *feeling of power*. . .'); III, 918 (*WM*, §1011, 'we have to realise. . .'). See also chapter 3, note 181.
171 See Pasley, 'Nietzsche's Use of Medical Terms', p. 126. For the reference to 'blond beasts', see Nietzsche, *Werke*, II, 786 (*GM*, I, §11). Examples of Nietzsche's praise of the Greeks are to be found throughout his writings; see, for example, I, 572 (*MA*, §214); I, 806 (*VMS*, §177); III, 463–4 (*WM*, §1051). In late texts, such as *Twilight of the Idols*, however, Nietzsche frequently praises the Romans above the Greeks; see II, 1028 (*GD*, 'What I Owe the Ancients', §2).
172 Nietzsche, *Werke*, II, 645–6 (*JGB*, §188); II, 1023 (*GD*, 'Expeditions', §48, 'not really a going-back. . .').
173 See Kaufmann, *Nietzsche*, pp. 220–2.
174 Nietzsche, *Werke*, I, 481 (*MA*, §40); II, 779 (*GM*, I, §7, 'Human history would be altogether too stupid a thing. . .').

175 Nietzsche, *Werke*, II, 566 (*JGB*, Preface).

176 Nietzsche, *Werke*, II, 965 (*GD*, 'Morality as Anti-Nature', §1).

177 Nietzsche, *Werke*, II, 987–8 (*GD*, 'What the Germans Lack', §6).

178 Nietzsche, *Werke*, II, 1019–20 (*GD*, 'Expeditions', §44).

179 Nietzsche, *Werke*, III, 589 (*WM*, §781).

180 Nietzsche, *Werke*, II, 797 (*GM*, I, §16, 'Napoleon'); II, 1024–5 (*GD*, 'Expeditions', §49, 'Goethe conceived. . .'). Like his mentor Schopenhauer, Nietzsche frequently displays great disdain for politics, particularly German politics; see II, 983 (*GD*, 'What the Germans Lack', §1). When he does praise political figures, however, it is usually because of their 'heroic' style, rather than because of specific political achievements; see the case of Bismarck (I, 1125 (*M*, §167, 'ein beweglicher Geist', 'an elastic mind')) or Cesare Borgia (II, 1012 (*GD*, 'Expeditions', §37, 'a "higher" man')).

181 Nietzsche, *Werke*, III, 697 (*WM*, §919, '*respecting* themselves. . .'); II, 160 (*FW*, §275); II, 878 (*GM*, III, §19, 'a genuine, resolute, "honest" lie. . .'); III, 438 (*WM*, §1059, 'It is also *our* work! – Let us be proud of it!'). The willingness to acknowledge that the production of 'appearance' (*Scheinbarkeit*) is the most fundamental human activity is an essential element of Nietzschean strength; see III, 555 (*WM*, §15); 477 (*WM*, §544).

182 Nietzsche, *Werke*, I, 1161 (*M*, §210); see I, 443 (*MA*, Preface, §6, 'how much *necessary* injustice there is in every for and against. . .').

183 See, for example, Nietzsche, *Werke*, I, 650 (*MA*, §402); I, 656 (*MA*, §421).

184 Nietzsche, *Werke*, II, 797 (*GM*, I, §17). This raises the problem, however, of how to evaluate many of Nietzsche's extreme statements on weakness, war and the sacrifice of human life to human greatness; see II, 312 (*ASZ*, I, 'Of War and Warriors', 'it is the good war that hallows every cause. . .'); II, 819 (*GM*, II, §12, 'The magnitude of an "advance". . .'). Is Nietzsche merely posing as bold, provocative and offensive to traditional morality? Or does he genuinely advocate his provocative suggestions? We know that Nietzsche delights in polemic, and we know, therefore, not to take everything he says at face value; but the problem of how we are to understand his more aggressive views is not easily resolved.

185 Nietzsche, *Werke*, II, 479 (*ASZ*, IV, 'The Honey Offering').

186 Nietzsche, *Werke*, II, 421 (*ASZ*, III, 'Of the Virtue that Makes Small', §3). Nietzsche's philosophy is thus directed at the production of a hierarchy of men with strong individuals at the top, and not at individual freedom and self-determination for all; see III, 907 (*WM*, §287). In this respect, of course, he differs strongly from his older contemporary, Kierkegaard.

187 Stern, *A Study of Nietzsche*, p. 117. See Hollingdale, pp. 183–4; and Heidegger, 'Wer ist Nietzsches Zarathustra?', pp. 110–13 (Magnus trans., pp. 70–1).

188 Nietzsche, *Werke*, II, 864 (*GM*, III, §14).

189 Stern, *A Study of Nietzsche*, p. 117.

190 See Deleuze, *Nietzsche*, p. 27; and A. Bullock, *Hitler: A Study in Tyranny* (Harmondsworth, 1962), pp. 159–60, 'Hitler, with an almost inexhaustible fund of resentment . . .'.

191 Nietzsche, *Werke*, III, 422 (*WM*, §966); III, 696 (*WM*, §46).

192 Nietzsche, *Werke*, I, 440–1 (*MA*, Preface, §4, 'health which does not care to dispense with sickness. . .'); III, 477 (*WM*, §1014); III, 592 (*WM*, §361, 'The *continuance* of the Christian ideal. . .'); II, 903–4 (*FWag*, Preface). See Pasley and Reed in *Nietzsche: Imagery and Thought*, edited by M. Pasley, pp. 130, 171.

193 Nietzsche, *Werke*, II, 1025 (*GD*, 'Expeditions', §49, 'tolerance . . . out of strength'); III, 461 (*WM*, §792, 'a mighty. . . spirit'). Although his idea of what constitutes true human freedom differs from that of Nietzsche in being social and communal rather than instinctual and 'heroically' individualistic, Hegel shares Nietzsche's distaste for resentment and envy; see *TWA*, XII, 47 (*PGesch*, Sibree trans., p. 31, 'The free man. . .').

194 Nietzsche, *Werke*, II, 819 (*GM*, II, §12, 'The magnitude of an "advance" . . .'); II, 1111 (*EH*, III, GT, §4, 'The relentless destruction . . .').

195 Nietzsche, *Werke*, II, 1166 (*A*, §2).

196 Nietzsche, *Werke*, III, 551 (*WM*, §449). For an excellent overall characterisation of Nietzsche's ideal of strength, see Schacht, p. 340.

197 Nietzsche, *Werke*, III, 481 (*WM*, §1048, 'an anti-metaphysical view of the world – yes, but an artistic one'). From Hegel's perspective, however, this fusion of philosophical insight and art makes Nietzsche's philosophy 'neither fish nor flesh' (*TWA*, III, 64 (*Phän*, Miller trans., p. 42)).

198 Nietzsche, *Werke*, II, 1104 (*EH*, III, §4). At times Nietzsche says he is interested in *method* (e.g. 'scientific' or 'critical' method) rather than just style, but it remains true that he is more interested in a mode or manner of being, thinking and writing, than in presenting propositional truths; see II, 1173, 1231 (*A*, §§13, 59).

199 Nietzsche, *Werke*, III, 476 (*WM*, §532); III, 501 (*WM*, §550); III, 502 (*WM*, §531). See chapter 3, note 44.

200 Nietzsche, *Werke*, III, 862 (*WM*, §522, '*We cease to think*. . .'); III, 751 (*WM*, §625, 'bloße Semiotik', 'mere signs'); III, 317 (*ÜWL*, Breazeale trans., p. 86, 'a suggestive transference. . .'); III, 365 (*PTZG*, §3, 'a metaphoric and entirely unfaithful translation. . .'). See Stern, *A Study of Nietzsche*, p. 184.

201 Nietzsche, *Werke*, II, 345 (*ASZ*, II, 'On the Blissful Islands').

202 Nietzsche, *Werke*, I, 1094 (*M*, §119). See Hayman, p. 358; and Wilcox, pp. 158–9.

203 Nietzsche, *Werke*, II, 119 (*FW*, §112, 'without reaching beyond the image or behind it. . .'); II, 961 (*GD*, ' "Reason" in Philosophy', §6, 'reality *once more*').

204 For a fuller discussion of Nietzsche's use of masks and his style of 'self-revelation and self-concealment', see W. D. Williams, 'Nietzsche's Masks', in *Nietzsche: Imagery and Thought*, edited by M. Pasley, pp. 83–103.

205 Nietzsche, *Werke*, II, 258 (*FW*, §382, 'plays naively . . . with all that was hitherto called holy, good, untouchable, divine. . .'); III, 321 (*ÜWL*, Breazeale trans., p. 90, 'shattering and mocking the old conceptual barriers').

206 Nietzsche, *Werke*, II, 585 (*JGB*, §21).

207 Nietzsche, *Werke*, III, 535 (*WM*, §569).

208 Other metaphysical terms which Nietzsche uses metaphorically are, for example, 'intelligible character' (II, 601 (*JGB*, §36)), 'soul' (I, 749 (*VMS*, §17)), 'becoming' (III, 914 (*WM*, §513)), 'atoms and monads' (III, 685 (*WM*, §715)) and of course 'truth' (III, 583 (*WM*, §272)). Nietzsche's metaphorical use of such metaphysical, mathematical and logical terms is designed both to undermine the apparent firmness of previous philosophical and scientific conceptions and also to lend manageable, but fictional stability to his own vision of life.

209 Nietzsche, *Werke*, II, 957 (*GD*, '"Reason" in Philosophy', §1, 'These senses . . . deceive us').

210 Nietzsche, *Werke*, III, 541 (*WM*, §552); 718 (*WM*, §586).

211 Nietzsche, *Werke*, III, 527 (*WM*, §308, 'Morality is just as "immoral" . . .'); III, 541 (*WM*, §552, 'morality is false'); III, 764 (*WM*, §583b, 'The supremacy of moral valuation would be refuted. . .').

212 Nietzsche, *Werke*, I, 440 (*MA*, Preface, §3).

213 Nietzsche, *Werke*, II, 958 (*GD*, ' "Reason" in Philosophy', §2, 'The "apparent" world is the only one. . .').

214 Nietzsche, *Werke*, III, 727 (*WM*, §584, 'And behold: now the world became false, and precisely on account of the properties that constitute its reality. . .'). Similarly, Nietzsche agrees that his mode of being seems 'evil' to the metaphysician, but he himself sees it as the embodiment of genuine freedom; see II, 343 (*ASZ*, II, 'The Child with the Mirror', 'Truly, my happiness and freedom come like a storm. . .'); II, 1156 (*EH*, IV, §5, 'the good and the just would call his superman – *devil*. . .').

215 Nietzsche, *Werke*, III, 691–2 (*WM*, §853). Nietzsche's employment of the terminology of the Platonic, metaphysical tradition in order to undermine that tradition demonstrates his belief that his new 'morality' 'must, if it is to be taught, appear in association with the prevailing moral laws, in the guise of their terms and forms' (III, 468 (*WM*, §957)).

216 Nietzsche, *Werke*, III, 689 (*WM*, §542). See also III, 497, where the word falsehood (*Falschheit*) could be interpreted in both of these two senses (*WM*, §616, 'as something in a state of becoming, as a falsehood always changing but never getting near the truth').

217 See M. Heidegger, *Nietzsche*, 2 Vols. (Pfullingen, 1961), I, 548, 'Denn, nur dann, wenn die Wahrheit im Wesen Richtigkeit ist . . .', 'For, only then, if the truth is in essence correctness. . .'. See also Stern, *A Study of Nietzsche*, p. 207, 'The idea that language is validated because it is a *system* or structure is not considered'.

218 Nietzsche, *Werke*, I, 1224 (*M*, §432); I, 1248 (*M*, §501); II, 72 (*FW*, §51).

219 Nietzsche, *Werke*, II, 115 (*FW*, §108); II, 127 (*FW*, §125); II, 161 (*FW*, §276); I, 439 (*MA*, Preface, §3); II, 1206 (*A*, §43).

220 Nietzsche, *Werke*, II, 601 (*JGB*, §36, '*my* proposition'); II, 949 (*GD*, 'Maxims', §44, 'Formula. . .').

221 Fink, p. 56.

222 Nietzsche, *Werke*, II, 344 (*ASZ*, II, 'On the Blissful Islands'). See III, 425 (*WM*, §1046, 'We want to hold fast to our senses. . .').

223 Fink, p. 134.

224 Nietzsche, *Werke*, II, 612–13 (*JGB*, §48); II, 729–33 (*JGB*, §260); III, 444–6 (*WM*, §943). T. J. Reed talks of Nietzsche's 'conjectural anthropology'; see 'Nietzsche's Animals', p. 172.

225 Nietzsche, *Werke*, I, 1191 (*M*, §307).

226 Nietzsche, *Werke*, I, 247 (*UB*, II, §6).

227 Examples of Nietzsche's 'creative' history are to be found on II, 963 (*GD*, 'How the "True World" at last Became a Myth'); and III, 509–12 (*WM*, §§97, 95). Hayman draws attention to the fact that Nietzsche would often indulge in grand generalisations on the basis of very inadequate research (p. 190); see also Stern, *A Study of Nietzsche*, p. 131.

228 Nietzsche, *Werke*, II, 1153 (*EH*, IV, §3). Nietzsche's most famous example of the fusion of history and metaphor is his declaration 'God is dead'; see II, 115 (*FW*, §108); II, 127 (*FW*, §125); II, 205 (*FW*, §343). The end of belief in God signals for Nietzsche the end of the belief in truth (II, 208 (*FW*, §344)); and that opens up the era of 'truth' or metaphorical understanding. Nietzsche's metaphorical account of the historical demise of Christianity is thus wholly appropriate to the new era.

229 See Hollingdale, p. 126; and *Nietzsche's Werke*, 16 Vols. (Leipzig, 1894–), XII, 65 ('Unpublished Material from the Period of *The Gay Science* 1881–2', §119, 'Wenn die Kreis-Wiederholung auch nur eine Wahrscheinlichkeit oder Möglichkeit ist', 'Even if circular repetition is only a probability or possibility'); XIV, 331 ('Unpublished Material from the Period of Revaluation 1882/3–1888', Part 2, 'Supplements, Plans, Variants and Prefaces', §168, 'Eine solche vorläufige Conception zur Gewinnung der höchsten Kraft ist der *Fatalismus* (ego – Fatum) – extremste Form "ewige Wiederkehr" ', 'One such provisional conception for the attainment of the greatest power is *fatalism* (ego – fate) – most extreme form "eternal recurrence" '). See also Schulz, pp. 107–9.

230 Nietzsche, *Werke*, III, 684 (*WM*, §708).

231 Nietzsche, *Werke*, III, 704 (*WM*, §1066). But compare III, 896 (*WM*, §617, 'the number of becoming elements not constant').

232 Nietzsche, *Werke*, II, 202–3 (*FW*, §341); II, 1128 (*EH*, III, ASZ, §1, 'this highest formula of affirmation. . .'). See Stern, *A Study of Nietzsche*, pp. 166–9; and Schulz, p. 108.

233 Nietzsche, *Werke*, II, 245–6 (*FW*, §370).

234 Nietzsche, *Werke*, II, 773 (*GM*, I, §2, 'Origin of language . . . as an expression of power on the part of the rulers'); II, 1005 (*GD*, 'Expeditions', §26, 'Speech, it seems, was devised only for the average').

235 Nietzsche, *Werke*, III, 895 (*WM*, §617).

236 See J. P. Stern, 'Nietzsche and the Idea of Metaphor', in *Nietzsche: Imagery and Thought*, edited by M. Pasley, p. 65.

237 Nietzsche, *Werke*, III, 486 (*WM*, §470); II, 1135 (*EH*, III, ASZ, §6). See also III, 509 (*WM*, §884).

238 See chapter 3, pp. 42–3. For Hegel's critique of the identification of wholeness with aggregation, see *TWA*, VII, 370 (*PRecht*, §216, Addition).

239 Nietzsche, *Werke*, II, 604 (*JGB*, §41); III, 434–5 (*WM*, §976); III, 512

(*WM*, §1031). Wholeness for Nietzsche means being as many-sided as one can be and encompassing as many different human possibilities as one can. It thus involves a multiplicity of levels of consciousness, which include being 'inquisitive in the most various directions' (III, 434 (*WM*, §976)), but also having the capacity to be 'ignorant' when it is necessary (II, 943 (*GD*, 'Maxims', §5, 'Once and for all, there is a great deal I do *not* want to know')). That Nietzsche's fragmented presentation is indeed intended to intimate a *whole* vision of man, and should not be taken to mean that his philosophy is mere piece-work (*Stückwerk*), is suggested clearly by I, 787 (*VMS*, §128).

240 Nietzsche, *Werke*, III, 434 (*WM*, §976, 'danger of going to pieces'); III, 1351 (Letter to J. Burckhardt, 6 January 1889, 'daß im Grund jeder Name in der Geschichte ich bin', 'that basically every name in history I am' – note Nietzsche's unusual syntax and positioning of the word 'I').

241 Nietzsche, *Werke*, I, 708 (*MA*, §586); III, 267 (*ÜPW*, Breazeale trans., p. 61, 'moments of sudden illumination. . .'). See Stern, *A Study of Nietzsche*, pp. 126–30.

242 See, for example, Nietzsche, *Werke*, III, 487 (*WM*, §556, 'Supposing one single creature. . .').

243 J. W. von Goethe, 'Urworte. Orphisch', in *The Penguin Book of German Verse*, introduced and edited by Leonard Forster (Harmondsworth, 1957; revised edition 1959), p. 230. The discontinuous quality of Nietzsche's thought can be seen most clearly in his collections of aphorisms, such as 'Maxims and Arrows' in *Twilight of the Idols*. It is also evident in the way that, for example, each of the paragraphs 26–34 in *Beyond Good and Evil* begins with a bold assertive judgement which is unconnected with the paragraph that precedes it. Indeed, Nietzsche's discontinuities are even present in an extended essay like *On the Uses and Disadvantages of History for Life*, where the discussions of 'the unhistorical', the various modes of historical consciousness, modern Germany and 'youth' are not always very well integrated with one another.

244 Nietzsche, *Werke*, III, 448 (*WM*, §424, 'The profoundest . . . books. . .'); II, 1131–2 (*EH*, III, ASZ, §3, 'like lightning. . .'). It should be said that it is not always clear whether Nietzsche's discontinuous style results from deliberate intention or simply from his failure to master his material over longer passages.

245 Nietzsche, *Werke*, II, 1027 (*GD*, 'What I Owe to the Ancients', §1).

246 Nietzsche, *Werke*, I, 786–7 (*VMS*, §127).

247 Nietzsche, *Werke*, I, 562 (*MA*, §178); I, 563 (*MA*, §188); I, 921 (*WS*, §106).

248 Nietzsche, *Werke*, II, 433 (*ASZ*, III, 'The Home-Coming').

249 Nietzsche, *Werke*, II, 246–7 (*FW*, §371).

250 Nietzsche, *Werke*, II, 1104 (*EH*, III, §4, 'the most multifarious art of style. . .'); II, 659 (*JGB*, §202, '*our* truths'); II, 697 (*JGB*, §231, '*my* truths'); II, 772 (*GM*, I, §1, 'For such truths do exist'); III, 844 (*WM*, §540). See Derrida, p. 103.

251 Nietzsche's attempt to preserve the freedom of the physiological 'sub-

ject' by insisting that all its perspectives are relative, that all its terms are
fictions and that the real character of the 'subject' is multiple and can
never be definitively determined, means that from a Hegelian perspective Nietzsche's philosophy rests on the foundation of the elusive, ironic
subject, and is thus the indirect heir of Fichte's philosophy. Nietzsche's
subject can thus be seen as 'the *ego* that sets up and dissolves everything
out of itself . . . the artist to whom no content of consciousness appears
as absolute and independently real, but only as a self-made and destruct-
ible show [*Schein*]' (*TWA*, XIII, 93–5 (*Ä*, Knox trans., I, 64–6)). The way in
which Nietzsche seeks to relativise the various positions he adopts and
retain his subjective freedom is seen, for example, in the separation of
the word 'I' from the verb with which it is associated: 'I – beware of
understanding it' (Nietzsche, *Werke*, II, 908 (*FWag*, §3)).

252 Nietzsche, *Werke*, II, 917 (*FWag*, §7). See Stern, *A Study of Nietzsche*,
     p. 157.
253 Nietzsche, *Werke*, II, 924 (*FWag*, §10).
254 Nietzsche, *Werke*, II, 917 (*FWag*, §7, 'Disgregation of the will. . .'); II, 933
     (*FWag*, Second Postscript, 'The decline of the power to organise. . .').
     See III, 696 (*WM*, §46).
255 Nietzsche, *Werke*, III, 486 (*WM*, §470); I, 1016 (*M*, Preface, §5).
256 Nietzsche, *Werke*, II, 696–7 (*JGB*, §230).
257 Nietzsche, *Werke*, III, 691–2 (*WM*, §853, 'There is only one world, and
     this is false . . . A world thus constituted is the true world [*die wahre
     Welt*]'); III, 693 (*WM*, §853, 'Der Wille zum Schein . . . gilt hier als tiefer
     . . . als der Wille . . . zum Schein', 'The will to appearance . . . here counts
     as more profound . . . than the will . . . to appearance').
258 Nietzsche, *Werke*, II, 1173 (*A*, §13).
259 Nietzsche, *Werke*, II, 256 (*FW*, §381). As we shall see in chapters 5 and 6,
     Hegel also wishes to disturb the ordinary expectations of his readers.
     However, his aim is not merely to leave some readers confused and to
     speak 'clearly' only to the initiated; it is rather to transform the
     understanding of all who encounter his thought.
260 Nietzsche, *Werke*, II, 1111 (*EH*, III, GT, §3).
261 Nietzsche, *Werke*, III, 313–14 (*ÜWL*, Breazeale trans., p. 83, 'even
     our contrast. . .').
262 The criticism that Nietzsche is a 'metaphysical' thinker has of course
     been made by Heidegger. Discussion of Heidegger's treatment of
     Nietzsche, and of whether he means the same by 'metaphysical' as Hegel
     and Nietzsche, would, however, take us beyond the scope of the
     present book.
263 Nietzsche, *Werke*, III, 543 (*WM*, §517); 458 (*WM*, §520, 'a world in a state
     of becoming. . .'); III, 685 (*WM*, §715, 'Linguistic means of expres-
     sion. . .'); II, 820 (*GM*, II, §13, 'only that which has no history is
     definable. . .').
264 Nietzsche, *Werke*, II, 115–16 (*FW*, §109). See Stern, *A Study of Nietzsche*,
     p. 147, 'Nietzsche's atheism at this point is "fixed" and dogmatic.'
265 Nietzsche, *Werke*, III, 497 (*WM*, §616, 'The world with which we are con-
     cerned is false. . .').

266 Nietzsche, *Werke*, III, 863 (*WM*, §473).

267 Nietzsche, *Werke*, III, 476 (*WM*, §532); II, 119 (*FW*, §111, 'denn es gibt an sich nichts Gleiches . . .', 'for nothing is really equal. . .').

268 Nietzsche, *Werke*, III, 524 (*WM*, §776); III, 431 (*WM*, §94, 'Much strength and energy *behind* the emphasis on forms [hinter *dem Formenwesen*]').

269 See I. Kant, *Prolegomena zu einer jeden künftigen Metaphysik* (Riga, 1783), §9. Whereas Kant is concerned with the transcendental conditions of knowledge, Nietzsche is concerned with the physiological conditions of knowledge. The mediating figure between Kant and Nietzsche is, of course, Schopenhauer, who combines both points of view. See chapter 4, note 75.

270 Nietzsche, *Werke*, III, 480 (*WM*, §254, '*Who interprets?* – our affects'); III, 903 (*WM*, §481, 'It is our needs *that interpret the world.* . .').

271 Similarly, Nietzsche can only assert that the terms 'ends' and 'means' are inventions by *means* of which we manipulate life by using those terms in a naive way, even though he might wish to claim he is only using them metaphorically; see III, 442 (*WM*, §503, 'With "end" and "means". . .'); III, 587 (*WM*, §707, 'becoming conscious is obviously only one more means. . .').

272 See also Fink, p. 57, 'Daß Hoffart . . .'.

273 The reason for Nietzsche's failure to undertake such a conceptual redefinition is that he deflects attention away from the question of the logical consistency of categories to their condition or source in life. In this way, Nietzsche argues himself out of the need to carry out the kind of critique of categories that Hegel carries out in the *Science of Logic*.

274 See Fink, p. 41, 'Das Sein gilt ihm als etwas Stehendes. . .'. Similarly, in his treatment of the opposition of egoism and altruism, Nietzsche privileges one side of the opposition – egoism – and interprets the other – altruism – as a sublimated mode of that fundamental egoistical 'reality'. Nietzsche thus 'resolves' the opposition between egoism and altruism by denying that altruism really exists. For Hegel, on the other hand, doing away with such an opposition means treating *both* sides as genuine realities, but seeing them as inseparable from one another. Hegel does not therefore reduce altruism to egoism, but understands it as the result of the transformation of individualistic self-interest into genuine social concern for the welfare of *all* selves; see chapter 1, pp. 14–15.

4   *Hegel and metaphysics*

1 Commentators who see Hegel and Nietzsche as allies in their criticisms of dualism, for example, include D. Breazeale and B.F. Beerling; see chapter 1, pp. 16–17.

2 For Hegel's treatment of the 'unhappy consciousness', see *TWA*, III, 163–77 (*Phän*, Miller trans., pp. 126–38).

3 See chapter 1, pp. 18–20.

4 See Hegel, *TWA*, XII, 241–5 (*PGesch*, Sibree trans., pp. 195–8); *TWA*, XVII, 50–96 (*PRel*, Speirs trans., II, 170–224). As is the case with his dis-

cussion of all forms of political and religious organisation, Hegel is concerned only with what he sees as the 'generic character' (*Grundbestimmung*) of Judaism, and he does not claim that his account is an exhaustive study of that religion; see *TWA*, XII, 63 (*PGesch*, Sibree trans., p. 44, 'that in all the divisions. . .').

5 Nietzsche, *Werke*, II, 1178 (*A*, §18).

6 Hegel, *TWA*, XII, 242 (*PGesch*, Sibree trans., p. 196).

7 Hegel, *TWA*, XVII, 50 (*PRel*, Speirs trans., II, 171). See also *TWA*, XII, 242 (*PGesch*, Sibree trans., p. 196, 'The spiritual speaks itself here absolutely free of the sensuous, and nature is reduced to something merely external and undivine'); and *TWA*, XVII, 61 (*PRel*, Speirs trans., II, 184, 'Nature is here undeified [*entgöttert*]').

8 Nietzsche, *Werke*, II, 431 (*ASZ*, III, 'Of the Apostates', §2).

9 Hegel, *TWA*, XII, 241–2 (*PGesch*, Sibree trans., p. 195).

10 The identity of the Christian God and the speculative Idea is maintained by Hegel throughout his philosophy, as is his desire to discover God in the natural and human world. For a passage in which the two points are made together, see *TWA*, XII, 27–9 (*PGesch*, Sibree trans., pp. 15–16, 'In the Christian religion. . .').

11 See *TWA*, XIII, 307–8 (*Ä*, Knox trans., I, 236–8). Just as they criticise the principle of exclusive divinity, so Hegel and Nietzsche also identify and criticise modes of consciousness which lay claim to exclusive possession of moral truth and which fail to take account of the value of other perspectives. Compare Nietzsche's treatment of 'The Good and the Just' ('who say and feel in their hearts: "we already know what is good and just, we possess it too; woe to those who are still searching for it!" ', *Werke*, II, 458 (*ASZ*, III, 'Of Old and New Law-Tables', §26)), and Hegel's treatment of the abstract good will ('further, just as the good is the abstract, so the bad too must be without content and derive its specification from my subjectivity; and it is in this way also that there arises the moral end of hating and uprooting the bad, the nature of the bad being left unspecified', *TWA*, VII, 270 (*PRecht*, §140, Remark d)).

12 Hegel, *TWA*, XIII, 311–12 (*Ä*, Knox trans., I, 240, 'If the man is not thus *one* in himself. . .').

13 Hegel, *TWA*, X, 23 (*E*, III, §381, Addition).

14 Nietzsche, *Werke*, II, 1183 (*A*, §24); II, 1208 (*A*, §44, 'The Christian is only a Jew of a "freer" confession').

15 Hegel, *TWA*, XII, 243 (*PGesch*, Sibree trans., p. 196, 'because the absolute itself is not comprehended as *concrete* spirit. . .').

16 The inadequacy of the Judaic religion in comparison with the Christian religion for Hegel is that 'the sensuous, the finite, the natural . . . has not yet been *taken up* into free subjectivity or *transfigured* within it' (*TWA*, XVII, 46–7 (*PRel*, Speirs trans., II, 167)).

17 Hegel, *TWA*, VIII, 93–4 (*E*, I, §§27, 28). See also *TWA*, V, 38 (*WL*, Miller trans., p. 45). The structure of the following section is based loosely on Hegel's arguments in §§26–60 of the *Encyclopaedia*, but reference is also made to the *Science of Logic* and to the *Lectures on the History of Philosophy*.

18 Hegel, *TWA*, VIII, 93 (*E*, I, §26).

19 Hegel, *TWA*, VIII, 97 (*E*, I, §30).

20 Hegel, *TWA*, V, 13 (*WL*, Miller trans., p. 25).

21 Hegel, *TWA*, VIII, 97 (*E*, I, §30).

22 Hegel, *TWA*, VIII, 100 (*E*, I, §34).

23 Hegel, *TWA*, VIII, 94 (*E*, I, §28).

24 Hegel, *TWA*, VIII, 94 (*E*, I, §28).

25 Hegel, *TWA*, VIII, 102 (*E*, I, §35, Addition).

26 Hegel, *TWA*, VIII, 98–9 (*E*, I, §32 and Addition).

27 Hegel, *TWA*, VIII, 95 (*E*, I, §28, Addition).

28 Hegel, *TWA*, VIII, 93 (*E*, I, §27). Similarly, Hegel considers Judaism to be 'the religion of the understanding in its most rigid and lifeless form' (*TWA*, XVII, 159 (*PRel*, Speirs trans., II, 294)). For Hegel's critique of the abstract notion of identity with which the understanding operates – that is, the notion that something is simply what it is and not mediated by its negation – see *TWA*, VI, 38–45 (*WL*, Miller trans., pp. 411–16).

29 Hegel, *TWA*, VIII, 121–2 (*E*, I, §45, Addition).

30 Hegel, *TWA*, VIII, 169 (*E*, I, §80; see also Addition).

31 Hegel, *TWA*, VIII, 99 (*E*, I, §32, Addition); VIII, 177 (*E*, I, §82, Remark); XI, 350 (*BS*, '*Aufheben der Gegensätze* überhaupt'). This does not of course mean that Hegel simply abolishes the conceptual distinctions of the understanding, but that he understands distinct moments as inseparable (*untrennbar*), as participating logically in one another; see *TWA*, V, 57 (*WL*, Miller trans., p. 60, 'These then are the two *moments* contained in logic. . .'). See also VIII, 102 (*E*, I, §35, Addition, 'A freedom involving no necessity, and mere necessity without freedom, are abstract and thus untrue determinations of thought').

32 For Hegel's speculative answer to the question of the divisibility of matter, see *TWA*, V, 225–7 (*WL*, Miller trans., pp. 197–9). Hegel's speculative resolution of the antinomy of freedom and necessity is that man is a natural being subject to the laws of natural and social existence, but that man gradually acquires freedom as he becomes self-conscious and as he becomes aware of the intrinsic character of freedom; see *TWA*, XII, 31 (*PGesch*, Sibree trans., p. 18, 'Man *as such* is free; and because they do not know this, they are not free'). An impression of the subtle way in which Hegel blends freedom and necessity can be gained from considering his treatment of the question of tragic responsibility; see chapter 8, pp. 205–6, 209–10, 215.

33 Hegel, *TWA*, VIII, 97 (*E*, I, §31).

34 Hegel, *TWA*, VIII, 98 (*E*, I, §31, Addition); XII, 476 (*PGesch*, Sibree trans., p. 397, 'But thus conditioned thought was not free. . .'); XIX, 591 (*GPhil*, Haldane trans., III, 98, 'insofar as the understanding keeps to the given religious content. . .').

35 Hegel, *TWA*, XII, 454–5, 495–6 (*PGesch*, Sibree trans., pp. 377–8, 416).

36 Hegel, *TWA*, XX, 120–3 (*GPhil*, Haldane trans., III, 216–19, 'Philosophy in its own proper soil separates itself entirely from philosophising theology . . . In this new period the universal principle . . . is the thought that proceeds from itself').

37 Hegel thinks that all the great post-Reformation metaphysicians proceed from given presuppositions or seek to reach a foundation of certainty; they include Descartes (*TWA*, XX, 127 (*GPhil*, Haldane trans., III, 224–5, 'and commence from thought, so that from it we should first attain to some fixed and settled basis')), Spinoza (XX, 172 (*GPhil*, Haldane trans., III, 263–4, 'The whole of Spinoza's philosophy is contained in these definitions')) and Leibniz (XX, 238 (*GPhil*, Haldane trans., III, 330, 'Thus the philosophy of Leibniz seems to be not so much a philosophical system...')). It should be noted that, although Hegel considers Leibniz to be a metaphysician because Leibniz proceeds from presupposed concepts and representations, he does not consider Leibniz's philosophy to be deductively 'necessary' in the manner of traditional metaphysics; see XX, 238 (*GPhil*, Haldane trans., III, 330).

38 Hegel believes that philosophy should not be founded on religious dogma; but equally he believes that the free development of thought which characterises speculative philosophy will confirm the truth of the Christian religion, since Christianity is the 'revelation of reason'; see *TWA*, VIII, 105–6 (*E*, I, §36, Addition).

39 Hegel, *TWA*, VIII, 94 (*E*, I, §28, Remark). For a discussion of Hegel's distinction between truth and correctness, see A. White, *Absolute Knowledge: Hegel and the Problem of Metaphysics* (Athens, Ohio/London, 1983), pp. 82–4. See also chapter 5, p. 131, and chapter 5, note 32.

40 Hegel, *TWA*, XIX, 557 (*GPhil*, Haldane trans., III, 64).

41 Hegel, *TWA*, XIX, 591–2 (*GPhil*, Haldane trans., III, 98).

42 Hegel, *TWA*, XIX, 238 (*GPhil*, Haldane trans., II, 220). Although Hegel believes that Aristotelian logic underlies metaphysical thinking, he does not believe that Aristotle himself can be classed as a metaphysician, since, Hegel argues, Aristotle did not actually think in accordance with his own logical principles; see *TWA*, XIX, 240–1 (*GPhil*, Haldane trans., II, 223). Aristotle, like Plato in Hegel's view, went beyond the distinctions of the understanding and produced genuinely speculative insights (*TWA*, VIII, 106 (*E*, I, §36, Addition)), though of course neither managed to think in as thoroughgoing a speculative manner as Hegel himself.

43 Hegel, *TWA*, VI, 511–41 (*WL*, Miller trans., pp. 793–818).

44 Hegel, *TWA*, VIII, 106–7 (*E*, I, §37 and Addition). Hegel is of course aware that empiricist thinkers such as Bacon and Locke seek to found knowledge on the experience or observation of both the outer, sensuous world, and the inner, mental one; see *TWA*, XX, 74, 204 (*GPhil*, Haldane trans., III, 170, 'Baconian philosophy thus usually means a philosophy which is founded on the observation of the external or spiritual nature of man...'; III, 299, 'das äußerlich und innerlich Wahrnehmbare', 'what is outwardly and inwardly perceptible'). However, for the purposes of this chapter I shall consider outer, sensuous experience to be of primary importance for the empiricists in Hegel's account.

45 Hegel, *TWA*, XX, 82 (*GPhil*, Haldane trans., III, 179). For a similar criticism of Scholasticism by Hegel himself, see *TWA*, XIX, 543 (*GPhil*,

Haldane trans., III, 42, 'In this scholastic activity thought pursues its work quite apart from all regard to experience').

46 Hegel, *TWA*, VIII, 108 (*E*, I, §38, Remark).
47 Hegel, *TWA*, VIII, 108 (*E*, I, §38, Remark).
48 Hegel, *TWA*, XX, 78–80 (*GPhil*, Haldane trans., III, 174–7). On Hegel's immense interest in empirical detail, see Findlay, pp. 348–51; and chapter 5, pp. 125–7.
49 Hegel, *TWA*, VIII, 109 (*E*, I, §38, Addition, 'Hence this instinct seized upon what is present, here, this, which has the infinite form implicit in itself, although not in the genuine existence of that form'). The true dialectical form inherent in sensuous immediacy is expounded by Hegel in the section on sense-certainty in the *Phenomenology* (see *TWA*, III, 82–92 (*Phän*, Miller trans., pp. 58–66); and chapter 7), and that dialectical form is articulated in purely conceptual terms in the *Science of Logic* (see chapter 5).
50 Hegel, *TWA*, VIII, 109 (*E*, I, §38, Addition).
51 Hegel, *TWA*, VIII, 110 (*E*, I, §38, Addition).
52 Hegel, *TWA*, XX, 209 (*GPhil*, Haldane trans., III, 298).
53 Hegel, *TWA*, XX, 222 (GPhil). No translation which corresponds exactly to this passage is to be found in the Haldane edition, but see Haldane, III, 298–9, for passages expressing similar ideas.
54 Hegel, *TWA*, XX, 209 (*GPhil*, Haldane trans., III, 298–9, 'Thus Locke has striven to satisfy a genuine necessity. . .'); XX, 223 (*GPhil*, Haldane trans., III, 299, 'derived. . .'); XX, 210–11 (*GPhil*, Haldane trans., III, 300–1, 'Locke *combats* the so-called innate ideas').
55 Hegel, *TWA*, XX, 211 (*GPhil*, Haldane trans., III, 300–1).
56 Hegel, *TWA*, XX, 217 (*GPhil*, Haldane trans., III, 305).
57 Hegel, *TWA*, VIII, 108 (*E*, I, §38).
58 Hegel, *TWA*, VIII, 110 (*E*, I, §38, Addition). In criticising the positivism of metaphysics, Hegel denies that there are infinite 'objects' to be known, and he comes to understand 'God' or 'reason' as the form of human and natural activity. In criticising the positivism of empiricism, on the other hand, Hegel does not deny that there are finite objects to be known (although he sees those objects as relational, rather than wholly independent entities); see *TWA*, IX, 334 (*E*, II, §336, 'the *relativity* of the immediate substances and properties'). Nor does he deny that it is correct for scientific knowledge to be based on the foundation of such objects; see *TWA*, XX, 209 (*GPhil*, Haldane trans., III, 298, 'The ordinary method adopted in the sciences'). Hegel's objection, as is evident in his discussion of Hume, is rather that founding cognition on the sensuous perceptions of those finite objects cannot yield the definitive knowledge that philosophy demands.
59 Hegel, *TWA*, XX, 83 (*GPhil*, Haldane trans., III, 180).
60 Hegel, *TWA*, VIII, 108–9 (*E*, I, §38, Remark). Although Hegel is concerned here with empiricism as a mode of philosophy, he is also aware that this method of analysis is employed throughout the natural sciences as well; see *TWA*, XX, 209 (*GPhil*, Haldane trans., III, 298). Hegel's

understanding of empirical analysis thus suggests some of the things he might have to say about natural science. Hegel believes that analysis uncovers the general determinations which are immediately contained in the object perceived; see *TWA*, VI, 503 (*WL*, Miller trans., pp. 787–8). But he thinks that the empiricists are wrong if they assume that the general propositions and laws which are arrived at by science are derived purely from passive observation; see *TWA*, VIII, 109–10 (*E*, I, §38, Addition). In the first place, analysis for Hegel involves the active transformation of what is empirically given to consciousness into the form of general empirical determinations; in Hegel's view, therefore, scientists can genuinely be said to *make* their observations. Secondly, as his comments on Kepler in the philosophy of history show, Hegel believes that the empirical observer must presuppose certain mathematical and logical principles in order to be able to produce 'immortal laws' from the observations he has made; see *TWA*, XII, 87 (*PGesch*, Sibree trans., p. 64). Hegel's understanding of natural science seems therefore to combine emphasis on the primacy of observation with the claim that a certain level of development of logical understanding is required for man to be able to formulate laws on the basis of those observations. It might be added that, since Hegel sees the great advances in science and empirical research as the distinctive achievement of the Renaissance and post-Renaissance world, he is pointing out that our openness to experience and readiness to observe what is the case is itself an attitude of mind which we have had to learn to develop in history, too; see *TWA*, XII, 488–91 (*PGesch*, Sibree trans., pp. 408–11); and XX, 11–12 (*GPhil*, Haldane trans., III, 108–9).

61 Hegel, *TWA*, VIII, 111 (*E*, I, §39).
62 Hegel, *TWA*, XX, 276–7 (*GPhil*, Haldane trans., III, 371).
63 B. Russell, *History of Western Philosophy* (London, 1946, second edition 1961), p. 646.
64 Hegel, *TWA*, XX, 280 (*GPhil*, Haldane trans., III, 374). For Hegel's treatment of induction, see *TWA*, VI, 384–7 (*WL*, Miller trans., pp. 689–92). Hegel agrees with Hume that generalisations based on empirical observation are relative to the present state of observed knowledge and therefore 'problematic'. Although he seems to consider such problematic conclusions to be satisfactory in empirical science (since he considers induction to be the appropriate method for such science), he does not consider them to be adequate for philosophy, whose task is to reach definitive conclusions. (On the definitiveness of speculative philosophy, see *TWA*, V, 42, 50 (*WL*, Miller trans., pp. 48, 54).) Where science treats its problematic empirical generalisations as natural laws, science has either smuggled in assumptions about the way things behave (*TWA*, VI, 386 (*WL*, Miller trans., p. 691, 'the syllogism by induction . . . is not based on that immediacy on which it is supposed to be based')), or its conclusions must have been supported by rational principles. Definitive legitimation for scientific theories is provided only by the philosophy of nature. Hegel's arguments about induction are meant to

show that empirical observations cannot justify necessary judgements about the world, or ground the pure concepts and categories of reason, that is to say that rational connections are not explicit in sense-perception. Since the mind formulates its contingent observations in linguistic judgements, however, the categories of thought do, through language, inform even simple empirical consciousness; see *TWA*, V, 20 (*WL*, Miller trans., p. 31, 'Into all that becomes something inward for men. . .').

65 See chapter 5, note 19.

66 G. W. Leibniz, *Philosophical Writings*, edited by G. H. R. Parkinson, translated by Mary Morris and G. H. R. Parkinson (London, 1973), p. 184 (*Monadology*, §33).

67 D. Hume, *An Inquiry Concerning Human Understanding*, edited with Introduction by Charles Hendel (New York, 1955), pp. 40, 'Propositions of this kind. . .', 42, 'nor does any man imagine that . . . the attraction of a loadstone could ever be discovered by arguments a priori'. However, for Hegel's *a priori* derivation of the existence of magnetism in nature, see *TWA*, IX, 202–17 (*E*, II, §§312–14).

68 For Nietzsche's critique of immediate certainty in general, see *Werke*, II, 580 (*JGB*, §16, 'Enough: this "I think". . .'). For a Nietzschean critique of the immediate certainty of '*this*' sun' or '*this*' window', but from a perspective different from that in Hegel's *Phenomenology*, see III, 316 (*ÜWL*, Breazeale trans., p. 86, 'Only by forgetting. . .'). See also Lamb, *Hegel: From Foundation to System*, pp. 26–8.

69 Nietzsche thus seems to be, like Hume, a sceptic who 'founds his remarks on the *truth* of the empirical element, on feeling and sensation, and proceeds to attack universal truths and laws, because they do not derive their authority from sense-perception' (*TWA*, VIII, 112 (*E*, I, §39)); see, for example, Nietzsche, *Werke*, II, 958 (*GD*, ' "Reason" in Philosophy', §2), though, in contrast to Hume, Nietzsche relies on the foundation of 'experience' in order to question the legitimacy of *all* judgements, not just necessary judgements. It should be remembered, however, that Nietzsche's attitude to sensation and feeling is actually ambiguous in that he treats them both as a more complex level of *interpretation* than consciousness and language, and as the physiological *reality* against which our linguistic judgements are declared to be mere interpretations; see chapter 3, pp. 51–3.

70 For a discussion of the similarity between Nietzsche and Hume, see Danto, pp. 93–5. For Nietzsche's own view of Hume and the similarities and differences between them, see, for example, *Werke*, III, 501 (*WM*, §550). Though Nietzsche clearly bases his critique of necessary judgements on a scepticism akin to Hume's, one should also remember the even greater debt that Nietzsche's notion of 'life' owes to Schopenhauer's idea of the will.

71 Hegel, *TWA*, VIII, 113 (*E*, I, §40 and Remark).

72 Hegel, *TWA*, XX, 331 (*GPhil*, Haldane trans., III, 424).

73 Hegel, *TWA*, VIII, 114 (*E*, I, §41, Addition 1).

74 Hegel, *TWA*, VIII, 115–16 (*E*, I, §41, Addition 2).

75 Hegel, *TWA*, XX, 206 (*GPhil*, Haldane trans., III, 300, 'Kant reproaches Locke with reason. . .'); *TWA*, VIII, 119 (*E*, I, §42, Addition 3, 'Although the categories (such as, for example, unity, cause and effect, and so on) belong to thought as such, it does not follow that they must be ours merely and not also the determinations of objects themselves'). Nietzsche, of course, inherits – albeit in a radically altered form – Kant's rather strange view that what the mind produces cannot be true of things in themselves, and this view underlies Nietzsche's philosophy of 'subjective' falsification and interpretation; see chapter 3, p. 92.

76 Hegel, *TWA*, XX, 355 (*GPhil*, Haldane trans., III, 447, 'for he remains confined within the conception of reality and being, according to which reality consists in being sensuous existence').

77 Hegel, *TWA*, VIII, 128 (*E*, I, §48, Addition). Many modern philosophers still retain this conception of contradiction, of course; see, for example, the passage by B. Russell quoted on p. 160.

78 Hegel applauds what he takes to be Kant's general insight into the inherent dialectic of reason, but is highly critical of the details of Kant's arguments in his discussion of the antinomies; see *TWA*, VIII, 129 (*E*, I, §48, Addition, 'The arguments which Kant offers for his thesis and antithesis are mere shams of demonstration [*Scheinbeweise*]'). See also *TWA*, V, 52 (*WL*, Miller trans., p. 56).

79 Hegel, *TWA*, VIII, 128 (*E*, I, §48, Addition).

80 Hegel, *TWA*, VIII, 126–7 (*E*, I, §48, Remark). Hegel's position, in contrast to that of Kant, is that the world does not exclude contradiction, but rather includes and resolves it; see *TWA*, VIII, 246–7 (*E*, I, §119, Addition 2).

81 Hegel, *TWA*, VIII, 135 (*E*, I, §51).

82 Hegel, *TWA*, XX, 360 (*GPhil*, Haldane trans., III, 452).

83 Hegel, *TWA*, VIII, 136 (*E*, I, §51, Remark).

84 Hegel, *TWA*, VIII, 136 (*E*, I, §51, Remark).

85 See chapter 4, note 10; and Hegel, *TWA*, XX, 362 (*GPhil*, Haldane trans., III, 454, 'an existence which is itself the concept').

86 Hegel, *TWA*, XX, 360 (*GPhil*, Haldane trans., III, 452).

87 Hegel, *TWA*, XX, 336–7 (*GPhil*, Haldane trans., III, 430).

88 Hegel, *TWA*, XX, 347–8 (*GPhil*, Haldane trans., III, 441).

89 Hegel, *TWA*, XX, 355 (*GPhil*, Haldane trans., III, 447).

90 Hegel, *TWA*, VIII, 120–1 (*E*, I, §44, Remark, 'The *negative* determination . . . is also enumerated among the categories of Kant').

91 Hegel, *TWA*, V, 40 (*WL*, Miller trans., p. 47, 'The forms of objective thinking. . .'); *TWA*, VIII, 113 (*E*, I, §41).

92 Hegel, *TWA*, V, 31 (*WL*, Miller trans., pp. 40–1, 'On the contrary. . .').

93 Hegel, *TWA*, VIII, 114 (*E*, I, §41, Addition 1).

94 Hegel, *TWA*, V, 50 (*WL*, Miller trans., p. 54).

95 Hegel, *TWA*, V, 27 (*WL*, Miller trans., p. 37).

96 Hegel, *TWA*, V, 41 (*WL*, Miller trans., p. 48, 'The content which is missing. . .').

97 Hegel, *TWA*, V, 61–2 (*WL*, Miller trans., pp. 63–4); *TWA*, VIII, 81 (*E*, I, §24). Strictly speaking, Hegel only says that the objective logic – the logic of being and essence – entails a critique of metaphysical categories; but in fact the subjective logic – the logic of the concept – also entails a critique of forms of thought, such as the judgement and the syllogism, which are employed by metaphysics. The major failing of Michael Theunissen's otherwise excellent book, *Sein und Schein: die kritische Funktion der Hegelschen Logik*, is that he underplays this critical moment in the subjective logic; see Theunissen, pp. 38, 41.
98 See chapter 1, note 97.

5 *Speculative thought and language in Hegel's philosophy*

1 Hegel, *TWA*, VIII, 121 (*E*, I, §44, Remark).
2 See, for example, *TWA*, XII, 23 (*PGesch*, Sibree trans., p. 11, 'To him who looks upon the world rationally, the world in its turn presents a rational aspect').
3 Hegel, *TWA*, V, 61 (*WL*, Miller trans., p. 63, 'The objective logic, then, takes the place rather of former *metaphysics*').
4 Hegel, *TWA*, VIII, 53 (*E*, I, §9, Remark, 'Speculative logic contains all previous logic and metaphysics. . .').
5 Hegel, *TWA*, VIII, 111 (*E*, I, §38, Addition). The definition of freedom in this quotation does not of course imply any solipsism on Hegel's part. It implies rather that freedom entails recognising the determinations of human reason as the determinations of the external world – '*pure* self-recognition in absolute otherness' (*TWA*, III, 29 (*Phän*, Miller trans., p. 14)). For the passage in which Hegel acknowledges his debt to empiricism, see chapter 4, pp. 105–6, and note 48.
6 On the difference between mere existence and rational actuality (*Wirklichkeit*), see *TWA*, VIII, 47–8 (*E*, I, §6, Remark). On the critical role of reason in history, see *TWA*, VIII, 71 (*E*, I, §19, Addition 3, 'Constitutions fell a victim to thought. . .').
7 Nietzsche, *Werke*, I, 263 (*UB*, II, §8).
8 Hegel, *TWA*, VI, 530 (*WL*, Miller trans., p. 809, 'the theorems of a synthetic science, especially of *geometry*'); XX, 209 (*GPhil*, Haldane trans., III, 298, 'the ordinary method adopted in the sciences').
9 Hegel, *TWA*, VI, 537–8 (*WL*, Miller trans., p. 815). See K. Popper, *The Logic of Scientific Discovery* (London, 1959), pp. 40–1. Although Hegel objects to natural science selecting its observations as examples to fit a presupposed theory, he does not object to science drawing on rational principles to formulate laws from the 'concrete totality' of its observations; see *TWA*, VI, 537 (*WL*, Miller trans., p. 815); and chapter 4, notes 60 and 64. But all laws, unless legitimated by the philosophy of nature, must presumably remain open to falsification by experience if they are to be classed as scientific.

10 Hegel, *TWA*, VIII, 47 (*E*, I, §6).
11 Hegel, *TWA*, IX, 15 (*E*, II, §246, Remark). See chapter 4, pp. 105–6.
12 Hegel, *TWA*, IX, 83 (*E*, II, §269, Remark, 'forces'); IX, 159–60 (*E*, II, §293, Remark, 'pores'); IX, 88 (*E*, II, §270, Remark, 'a monstrous metaphysic . . . contrary to both experience and to the concept'); IX, 191 (*E*, II, §305, Remark, 'the metaphysics of independence is set up against the experience mentioned, and is indeed presupposed a priori'). This last quotation corrects M. J. Petry's mistranslation of the phrase, *ja a priori der Erfahrung vorausgesetzt*, which reads 'and the experience is indeed presupposed a priori'.
13 Hegel, *TWA*, IX, 90–1 (*E*, II, §270, Remark).
14 Hegel, *TWA*, IX, 15 (*E*, II, §246 and Remark); IX, 117 (*E*, II, §276, Remark). A similar procedure is employed in Hegel's philosophy of history, too; see *TWA*, XII, 87 (*PGesch*, Sibree trans., pp. 63–4), where Hegel says that the philosopher seeking to understand the specific principles or characters of historical cultures must be 'familiar a priori (if we like to call it so) with the whole circle of conceptions to which the principles in question belong', that is with the speculative Idea, and that he must at the same time adhere closely to the historical material at hand in order to tell whether a particular principle does indeed constitute the specific principle of a particular culture.
15 Hegel, *TWA*, IX, 20 (*E*, II, §246, Addition, 'without treating experience as the ultimate basis of verification'); IX, 42 (*E*, II, §254, Addition, 'Even if we should deceive ourselves in this respect, this would in no way affect the truth of our thought').
16 See, for example, M. J. Petry's introduction to his translation of the philosophy of nature, pp. 49–53.
17 The fact that Hegel acknowledges that contemporary natural science was limited in many respects can be seen, for example, from *TWA*, IX, 82 (*E*, II, §268, Addition, 'There is still much that cannot be grasped, and this has to be admitted in the philosophy of nature'); and IX, 106 (*E*, II, §270, Addition, 'philosophy need not be disturbed if the explanation of each and every phenomenon has not yet been completed').
18 See Hegel, *TWA*, IX, 15 (*E*, II, §246, Remark, 'The procedure involved in the formation and preliminaries of a [philosophical] science is not the same as the science itself, however, for in this latter case it is no longer experience, but rather the necessity of the concept, which must emerge as the foundation').
19 Hegel, *TWA*, XX, 211 (*GPhil*, Haldane trans., III, 301). The goal of philosophy is not therefore completeness of contingent, empirical detail, but insight into 'the essence of the thing itself, the essence implied by the concept' (*das begriffsgemäße Wesen der Sache selbst*) (*TWA*, XIV, 265 (*Ä*, Knox trans., II, 629)); see VII, 370 (*PRecht*, §216, Addition). Hegel is thus not aiming at the kind of all-inclusive 'holism' which Russell accuses him of. For Hegel, we do not need to know all about something in order to understand its conceptual structure, any more than we need to know all about the relations into which John and James

enter with other people and things in order to understand the statement 'John is the father of James' (Russell, *History of Western Philosophy*, p. 714); see D. Lamb, *Language and Perception in Hegel and Wittgenstein* (Avebury, 1979), pp. 5–6.

20 Hegel, *TWA*, VIII, 41 (*E*, I, §1).

21 Hegel, *TWA*, V, 35 (*WL*, Miller trans., p. 43, 'Logic, on the contrary, cannot presuppose any of these forms of reflection and laws of thinking').

22 Hegel, *TWA*, V, 75 (*WL*, Miller trans., p. 75).

23 Hegel, *TWA*, XII, 87, 92–4 (*PGesch*, Sibree trans., pp. 64, 67–9); XX, 63–5 (*GPhil*, Haldane trans., III, 159–62, 'It was only in the sixteenth and seventeenth centuries that genuine philosophy re-appeared').

24 Hegel, *TWA*, VIII, 41 (*E*, I, §1, 'Some acquaintance or outside familiarity. . .'); V, 19 (*WL*, Miller trans., p. 31, 'but this traditional material, the familiar forms of thought. . .'). Hegel's dictum that philosophy is its own age conceived in thought (*TWA*, VII, 26 (*PRecht*, Preface)) does not therefore mean that speculative philosophy is essentially limited by its historical situation, but rather that modern society and the modern insistence on self-determination are the essential conditions of absolute self-understanding; see *TWA*, V, 23 (*WL*, Miller trans., p. 34, 'As a matter of fact. . .'); VII, 28 (*PRecht*, Preface, 'As the thought of the world, it [philosophy] appears only when actuality is already there . . . after its process of formation has been completed').

25 Hegel, *TWA*, XII, 394 (*PGesch*, Sibree trans., pp. 325–6, 'Make of Christ what you will, exegetically. . .'); XII, 400 (*PGesch*, Sibree trans., p. 331, 'It is a matter of perfect indifference where a thing originated; the only question is: "is it true in and for itself?"'). This does not mean, however, that Hegel is completely uninterested in the source of ideas, but that, for him, knowing about the source of ideas does not of itself allow you to determine their truth, that is to say 'the whence . . . does not exhaust the whole question' (*das Woher erschöpft die Frage nicht*) (*TWA*, XX, 214 (*GPhil*, Haldane trans., III, 312)). For a statement of Nietzsche's genetic method, on the other hand, see *Werke*, I, 1073–4 (*M*, §95).

26 The failure of Nietzsche is that he is unable to evaluate systems in their own terms as *systems*, but always has to 'interpret' those systems in the light of the mode of life that produced them: 'the only thing of interest in a refuted system is the personal element' (*Werke*, III, 352 (*PTZG*, A Later Preface)).

27 Hegel, *TWA*, V, 72–3 (*WL*, Miller trans., pp. 72–3). The beginning of speculative philosophy is not to be understood as provisional or hypothetical, however; it is merely the beginning, but its character as indeterminate immediacy is necessarily what it is, since it *is* merely the beginning; see *TWA*, V, 71–2 (*WL*, Miller trans., p. 72).

28 Hegel, *TWA*, V, 42–3, 67 (*WL*, Miller trans., pp. 48–9, 68–9). For a fuller discussion of the *Phenomenology* than is offered here, see chapter 7.

29 Hegel, *TWA*, V, 43 (*WL*, Miller trans., p. 49); V, 57 (*WL*, Miller trans., p. 60, 'This unity also constitutes the logical principle as *element*. . .'). In this book I have sought a Hegelian alternative to Nietzsche's critique of

metaphysics by concentrating mainly on Hegel's *Science of Logic*, in which Hegel undertakes a critique of all conceptual oppositions or *Gegensätze*, including the abstract categories of metaphysics, and the opposition of being and becoming on which Nietzsche relies in order to carry out his own critique of metaphysical categories. However, it should be noted that the *Phenomenology* also offers a critique of the Kantian (and Nietzschean) separation of consciousness and reality, in particular.

30 See P. F. Strawson, *The Bounds of Sense* (London, 1966, second edition 1975), p. 131.

31 See chapter 4, p. 107.

32 Hegel does not of course deny that ordinary statements can be true in the perfectly straightforward sense of 'correct' (see *TWA*, III, 41 (*Phän*, Miller trans., p. 23, 'To such questions. . .')), but he says that the form of the ordinary judgement or proposition is inadequate to the statement of *philosophical* truth; see *TWA*, V, 93 (*WL*, Miller trans., pp. 90–1); VIII, 98 (*E*, I, §31 Remark). Hegel is fully aware that his understanding of philosophical truth as the 'correspondence [*Übereinstimmung*] of a content with itself' is unconventional, but he also claims that such a conception of truth is anticipated in ordinary phrases such as 'a true friend' or 'a true work of art'; see *TWA*, VIII, 85–6 (*E*, I, §24, Addition 2); VIII, 100 (*E*, I, §33, Remark); VIII, 323–4 (*E*, I, §172, Addition); XIII, 151 (*Ä*, Knox trans., l, 110–11, 'And truth not at all in the *subjective* sense. . .').

33 Hegel, *TWA*, V, 68–9 (*WL*, Miller trans., pp. 69–70).

34 Hegel, *TWA*, V, 72 (*WL*, Miller trans., p. 72).

35 Hegel, *TWA*, V, 79, 82–3 (*WL*, Miller trans., pp. 78, 'empty word', 82).

36 Hegel, *TWA*, V, 83 (*WL*, Miller trans., pp. 82–3). In contrast to Nietzsche, who sees 'becoming' as opposed to 'being' and who considers the dynamism of life to be opposed to abstract thought, Hegel sees 'becoming' as inherent in the very notion of 'being' and thus sees abstract thought itself as inherently dynamic.

37 Hegel, *TWA*, VIII, 194 (*E*, I, §89, Remark).

38 Hegel, *TWA*, V, 111–17 (*WL*, Miller trans., pp. 105–10).

39 Hegel, *TWA*, VIII, 184 (*E*, I, §86, Addition 1).

40 Hegel, *TWA*, V, 82 (*WL*, Miller trans., p. 82); V, 68 (*WL*, Miller trans., p. 69, 'Simple immediacy is itself an expression of reflection [*Reflexionsausdruck*] and contains a reference to its distinction from what is mediated. This simple immediacy, therefore, in its true expression is *pure being*'). See White, pp. 35–41. D. Henrich says of Hegel's use of reflective terms like 'indeterminate immediacy' or 'equality with itself' to characterise pure being that 'a category of reflection is qualified by a determination which is intended precisely to negate [*aufheben*] the reflective character of that category'; see 'Anfang und Methode der Logik', *Hegel-Studien*, Beiheft 1 (1964), 28. Another example of what Henrich means is Hegel's description of the difference between pure being and pure nothingness as 'the completely abstract difference which is at the same time no difference' (*TWA*, VIII, 187 (*E*, I, §87, Addition)).

41 Hegel, *TWA*, V, 95 (*WL*, Miller trans., p. 92, 'Their difference is therefore

completely empty. . .'); VIII, 186–7 (*E*, I, §87, Remark, 'its distinction from nothing lies in opinion [*Meinung*] only').

42 Hegel, *TWA*, V, 111 (*WL*, Miller trans., p. 105, 'But we call dialectic the higher movement of reason in which such seemingly utterly separate terms pass over into each other spontaneously, through what they are. . .'). Although it is the philosopher who does the thinking in the *Logic* (*TWA*, VIII, 63 (*E*, I, §17)), that philosopher follows the intrinsic logic of thought itself. In this sense, therefore, the philosopher renders explicit the logical 'activity' of the categories themselves.

43 Strictly speaking, the term 'category' should only be applied to the determinations of the logic of being and perhaps also to the determinations of the logic of essence (*TWA*, IV, 87 (*NHS*)), though Hegel also refers to certain of these latter determinations as 'determinations of reflection' (*Reflexionsbestimmungen*) (*TWA*, IV, 164 (*NHS*); VI, 36–8 (*WL*, Miller trans., pp. 409–11)). The determinations of the logic of concept are called 'concepts' (*Begriffe*). In this book, however, the terms 'category' and 'concept' will often be used interchangeably.

44 Hegel, *TWA*, V, 70 (*WL*, Miller trans., p. 71).

45 See Hegel, *TWA*, VI, 571 (*WL*, Miller trans., p. 841, 'The method of truth, too, knows the beginning to be incomplete, because it is a beginning; but at the same time it knows this incomplete beginning [*dies Unvollkommene*] to be something necessary [*ein Notwendiges*], because truth only comes to be itself through the negativity of immediacy'). For an interpretation of Hegel's philosophy which stresses its *ex ante* character, but which nevertheless denies that dialectical logic is rational in any ordinary sense, see M. Rosen, *Hegel's Dialectic and its Criticism* (Cambridge, 1982). For a critique of Rosen, see my review in *The Owl of Minerva* (Journal of the Hegel Society of America), 15, 1 (Autumn 1983), 117–21.

46 Hegel, *TWA*, VIII, 181 (*E*, I, §85).

47 Hegel, *TWA*, V, 248 (*WL*, Miller trans., p. 216, 'But the perversity of employing mathematical categories. . .'); VI, 294 (*WL*, Miller trans., p. 617, 'Their determinations are not inert entities like numbers. . .').

48 Hegel, *TWA*, VIII, 96 (*E*, I, §28, Addition, 'finite things. . . characterised through finite predicates').

49 Hegel, *TWA*, VIII, 53 (*E*, I, §9, Remark); VIII, 169 (*E*, I, §80, Addition, 'It is by referring to this opposition of understanding to sensation and feeling that we must explain the frequent attacks made upon thought').

50 Hegel, *TWA*, VIII, 308–9 (*E*, I, §161 and Addition); VIII, 391 (*E*, I, §240); V, 130–1 (*WL*, Miller trans., pp. 121–2).

51 Hegel, *TWA*, VI, 550–3 (*WL*, Miller trans., pp. 825–7). Forms of thought such as quantitative analysis or the reflective understanding of causality are perfectly appropriate for understanding finite things in Hegel's view. The things in the world of the dialectical philosopher do, therefore, have quantifiable size and do cause other things to happen. The implication of Hegel's logical analysis, however, is that the speculative philosopher understands that there is more to quantity and causality than meets the

eye of ordinary thought; see *TWA*, VIII, 249 (*E*, I, §121, Addition, 'In common life, and . . . in the finite sciences. . .'), where this point is made with reference to the category of 'ground'.

52 Hegel, *TWA*, V, 70 (*WL*, Miller trans., p. 71).

53 Hegel, *TWA*, V, 58 (*WL*, Miller trans., p. 61, 'it is only in inorganic nature that it [the concept] is *implicit* [*Begriff* an sich]').

54 Röttges, pp. 42–4.

55 The similarity between Nietzsche and Fichte was already suggested in chapter 3, note 251.

56 Hegel, *TWA*, VI, 418 (*WL*, Miller trans., p. 718, '*in general*, it is *only as a product* that the mechanical object is an *object*; because it is only *through the mediation of an other* in it that it is what it is'); VIII, 96 (*E*, I, §28, Addition, 'Similarly, finite things stand to each other as cause and effect. . .').

57 Hegel, *TWA*, XII, 30 (*PGesch*, Sibree trans., p. 17).

58 See, for example, *TWA*, XII, 78 (*PGesch*, Sibree trans., p. 57, 'but *only* possibility. . .').

59 On the category of contingency in Hegel's *Logic*, see G. di Giovanni, 'The Category of Contingency in the Hegelian Logic', in *Art and Logic in Hegel's Philosophy*, edited by W. E. Steinkraus and K. I. Schmitz (New Jersey, 1980), pp. 179–200.

60 Hegel grounds the possibility of tentativeness and caution in his treatment of, for example, the problematic conclusions of induction and the form of the problematic judgement itself; see *TWA*, VI, 347–9, 386 (*WL*, Miller trans., pp. 660–1, 691). The self-critical caution Hegel evinces with regard to his own philosophy can be seen from the fact that, although he considers the method of speculative philosophy to be absolute, he does not put the details of his philosophical exposition beyond criticism; see *TWA*, V, 19, 50 (*WL*, Miller trans., pp. 31, 54).

61 *The Linguistic Turn*, edited and with an introduction by R. Rorty (Chicago, 1967), pp. 8–9.

62 *The Linguistic Turn*, edited by R. Rorty, p. 11.

63 Hegel, *TWA*, X, 257–71 (*E*, III, §§451–8).

64 Hegel, *TWA*, X, 278 (*E*, III, §462, Remark); X, 280 (*E*, III, §462, Addition, 'words thus attain an existence animated by thought. This existence is absolutely necessary to our thoughts').

65 Hegel, *TWA*, X, 280 (*E*, III, §462, Addition, 'Accordingly, the word gives to thoughts their highest and truest existence'); VIII, 152 (*E*, I, §63, Remark, 'we must not let ourselves be deceived . . . by . . . a merely verbal similarity'). See Cook, *Language in the Philosophy of Hegel*, pp. 156–8. Hegel was thus as conscious as Nietzsche or Wittgenstein that we must guard against being misled by the superficial form of language, but, like Wittgenstein, he has no sympathy for any general linguistic scepticism of the kind adopted by Nietzsche.

66 Hegel, *TWA*, X, 268 (*E*, III, §457, '*the imagination which produces signs*'); X, 271 (*E*, III, §459, Remark, 'Language here comes under discussion. . .'). See also *TWA*, IV, 322 (*NHS*); XII, 85 (*PGesch*, Sibree trans., p. 62, 'For grammar, in its extended and consistent form, is the work of thought,

which makes its categories distinctly visible therein. . .'). As I. Fetscher points out, by grammar we are to understand here not the scientific analysis of grammatical forms, but the unreflected development of these forms in language itself; see *Hegels Lehre vom Menschen* (Stuttgart, 1970), p. 172.

67 Compare Bertrand Russell: 'In order to understand a sentence, it is necessary to have knowledge both of the constituents and of the particular instance of the form. It is in this way that a sentence conveys information, since it tells us that certain known objects are related according to a certain known form. Thus some kind of knowledge of logical forms, though with most people it is not explicit, is involved in all understanding of discourse' (*Our Knowledge of the External World* (Chicago/London, 1914), pp. 43–4). See also P. F. Strawson, *Logico-Linguistic Papers* (London, 1971), p. 131.

68 *Hegel's Philosophy of Subjective Spirit*, edited and translated with an introduction and explanatory notes by M. J. Petry, 3 Vols. (Dordrecht, 1978), III, 429. Although he sees grammar as founded in logical categories, Hegel is aware that grammatical rules often involve a high degree of irregularity; see *Hegel's Philosophy of Subjective Spirit*, III, 194–5, 'Now in every language there are certain anomalies within which the universal does not prevail'; *TWA*, VIII, 286 (*E*, I, §145, Addition, 'thus in language . . . there is unquestionably considerable room for chance').

69 Hegel, *TWA*, V, 20 (*WL*, Miller trans., p. 31, 'everything that he has transformed into language and expresses in it contains a category').

70 Hegel, *TWA*, VI, 311–17, 328, 335–7, 346–7 (*WL*, Miller trans., pp. 631–6, 645, 650–2, 659–60).

71 Hegel would here seem to satisfy one of Strawson's criteria for being a philosopher, namely that he is someone who has 'tried to reach through surface similarities of grammatical form to the semantico-logical differences which lie below them' (*Logico-Linguistic Papers*, p. 142). See also Findlay, p. 231.

72 See chapter 6 on Hegel and judgement.

73 Hegel, *TWA*, X, 197 (*E*, III, §411, Addition).

74 Hegel, *TWA*, X, 280 (*E*, III, §462, Addition, 'But it is also ridiculous to regard as a defect of thought and a misfortune, the fact that it is tied to the word').

75 L. Wittgenstein, *Philosophical Investigations* (dual language edition), translated by G. E. M. Anscombe (Oxford, 1958), §23. Hegel does, however, provide the general categories for such a study. The logical form of a command, for example, is in Hegel's view that of a proposition or *Satz*; see *TWA*, VIII, 319 (*E*, I, §167, Remark). So the concept required to understand the form of a command is that of 'positing' (*Setzen*). On the difference between a proposition and a judgement, see *TWA*, VI, 305 (*WL*, Miller trans., p. 626); and VIII, 319 (*E*, I, §167 and Remark).

76 Hegel, *TWA*, X, 270 (*E*, III, §458, Remark, 'treating the intuition as its own property. . .'); X, 271 (*E*, III, §459 and Remark, 'Language . . . a product of intelligence for manifesting its ideas [*Vorstellungen*] in an

external medium'). See Cook, *Language in the Philosophy of Hegel*, pp. 180–2, 'Hegel's appreciation . . .'.

77 Hegel, *TWA*, X, 269 (*E*, III, §457, Addition, 'The arbitrary nature of the connection. . .').

78 Hegel, *TWA*, IV, 52 (*NHS*).

79 See *TWA*, I, 365 (*FS*, Knox trans., p. 248), where Hegel describes signs as 'conventional'; and IV, 52 (*NHS*, 'der in allen vorstellenden Wesen wiederklingt'). On Hegel's understanding of the sign as conventional, see T. Bodammer, *Hegels Deutung der Sprache* (Hamburg, 1969), pp. 41, and 253, note 114. On the importance of the sign in general for Hegel's philosophy of language, see M. Rosen, pp. 122–35.

80 Hegel, *TWA*, VII, 352. See also the parallel drawn by Fetscher 'between the *liberating role of labour* for the "slavish consciousness" and the *liberating role of language* for the human spirit' (p. 163).

81 Hegel, *TWA*, IV, 319–20 (*NHS*).

82 Hegel, *TWA*, XIII, 243 (*Ä*, Knox trans., I, 185).

83 Hegel, *TWA*, XIII, 301 (*Ä*, Knox trans., I, 232).

84 Cook, *Language in the Philosophy of Hegel*, pp. 163–4; 'languages' is misspelt as 'language' in the text.

85 Hegel, *TWA*, V, 20 (*WL*, Miller trans., p. 31).

86 Hegel, *TWA*, VIII, 62 (*E*, I, §16, Remark, 'Sciences are positive in conse-quence of the inadequate and limited ground on which their statements rest. Their statements are based upon formal inference, or upon feeling, faith and authority'); *TWA*, X, 248 (*E*, III, §447, Remark, 'If a man on any topic appeals. . . to his feeling. . .'). Hegel does at times refer to 'intellec-tual intuition' (*intellektuelle Anschauung*), but he equates this with Schellingian intuition of the outside world, not with introspection, and he does not see it as the foundation of philosophical thought; see *TWA*, X, 254 (*E*, III, §449, Addition); VI, 286 (*WL*, Miller trans., p. 611).

87 Hegel, *TWA*, III, 19–20 (*Phän*, Miller trans., pp. 7–8); III, 65 (*Phän*, Miller trans., p. 43, 'truth ripened to its properly matured form so as to be cap-able of being the property of all self-conscious reason'). In this respect Hegel's views have a strong affinity with those of the later Wittgenstein. Wittgenstein also insists that thought is public and that it is not to be confused with certainties and convictions which we have in the private space of our minds. Wittgenstein also explicitly rejects the view that we gain insight into the nature of thought directly by an act of intro-spection; see, for example, *Philosophical Investigations*, §§316, 329; and *On Certainty* (dual language edition), edited by G. E. M. Anscombe and G. H. von Wright, translated by Denis Paul and G. E. M. Anscombe (Oxford, 1979), §§15, 245, 308. Comparisons between Hegel and Wittgenstein have been suggested by C. Taylor and D. Lamb; see Taylor, 'The Open-ing Arguments of the *Phenomenology*', in *Hegel: A Collection of Critical Essays*, edited by A. MacIntyre (New York, 1972, second edition 1976), pp. 151–87; and Lamb, *Language and Perception in Hegel and Wittgenstein*, and *Hegel: From Foundation to System*. For a further comparison between Hegel and Wittgenstein in this book, see chapter 7.

88 See, for example, the section on judgement in the *Logic*; see *TWA*, VI, 311–51 (*WL*, Miller trans., pp. 630–63).

89 Hegel, *TWA*, V, 82; VI, 213 (*WL*, Miller trans., pp. 81, 550); III, 59–61 (*Phän*, Miller trans., pp. 38–40). The sentence form is crucial for Hegel since it reveals that categories are not distinct units, but are 'reflected' into one another (*TWA*, III, 26–7 (*Phän*, Miller trans., pp. 12–13)). See *TWA*, V, 93 (*WL*, Miller trans., p. 90, 'Now insofar as the proposition. . .'), where Hegel draws explicit attention to the fact that the form of the sentence in which the categories of 'being' and 'nothing' are stated to be identical redefines those categories as 'becoming'. Hegel's study of the categories of being – his ontology – is thus not a study of metaphysical 'objects' (*Gegenstände*), but an 'exercise in linguistic analysis' (*sprachanalytisches Geschäft*) (Theunissen, p. 52). It studies the dialectical form of being by studying the form of speculative sentences and speculative thought. Hegel's treatment of judgement even suggests that the dialectical form of thought and being is anticipated – though not fully manifested – in the copula of the judgement; see *TWA*, VI, 309, 351 (*WL*, Miller trans., pp. 629–30, 'If the *is* of the copula. . .', 663, 'The *unity* of the concept as the *determinateness* constituting the copula. . .').

90 Hegel, *TWA*, III, 60 (*Phän*, Miller trans., p. 39). Speculative sentences are also distinguished from judgements with a given *conceptual* content, as the lines quoted on p. 147 show; see *TWA*, III, 60 (*Phän*, Miller trans., p. 39, 'The universal is not meant to have. . .').

91 Hegel, *TWA*, III, 59, 62 (*Phän*, Miller trans., pp. 38, 40–1).

92 For Hegel's treatment of the positive infinite judgement, see *TWA*, VI, 325 (*WL*, Miller trans., pp. 642–3); and VIII, 324–5 (*E*, I, §173 and Remark), where a tautology is called an '*identical* judgement'.

93 Hegel, *TWA*, III, 59 (*Phän*, Miller trans., p. 38, 'So, too, in the philosophical proposition. . .').

94 For a summary of Hegel's view of the contradiction at the heart of the judgement, see *TWA*, VI, 309–10 (*WL*, Miller trans., p. 630).

95 Hegel, *TWA*, III, 57 (*Phän*, Miller trans., p. 37). This tension reveals that there are finite things which are the subjects of judgements – whereas the subjects of speculative sentences are not infinite 'things' – but that finite things are nevertheless to be determined as specific complexes of qualities and relations; compare R. Aquila, 'Predication and Hegel's Metaphysics', *Kant-Studien*, 64, 2 (1973), 239, 'There is only one alternative . . .'.

96 Hegel, *TWA*, III, 58 (*Phän*, Miller trans., p. 37).

97 Hegel, *TWA*, III, 60 (*Phän*, Miller trans., p. 39).

98 Hegel, *TWA*, III, 58 (*Phän*, Miller trans., p. 37).

99 Hegel, *TWA*, III, 59 (*Phän*, Miller trans., p. 38).

100 Hegel, *TWA*, III, 59 (*Phän*, Miller trans., p. 38).

101 Hegel, *TWA*, III, 59 (*Phän*, Miller trans., p. 38).

102 Hegel, *TWA*, III, 60 (*Phän*, Miller trans., p. 39).

103 The way to test speculative sentences, therefore, is to examine whether the predicate does actually render explicit what is implied by the subject,

and whether the redefinition of the subject does actually follow from the identity of the categories.

104 The sentence 'the actual is the universal' mentioned in the preface to the *Phenomenology* is in fact a rather unhappy example for Hegel to have chosen, since at the point in the *Logic* at which the speculative logician is explaining 'actuality' the structure of 'universality' has not yet been determined and so cannot be recognised in the structure of the category under discussion. Indeed, as far as I know, the sentence does not appear in the *Logic*. The principle of Hegel's argument is what is important, however, and other examples such as 'the necessary is an *actual*' (*das Notwendige ist ein* Wirkliches) (*TWA*, VI, 207 (*WL*, Miller trans., p. 545)) could be substituted for the sentence chosen by Hegel.

105 Hegel, *TWA*, VI, 294 (*WL*, Miller trans., p. 617, 'lebendige Bewegungen', 'living movements').

106 Hegel, *TWA*, III, 61 (*Phän*, Miller trans., pp. 39–40).

107 Hegel, *TWA*, III, 61 (*Phän*, Miller trans., p. 40, 'Here we should bear in mind that the dialectical movement likewise has propositions for its parts or elements'); see L. B. Puntel, *Darstellung, Methode und Struktur* (Bonn, 1973), *Hegel-Studien*, Beiheft 10, p. 33.

108 Hegel, *TWA*, III, 27–8 (*Phän*, Miller trans., pp. 13–14).

109 Hegel, *TWA*, III, 41 (*Phän*, Miller trans., p. 23, 'To such questions as...').

110 Russell, *History of Western Philosophy*, p. 701. See *TWA*, VIII, 47 (*E*, I, §6).

111 Hegel, *TWA*, V, 25 (*WL*, Miller trans., p. 35, 'what is there more in *us* as against them...').

112 Hegel does not deny the place of instinct and nature in human life, but he believes that man only acquires true freedom and true individuality when his nature is *aufgehoben* in a genuine social relationship of mutual recognition; see *TWA*, XII, 58–9 (*PGesch*, Sibree trans., pp. 40–1); and *Vorlesungen über Rechtsphilosophie 1818–1831*, edited by K. H. Ilting, 4 Vols. (Stuttgart, 1973–), I, 322, §113. On the ever-present influence of natural passions (*Leidenschaften*) on the associations of the mind, see *TWA*, X, 265 (*E*, III, §455, Addition).

113 Hegel, *TWA*, III, 23 (*Phän*, Miller trans., p. 10). This sentence shows that speculative sentences may be more complex than the simple forms such as 'the actual is the universal' discussed above.

114 Hegel, *TWA*, III, 60 (*Phän*, Miller trans., p. 39).

115 Hegel, *TWA*, III, 60 (*Phän*, Miller trans., p. 39).

116 In speculative sentences, therefore, what is important is that the subject and predicate – the concepts thematised in the *Logic* – are not conceived merely as given elements but as concepts constituted by the speculative development of the *Logic* itself. Many other words in speculative sentences, however, such as *dasselbe* and *insofern* in the sentence quoted on p. 152, will obviously have given meanings defined by their role in ordinary language. See White, p. 36, 'That the names for the pure thoughts must in most cases be selected from the words already available in a given language is not of crucial logical importance, since the signification of each thought must in every case be determined by the movement lead-

ing to it. The names of the pure thoughts are not destructively ambiguous in that the process of Hegel's *Logic* never requires that either concepts or the names of concepts be analysed in terms of their various historical, philosophical or colloquial significations. On the contrary, the difficulty of the *Logic* stems to a great extent from the stringent requirement that only what is "present at hand" – only what has been dialectically developed – be considered at any given point.'

117 It is thus false to say that for Hegel 'the universe is posited by a Spirit whose essence is rational necessity' (Taylor, *Hegel* (Cambridge, 1975), p. 538).

118 Schopenhauer, *Sämtliche Werke*, II, 508 (*WWV*, I, 'Criticism of the Kantian Philosophy', Payne trans., I, 429, 'But the greatest effrontery. . .').

119 Puntel, p. 65.

120 See, for example, Hegel, *TWA*, VIII, 109 (*E*, I, §38, Addition, 'Spinnengeweben und Nebelgestalten des abstrakten Verstandes. . .', 'Spiders' webs and phantasms of the abstract understanding . . .'). Compare also Hegel's comments on envy (*TWA*, XII, 48 (*PGesch*, Sibree trans., p. 32, 'The Thersites of Homer. . .')) with Nietzsche's judgement on jealousy (*Werke*, II, 303 (*ASZ*, II, 'Of Joys and Passions', 'He whom the flames of jealousy. . .')). See also chapter 5, p. 125.

121 Hegel, *TWA*, III, 23 (*Phän*, Miller trans., p. 10).

122 Hegel, *TWA*, VI, 67 (*WL*, Miller trans., p. 433).

123 Nietzsche, *Werke*, II, 790 (*GM*, I, §13); see chapter 3, note 21.

124 Nietzsche, *Werke*, III, 917 (*WM*, §1067); see also, for example, III, 896 (*WM*, §617, 'Werden als Erfinden . . .', 'becoming as inventing . . .').

125 Nietzsche, *Werke*, III, 685 (*WM*, §715, 'Linguistic means of expression are useless for expressing "becoming" ' – including, of course, the word 'becoming' itself).

126 Nietzsche, *Werke*, III, 916–17 (*WM*, §1067).

127 Sober – 'the cold march of necessity in the thing itself' (*TWA*, III, 16 (*Phän*, Miller trans., p. 5)) – despite Hegel's 'Nietzschean' claim that 'the true is . . . the Bacchanalian revel in which no member is not drunk' (*TWA*, III, 46 (*Phän*, Miller trans., p. 27)).

128 Hegel does not deny the value of the associations of the imagination (see *TWA*, X, 265 (*E*, III, §455, Addition)), but he thinks that argument should rely on logical connections rather than association or analogy. Furthermore, Hegel would repudiate the fashionable modern view that logical connections can invariably be undermined by the associative play of metaphors which is alleged to underlie such connections. For Hegel's critique of argument by analogy, see *TWA*, VI, 387–91 (*WL*, Miller trans., pp. 692–5). On Nietzsche's extensive use of metaphorical association and analogy in the argument of *The Birth of Tragedy*, on the other hand, see M. S. Silk and J. P. Stern, *Nietzsche on Tragedy* (Cambridge, 1981), pp. 188–209.

129 Nietzsche, *Werke*, III, 917 (*WM*, §1067).

130 Hegel's judgement on Nietzsche's juxtaposition of frequently contradictory metaphors and propositions about life would probably be 'that these propositions are not connected and therefore exhibit their

content only in the form of an antinomy, whereas their content refers to one and the same thing, and the determinations which are expressed in the . . . propositions are supposed to be in complete union – a union which can only be stated as an *unrest* of *incompatibles*, as a *movement*' (*TWA*, V, 94 (*WL*, Miller trans., p. 91)).

131 Hegel, *TWA*, V, 41 (*WL*, Miller trans., p. 48, 'When they are taken as fixed determinations . . . they [logical forms] lack a substantial content – a matter which would be substantial in itself. The content which is missing in the logical forms is nothing else than a solid foundation and a concretion of these abstract determinations, and such a substantial being for them is usually sought outside them').

6 *Hegel's conception of the judgement*

1 For Hegel's discussion of other linguistic forms such as metaphor and simile, see *TWA*, XIII, 516–39 (*Ä*, Knox trans., I, 402–21).

2 See chapter 3, pp. 45, 77.

3 Hegel, *TWA*, VI, 302 (*WL*, Miller trans., pp. 623–4, 'two self-subsistents which are called subject and predicate'); VI, 304–5 (*WL*, Miller trans., pp. 625–6, 'The judgement has in general for its sides totalities which to begin with are essentially self-subsistent. . .', 'From this *subjective* standpoint, then, subject and predicate are considered to be complete, each on its own account, apart from the other').

4 Hegel, *TWA*, VI, 303 (*WL*, Miller trans., p. 624, 'for *what it is* is first enunciated by the predicate. . .'); VI, 308 (*WL*, Miller trans., p. 628, 'The subject is determined only in its predicate, or, only in the predicate is it a subject').

5 Hegel, *TWA*, VIII, 317 (*E*, I, §166, Remark, 'No doubt there is also a distinction between the categories of individual and universal, of subject and predicate: but it is nonetheless a universal fact that every judgement states them to be identical').

6 Hegel, *TWA*, VIII, 316–18 (*E*, I, §166, Remark and Addition).

7 E. Tugendhat, *Vorlesungen zur Einführung in die sprachanalytische Philosophie* (Frankfurt, 1979), p. 192.

8 D. Bell, *Frege's Theory of Judgement* (Oxford, 1979), p. 2.

9 Hegel, *TWA*, VI, 301–2 (*WL*, Miller trans., p. 623, 'this positing. . .', 'the proximate *realisation*. . .'). See also Theunissen, pp. 66–7; J. P. Surber, 'Hegel's Speculative Sentence', *Hegel-Studien*, 10 (1975), 213; and M. Rosen, p. 139. In the *Logic* Hegel argues that the judgement is 'prior' to the concept but not that the judgement is the fundamental unit of meaning. The subsequent development of the *Logic* shows, for example, that rational syllogisms constitute units of meaning in their own right and cannot simply be regarded as 'composed' of judgements; see *TWA*, VI, 357–8 (*WL*, Miller trans., p. 669). Furthermore, as I suggested in chapter 5 (pp. 142–4), Hegel believes that all thought is linguistic and therefore occurs within the context of social and historical existence. Judgements

cannot therefore be considered as meaningful in isolation from the context of discourse within which they are uttered. Hegel's position is thus much closer to Wittgenstein's interest in the context of utterances than, for example, to Russell's rather academic study of isolated sentences; see chapter 7.

10 Hegel, *TWA*, VI, 301 (*WL*, Miller trans., p. 623).

11 Hegel, *TWA*, X, 286 (*E*, III, §467, Addition, 'as a totality. . .'). See Lamb, *Hegel: From Foundation to System*, p. 194. Hegel agrees that *words* are connected in judgements, but he insists that the *concepts* in judgements are moments of one thought; see *TWA*, VI, 304–5 (*WL*, Miller trans., p. 625, 'judgement . . . is the *original division* [*ursprüngliche Teilung*] of what is originally one', 626, 'for it is *words* that are here externally combined'). The view that concepts are 'moments' of judgements rather than isolated units is of course anticipated throughout the logics of being and essence in Hegel's demonstration that all determinations are to be understood as inseparable from their negations.

12 Cook, *Language in the Philosophy of Hegel*, pp. 143–4; Hegel, *TWA*, VI, 309 (*WL*, Miller trans., p. 629, 'But this *differenceless identity* [*unterschiedslose Identität*] really constitutes the *true* relation of the subject to the predicate. . .').

13 Hegel, *TWA*, VI, 308 (*WL*, Miller trans., p. 628, 'the copula expresses. . .'); VI, 312 (*WL*, Miller trans., p. 632, 'their relation, the *is* or *copula*. . .'); VI, 321 (*WL*, Miller trans., p. 639, 'their relation, *the form of the judgement*'). See also Theunissen, p. 395. The degree of formal identity between subject and predicate becomes more explicit as the forms of judgement with which Hegel deals become more complex; see *TWA*, VI, 309 (*WL*, Miller trans., p. 630, 'To restore this *identity* of the concept, or rather to *posit* it, is the goal of the *movement* of the judgement'). However, there is not space here to discuss these different forms in detail, so my remarks are confined to what Hegel sees as the general form of the judgement as such; see *TWA*, VI, 312 (*WL*, Miller trans., p. 632, 'every judgement is also in general an abstract judgement. . .'). Though he rejects the idea that the copula always indicates *identity* between terms, Bertrand Russell agrees with Hegel that the copula is not to be understood as a separate constituent of the judgement: 'If I say, "Socrates is mortal", "Jones is angry", "the sun is hot", there is something in common in these three cases, something indicated by the word "is". What is in common is the *form* of the proposition, not an actual constituent' (*Our Knowledge of the External World*, p. 42).

14 Russell, *Our Knowledge of the External World*, pp. 39–40. Findlay, on the other hand, praises Hegel's idea of identity in predication for being 'so much more like the identity of ordinary speech than the rigid concept of the logicians' (pp. 228–9).

15 Hegel, *TWA*, VI, 308 (*WL*, Miller trans., p. 628, 'the predicate is this *posited* determinateness [*gesetzte Bestimmtheit*] of the subject').

16 Hegel, *TWA*, VI, 307 (*WL*, Miller trans., p. 628, '*The subject without the predicate*, is what the *thing without qualities*, the *thing in itself* is in the sphere

of appearance – an empty, indeterminate ground'). See Aquila, pp. 234–5.

17 Hegel, *TWA*, VI, 305 (*WL*, Miller trans., p. 626, 'The predicate which is attached to the subject should, however, also *belong* to it, that is, be in and for itself identical with it'); VI, 308 (*WL*, Miller trans., p. 628, '*posited* determinateness. . .').

18 Hegel, *TWA*, VI, 308 (*WL*, Miller trans., p. 628).

19 Hegel, *TWA*, VI, 301 (*WL*, Miller trans., p. 623).

20 A similar argument is put forward by John Searle: 'To understand the *name of a universal* it is necessary to understand the use of the corresponding general term . . . "Kindness" is parasitic on "is kind"; "is kind" is prior to "kindness" ' (*Speech Acts*, (Cambridge, 1969), p. 119).

21 G. Frege, *Nachgelassene Schriften*, edited by H. Hermes and others (Hamburg, 1969), p. 129 (Long trans., p. 119). See Tugendhat, p. 192.

22 Theunissen, pp. 66–7.

23 Hegel, *TWA*, VI, 308 (*WL*, Miller trans., p. 628).

24 Searle, p. 119.

25 Hegel, *TWA*, VI, 303 (*WL*, Miller trans., p. 625); VIII, 320 (*E*, I, §169, Remark).

26 Findlay, p. 229.

27 Hegel, *TWA*, VIII, 316–17 (*E*, I, §166, Remark); VI, 312–13 (*WL*, Miller trans., p. 632, 'that the individual is a universal').

28 Hegel, *TWA*, VI, 316 (*WL*, Miller trans., p. 635).

29 Hegel, *TWA*, VI, 313–14, 316–17 (*WL*, Miller trans., pp. 632–3, 635–6).

30 Judgements are thus not themselves suited to articulate the dialectical, dynamic form of nature, thought and consciousness. But they are suited to describe finite things and the finite qualities and relations of conscious human beings; and as we spell out the character of finite things in judgements, we imply that the subject is speculative to the extent that what we mean by the subject is only fully understandable in terms of qualities and relations which are expressible in language. We imply, therefore, that even finite, empirical things are relational in character, and that empirical reality is thus not something 'pure' which is distorted by being expressed in language, but rather that in language we state explicitly the relations in terms of which we actually perceive objects. This position, however, does not commit Hegel to the view that a subject is reducible to a simple aggregate of predicates, but rather to the view that the finite subject is to be conceived as the coherent unity and continuity of its predicates; see Hegel, *TWA*, VI, 314 (*WL*, Miller trans., p. 633, 'the thing . . . is reflected into itself in its qualities, properties or accidents; or it *continues* itself through them').

31 Hegel thus endeavours as much as possible to use words from ordinary language to name the concepts developed in the *Logic* in order to make people realise that in philosophy they are being shown in a new light what they are already familiar with; see *TWA*, V, 20–1 (*WL*, Miller trans., pp. 31–3); XX, 16–17, 52–3, 259 (*GPhil*, Haldane trans., III, 114, 150,

351–2). Hegel insists, however, that these words have not to be understood in their ordinary or 'original' meaning, since the philosophical exposition of concepts does not remain at the level of ordinary understanding; see VI, 406–7 (*WL*, Miller trans., pp. 708–9, 'Philosophy has the right. . .'); XX, 188 (*GPhil*, Haldane trans., III, 284, 'This proof from the usage of language – that we also understand this to be the meaning in everyday life . . . – has no philosophical significance'). Hegel's use of terms from ordinary language to name concepts is thus designed to provide a familiar point of departure from which to begin philosophising and a 'familiar cultural universe out of which philosophy may grow' (Cook, *Language in the Philosophy of Hegel*, pp. 67, 70). Hegel's attitude to ordinary language may be summarised as follows: the concepts people use do not always mean quite what people think they mean, but they do at least mean something like it, and it is the task of philosophy to clarify what that is; see VIII, 79 (*E*, I, §22, Addition, 'The business of philosophy is to bring to explicit consciousness. . .').

7 *Context and the immanence of rationality in Hegel's* Phenomenology

1 Hegel, *TWA*, III, 145 (*Phän*, Miller trans., p. 110).
2 Hegel, *TWA*, III, 82 (*Phän*, Miller trans., p. 58). The term 'sensory realism' is taken from Lamb, *Hegel: From Foundation to System*, pp. 76–7. See also Taylor, 'The Opening Arguments of the *Phenomenology*', in *Hegel: A Collection of Critical Essays*, pp. 161–8.
3 Hegel, *TWA*, III, 83 (*Phän*, Miller trans., pp. 58–9).
4 Hegel, *TWA*, III, 84 (*Phän*, Miller trans., pp. 59–60).
5 Hegel, *TWA*, III, 84–5 (*Phän*, Miller trans., pp. 59–61). G. Patzig takes exception to Hegel's suggestion that we test the 'truths' of sense-certainty by writing those 'truths' down. Patzig argues that the word 'truth' cannot be applied to a sentence like 'now is night' because a sentence cannot be judged to be true or false without explicit reference to the time and place of the utterance. By themselves, Patzig maintains, the words 'now' and 'here' do not make a sentence stable or 'tenable' (*haltbar*), whereas the introduction of names and dates – 'On the 19.4.70 at 1.24 Central European Time it is nighttime in Göttingen' – would yield a sentence which refers to a definite place and time and which, if true, could not become 'stale' later on; see *Tatsachen, Normen, Sätze* (Stuttgart, 1980), pp. 142–3. It should be clear from what has been said, however, that this is not an objection to Hegel at all, but a restatement of a point Hegel himself is making. After all, Hegel's argument is designed precisely to show that the words 'now' and 'here' are indeterminate when used in isolation. Like Patzig, therefore, Hegel implies that a sentence which only says 'now is night' cannot have a definite truth-value because it does not determine any specific time against which to measure the claim that it *is* night.
6 Hegel, *TWA*, VIII, 74 (*E*, I, §20, Remark). See also *TWA*, V, 126 (*WL*,

Miller trans., p. 117), and XVIII, 536–7 (*GPhil*, Haldane trans., I, 466–7).

7 Hegel, *TWA*, III, 88–91 (*Phän*, Miller trans., pp. 63–4).

8 Hegel, *TWA*, III, 85 (*Phän*, Miller trans., p. 60). See Lamb, *Hegel: From Foundation to System*, pp. 84–7.

9 Hegel, *TWA*, III, 89–90 (*Phän*, Miller trans., p. 64).

10 J. N. Findlay, 'Analysis of the Text', appended to A. V. Miller's translation of Hegel's *Phenomenology of Spirit*, p. 510.

11 Hegel, *TWA*, III, 90 (*Phän*, Miller trans., p. 64, 'just as the day is a simple plurality of nows').

12 See Cook, *Language in the Philosophy of Hegel*, p. 34, 'a nexus of various relations and universal concepts'. The value of judgements of 'reflection' for Hegel – judgements such as 'this instrument is useful' which predicate a relational property of a subject – is that they render explicit the fact that the subject 'is in *existence*, in *relation* and *inter-connection* with another thing – with an external world' (*TWA*, VIII, 326 (*E*, I, §174)).

13 Hegel, *TWA*, X, 275–6 (*E*, III, §459, Remark).

14 Hegel, *TWA*, VIII, 41 (*E*, I, §1, 'it is only through representations [*Vorstellungen*], and by having constant recourse to them, that the thinking mind goes on to know and comprehend in the strict meaning of thought'); X, 243 (*E*, III, §445, Remark, 'the truth... lies in this, that the intuition, representation, etc. are not isolated, and exist only as "moments" in the totality of cognition itself').

15 Hegel, *TWA*, V, 20 (*WL*, Miller trans., p. 31, 'Into all that becomes something inward for men...').

16 Lamb, *Hegel: From Foundation to System*, p. 213.

17 Wittgenstein, *Philosophical Investigations*, §28.

18 Lamb, *Language and Perception in Hegel and Wittgenstein*, p. 31.

19 Wittgenstein, *Philosophical Investigations*, §§30, 31, 257, 454. See A. Kenny, *Wittgenstein* (London, 1973), p. 157, 'So in the acquisition ...'.

20 Wittgenstein, *Philosophical Investigations*, §§40, 43.

21 Wittgenstein, *Philosophical Investigations*, §49.

22 Wittgenstein, *Philosophical Investigations*, §20.

23 Wittgenstein, *Philosophical Investigations*, §7.

24 Wittgenstein, *Philosophical Investigations*, §§19, 23.

25 For Hegel the meaning of a sign is not identified with an object referred to either, but rather with the representation (*Vorstellung*) or form of thought which the sign signifies; see *TWA*, X, 270 (*E*, III, §458); X, 280 (*E*, III, §462, Addition, 'words thus attain an existence animated by thought...'). Moreover, Hegel's awareness of the conventional nature of signs, and of the importance of grammar for the systematic form of language, suggests that he also understands Wittgenstein's point that we learn the meaning of a sign by learning how it is to be used within a community. Where Hegel differs from Wittgenstein, however, is in his belief that we only understand conceptual terms fully when we understand not merely the different ways in which these terms are employed in different contexts, but also the intrinsic logical character of the thoughts themselves.

26 Wittgenstein, *Philosophical Investigations*, §§89, 97, 108. The target of Wittgenstein's criticism is of course primarily the a priori 'logic' of his own *Tractatus* (see *Philosophical Investigations*, p. x, Preface) but his criticism also encompasses the general metaphysical concern for 'essences'.

27 D. Pears, *Wittgenstein* (London, 1971), pp. 134, 138–9; and Wittgenstein, *Philosophical Investigations*, §83.

28 Wittgenstein, *Philosophical Investigations*, §103.

29 Wittgenstein, *Philosophical Investigations*, §§66, 106, 109, 116, 124, 126. See also Pears, *Wittgenstein*, pp. 172–3. Pears calls Wittgenstein's method 'a subtle kind of positivism' (p. 104).

30 Wittgenstein, *Philosophical Investigations*, §109.

31 Wittgenstein, *Philosophical Investigations*, §118. Pears argues that Wittgenstein is not intending to prevent people from ever philosophising in the first place, but rather to bring them back to ordinary language when they do philosophise. On this view, the activity of trying to overstep the limits of ordinary language in philosophy is essential to the task of finding out where those limits lie; see Pears, *Wittgenstein*, pp. 123–4.

32 J. L. Austin, *Philosophical Papers* (Oxford, 1961, third edition 1979), p. 181.

33 Pears, *Wittgenstein*, p. 126.

34 Wittgenstein, *Philosophical Investigations*, §§92, 129. See D. Pears, 'Wittgenstein and Austin', in *British Analytical Philosophy*, edited by B. Williams and A. Montefiore (London, 1966), p. 38.

35 R. Rorty, *Philosophy and the Mirror of Nature* (Princeton, 1980), p. 315.

36 Wittgenstein, *Philosophical Investigations*, §108.

37 Wittgenstein, *Philosophical Investigations*, §67. For Hegel's treatment of 'something' and 'identity', see *TWA*, V, 122–7 (*WL*, Miller trans., pp. 114–19); and VI, 38–45 (*WL*, Miller trans., pp. 411–16). The activity of abstracting and generalising provides a useful focus for comparing the philosophical positions of Hegel, Nietzsche and Wittgenstein. For Hegel the activity of abstracting is a perfectly normal activity rooted in the fact that we think and speak at all; see *TWA*, V, 126 (*WL*, Miller trans., p. 117, 'Speech . . . gives expression only to universals'); VIII, 77 (*E*, I, §21, Addition, 'To reflect is a lesson even the child has to learn'). The task of philosophy, therefore, is to draw out the concreteness in the abstract, universal concepts with which we think. Nietzsche agrees that the activity of abstracting is a 'normal' human activity by arguing that our universal, metaphysical concepts are intimately bound up with the grammar of everyday language; see *Werke*, II, 960 (*GD*, ' "Reason" in Philosophy', §5). Nietzsche differs from Hegel, however, in insisting that man should be strong enough to acknowledge his abstract concepts as fictions and falsifications of life. Wittgenstein also sees the activity of abstracting as deriving from our language, but he considers that activity to be the deviant product of the malfunctioning of language rather than the product of ordinary usage itself (*Philosophical Investigations*, §§38, 132). Wittgenstein's own philosophy therefore endeavours to make

people aware of how the malfunctioning of language misleads us into making philosophical assumptions and asking philosophical questions which deviate from what is implied by our ordinary understanding of things and our ordinary usage of words (§§109, 116). Ordinary language for Hegel, as I indicated in chapter 6, note 31, does not provide an alternative to philosophical understanding, but constitutes rather a form of experience whose concepts it is philosophy's task to clarify.

38 Hegel, *TWA*, III, 70–1 (*Phän*, Miller trans., p. 48).
39 Cook, *Language in the Philosophy of Hegel*, p. 160.
40 Hegel, *TWA*, III, 24 (*Phän*, Miller trans., p. 10).
41 Taylor points to the 'dialectic' in Wittgenstein, but does not explicitly identify dialectic as the form of free play; see 'The Opening Arguments of the *Phenomenology*', in *Hegel: A Collection of Critical Essays*, p. 160.
42 Hegel, *TWA*, III, 76–9 (*Phän*, Miller trans., pp. 53–5). On the difference between the *Phenomenology* and the section entitled 'Phenomenology' in the *Encyclopaedia*, see White, pp. 164–5, note 10. Phenomenology in Hegel's sense is not to be confused with Husserl's science of the same name.
43 Hegel, *TWA*, III, 29–30 (*Phän*, Miller trans., p. 15).
44 Hegel, *TWA*, III, 78–9 (*Phän*, Miller trans., p. 55).
45 Hegel, *TWA*, III, 77 (*Phän*, Miller trans., pp. 53–4).
46 Hegel, *TWA*, III, 79–80 (*Phän*, Miller trans., pp. 55–6).
47 Hegel, *TWA*, III, 74 (*Phän*, Miller trans., p. 51, 'the *goal*. . .').
48 Lamb, *Hegel: From Foundation to System*, p. 13.
49 Lamb, *Hegel: From Foundation to System*, p. 34.
50 Nietzsche, *Werke*, II, 941 (*GD*, Preface).
51 Nietzsche, *Werke*, II, 601 (*JGB*, §36).
52 Nietzsche, *Werke*, II, 729 (*JGB*, §259, 'life itself is *essentially* appropriation, injury, overpowering of the strange and weaker. . .').
53 Nietzsche, *Werke*, I, 245 (*UB*, II, §6).
54 Hegel, *TWA*, VI, 250 (*WL*, Miller trans., p. 581).
55 Nietzsche, *Werke*, I, 246 (*UB*, II, §6).
56 Nietzsche, *Werke*, I, 247 (*UB*, II, §6).
57 Hegel, *TWA*, III, 71 (*Phän*, Miller trans., p. 49). From a Hegelian perspective, indeed, Nietzsche's approach bears signs of being 'an external, negative activity which does not pertain to the subject matter itself, having its ground in mere conceit as a subjective itch for unsettling and destroying what is fixed and substantial' (*TWA*, V, 51 (*WL*, Miller trans., p. 56)). Compare Nietzsche's remarks on the need for 'the lion of the spirit' to destroy traditional values in order to assert the freedom of his own will; see *Werke*, II, 293–4 (*ASZ*, I, 'Of the Three Metamorphoses'). See also I, 439–40 (*MA*, Preface, §3, 'he tears to pieces whatever attracts him. . .'; 'Can one not reverse *all* values?'). It should be said, however, that this wilful, leonine destructiveness is not the goal of Nietzsche's philosophy, but merely the means to that goal. The goal, as I suggested in chapter 3, is the aesthetic creativity and openness of 'strength' – 'that *mature* freedom of spirit which is equally self-control and discipline of the

heart, and gives access to many and opposed modes of thought' (I, 441 (*MA*, Preface, §4)); see also II, 293–4 (*ASZ*, I, 'Of the Three Metamorphoses', 'The child is innocence...'). However, such creative freedom still retains that leonine moment and thus still *confronts* what it is opposed to with its superior strength. Nietzschean 'strength' does not meet its opponent on his own ground, therefore, even when, as in Nietzsche's critique of metaphysics and morality, it exploits its opponent's vocabulary for its own ends; see chapter 3, pp. 78–81.

58 Nietzsche, *Werke*, I, 1137–8 (*M*, §190).
59 Hegel, *TWA*, III, 54–5 (*Phän*, Miller trans., p. 34, '*logical necessity* . . . is the rational element and the rhythm of the organic whole').
60 Hegel, *TWA*, III, 53–4 (*Phän*, Miller trans., p. 33). See Puntel, p. 41, ' "System" hat bei Hegel nichts zu tun mit apriorisch-deduktiver Konstruktion der Wirklichkeit. . .', ' "System" in Hegel has nothing to do with an a priori, deductive construction of reality. . .'.
61 Hegel, *TWA*, III, 72 (*Phän*, Miller trans., p. 49).
62 Without the aid of the *Logic*, therefore, 'the phenomenologist may not fully understand *why* the stances of consciousness organise themselves as they do, but he must be able to see *that* they so organise themselves' (White, p. 22).
63 Hegel, *TWA*, VIII, 82 (*E*, I, §24, Addition 1).
64 Hegel, *TWA*, XIII, 191 (*Ä*, Knox trans., I, 143–4). See also VIII, 59 (*E*, I, §13).
65 Hegel, *TWA*, V, 45 (*WL*, Miller trans., p. 51, 'But inasmuch as it is said. . .').
66 Hegel, *TWA*, VIII, 78 (*E*, I, §21, Addition).
67 Hegel, *TWA*, VIII, 85 (*E*, I, §24, Addition 2). See Cook, *Language in the Philosophy of Hegel*, p. 180, 'The Absolute, whatever its final status, is nothing but the experience and expression of consciousness – individual and collective – and has no existence or meaning beyond them.' For Hegel, it is clearly an error of the understanding to regard 'the metaphysical' as 'a mere figment of thought, which *fringes* actuality and is therefore *external* to it' ([*der*] *Irrtum des Verstandes, daß das Metaphysische nur ein Gedankending neben, d.i, außer der Wirklichkeit sei*) (IX, 169 (*E*, II, §298, Remark)).

8 *Hegel and Nietzsche on tragedy*

1 Nietzsche, *Werke*, II, 1109 (*EH*, III, GT, §1).
2 Nietzsche, *Werke*, III, 463 (*WM*, §1051, 'Dionysus is a *judge*!').
3 Nietzsche, *Werke*, II, 1110–11 (*EH*, III, GT, §3); III, 432 (*WM*, §1029).
4 Nietzsche, *Werke*, II, 1152 (*EH*, IV, §1).
5 The most comprehensive treatment of Nietzsche's book – and its confusions – is without doubt M. S. Silk and J. P. Stern, *Nietzsche on Tragedy* (Cambridge, 1981).

6 Although in his earlier period he is critical of traditional, Christian metaphysics, and prefers to see the world as the product of a chaotic, energetic will rather than as the product of an underlying rationality, the early Nietzsche, under the spell of Schopenhauerian metaphysics, still considered his own position to be metaphysical. The Apolline and the Dionysiac drives were thus thought of as modalities of the fundamental metaphysical reality 'behind' appearance; see *Werke*, I, 32–3 (*GT*, §4). It is only with the later Nietzsche that we find the attempt at a wholescale rejection of all metaphysical notions.

7 Nietzsche, *Werke*, I, 21–3 (*GT*, §1).

8 Nietzsche, *Werke*, I, 22 (*GT*, §1).

9 Nietzsche, *Werke*, I, 88 (*GT*, §16).

10 Nietzsche, *Werke*, I, 55 (*GT*, §9).

11 Nietzsche, *Werke*, I, 24–5 (*GT*, §1).

12 Nietzsche, *Werke*, I, 40 (*GT*, §5).

13 Nietzsche, *Werke*, I, 131 (*GT*, §24).

14 Nietzsche, *Werke*, I, 93 (*GT*, §17).

15 Nietzsche, *Werke*, I, 24–6, 52, 121 (*GT*, §§1, 2, 8, 22).

16 Nietzsche, *Werke*, I, 25 (*GT*, §1, 'Now . . . each one feels himself not only united, reconciled, and fused with his neighbour, but as one with him, as if the veil of *maya* had been torn aside').

17 Nietzsche, *Werke*, I, 133 (*GT*, §25).

18 Nietzsche, *Werke*, I, 130 (*GT*, §24).

19 Nietzsche, *Werke*, I, 40 (*GT*, §5).

20 Nietzsche, *Werke*, I, 115–20 (*GT*, §21).

21 Leon Rosenstein points out that tragedy makes life *bearable* for Nietzsche, but makes life *intelligible* for Hegel ('Metaphysical Foundations of the Theories of Tragedy in Hegel and Nietzsche', in *Journal of Aesthetics and Art Criticism*, 28, 4 (Summer 1970), 527.

22 Nietzsche, *Werke*, I, 121 (*GT*, §22).

23 Nietzsche, *Werke*, I, 47, 93 (*GT*, §§7, 17, 'metaphysical comfort'); 120–1 (*GT*, §22, 'He beholds the transfigured world of the stage and nevertheless denies it'). See Schacht, p. 499.

24 Nietzsche, *Werke*, I, 122 (*GT*, §22, 'but they never tire of characterising . . . the triumph of the moral world order [*den Sieg der sittlichen Weltordnung*] or the purgation of the emotions through tragedy, as the essence of the tragic').

25 Nietzsche, *Werke*, I, 37–40 (*GT*, §5).

26 Nietzsche, *Werke*, I, 32 (*GT*, §4, 'those omnipotent art impulses', 'an ardent longing for illusion').

27 Nietzsche, *Werke*, I, 121 (*GT*, §22, 'Urfreude im Schoße des Ur-Einen', 'primal joy in the bosom of the primordially One').

28 Nietzsche, *Werke*, I, 16 (*GT*, 'Attempt at a Self-Criticism', §6).

29 Nietzsche, *Werke*, I, 59 (*GT*, §9). See Silk and Stern, pp. 273, 296.

30 Nietzsche, *Werke*, I, 122 (*GT*, §22).

31 Nietzsche, *Werke*, I, 59 (*GT*, §9).

32 Nietzsche, *Werke*, I, 58 (*GT*, §9).

33 Nietzsche, *Werke*, I, 58 (*GT*, §9).
34 Nietzsche, *Werke*, I, 23 (*GT*, §1, 'measured restraint'); 58 (*GT*, §9, 'cheerfulness of artistic creation').
35 See Stern, *A Study of Nietzsche*, p. 174.
36 Nietzsche, *Werke*, I, 37 (*GT*, §5).
37 See Silk and Stern, pp. 226, 230, 345–6.
38 For a more detailed discussion of Nietzsche's later views of *The Birth of Tragedy*, see Silk and Stern, pp. 117–25.
39 Nietzsche, *Werke*, I, 17–18 (*GT*, 'Attempt at a Self-Criticism', §7).
40 Nietzsche, *Werke*, II, 244 (*FW*, §370).
41 Nietzsche, *Werke*, I, 101–2 (*GT*, §18).
42 Nietzsche, *Werke*, I, 9, 18 (*GT*, 'Attempt at a Self-Criticism', §§1, 7). Together with this change in the character of tragic mood, there is a change in the later Nietzsche in the character of Dionysiac reality itself. The pessimistic reality which the tragic soul now confronts is no longer the metaphysical realm 'behind' experience into which man previously sought to dissolve; rather it is the disturbing reality of *this* world, the irreducible instability and restless creativity of life.
43 Nietzsche, *Werke*, II, 372 (*ASZ*, II, 'Of Self-Overcoming', 'And he who has to be a creator. . .').
44 Nietzsche, *Werke*, II, 1032 (*GD*, 'What I Owe to the Ancients', §5).
45 Nietzsche, *Werke*, II, 1110 (*EH*, III, GT, §3). See Silk and Stern, p. 296.
46 Nietzsche, *Werke*, III, 834 (*WM*, §1041).
47 Nietzsche, *Werke*, III, 773 (*WM*, §1052, 'The tragic man affirms even the harshest suffering; he is sufficiently strong, rich and capable of deifying [*vergöttlichend*] to do so'). From Hegel's perspective, Nietzsche's high evaluation of suffering as a test of human character is evidence, perhaps, of 'a certain superior sentimentality [*vornehme Empfindlichkeit*] which indulges itself in pain and suffering and finds more interest in them than in the painless situations that it regards as commonplace' (Hegel, *TWA*, XV, 567 (*Ä*, Knox trans., II, 1232)).
48 Nietzsche, *Werke*, III, 773 (*WM*, §1052, 'One will see that the problem is that of the meaning of suffering: whether a Christian meaning or a tragic meaning').
49 Nietzsche, *Werke*, I, 1171–2 (*M*, §240).
50 Nietzsche, *Werke*, II, 1109 (*EH*, III, GT, §2, 'a Yes-saying . . . even to guilt').
51 Nietzsche, *Werke*, II, 132 (*FW*, §135); II, 834–5 (*GM*, II, §23); III, 495 (*WM*, §845, 'the idealisation of the man of *great sacrilege*').
52 Nietzsche, *Werke*, II, 1140 (*EH*, III, ASZ, §8, 'the *joy even in destroying*'); III, 432 (*WM*, §982); III, 539 (*WM*, §1028).
53 Nietzsche, *Werke*, I, 93 (*GT*, §17, 'We are really for a brief moment primordial being itself, feeling its raging desire for existence . . . The struggle, the pain, the destruction of phenomena now appears necessary to us').
54 Nietzsche, *Werke*, II, 245 (*FW*, §370).

55 Nietzsche, *Werke*, II, 102–3 (*FW*, §98). See also II, 1032 (*GD*, 'What I Owe to the Ancients', §5, 'the *sacrifice* of its highest types. . .').

56 Nietzsche, *Werke*, II, 161 (*FW*, §276, '*Amor fati*'); III, 463 (*WM*, §1051, 'from that height of joy. . .'); III, 574–5 (*WM*, §852, 'to experience suffering as a *pleasure*').

57 Nietzsche, *Werke*, III, 495 (*WM*, §845).

58 Nietzsche, *Werke*, III, 755–6 (*WM*, §800).

59 Nietzsche, *Werke*, III, 575 (*WM*, §852).

60 Hegel, *TWA*, XV, 535–7 (*Ä*, Knox trans., II, 1206–7).

61 This point is, however, made by Rosenstein (p. 525).

62 Hegel, *TWA*, XV, 523 (*Ä*, Knox trans., II, 1196, 'The original essence of tragedy. . .').

63 Hegel, *TWA*, XV, 545 (*Ä*, Knox trans., II, 1213–14). See also XIII, 278–9 (*Ä*, Knox trans., I, 213–14), where Hegel cites the tragedy of Ajax as another example of the antagonism between the hero's consciousness and intention in his act and his later consciousness of what the act really was.

64 Hegel, *TWA*, XV, 545 (*Ä*, Knox trans., II, 1214).

65 Hegel, *TWA*, XVII, 133 (*PRel*, Speirs trans., II, 265).

66 Hegel, *TWA*, XV, 521 (*Ä*, Knox trans., II, 1194).

67 Hegel, *TWA*, XV, 522 (*Ä*, Knox trans., II, 1195, 'for if we take the ethical order in its direct genuineness [*das Sittliche . . . in seiner unmittelbaren Gediegenheit*], and do not interpret it from the point of view of subjective reflection as abstract morality [*das formell Moralische*]. . .'). See also, for example, *TWA*, VII, 87–8 (*PRecht*, §33); and chapter 1, note 98.

68 Greek tragic heroes are thus 'living representatives of the substantial spheres of life' (*TWA*, XV, 522 (*Ä*, Knox trans., II, 1195)).

69 Hegel, *TWA*, XV, 524 (*Ä*, Knox trans., II, 1197, 'for although the characters have a purpose. . .'); 544 (*Ä*, Knox trans., II, 1213, 'But an individual's decision, justified by the object he aims at, is carried out in a one-sided, particular way. . .').

70 Silk and Stern, pp. 319–21.

71 Hegel, *TWA*, XV, 544 (*Ä*, Knox trans., II, 1213).

72 Sophocles, 'Antigone', in *Greek Tragedies*, Vol. I, edited by David Grene and Richard Lattimore (Chicago, 1968), p. 190, lines 285–7. See also Hegel, *TWA*, XV, 544 (*Ä*, Knox trans., II, 1213, 'Creon honours Zeus alone, the dominating power over public life and common welfare').

73 Hegel, *TWA*, XV, 549 (*Ä*, Knox trans., II, 1217, 'so that she ought to pay obedience to the royal command').

74 Hegel, *TWA*, XV, 545, 551 (*Ä*, Knox trans., II, 1214, 1219); XVII, 133 (*PRel*, Speirs trans., II, 265).

75 Hegel, *TWA*, XV, 524 (*Ä*, Knox trans., II, 1197, 'Therefore what is sublated [*aufgehoben*] in the tragic dénouement is only the *one-sided* particularity. . .'); 547 (*Ä*, Knox trans., II, 1215, 'this one-sidedness is stripped away').

76 Sophocles, *The Theban Plays*, translated by E. F. Watling (Harmondsworth, 1947), Introduction, p. 16.

77 For Hegel's discussion of these three modes of resolution, see *TWA*, XV, 532–3, 550–2 (Ä, Knox trans., II, 1203–4, 1218–20).
78 G. Steiner, *The Death of Tragedy* (London, 1961), p. 8.
79 Hegel, *TWA*, XV, 532 (Ä, Knox trans., II, 1203).
80 Hegel, *TWA*, XV, 533 (Ä, Knox trans., II, 1204, 'plays'); 568 (Ä, Knox trans., II, 1232, 'plays and dramas'); 532 (Ä, Knox trans., II, 1204, 'the Greeks had tragedies... for example ... *The Eumenides* ... and ... *Philoctetes*'); 550–1 (Ä, Knox trans., II, 1218, 'tragic dénouement').
81 Hegel, *TWA*, XV, 532–3, 567 (Ä, Knox trans., II, 1204, 1232).
82 Hegel, *TWA*, XV, 524 (Ä, Knox trans., II, 1197, 'in der Tragik ihres Handelns, kann sie von sich selbst und ihrem Vorhaben nicht ablassen...', 'and now, in the tragic circumstances of their action, if they are unable to renounce themselves and their intentions...'). See also XV, 533 (Ä, Knox trans., II, 1204, 'conflicts... meant to proceed via their own discord to a peaceful end and therefore from the start... not such sharp oppositions as those in tragedy').
83 Hegel, *TWA*, XV, 532, 551 (Ä, Knox trans., II, 1203, 1219).
84 Hegel, *TWA*, XV, 532 (Ä, Knox trans., II, 1197, 'The truly substantial thing which has to be actualised... is... the reconciliation in which the specific individuals and their aims work together harmoniously').
85 Hegel, *TWA*, XV, 549–50 (Ä, Knox trans., II, 1217–18).
86 Sophocles, 'Antigone', in *Greek Tragedies*, Vol. I, p. 217, line 1069 (line not quoted by Hegel himself).
87 Hegel, *TWA*, XV, 524, 547 (Ä, Knox trans., II, 1197, 1215–16).
88 Hegel, *TWA*, XV, 547 (Ä, Knox trans., II, 1215–16). See Rosenstein, p. 524.
89 A. C. Bradley, 'Hegel's Theory of Tragedy', in *Oxford Lectures on Poetry* (London, 1959), p. 90; and Aristotle, 'On The Art of Poetry', in *Classical Literary Criticism*, translated with Introduction by T. S. Dorsch (Harmondsworth, 1965), chapter 13, p. 48.
90 Hegel, *TWA*, XV, 545–6 (Ä, Knox trans., II, 1214–15). Characters who are mere victims of human oppression, or indeed of any transcendent *Geist*, can present a heart-rending sight, but cannot in Hegel's view be tragic, because 'truly *tragic* action necessarily presupposes a live conception of *individual* freedom and independence or at least an individual's self-determination and willingness to accept freely and on his own account the responsibility for his own act and its consequences' (XV, 534–5 (Ä, Knox trans., II, 1205–6)). For characters to be tragic they must not be purely evil, but they must suffer as a result of their own 'blameworthy deed' (*schuldvolle Tat*) (XV, 526 (Ä, Knox trans., II, 1198)).
91 Hegel, *TWA*, XV, 547 (Ä, Knox trans., II, 1215–16, 'absolute rationality').
92 Hegel, *TWA*, XV, 523 (Ä, Knox trans., II, 1196, '[we can only be] really serious about those gods... when they now come to life as a specific "pathos" in a human individual...'). See also XIII, 236–52 (Ä, Knox trans., I, 179–93).
93 A similar point is made in Hegel's treatment of the master–slave dialectic

in the *Phenomenology*, where he argues that the 'fear of death' and the 'hard discipline of service' are essential to free the slave from narrow self-interest and to set consciousness on the path to true freedom and *Sittlichkeit*; see *TWA*, III, 154–5 (*Phän*, Miller trans., pp. 118–19). See also III, 36 (*Phän*, Miller trans., p. 19, 'But the life of spirit is not the life that shrinks from death and keeps itself untouched by devastation. . .'). See also chapter 1, note 98.

94 Aeschylus, 'Agamemnon', in *Oresteia*, translated with Introduction by R. Lattimore (Chicago, 1953), p. 40, lines 177–8 (lines not quoted by Hegel). The chorus's words have an obvious application to plays which end in catastrophe, but they can also apply to a varying extent to those plays which end peacefully. In *Oedipus Rex* (*c.* 427 BC), Oedipus is broken by the discovery of what he has done, and is thereby caused to acknowledge his guilt and to heal the breach with Creon; see Sophocles, 'Oedipus Rex', in *Greek Tragedies*, Vol. I, pp. 170, 172, lines 1397–8, 1431–5. In *Oedipus at Colonus* (*c.* 408 or 407 BC), on the other hand, Oedipus protests his innocence and participates in a fresh conflict with Creon and Polynices. Although this conflict does not itself result in further catastrophe for Oedipus, the hero has to suffer for the catastrophic discoveries made in *Oedipus Rex*, and thus has to be 'slave . . . to such unending pain as no man had before', before he is transfigured; see Sophocles, 'Oedipus at Colonus', in *Greek Tragedies*, Vol. III, edited by David Grene and Richard Lattimore (Chicago, 1968), p. 116, lines 105–6.

95 See Hegel, *TWA*, XV, 551 (*Ä*, Knox trans., II, 1219, 'these unconsciously committed crimes do not make him unhappy; but of old he had solved a riddle and now he forcibly extracts . . . a knowledge of his own dark fate and acquires the dreadful realisation that it has been accomplished in himself').

96 Hegel, *TWA*, XV, 547 (*Ä*, Knox trans., II, 1215). Otto Pöggeler is thus wrong to claim that Hegel's 'teleological–dialectical thinking obscures the seriousness of discord [*Entzweiung*] in history', for it is the very factor which makes conflict tragic and so deeply agonising – namely the hero's own responsibility for his fate – that also makes his end a just one. We understand man's fate as just, therefore, when we take man's responsibility for conflict seriously, not when we endeavour to conceal conflict from view. See O. Pöggeler, 'Hegel und die griechische Tragödie', *Hegel-Studien*, Beiheft I (1964), p. 303.

97 Bradley, p. 83.

98 Nietzsche, *Werke*, I, 121 (*GT*, §22).

99 Hegel, *TWA*, XV, 524–6 (*Ä*, Knox trans., II, 1197–8). See Aristotle, chapter 13, p. 48.

100 Hegel, *TWA*, XV, 536–7 (*Ä*, Knox trans., II, 1206–7).

101 Hegel, *TWA*, XV, 556–8 (*Ä*, Knox trans., II, 1223–5, 'what presses for satisfaction is the *subjectivity* of their heart and mind, and the particularity of their own character').

102 Hegel, *TWA*, XV, 559 (*Ä*, Knox trans., II, 1225–6).

103 Bradley, p. 77.
104 Hegel, *TWA*, XV, 560 (*Ä*, Knox trans., II, 1226).
105 Hegel, *TWA*, XIII, 289 (*Ä*, Knox trans., I, 222–3).
106 Hegel, *TWA*, XIV, 200 (*Ä*, Knox trans., I, 577–8, 'supremely admirable');
   XV, 546 (*Ä*, Knox trans., II, 1215, 'excites our admiration'); XV, 536–7,
   560–2 (*Ä*, Knox trans., II, 1206–7, 1226–8). Compare Bradley, pp. 86–8.
   In what is presumably a reference to *Macbeth*, Hegel clarifies his view of
   the extent to which the hero can be both a criminal and tragic. Modern
   tragic heroes, he says, may resort to crime and injustice to achieve their
   goal, but they do not make crime and injustice into their goal (*TWA*, XV,
   557 (*Ä*, Knox trans., II, 1224)). The implication, therefore, is that where
   they do make crime into their goal they cease being tragic.
107 Hegel, *TWA*, XV, 559–60 (*Ä*, Knox trans., II, 1226).
108 Hegel, *TWA*, XIV, 202 (*Ä*, Knox trans., I, 579); XV, 527 (*Ä*, Knox trans.,
   II, 1199, 'in tragedy the individuals destroy themselves. . .'); XV, 564–5
   (*Ä*, Knox trans., II, 1230, 'the picture of its self-destructive struggle. . .')
109 Hegel, *TWA*, XIV, 202–3; XV, 562–4 (*Ä*, Knox trans., I, 579–80; II, 1228–
   30).
110 Hegel, *TWA*, XIV, 207–8 (*Ä*, Knox trans., I, 583–4). See also XV, 559 (*Ä*,
   Knox trans., II, 1225–6); XIII, 316 (*Ä*, Knox trans., I, 244).
111 Bradley, p. 80. See Hegel, *TWA*, XV, 566–7 (*Ä*, Knox trans., II,
   1231–2).
112 Hegel, *TWA*, XV, 559 (*Ä*, Knox trans., II, 1226).
113 Hegel, *TWA*, XV, 565 (*Ä*, Knox trans., II, 1230).
114 Hegel, *TWA*, XV, 566 (*Ä*, Knox trans., II, 1231). See Bradley, p. 79.
115 Hegel, *TWA*, XV, 539 (*Ä*, Knox trans., II, 1208–9, '*heroic* age'). In modern
   society, where an individual's life is circumscribed by law and where substantial interests are embodied in institutions rather than heroic agency,
   tragedy is difficult to generate, in Hegel's view, but it is not, as one might
   expect, impossible. Hegel says that our interest in, and need for, the
   spectacle of heroic individuality is always present, and one obvious way
   in which such individuality can express itself in modern society, he
   believes, is 'by a revolt against the whole of civil society itself' (*TWA*,
   XIII, 255 (*Ä*, Knox trans., I, 195)). For Hegel's views on alternative
   possibilities for tragic drama in the modern rational state, see *TWA*, XIII,
   255–7; and XV, 557–8 (*Ä*, Knox trans., I, 195–6; II, 1224–5).
116 Hegel, *TWA*, XV, 547 (*Ä*, Knox trans., II, 1216, 'neither is the necessity
   of the outcome a blind fate. . .').
117 Hegel, *TWA*, XV, 548 (*Ä*, Knox trans., II, 1216, 'fate drives individuality
   back within its limits and destroys it if these are crossed').
118 Hegel, *TWA*, XV, 549 (*Ä*, Knox trans., II, 1217–18).
119 Hegel, *TWA*, XV, 526 (*Ä*, Knox trans., II, 1198, 'A truly tragic
   suffering. . .').
120 Hegel, *TWA*, I, 343 (*FS*, Knox trans., p. 229).
121 Hegel, *TWA*, XV, 526 (*Ä*, Knox trans., II, 1198, 'Above mere fear and
   tragic sympathy. . .').
122 See Stern, *A Study of Nietzsche*, p. 148, 'Taking no warning from Greek

tragedy . . . Nietzsche has no fear of hubris (*GM*, III, §9). His ultimate indictment of Christian belief (the basis of his charge that it is against life and against the earth) is that Christianity does not recognise man as master of the universe.'

123   Nietzsche, *Werke*, II, 595 (*JGB*, §30).

124   Hayman, pp. 128–9.

125   For some of Nietzsche's views on war and suffering, see, for example, *Werke*, I, 950 (*WS*, §187); II, 967 (*GD*, 'Morality as Anti-Nature', §3); III, 432 (*WM*, §982); III, 921 (*WM*, §1040); II, 689 (*JGB*, §225); II, 744 (*JGB*, §270).

126   Nietzsche, *Werke*, II, 773 (*GM*, II, §2); II, 866 (*GM*, III, §14); II, 1014 (*GD*, 'Expeditions', §37).

127   See Silk and Stern, p. 359.

128   Nietzsche, *Werke*, II, 1190–2 (*A*, §§29, 30).

129   Nietzsche, *Werke*, II, 1159 (*EH*, IV, §9).

130   Nietzsche, *Werke*, II, 1191 (*A*, §29). See also, for example, II, 447 (*ASZ*, III, 'Of Old and New Law-Tables', §7, 'Wahr sein – das *können* wenige!', 'Be truthful – few *can* do it!').

131   Nietzsche, *Werke*, III, 535 (*WM*, §569, 'hypothesis that only subjects exist. . .').

132   The essential inwardness of Nietzsche's whole philosophy is evident from the fact that it is geared primarily to the furtherance of a mode of *will*; see, for example, *Werke*, II, 394–5 (*ASZ*, II, 'Of Redemption', 'Will – that is what the liberator and bringer of joy is called. . .'). Although, of course, Nietzsche does not ignore social and political issues altogether, he does not concern himself to the extent that Hegel does with the ways in which this inner will expresses itself in specific courses of action or forms of social organisation; see Stern, *A Study of Nietzsche*, pp. 105–6.

133   Rosenstein puts this point succinctly: 'Hegel's entire philosophic system could be said to work on the principle of eternal justice: the inadequate notion, claiming more than its due, is overturned and, collapsing from within, yields to the larger view, the more complete reality' (p. 524).

134   Hegel, *TWA*, XII, 392 (*PGesch*, Sibree trans., p. 324, 'Man is only God insofar. . .').

135   Nietzsche, *Werke*, II, 801 (*GM*, II, §2, 'If we place ourselves at the end of this tremendous process . . . where society and the morality of custom at last reveal *what* they have simply been the means to: then we discover that the ripest fruit is the *sovereign individual*. . .').

136   See Nietzsche, *Werke*, II, 1190 (*A*, §29, 'If anything is unevangelic, it is the concept hero').

Bibliography

This bibliography includes all the works cited in the notes (whether they have been consulted in full or only in part) and a selection of other works which I have found useful in the preparation of this book.

Abendroth, W. *Schopenhauer*, Hamburg, 1967

Aeschylus. *Oresteia*, translated with Introduction by R. Lattimore, Chicago, 1953

Allison, D. (ed.). *The New Nietzsche*, New York, 1977

Aquila, R. 'Predication and Hegel's Metaphysics', *Kant-Studien*, 64, 2 (1973), 231–45

Aristotle. 'On the Art of Poetry', in *Classical Literary Criticism*, translated with Introduction by T. S. Dorsch, Harmondsworth, 1965

Austin, J. L. *Philosophical Papers*, Oxford, 1961, third edition 1979

Avineri, S. *Hegel's Theory of the Modern State*, Cambridge, 1972

Axelos, C. 'Zu Hegels Interpretation der Tragödie', *Zeitschrift für philosophische Forschung*, 19, 4 (October–December 1965), 655–67

Beerling, B. F. 'Hegel und Nietzsche', *Hegel-Studien*, 1–2 (1961), 229–46

Bell, D. *Frege's Theory of Judgement*, Oxford, 1979

Benz, E. *Nietzsches Ideen zur Geschichte des Christentums und der Kirche*, Leiden, 1956

Bernoulli, C. A. *Franz Overbeck und Friedrich Nietzsche: eine Freundschaft*, 2 Vols., Jena, 1908

Bodammer, T. *Hegels Deutung der Sprache*, Hamburg, 1969

Bradley, A. C. 'Hegel's Theory of Tragedy', in *Oxford Lectures on Poetry*, London, 1959, pp. 69–95

Brann, H. W. 'Hegel, Nietzsche and the Nazi Lesson', *Humanist*, 12 (1952), 111–15 and 179–82

Breazeale, D. 'The Hegel–Nietzsche Problem', *Nietzsche-Studien*, 4 (1975), 146–64

Brose, K. *Geschichtsphilosophische Strukturen im Werke Nietzsches*, Bern/Frankfurt, 1973

   Kritische Geschichte: Studien zur Geschichtsphilosophie Nietzsches und Hegels, Frankfurt, 1978

Bullock, A. *Hitler: A Study in Tyranny*, Harmondsworth, 1962

Burckhardt, J *Weltgeschichtliche Betrachtungen*, edited with Afterword by W. Kaegi, Basle, 1970

Reflections on History, translated by M. D. H., London, 1943

Cook, D. *Language in the Philosophy of Hegel*, The Hague, 1973

'Leibniz and Hegel on Language', in *Hegel and the History of Philosophy*, edited by J. O'Malley and others, The Hague, 1974, pp. 95–108

Danto, A. *Nietzsche as Philosopher*, Columbia, 1965

Deleuze, G. *Nietzsche*, [Paris], 1965

Nietzsche et la philosophie, Paris, 1962

Nietzsche and Philosophy, translated by Hugh Tomlinson, London 1983

Derrida, J. *Éperons*, Paris/Chicago, 1979

Dühring, E. *Gesamtcursus der Philosophie*, 2 Vols., Leipzig, 1894–5

Fackenheim, E. *The Religious Dimension in Hegel's Thought*, Bloomington, 1967

Feldkeller, P. 'Hegel und Nietzsche', *Neue Preußische Kreuzzeitung* (1920), Vol. 410–11

Fetscher, I. *Hegels Lehre vom Menschen*, Stuttgart, 1970

Findlay, J. N. *Hegel: A Re-examination*, London 1958

Fink, E. *Nietzsches Philosophie*, Stuttgart, 1960, fourth edition 1979

Forbes, D. Introduction to translation by H. B. Nisbet of Hegel's Introduction to his *Lectures on the Philosophy of World History*, Cambridge, 1975, pp. vii–xxxv

Frege, G. *Nachgelassene Schriften*, edited by H. Hermes and others, Hamburg, 1969

Posthumous Writings, edited by H. Hermes and others, translated by Peter Long and Roger White with the assistance of Raymond Hargreaves, Oxford 1979

Frenzel, I. *Nietzsche*, Hamburg, 1966

Gadamer, H. *Hegels Dialektik*, Tübingen, 1971

Gilman, S. L. 'Hegel, Schopenhauer and Nietzsche see the Black', *Hegel-Studien*, 16 (1981), 163–88

Giovanni, G. di. 'The Category of Contingency in the Hegelian Logic', in *Art and Logic in Hegel's Philosophy*, edited by W. E. Steinkraus and K. I. Schmitz, New Jersey, 1980, pp. 179–200

Goedert, G. *Nietzsche critique des valeurs chrétiennes: souffrance et compassion*, Paris, 1977

Goethe, J. W. von. 'Urworte. Orphisch', in *The Penguin Book of German Verse*, edited with Introduction by Leonard Forster, Harmondsworth, 1957, revised edition, 1959

Graef, H. C. 'From Hegel to Hitler', *Contemporary Review*, 158 (July–December 1940), 550–6

Greene, M. 'Hegel's "Unhappy Consciousness" and Nietzsche's "Slave Morality"', in *Hegel and the Philosophy of Religion*, edited by D. Christensen, The Hague, 1970, pp. 125–41

Günther, J. 'Nietzsche und der Nationalsozialismus', in 'Hegel und Nietzsche', *Nationalsozialistische Monatshefte*, 21 (December 1931), 560–3

Haar, M. 'Nietzsche and Metaphysical Language', in *The New Nietzsche*, edited by D. Allison, New York, 1977, pp. 5–36

Habermas, J. *Erkenntnis und Interesse*, Frankfurt, 1968

Hartmann, E. von *Philosophie des Unbewußten*, Berlin, 1869

Hartmann, K. 'Hegel: a Non-metaphysical View', in *Hegel: a Collection of Critical Essays*, edited by A. MacIntyre, New York, 1972, second edition 1976, pp. 101–24

Hayman, R. *Nietzsche: a Critical Life*, London, 1980

Hegel, G. W. F. *Theorie Werkausgabe*, edited by E. Moldenhauer and K. Michel, 20 Vols. and Index, Frankfurt, 1969–

  Aesthetics: Lectures on Fine Art, translated by T. M. Knox, 2 Vols., Oxford, 1975

  Lectures on the History of Philosophy, translated from the German by E. S. Haldane, 3 Vols., London, 1892–6

  Lectures on the Philosophy of Religion. Together with a Work on the Proofs of the Existence of God, translated from the second German edition by the Rev. E. B. Speirs and J. Burdon Sanderson, edited by the Rev. E. B. Speirs, 3 Vols., London, 1895

  On Christianity: Early Theological Writings, translated by T. M. Knox, with Introduction, and Fragments translated by Richard Kroner, Chicago, 1948, New York, 1961

  The Philosophy of History, with Prefaces by Charles Hegel and the translator, J. Sibree, and new Introduction by C. J. Friedrich, New York, 1956

  Vorlesungen über Rechtsphilosophie, edited by K. H. Ilting, 4 Vols., Stuttgart, 1973–

  Hegel's Phenomenology of Spirit, translated by A. V. Miller, with Analysis of the Text and Foreword by J. N. Findlay, Oxford, 1977

  Hegel's Philosophy of Mind, being Part Three of the *Encyclopaedia* (1830), translated by W. Wallace, together with the *Zusätze* in Boumann's text (1845), translated by A. V. Miller, with Foreword by J. N. Findlay, Oxford, 1971

  Hegel's Philosophy of Nature, edited and translated with Introduction and Explanatory Notes by M. J. Petry, 3 Vols., London, 1970

  Hegel's Philosophy of Right, translated with Notes by T. M. Knox, Oxford, 1952

  Hegel's Philosophy of Subjective Spirit, edited and translated with Introduction and Explanatory Notes by M. J. Petry, 3 Vols., Dordrecht, 1978

  Hegel's Science of Logic, translated by A. V. Miller, with Foreword by J. N. Findlay, London, 1969

  The Logic of Hegel, translated from the *Encyclopaedia* with Prolegomena by W. Wallace, Oxford, 1874

Heidegger, M. *Nietzsche*, 2 Vols., Pfullingen, 1961

  'Wer ist Nietzsches Zarathustra?', in *Vorträge und Aufsätze*, Pfullingen, 1954, pp. 101–26

  'Who is Nietzsche's Zarathustra?', translated by B. Magnus, in *The New Nietzsche*, edited by D. Allison, New York, 1977, pp. 64–79

Hennemann, G. *Von der Kraft des deutschen Geistes: Fichte–Hegel–Nietzsche*, Cologne, 1940

Henrich, D. 'Anfang und Methode der Logik', *Hegel-Studien*, Beiheft 1 (1964), 19–35

Hillebrand, K. 'Über historisches Wissen und historischen Sinn', in *Zeiten, Völker und Menschen*, 2 Vols., Berlin, 1874–5, II (*Wälsches und Deutsches*), pp. 311–38

Hollingdale, R. *Nietzsche*, London, 1973
    Nietzsche: The Man and his Philosophy, London, 1965, revised edition, 1985

Houlgate, S. Review of *Hegel's Dialectic and its Criticism* by M. Rosen, in *The Owl of Minerva* (Journal of the Hegel Society of America), 15, (Autumn 1983), 117–21

    Review of *Absolute Knowledge: Hegel and the Problem of Metaphysics* by A. White, in *Bulletin of the Hegel Society of Great Britain*, 9 (Spring–Summer 1984), 36–41

Hume, D. *An Inquiry Concerning Human Understanding*, edited with Introduction by Charles Hendel, New York, 1955

Janz, C. P. *Friedrich Nietzsche: Biographie*, 3 Vols., Munich, 1978–9

Jaspers, K. *Nietzsche: Einführung in das Verständnis seines Philosophierens*, Berlin, 1936, second edition 1947

Kant, I. *Kritik der reinen Vernunft*, Riga, 1781, second edition 1787
    Prolegomena zu einer jeden künftigen Metaphysik, Riga, 1783

Kaufmann, W. *Hegel: Re-interpretation, Texts and Commentary*, London, 1965
    Nietzsche: Philosopher, Psychologist, Antichrist, Princeton, 1950
    'Hegel's Ideas about Tragedy', in *New Studies in Hegel's Philosophy*, edited by W. E. Steinkraus, New York, 1971, pp. 201–20

Kenny, A. *Wittgenstein*, London, 1973

Krell, D. 'Heidegger, Nietzsche, Hegel: an Essay in Descensional Reflection', *Nietzsche-Studien*, 5 (1976), 255–62

Kremer-Marietti, A. 'Hegel et Nietzsche', *La revue des lettres modernes*, 76–7 (Winter 1962–3), 17–24

Krummel, R. F. *Nietzsche und der deutsche Geist*, Berlin, 1974

Küng, H. *Christ sein*, Munich, 1974, fifth edition 1980

Lamb, D. *Hegel: From Foundation to System*, The Hague, 1980
    Language and Perception in Hegel and Wittgenstein, Avebury 1979

Lange, F. A. *Geschichte des Materialismus und Kritik seiner Bedeutung in der Gegenwart*, Iserlohn, 1866
    The History of Materialism, authorised translation by E. C. Thomas, with Introduction by Bertrand Russell, London, 1925

Leibniz, G. W. *Philosophical Writings*, edited by G. H. R. Parkinson, translated by Mary Morris and G. H. R. Parkinson, London, 1973

Lévy, A. *Stirner et Nietzsche*, Paris, 1904

Lingis, A. 'The Will to Power' in *The New Nietzsche*, edited by D. Allison, New York, 1977, pp. 37–63

Locke, J. *An Essay Concerning Human Understanding*, abridged and edited with Introduction by A. D. Woozley, Glasgow, 1964

Löwith, K. *Von Hegel zu Nietzsche*, Stuttgart, 1941, third edition 1953
    From Hegel to Nietzsche, translated by David E. Green, London, 1965

Lyotard, J-F. 'Analysing Speculative Discourse as Language-game', translated by G. Bennington, *Oxford Literary Review*, 4, 3 (1981), 59–67

MacIntyre, A. (ed.). *Hegel: A Collection of Critical Essays*, New York, 1972, second edition 1976

Marion, J-L. 'Généalogie de la "Mort de Dieu" ', *Résurrection: revue de doctrine chrétienne*, 16, 36 (1971), 30–53

Martensen, H. *Grundriß des Systems der Moralphilosophie*, Kiel, 1845

Martin, A. von. *Geistige Wegbereiter des deutschen Zusammenbruchs: Hegel–Nietzsche–Spengler*, Recklinghausen, 1948

Mure, G. R. G. *The Philosophy of Hegel*, London, 1965

Nietzsche's Werke, 16 Vols., Leipzig, 1894–

Nietzsche, F. W. *Werke und Briefe: Historisch-kritische Gesamtausgabe*, edited by H. J. Mette, W. Hoppe and others, 9 Vols., Munich, 1933–

  Werke, edited by K. Schlechta, 3 Vols. and Index, Munich, 1954–

Werke: Kritische Gesamtausgabe, edited by C. Colli and M. Montinari, Berlin, 1967–

Beyond Good and Evil: Prelude to a Philosophy of the Future, translated with Introduction and Commentary by R. J. Hollingdale, Harmondsworth, 1973

Daybreak: Thoughts on the Prejudices of Morality, translated by R. J. Hollingdale, with Introduction by Michael Tanner, Cambridge, 1982

Human, All-too Human: A Book for Free Spirits, Part 1, translated by Helen Zimmern, with Introduction by J. M. Kennedy, Edinburgh and London, 1909, in *The Complete Works of Friedrich Nietzsche*, edited by Oscar Levy, Vol. VII, Part 1

Human, All-too Human: A Book for Free Spirits, Part 2, translated by Paul V. Cohn, Edinburgh and London, 1911, in *The Complete Works of Friedrich Nietzsche*, edited by Oscar Levy, Vol. VII, Part 2

On the Future of our Educational Institutions; Homer and Classical Philology, translated with Introduction by J. M. Kennedy, Edinburgh and London, 1909, in *The Complete Works of Friedrich Nietzsche*, edited by Oscar Levy, Vol. VI

On the Genealogy of Morals, translated by W. Kaufmann and R. J. Hollingdale, and *Ecce Homo*, translated by W. Kaufmann, edited with Commentary by W. Kaufmann, New York, 1969

Philosophy in the Tragic Age of the Greeks, translated with Introduction by Marianne Cowan, Chicago, 1962

The Birth of Tragedy and *The Case of Wagner*, translated with Commentary by W. Kaufmann, New York, 1967

The Gay Science. With a Prelude in Rhymes and an Appendix of Songs, translated with Commentary by W. Kaufmann, New York, 1974

The Will to Power, translated by W. Kaufmann and R. J. Hollingdale, edited with Commentary by W. Kaufmann, London, 1968

Thus Spoke Zarathustra: A Book for Everyone and No-one, translated with Introduction by R. J. Hollingdale, Harmondsworth, 1961, reprinted with new Introduction, 1969

Twilight of the Idols and *The Anti-Christ*, translated with Introduction and Commentary by R. J. Hollingdale, Harmondsworth, 1968

Untimely Meditations, translated by R. J. Hollingdale, with Introduction by J. P. Stern, Cambridge, 1983

Philosophy and Truth: Selections from Nietzsche's Notebooks of the early 1870s, translated and edited with Introduction and Notes by Daniel Breazeale and Foreword by W. Kaufmann, New Jersey and Sussex, 1979

O'Brien, G. *Hegel on Reason and History*, Chicago, 1975

Oehler, M. *Nietzsches Bibliothek*, 14. Jahresgabe der Gesellschaft der Freunde des Nietzsche-Archivs, Weimar, 1942

Pasley, M. (ed.). *Nietzsche: Imagery and Thought*, Cambridge, 1978

'Nietzsche's Use of Medical Terms', in *Nietzsche: Imagery and Thought*, edited by M. Pasley, Cambridge, 1978, pp. 123–58

Patzig, G. *Tatsachen, Normen, Sätze*, Stuttgart, 1980

Pears, D. *Wittgenstein*, London, 1971

'Wittgenstein and Austin', in *British Analytical Philosophy*, edited by B. Williams and A. Montefiore, London, 1966, pp. 17–39

Pfeil, H. *Von Christus zu Dionysus: Nietzsches religiöse Entwicklung*, Meisenheim am Glan, 1975

Plant, R. *Hegel*, London, 1972, second edition 1983

Pöggeler, O. 'Hegel und die griechische Tragödie', *Hegel-Studien*, Beiheft 1 (1964), 285–305

Popper, K. *The Logic of Scientific Discovery*, London, 1959

The Open Society and its Enemies, London, 1945

'What is Dialectic?', *Mind*, 49 (1940), 403–26

Puntel, L. B. *Darstellung, Methode und Struktur*, Bonn, 1973, *Hegel-Studien*, Beiheft 10

Reed, T. J. 'Nietzsche's Animals: Idea, Image and Influence', in *Nietzsche: Imagery and Thought*, edited by M. Pasley, Cambridge, 1978, pp. 159–219

Rimke, H. 'Was bedeutet uns Hegel?', in 'Hegel und Nietzsche', *Nationalsozialistische Monatshefte*, 21 (December 1931), 559–60

Ritter, J. *Hegel und die französische Revolution*, Frankfurt, 1965

Robert, E. de. *L'ancienne et la nouvelle philosophie: essai sur les lois générales du développement de la philosophie*, Paris, 1887

Rohrmoser, G. 'Das Atheismusproblem bei Hegel und Nietzsche', *Der evangelische Erzieher*, 18, 9 (1966), 345–53

Rorty, R. *Philosophy and the Mirror of Nature*, Princeton, 1980

Rorty, R. (ed.). *The Linguistic Turn*, Chicago, 1967

Rosen, M. *Hegel's Dialectic and its Criticism*, Cambridge, 1982

Rosen, S. *G. W. F. Hegel: An Introduction to the Science of Wisdom*, Yale, 1974

Rosenstein, L. 'Metaphysical Foundations of the Theories of Tragedy in Hegel and Nietzsche', *Journal of Aesthetics and Art Criticism*, 28, 4 (Summer 1970), 521–33

Röttges, H. *Nietzsche und die Dialektik der Aufklärung*, Berlin, 1972

Russell, B. *History of Western Philosophy*, London, 1946, second edition 1961

Our Knowledge of the External World, Chicago/London, 1914

Salaquarda, J. 'Nietzsche und Lange', *Nietzsche-Studien*, 7 (1978), 236–53

Schacht, R. *Nietzsche*, London, 1983

Schaller, H. 'Geschichte und das Wesen des Menschen: Beitrag zu einem großen Problem in Form einer Darstellung der Gedanken Hegels, Schopenhauers, Nietzsches über dasselbe', Dissertation, Leipzig, [1924]

Schlechta, K. *Nietzsche-Chronik*, Munich, 1975

Schlechta, K. and Anders, A. *Friedrich Nietzsche: von den verborgenen Anfängen seines Philosophierens*, Stuttgart, 1962

Schlechta, K. and Reichert, H. W. *Internationale Nietzsche-Bibliographie*, Chapel Hill, 1968

Schopenhauer, A. *Sämtliche Werke*, edited by J. Frauenstädt, 6 Vols., Leipzig, 1873–4

  On the Basis of Morality, translated by E. F. J. Payne, with Introduction by Richard Taylor, Indianapolis, 1965

  On the Fourfold Root of the Principle of Sufficient Reason, translated by E. F. J. Payne, with Introduction by Richard Taylor, La Salle, Illinois, 1974

  Parerga and Paralipomena: Short Philosophical Essays, translated by E. F. J. Payne, 2 Vols., Oxford, 1974

  The World as Will and Representation, translated by E. F. J. Payne, 2 Vols., New York, 1958, revised edition, 1966

Schulz, W. *Der Gott der neuzeitlichen Metaphysik*, Pfullingen, 1957, seventh edition 1982

Searle, J. *Speech Acts*, Cambridge, 1969

Seeberger, W. *Hegel und die Entwicklung des Geistes zur Freiheit*, Stuttgart, 1961

Silk, M. S. and Stern, J. P. *Nietzsche on Tragedy*, Cambridge, 1981

Simon, J. 'Die Kategorien im "gewöhnlichen" und im "spekulativen" Satz', *Wiener Jahrbuch für Philosophie*, 3 (1970), 9–37

Sluga, H. *Gottlob Frege*, London, 1980

Soll, I. *An Introduction to Hegel's Metaphysics*, Chicago, 1969

Sophocles. 'Antigone' and 'Oedipus Rex', in *Greek Tragedies*, Vol. I, edited by David Grene and Richard Lattimore Chicago, 1968

  'Oedipus at Colonus', in *Greek Tragedies*, Vol. III, edited by David Grene and Richard Lattimore, Chicago, 1968

  The Theban Plays, translated by E. F. Watling, Harmondsworth, 1947

Stack, G. *Lange and Nietzsche*, Berlin, 1983

Steiner, G. *The Death of Tragedy*, London, 1961

Steinhauer, K. *Hegel-Bibliographie*, Munich/London, 1980

Stern, J. P. *A Study of Nietzsche*, Cambridge, 1979

  'Nietzsche and the Idea of Metaphor', in *Nietzsche: Imagery and Thought*, edited by M. Pasley, Cambridge, 1978, pp. 64–82

Strawson, P. F. *The Bounds of Sense*, London, 1966, second edition 1975

  Logico-Linguistic Papers, London, 1971

Surber, J. P. 'Hegel's Speculative Sentence', *Hegel-Studien*, 10 (1975), 211–30

Szondi, P. 'Zu Hegels Bestimmung des Tragischen', *Archiv für das Studium der Neueren Sprachen und Literaturen*, 198 (1961–2), 22–9

Taylor, C. *Hegel*, Cambridge, 1975

'The Opening Arguments of the *Phenomenology*', in *Hegel: A Collection of Critical Essays*, edited by A. MacIntyre, New York, 1972, second edition 1976, pp. 151–87

Tchijewsky, D. 'Hegel et Nietzsche', *Revue d'histoire de la philosophie*, 3 (1929), 321–47

Teichmüller, G. *Die wirkliche und die scheinbare Welt: neue Grundlegung der Metaphysik*, Breslau, 1882

Theunissen, M. *Sein und Schein: die kritische Funktion der Hegelschen Logik*, Frankfurt 1980

Tugendhat, E. *Vorlesungen zur Einführung in die sprachanalytische Philosophie*, Frankfurt, 1979

Überweg, F. *Grundriß der Geschichte der Philosophie*, edited by M. Heinze, 4 Vols., Berlin, 1876–1902

Ushenko, A. 'The Logics of Hegel and Russell', *Philosophy and Phenomenological Reaseach*, 10, 1 (September 1949), 107–14

Wagner, R. *Mein Leben*, edited by M. Gregor-Dellin, Munich 1963, second edition 1976

My Life, authorised translation from the German, London, 1911, reissued 1963

Warnock, M. 'Nietzsche's Conception of Truth', in *Nietzsche: Imagery and Thought*, edited by M. Pasley, Cambridge, 1978, pp. 33–63

White, A. *Absolute Knowledge: Hegel and the Problem of Metaphysics*, Athens, Ohio/London, 1983

Wilcox, J. T. *Truth and Value in Nietzsche*, Michigan, 1974

Williams, B. and Montefiore, A. (eds.). *British Analytical Philosophy*, London 1966

Williams, W. D. 'Nietzsche's Masks' in *Nietzsche: Imagery and Thought*, edited by M. Pasley, Cambridge, 1978, pp. 83–103

Wittgenstein, L. *On Certainty*, edited by G. E. M. Anscombe and G. H. von Wright, translated by Denis Paul and G. E. M. Anscombe, Oxford, 1979

Philosophical Investigations, translated by G. E. M. Anscombe, Oxford, 1958

Zimmermann, R. 'On Nietzsche', *Philosophy and Phenomenological Research*, 29, 2 (December 1968), 274–81

Index